D1049557

PAUL T. MENZEL
ROUTE 1
MANCHESTER, MICHIGAN

BRITISH PHILOSOPHY IN
THE MID-CENTURY

BRITISH PHILOSOPHY IN THE MID-CENTURY

A Cambridge Symposium

639040

EDITED BY

C. A. MACE

Professor (Emeritus)
University of
London

London
GEORGE ALLEN AND UNWIN LTD
Ruskin House Museum Street

Printed in Great Britain
in 12 on 13 point Fournier type
by The Alden Press in the City of Oxford

FOREWORD

THE essays published in this volume had their origin in a course of lectures organized by the British Council at Peterhouse, Cambridge, in the summer of 1953. This course, the first of its kind, was attended by professors, lecturers and teachers of philosophy from such countries as France, Belgium, Italy, Austria, China and the United States. The Faculty of Moral Science was responsible for the programme of lectures and discussions. Miss Margaret Masterman and Dr. Theodore Redpath were nominated by the Faculty as joint Directors of Studies.

The lectures discussed proved of such interest and importance that their circulation among a wider public will be welcome. It was agreed, not least by the overseas members, that the exchange of ideas on so many philosophical themes was both necessary and fruitful, and it is hoped that this gathering may be the prelude to others. Those who took part will recall with especial interest the fact that the lectures included one of the last public utterances of C. D. Broad as the Knightbridge Professor of Moral Philosophy, and one of the rare appearances of Professor G. E. Moore. The British Council wishes to record its thanks to the Faculty of Moral Science for having made the course possible.

E. W. F. TOMLIN

EDITORIAL PREFACE TO THE FIRST EDITION

THIS volume records a 'Cambridge Symposium' in a literal topographical sense. The papers are all based on lectures delivered at Cambridge under the circumstances explained in Mr. Tomlin's Foreword. The lecturers were in the main Cambridge philosophers, but contributions were invited from representatives of Bristol, London and Oxford. It was at first intended that the lectures should be published as delivered, but many lecturers wished to expand or redraft their papers. In some cases the changes were extensive. The Symposium may in consequence claim to reflect not merely the state of philosophical thought at a point in time, but also some trends of philosophy throughout the earlier years of the first decade of the second half of the century.

The subjects selected for discussion do not dictate an inevitable order of presentation, but Professor Broad's contribution was obviously the most appropriate with which to begin, and the two lectures that follow are also concerned in some measure with developments and trends. Thereafter the sequence was a matter for arbitrary choice. The four following lectures are concerned with method in philosophy and science. Next in order are two papers on sense-data and perception. G. E. Moore's paper was written especially for this volume, but is concerned with the subject of an informal discussion with students who attended the Peterhouse course. The following group of three papers take up questions of Language and Meaning, and the concluding contributions some questions of Aesthetics. The position assigned to Dr. Redpath's paper might be taken to reflect the comparative neglect of Aesthetics in British philosophy, but more significant is the fact that the subject is represented at all. Its presence is one of several signs of resurgence and vitality in this Cinderella of the philosophical disciplines.

June 1956   C. A. MACE

PREFACE TO THE SECOND EDITION

THERE have been several changes in this new edition of *British Philosophy in the Mid-Century*. The biographical and bibliographical details have been brought up to date. Some contributors have added 'postscripts' noting developments in their special fields of interest or in their own philosophical opinions. A major change has been the replacement of Professor (now Sir Karl) Popper's paper *Philosophy of Science: A Personal Report* by a paper by Professor Alice Ambrose and Professor Morris Lazerowitz on *Wittgenstein*. Owing to special copyright arrangements, Professor Popper's paper could not be reprinted in this edition. Its place is taken by a new, and important contribution which meets the charge that the first edition was a sort of 'Hamlet without the Prince of Denmark'. Most of the papers in the first edition had been directly or indirectly influenced by Wittgenstein.

Since 1957 two of the most influential of British philosophers have died — G. E. Moore (1958) and Ludwig Wittgenstein (1951). For them, as for all the candidates for immortality, the critical years are those that follow immediately upon life on earth. Some philosophers influential in their day are forgotten as soon as their obituaries have been written. For others these are the years in which immortality is conferred. For Moore and Wittgenstein the interval between the first and the present edition of this book has been one in which the influence of their thoughts has extended to places remote from those in which they taught. Both had published very little. Their influence had been in face to face contacts in which their intellectual powers were reinforced by their (very different) personalities. Happily both left material for posthumous publications. (These are listed in this volume).

The ten years interval between the first and the present edition have not been years of stagnation in philosophy. Philosophers today are distrustful of overall generalizations, and of overall descriptions of the universe and of 'the nature of philosophy'. But if a general statement could be made these years might be described as years in which British Philosophy has come to be seen in perspective in the wider history of philosophy in general. (See, for example, Ayer's editorial introduction to *Positivism*, 1959.)

They could also be described as years of assessment, re-assessment and of consolidation. The more revolutionary forces of Positivism and of the so-called 'Linguistic' schools are retiring to positions of strength established earlier in the century. The age is one of a sort of Last Judgment. The protracted process of this Last (Human) Judgment may well continue to the end of the century; but whatever may be the exact form of this Judgment there can be little doubt that after Moore and Wittgenstein philosophy can never be quite the same again.

C. A. MACE

1965

CONTENTS

Foreword by E. W. F. Tomlin   5

Editorial Preface to First Edition   7

Preface to the Second Edition   8

C. D. BROAD
The Local Historical Background of Contemporary
British Philosophy   11

A. C. EWING
Recent Developments in British Ethical Thought   63

    (i) The Good and the Right
    (ii) The Nature of Ethical Judgments

    Postscript   95

C. A. MACE
Some Trends in the Philosophy of Mind   97

    Postscript   112

S. KÖRNER
Some Types of Philosophical Thinking   113

    Postscript   131

R. B. BRAITHWAITE
Probability and Induction   135

A. AMBROSE and M. LAZEROWITZ
Ludwig Wittgenstein: Philosophy, Experiment and Proof   153

G. E. MOORE
Visual Sense-Data   203

A. J. AYER
Perception   213

10 CONTENTS

GILBERT RYLE
The Theory of Meaning 237

STUART HAMPSHIRE
The Interpretation of Language: Words and Concepts 265

Postscript 279

MARGARET MASTERMAN
Metaphysical and Ideographic Language 281

(i) Towards a Logical Definition of Metaphysics
(ii) Metaphysical Sequences in Language

Postscript 357

THEODORE REDPATH
Some Problems of Modern Aesthetics 359

(i) The Meaning of a Poem
(ii) The Relation between Evaluations, Reason and
Description in Aesthetics

H. BONDI
Some Philosophical Problems of Cosmology 391

Postscript 399

Index 401

C. D. BROAD

*The Local Historical
Background of
Contemporary
Cambridge Philosophy*

CHARLIE DUNBAR BROAD, M.A., LITT.D. (Cantab.): born London, December 30th, 1887; educated at Dulwich College and Trinity College, Cambridge; Fellow of Trinity College, Cambridge; Professor Emeritus of Moral Philosophy in the University of Cambridge; Fellow of the British Academy; Fellow of the Royal Swedish Academy of Science; President of the Society for Psychical Research, 1935-36 and 1957-60; Visiting Professor in Philosophy, University of Michigan, 1953-54; Flint Professor of Philosophy, University of California in Los Angeles, 1954; Nicholas Murray Butler Gold Medal, Columbia University, 1960.

Chief publications: *Perception, Physics and Reality. Scientific Thought. The Mind and its Place in Nature. Five Types of Ethical Theory. Examination of McTaggart's Philosophy. Ethics and the History of Philosophy* (Essays). *Psychical Research, Religion and Philosophy* (Essays). *Lectures on Psychical Research*, 'G. E. Moore's Latest Published Views on Ethics', *Mind*, Vol. LXX. Many other contributions to that and other philosophical journals.

The Philosophy of C. D. Broad in the Library of Living Philosophers (Ed. Schillp) contains his 'Autobiography' and 'Reply to Critics' together with a comprehensive bibliography (up to 1959).

C. D. BROAD

THE LOCAL HISTORICAL
BACKGROUND OF
CONTEMPORARY
CAMBRIDGE PHILOSOPHY

Hi motus animorum, atque haec certamina tanta,
Pulveris exigui iactu compressa quiescunt.

IN the two papers which I am to give by way of introduction to
the present course I shall confine myself within the following
limits. I shall consider only those Cambridge philosophers who
have ceased to be actively engaged in university teaching here or
elsewhere, and I shall include all those and only those whose death
or retirement took place in the first half of the present century. A
selection made on these principles just includes Sidgwick, who
died in 1900, and Wittgenstein, who retired in 1947 and died four
years later, and it just excludes myself. The other names in it are
Venn, Ward, John Neville Keynes, Sorley, Johnson, Stout,
Whitehead, McTaggart, Lord Russell, Professor Moore, John
Maynard Keynes and Ramsey. (These names are mentioned in
the order in which those who were known by them were born.)
Three of the men in this list, viz. Stout, Whitehead and Lord
Russell, spent the most important part of their time as active philo-
sophical teachers and writers away from Cambridge. One of them,
John Maynard Keynes, is more widely known as an economist
and a man of affairs than as a philosopher.

To be a Cambridge philosopher during the last 100 years seems
to have been a healthy occupation. Of the two men in my list who
are still living, Lord Russell is in his eighty-first year and Professor
Moore in his eightieth. Of the remaining twelve no less than six,

viz. Venn, Ward, John Neville Keynes, Sorley, Stout and White-head, had reached or passed their eightieth birthday. Venn died in his ninetieth year and Keynes in his ninety-seven. Of the rest none died before the age of fifty-nine, except Ramsey, whose sudden death through illness in 1930 in his twenty-seventh year was a grievous loss to philosophy in general and to logic in particular.

Before considering the work of these philosophers in detail I will make some general remarks about the study and teaching of philosophy in Cambridge. The first is a purely terminological one. What is elsewhere called 'philosophy' is known officially here as 'moral science' or 'the moral sciences'. A more substantial point is this. During the whole of the period under consideration philosophy in Cambridge has, for good or for ill, been the business of a very small group of specialists. It has not, as in Oxford and in the Scottish universities, been a subject taken along with others by all or most students of arts at some stage or other of their curriculum.

Closely connected with this is the fact that the number of teaching posts in this subject has always been very small in Cambridge. Up to 1896 there was only one professorial chair, viz. the Knightbridge Professorship of Moral Philosophy. From its original foundation in 1693 to the accession of Sidgwick the only outstanding Knightbridge Professors were Wm. Whewell, John Grote and F. D. Maurice. In 1896 a second chair was founded, largely through the efforts of Sidgwick and partly through his generous personal contribution in money. This was at first entitled the Professorship of Mental Philosophy and Logic, and latterly the Professorship of Philosophy. It was originally created for Ward, and since his death it has been held successively by Moore, Wittgenstein, and von Wright, and is now occupied by Wisdom.

Just as there have never been more than two professors at any one time, so too there have never been more than a very few university or college lecturers in philosophy. It is worth noting that certain lecturers, who were never professors, have had considerably greater influence on Cambridge philosophy than their professorial contemporaries. When I was a student, e.g. McTaggart and Johnson and Russell meant far more to most of us than

Ward and Sorley, the two professors. This is partly due to the Cambridge system of tuition, which brings the lecturers into close and regular personal contact with undergraduates who are studying the subject, whilst it tends to isolate the professors from them.

It is evident that the features which I have noted have their drawbacks. Cambridge philosophy tends to be a thin stream, confined to a rather narrow and isolated, if sometimes deep, channel, and always in danger of almost drying up for considerable periods. Other things being equal, one would expect that Oxford, e.g. with its numerous and varied professors and lecturers, and with its wide range of students of philosophy, would make a better balanced and more continuous contribution to the subject. On the whole I think it must be admitted that this reasonable expectation has been justified by the historical facts.

From about 1860 to 1906 there was a very close connection in Cambridge between the study of moral science and that of economics. It was not until the latter date that economics became a completely independent branch of study in the university. Sidgwick, John Neville Keynes and Johnson all lectured on economics and made valuable contributions in their published writings to economic theory. Long after the separation John Maynard Keynes, who was an economist *par excellence*, wrote an important work on the philosophy of probability; whilst Ramsey, who was primarily a pure mathematician and a logician, published two important papers in which he applied mathematical analysis to particular problems of theoretical economics.

It was doubtless inevitable that economics, when it grew up to be a huge and highly complex subject, should leave the home of its childhood and set up house for itself. I do not know whether this separation from moral science has been harmful to Cambridge economics, but I am inclined to think that it may have been unfortunate in certain respects for Cambridge philosophy. It is noteworthy that since those days philosophy in Cambridge has been almost completely out of touch with general history, with political theory and sociology, and with jurisprudence. This has no doubt saved it from many temptations to vague and pretentious verbiage, and from the danger of philosophizing with one eye on contemporary politics. But it has involved the complete neglect of much that is a proper subject for philosophic analysis and speculation, and which has in fact always formed an important part of philosophy in other places and in Cambridge itself at other times.

On the whole it would be true to say that the Cambridge philosophers who have had most influence in the later part of the period under discussion have tended to approach the subject from the side of mathematics or of mathematical physics, rather than from that of biology or history or the social sciences or the arts. But it may fairly be added that these men have been by no means narrow specialists, but persons of wide general culture and interests. It is enough to mention the names of Lord Russell and of Whitehead by way of illustration.

There is one more general remark that I would make about Cambridge philosophy in the last fifty years. This concerns the complete separation which prevails between the study of ancient and of modern philosophy. To this day the history of philosophy begins for the student of moral science here with Descartes, whilst Greek philosophy is a branch of classical studies. There is practically no overlapping either of teachers or of students. It happens, indeed, that a number of eminent Cambridge philosophers had distinguished themselves in classical studies before taking philosophy. Examples are Sidgwick, Stout and Professor Moore. It has happened also from time to time that a classical scholar working in Greek philosophy was interested in certain aspects of the work of his philosophical colleagues. But in the main, ancient philosophy, on the one hand, and general philosophy and the history of modern philosophy, on the other, are in almost watertight compartments. I should suppose that this fact will strike most of my audience as extremely paradoxical. It has never ceased to astonish and to shock me.

I have now said enough of the general features of Cambridge philosophy to show that it has been and is a somewhat peculiar growth, in fact a kind of hot-house plant. It is perhaps surprising that it should have borne so much excellent fruit as it has done in the last fifty years. This must be ascribed to the contingent fact that this half-century has been marked by a sequence of Cam-

bridge philosophers of quite outstanding ability, originality and
personality. The names of Professor Moore, Lord Russell and
Wittgenstein are enough to substantiate this statement.

Let us now leave generalities and come down to concrete
details. It will be convenient to begin by dividing the Cambridge
philosophers of the period into the following six groups. In the
first of these I place those whose main interest has been in *logic*,
formal or inductive, and the theory of probability. These are
Venn, the two Keyneses, Johnson and Ramsey. In the second I
group together two men who approached philosophy from the
side of *psychology* and made extremely important contributions to
it, but were also eminent as epistemologists and metaphysicians.
These are Ward and Stout. Next, in a class by himself, comes
McTaggart, the one *pure metaphysician*. In the fourth group I
put the two philosophers whose main work was in *ethics*, viz.
Sidgwick and Sorley. Then, in a class by himself, comes *Professor
Moore*, who has had a more profound and many-sided influence
than any one other Cambridge philosopher. In my sixth and last
class I group together three men, who originally approached
philosophy from the side of mathematics and mathematical logic
and made important contributions to those subjects, but went on
to deal with epistemological and metaphysical problems. These
philosophers are Whitehead, Lord Russell and Wittgenstein.
Our six classes may therefore be briefly described as follows:
(1) *Logicians*, (2) *Psychologist-Philosophers*, (3) *Pure Metaphysicians*, (4) *Moralist-Philosophers*, (5) the class whose only member is *Professor Moore*, and (6) *Logico-mathematical Philosophers*.

I shall now treat each of these groups in turn. The amount of
space which I shall allot to any particular member of any particular group will be determined partly by the importance which I
ascribe to him in the development of contemporary Cambridge
philosophy, and partly by the extent of my knowledge of his
work and by the degree of interest which I feel for it.

(1) *The Logicians.* It is fitting that a University at which Francis
Bacon was a student and Isaac Newton a professor, and in which
mathematics and physics have always been principal subjects of

study and research, should have made important contributions to the development of logic and the theory of scientific method.

Before the beginning of our period the most outstanding inductive logician in Cambridge was William Whewell. He came just at the end of the time when it was still possible to have a first-hand knowledge of the whole of existing science. Whewell did have that knowledge and much besides. He was born in 1794 and died, as Master of Trinity College, in 1866. The wide range of his knowledge and his interests is testified by the fact that he held the chair of Mineralogy from 1828 to 1832 and the Knightbridge Professorship of Moral Philosophy from 1838 to 1855. His most important contributions to the theory of induction are his *History of the Inductive Sciences*, published in 1837, and his *Philosophy of the Inductive Sciences*, published in 1840. Both these works are of great interest and importance, and are still well worth reading. Most of us nowadays are acquainted with his views only at second-hand through the controversial references to them in Mill's *Logic*. There is no doubt that he emphasized certain features in scientific reasoning, e.g. the importance of what he called 'colligating concepts', which Mill was inclined to neglect. His philosophy of induction is at any rate based upon a profound knowledge of the history of science and a first-hand acquaintance with the mathematics and physics of his time, to which Mill can make no comparable claim.

The two men in England who did most to initiate modern symbolic logic were Boole and de Morgan. Of these de Morgan was a Cambridge mathematician by origin, and his earlier papers were contributed to the *Proceedings* of the Cambridge Philosophical Society. He became Professor of Mathematics at University College, London, at a very early age, and most of his later work was done in London.

The first Cambridge logician who falls within our period is John Venn. He was born in 1834 and lived till 1923. He became Fellow of Caius College, Cambridge, in 1857 and university lecturer in moral science in 1862. He made important and characteristic contributions both to formal logic and to inductive logic and the philosophy of probability.

His first book, *The Logic of Chance*, published in 1866, is his main contribution to the last named subject. Venn is one of the earliest exponents of what may be called the 'limiting-frequency' interpretation of probability. On his view, the notion of probability applies where and only where the following conditions are fulfilled. (i) There must be a potentially unlimited class of things or events marked out by the presence in all its members of a certain defining characteristic *P*. This characteristic must be accompanied in some, but not in all, its instances by a certain other characteristic *Q*. (E.g. *P* might be the property of being a man, and *Q* that of being left-handed.) (ii) There must be no means of inferring with certainty from any available premisses, with regard to any *individual* member, either that it has or that it has not *Q*. (iii) Suppose that a sequence of larger and larger selections, each including all that was selected before and more besides, is made from the original class. Suppose that in each successive selection the proportion of individuals possessing *Q* is noted. Then the third condition is that these proportions should approach a certain limiting value as the selections become larger and larger. Venn says that it is an empirical fact that there are many classes in nature which answer to these conditions, and that this empirical fact is at the basis of the notion of numerical probability and of all valid applications of that notion.

This doctrine has been widely accepted since Venn's time, and it has been greatly elaborated and subtilized in order to meet the many criticisms to which it has been subjected. It had been adumbrated by another Cambridge man, Leslie Cliffe Ellis, but I believe that Venn was the first to state it and to argue it in detail. Venn considers that the only important rival to his theory is that which de Morgan had put forward in his *Formal Logic*. De Morgan tried to assimilate probable to demonstrative reasoning by an analogy and a contrast between partial belief and complete conviction. He seems to have regarded the probability-calculus as providing a measure of the degree of belief which a reasonable person would actually have when presented with evidence which was persuasive but not coercive. Venn has little difficulty in showing the extreme difficulties of any such theory.

In 1889 Venn embodied his thoughts on inductive logic and scientific method in a substantial volume entitled *Principles of Empirical Logic*. I suspect that this work is little read nowadays, but it had considerable influence on generations of Cambridge students and there is much in it that would still repay attentive study. Apart from its very full discussion of the physical and the psychological pre-conditions of induction, and its revision of the inductive methods as formulated by Mill, it contains most interesting matter on language, on definition, on scientific classification and division, and on standards and units both in physical and in psychological measurement. There is also to be found in it a very interesting account of the nature of the ideal concepts of pure geometry and of their applicability to the actual things and processes in nature.

Venn's main contribution to formal logic was his book entitled *Symbolic Logic*, published in 1881. It was a standard work on the subject until the innovations introduced by Whitehead and Russell in the early years of the present century. Venn was greatly interested in the representation by means of diagrams of the logical relations between classes. For this purpose he introduced a method which superficially resembles that of Euler, in so far as it uses circles to represent classes, and their intersections and other geometrical relationships to represent the logical relations between classes. But this resemblance is only superficial. The method of representing propositions asserting relations between classes is fundamentally different. It consists in regarding such propositions as asserting or denying the presence of instances in one or another of the four mutually exclusive and collectively exhaustive conjunctive sub-classes $S\&P$, $S\&not\text{-}P$, $not\text{-}S\&P$ and $not\text{-}S\&not\text{-}P$. Venn represents absence of instances by shading the corresponding segment of the two intersecting circles which severally represent S and P, and he represents presence of at least one instance by putting a short line in the corresponding segment. This method is far better than Euler's even when only two classes are under consideration. When three or more have to be considered, as in the treatment of the syllogism, Venn's method remains simple and elegant, whilst Euler's becomes intolerably clumsy if all the possibilities are to be represented.

It is of some interest to remark that a system of diagrammatic representation, based on the same principle as Venn's but even more elegant, was invented independently by the Oxford logician C. L. Dodgson, better known as Lewis Carroll, the author of *Alice in Wonderland* and other world-famous books for children of all ages.

Venn was a singularly honest and independent thinker, who expressed his thoughts in simple straightforward language, which makes his works a pleasure to read and a model of English philosophic writing.

I turn now to John Neville Keynes. He was born in 1852, became Fellow of Pembroke College, Cambridge, in 1876, and held a university lectureship in moral science from 1884 to 1911, when he became Registrary of the University and ceased to lecture. He died in 1950, having survived by four years his still more famous son, John Maynard Keynes, the economist. John Neville Keynes is best known for his book *Studies and Exercises in Formal Logic.* This was first published in 1884. It was several times re-written and enlarged, and was last re-printed in 1930. It was the text-book in formal logic for many generations of Cambridge moral scientists. It is far and away the best book that exists in English on the old-fashioned formal logic and the earlier stages of the more recent developments.

Keynes does not enter deeply into philosophical problems. He settled a number of ancient and troublesome controversies by drawing certain important distinctions and clearly defining certain terms which had hitherto been vague. His discussion of the notions of connotation and denotation, in connection with which he distinguished between 'conventional', 'subjective' and 'objective' intension, is an excellent example of this. Other outstanding examples are his account of the notion of the existential import of propositions, and his distinction between what he calls 'conditional' and 'true hypothetical' propositions.

Keynes was well acquainted with the work of Boole, de Morgan, Jevons and Schröder. There is a long appendix to his book, entitled *A Generalisation of Logical Processes in their Application to Complex Propositions*, in which he devotes six chapters to the formal logic of such propositions. By a 'complex proposition' he means a proposition of one of the four canonical forms A, E, I and O, in which either the subject or the predicate or both consists of a conjunction or a disjunction of classes. An example would be 'Everything which is either $A \& B$ or $C \& D$ is either $X \& Y$ or $Z \& W$.' He developed a method for dealing with such propositions, which departs in the least degree possible from the traditional treatment of propositions with non-complex terms. In this way he is able to solve, without any algebraical apparatus, all the problems for which other logicians, such as Boole, had employed a kind of algebraical calculus. For my own part I should regard this as a kind of technical *tour de force*. It was well worth doing once and for all, to show that it could be done. But for the future it would seem better to employ a convenient general calculus, and to regard the traditional propositions with non-complex terms as simplified special cases.

Keynes greatly simplified and systematized the traditional doctrine of the syllogism by the use of the notion of *antilogism*, which he took over from the American logician Mrs. Ladd-Franklin. By this means it can easily be shown that to each valid syllogism in any of the first three figures there necessarily corresponds one and only one valid syllogism in each of the other two. It can also be shown that to each special rule for any of the first three figures there corresponds a logically equivalent rule for each of the other two. By this means the traditional doctrine of the syllogism was transformed from something that looks very much like the receipts in a cookery-book to something which can claim to be a fairly coherent system.

The one book which Keynes published on economics, *Political Economy, its Scope and Relations*, has the same kind of merits as his work on formal logic. It remains to this day the most important contribution made by an Englishman to the discussion of the nature of economics and the logic and methodology of that science. Keynes supplemented the book by contributing a number of articles on allied topics to Palgrave's *Dictionary of Political Economy*. His main interests are well indicated by the following titles: 'Analytical Method', 'A Posteriori Reasoning', 'A Priori Reasoning', 'Deductive Method'.

The next logician on our list is William Ernest Johnson. He is the first of them whom I knew personally. He had been teaching for many years when I began to study moral science in 1908, and he continued to do so for many years afterwards. As an undergraduate I attended his lectures on Advanced Logic, and later I came to know him well.

Johnson was born in 1858 and died in 1931. He came of a well-known Nonconformist family of Cambridge school-masters. He started his career as a mathematical scholar of King's College, Cambridge, and took his degree with high honours in mathematics. His first published book was an advanced text-book in *Trigonometry*. He lectured for many years in the University on the mathematical theory of economics, and he contributed to the *Economic Journal* a long and important paper entitled 'The Pure Theory of Utility Curves'. He became a university lecturer in moral science in 1896 and continued to hold that office until his death in 1931. Although he is known to philosophers mainly as a logician, it is important to notice that it was in *psychology* that he gained special distinction in his honours examination in moral science, and that for many years it was *psychology* on which he lectured. It was not until Keynes gave up his lectureship on becoming Registrary in 1911 that Johnson began to lecture on logic. Thereafter his lecturing was confined to that subject.

Johnson was a most acute thinker and a very hard and conscientious worker. He wrote much, but owing to ill-health and excessive diffidence and self-criticism he published very little. After contributing a series of three important articles, entitled 'The Logical Calculus,' to the first three volumes of *Mind* in 1892 to 1894, he published nothing in philosophy until 1918, when he broke his long silence with two articles in *Mind* entitled 'The Analysis of Thinking'. This was the prelude to the publication of his great work entitled *Logic*, of which the first volume appeared in 1921, the second in 1922 and the third in 1924. This embodied much of his lecture-notes and of scattered manuscripts in which he had worked out his own thoughts without any view to publication. There was to have been a fourth volume dealing with probability, a subject to which Johnson had devoted a vast amount of thought. But the physical and mental strain involved in preparing the first three volumes had been too much for a life-long invalid now in his sixties. Notwithstanding the help given by devoted pupils, who sought to relieve him as much as possible of the drudgery of preparing his writings for the press, he was unable to compose a sustained and coherent presentation of his work on probability. The little that could be rescued was published after his death by Braithwaite in 1932 in three articles in *Mind* entitled 'Probability; 'The Relations of Proposal to Supposal', 'Axioms' and 'The Deductive and Inductive Problems'.

During the quarter of a century in which Johnson published nothing and was practically unknown outside a small circle in Cambridge he exerted a strong and continuous influence on philosophy within the university. This he did in two ways. In the first place, practically every student of moral science attended his lectures, and many of them went to him for private tuition, not only in logic but in all the other branches of the subject. Secondly, he was immensely generous in help, fertile in suggestion, and acute in criticism, when consulted by colleagues who were working on philosophical problems. The elder Keynes, in each successive edition of his *Studies and Exercises in Formal Logic*, mentions with gratitude the help which he had received from Johnson; and the younger Keynes has put on record Johnson's extreme helpfulness and generosity to him when he was writing his *Treatise in Probability*. For my own part I can say that I gained more from a course of lectures by Johnson under the title of *Advanced Logic* than from any one other course that I attended. The form of the lectures was not particularly happy, but the matter was extraordinarily rich, varied and original. Much of it was afterwards embodied in the *Logic*, but the lectures included much besides. In particular, there was an elaborate and acute discussion of the main doctrines of Russell's *Principles of Mathematics* and of questions arising from them, and a whole treatise on the philosophy and the formal development of the calculus of probability, which later formed the background of Lord Keynes's book on that subject. Johnson was not merely a logician of outstanding originality and technical ability, a psychologist and a metaphysician. He was also a man of very wide and thorough general culture. He was an accomplished pianist and an excellent chess-player, and he had a profound knowledge and a critical appreciation of all the classics in English literature. To know him and to converse with him was a liberal education.

Johnson's *Logic* is very much more than a treatise on deductive and inductive logic, as ordinarily understood. It contains most valuable and original chapters on fundamental problems of epistemology, metaphysics and even psychology. Johnson holds that logic is primarily concerned with *propositions*. He distinguishes these from *judgments*, which are part of the subject-matter of psychology; from *sentences*, which are part of the subject-matter of grammar, and from *facts*.

The first volume is concerned mainly with the analysis and classification of propositions, with terms and with relations. An important chapter is devoted to what Johnson calls 'determinables' and 'determinates', e.g. colour and the various colours, such as red, blue, etc., and to the analogies and differences between these correlated notions and those of genus and species, e.g. animal, on the one hand, and cat, dog, lion, etc., on the other. Another important chapter is concerned with the distinction between what Johnson calls 'enumerations', which, he thinks, lie at the basis of arithmetic, and genuine 'classes', such as men or red things.

The second volume deals with the general principles and the various forms of demonstrative inference. Under this heading Johnson includes those types of demonstrative argument, commonly treated in works on inductive logic, of which Mill's four Methods are crude examples. Johnson cleared up the logical principles of demonstrative induction, which had been left in such obscurity by Mill. He made explicit the concealed premises and showed the purely deductive character of these arguments. He formulated the possible varieties of such arguments under four headings, which he called the Figures of *Agreement*, of *Difference*, of *Composition* and of *Resolution*, and he showed, by means of a single antilogism, the logical interconnections of the four. This work may be regarded as forming an intermediate stage between the earlier crudities of Mill and the later subtleties of Professor von Wright, who has exhaustively handled the logic of necessary and of sufficient conditions. In the same volume Johnson deals with the logic of algebraical reasoning and with that of the old-fashioned Euclidean geometry in a way which is highly original but also highly controversial. In connection with these topics there is an interesting chapter on the nature of magnitude and the notion of 'dimensions' in physics, and a most illuminating discussion of the notions of absolute and relative space and time.

The third volume is primarily concerned with what Johnson calls 'problematic induction', i.e. generalization from instances where the argument cannot be made demonstrative even by appealing to suppressed universal premisses. It begins with an important discussion of the notion of a natural law, and the distinction between universals of law and merely factual general propositions. From this it passes on to discuss the various criteria by which the probability of the conclusion of a problematic induction is estimated.

But the greater part of this volume is devoted to a most interesting analysis of the notions of cause and of substance. Johnson regarded these as two complementary features in a single category. A substance, or as Johnson called it a 'continuant', is something which can significantly be said to have *dispositional* properties, and these are essentially *causal*. On the other hand, causal laws can be stated only in terms of *continuants* and their states and their spatio-temporal and other non-causal relationships. The actual history of any continuant is determined jointly by its dispositional properties and its non-causal relationships. It is one possible manifestation of its nature out of an unlimited number of alternative manifestations, each of which would have been actualized if and only if the non-causal relationships had been different in one or another of the innumerable different possible ways. Johnson gave a thorough analysis also of the notion of an 'occurrent', as he calls it, which is correlative to that of a continuant. He carefully distinguished between the notion of continuant and occurrent, on the one hand, and that of substantive and adjective, on the other. Failure to distinguish clearly between these two pairs of correlatives has been, as he points out, a fruitful source of confusion and error in philosophy. An *occurrent*, e.g. a flash of lightning or a twinge of toothache, is a dated, and it may be a localized, *particular*. An adjective, e.g. red or throbbing, even when it is completely determinate and specific, is a *universal*, which characterizes some occurrent or continuant.

Having thus discussed the general notions of cause and of substance, and their intimate interconnections, Johnson proceeds to consider a number of important philosophical questions concerning causation. He begins by drawing a valuable distinction between a plurality of coincident *cause-factors* or *effect-factors*, on the one hand, and the *total cause* or the *total effect* which they together constitute, on the other. In terms of this distinction he is able to deal clearly with the confused notions of plurality of causes for a single effect and plurality of effects of a single cause. He went on from this to consider the application of the notions of cause and continuant to minds and mental processes. These two chapters contain all the information now available about Johnson's highly characteristic views on the philosophy of mind. I cannot attempt to give any adequate account of these, but must confine myself to the following brief summary.

Johnson held that a human mind is a psychical continuant, which neither contains other continuants as parts nor is itself part of any other continuant. In this it contrasts with a material thing. For any finite body is a physical continuant, which consists of other such continuants, viz. material particles of various kinds, and is itself part of a larger physical continuant, e.g. the solar system. He held that a person's mind acts directly on his brain when a volition passes into overt action; that his body acts on his mind when a stimulus evokes a sensation; and that there is purely immanent causation within a person's mind in the process of deliberation which leads up to a voluntary decision. Johnson claimed to refute the doctrine that to every different event in a person's mind there corresponds a different event in his brain. He thinks that there probably is this one-to-one correlation in the case of *sensations*. But for that very reason, he argues, there cannot *also* be detailed brain-correlates to all the various judgments which a person may make about any one of his sensations or to all the various emotions and shades of emotion with which he may react to it.

Notwithstanding this denial, Johnson was a convinced determinist. Our voluntary decisions are, according to him, completely determined, but their causes are other states of our own minds, to which there are no detailed correlates in our brains.

I have now devoted as much time as I can afford, though less than I could wish, to Johnson, and so I pass to our next logician, the younger Keynes. John Maynard, afterwards Baron Keynes of Tilton, was born in 1883 and died in 1946. He became Fellow of King's College, Cambridge, in 1909. He was for a time a high official at the India Office, and much of his life was spent in London in the service of the state and in high finance. We are not concerned here with his notable contributions to economic theory, with his work at the Treasury in the two world wars, or with his eminent services to his College, which he greatly enriched by the skill and devotion with which, as its Bursar, he managed its finances for many years. It will suffice here to record, for what it may be worth, my conviction that he was, taking him all round, the ablest Englishman and one of the ablest men of his generation. He was never a teacher of philosophy in the University, and he would not have reckoned himself a professional philosopher, though the mental powers which he displayed in economic theory were philosophic in the highest sense. We are concerned here only with his one published contribution to philosophy, *A Treatise on Probability*, published in 1921. The proofs of this work were complete by the summer of 1914, and I well remember going over some of them in the long vacation of that year with Keynes himself and Bertrand Russell. From these innocent pleasures Keynes was reft away by the outbreak of the first world war to advise the financial authorities in London on the moratorium and the foreign exchanges.

Keynes had been trained first as a mathematician and later as an economist. From his childhood he had been associated with Johnson, first as his father's friend and colleague who often visited the paternal house to discuss logical problems with the elder Keynes, and later as a greatly senior Fellow of his own College. Keynes generously acknowledged his great obligations to Johnson, and they are indeed obvious to anyone who attended Johnson's lectures on Advanced Logic, as I did. The notation used throughout the *Treatise* is that which Johnson invented; many of the theorems proved in Part II of the book were first discovered and proved by him; and the notions of 'groups' and of 'requirement', in terms of which Keynes discusses the conditions for non-circular logical inference, were first introduced by Johnson in dealing with the so-called 'paradoxes of implication' and with Mill's attack on the traditional view of the syllogism.

Keynes considered and deliberately rejected the limiting-frequency view of probability. His own view is that probability is an unanalysable logical relation between two propositions, which, following Johnson, we may call the 'proposal' and the 'supposal'. It is analogous to the relation between the premisses and the conclusion of a valid demonstrative argument, but there is this fundamental difference. A person who fully accepts any premiss is justified in fully accepting any proposition which it entails. But, when the logical relation is that of 'probabilification', complete acceptance of the supposal justifies only some degree of partial belief in the proposal. The relation of probabilification is capable of degrees, since complete acceptance of a supposal justifies in some cases a higher and in some cases a lower degree of belief in a proposal. Keynes argued that there is no reason to think that all probabilities are comparable with each other in respect of magnitude, and *a fortiori* that there is no reason to believe that they are all in principle capable of numerical measurement. Measurement is possible only in the important, but comparatively rare, cases where we have a field of possibilities, which can be split up into a set of mutually exclusive, collectively exhaustive and equi-probable alternatives.

This leads Keynes to consider the famous Principle of Indifference, which has often been put forward as a safe criterion for equiprobability of alternatives. Von Kries had already pointed out the absurdities and inconsistencies to which an uncritical use of this principle leads, particularly in geometrical applications of probability. By considering such cases, and generalizing from them, Keynes endeavoured to elicit and state the conditions under which alone the principle is valid. In effect the conditions come to this. The alternative proposals must be determinates of the same degree of determinateness under some one determinable, and the supposal must be symmetrically related to *all* of them in every respect in which it is relevant to the probability of *any* of them. Thus any valid application of the Principle of Indifference requires prior judgments as to relevance and irrelevance. These in the end rest on direct insight, and cannot be made by mechanically applying any general rule.

Keynes's contributions to the philosophy of induction may be briefly summarized as follows. Consider any proposed general law: All S is P. Suppose that n instances of S have been observed and that all of them have been found to be P. What is the relevance to the probability of the proposed law of observing further instances of S and finding that they too are P?

In the first place, the original n instances of S certainly had other properties, e.g. T, common to them, beside S and P. It is therefore possible that some of these are necessary conditions for the presence of P in instances of S, and that, if there is a law at all connecting S with P, it is of the more restricted form: All S which is T is P. To eliminate this possible source of doubt, further instances of S which are P are relevant only if they *differ* from the original n instances in *lacking* some character, e.g. T, which these all had in common. Further instances of S which, so far as we can tell, *resemble* the original n instances in every respect in which they are known to resemble each other, can be relevant only in the following roundabout way. It is very likely that the original n instances of S may have had certain features in common which we did not, and perhaps could not, observe. Some of these may have been necessary conditions for the presence of P in instances of S. Now a new instance of S, which *seems* to resemble the original n instances in every respect in which they are *known* to resemble each other, may in fact differ from them all in lacking some *unobserved* feature which they all in fact had in common. If so, it does in fact serve to eliminate the possibility that this unrecognized common feature in the original n instances is a necessary condition of the presence of P in instance of S. So an increase in the number of observed instances according with a proposed law is relevant here only in so far as it introduces actual or possible *variety*, and thus actually or possibly eliminates various suggestions to the effect that the true law connecting S with P may be of a more restricted form than the proposed law: All S is P. This type of argument Keynes calls 'analogical'. I should prefer to call it 'eliminative'.

Plainly this line of argument at best enables us only to eliminate suggested laws which are too general. It does not by itself provide any positive evidence for any proposed law which has so far escaped elimination. For this purpose a different line of argument is needed, and in it multiplication of instances plays a different part. Keynes calls such arguments 'purely inductive'. His account of them may be summarized as follows:

If the proposed law that all S is P were true, it would necessarily follow that *any* instance of S which might be observed would be found to be P. It is easy to prove, from the accepted axioms of the calculus of probability, the following proposition. Subject to a certain two conditions, the probability of the proposed law that all S is P, relative to the supposal that n instances of S have been observed and that all of them have been found to be P, increases with every increase of n. Moreover, as n is increased indefinitely this probability tends to the limiting value of unity. This result may seem at first sight promising, but the promise fades when we consider the two conditions under which alone it holds. The first is that the proposed law shall have an antecedent probability, *prior to* all observations on instances of S, which is greater than some fraction which is itself greater than O. The second condition is that the probability that n observed instances of S would all be found to be P, relative to the supposition that the law is *false*, should diminish with every increase in n and should tend to the limiting value zero as n is increased indefinitely.

Keynes did not pay much attention to the second condition, though it does in fact raise some awkward questions. Nor did he state the first condition so carefully as I have done in view of the criticisms of Nicod and others on Keynes's argument. What he proceeded to do was to consider what general supposition about the constitution of nature would give a finite antecedent probability to any proposed law connecting any two characteristics which occur in nature. The supposition which he held to be necessary and sufficient for this purpose he called the *Principle of Limited Variety*.

The essential point of this is the assumption that the vast variety of perceptible properties are manifestations of a comparatively few non-perceptible 'generating properties'. Each generating property thus manifests itself in a whole group of associated perceptible properties. Suppose now that the perceptible property S has been observed only once, and that it was then found to be accompanied by the perceptible property P. Then, relative to the supposal of limited variety, there is a finite probability that S and P are both manifestations of a single generating property. If so, they must occur together in every instance in which either of them occurs. (This argument rests on the simplifying assumption that the two sets of perceptible properties which correspond to two generating properties never overlap. If this assumption be not made, the above argument cannot be used; but we could still assign a finite probability to propositions of the form: 'The next S to be observed will be P.')

A final question remained for Keynes. Let it be granted that the Principle of Limited Variety would suffice to provide any proposed law with that finite antecedent probability which is needed in order that it shall be possible, with sufficient verification, to make the law practically certain. What ground, if any, have we for accepting the principle? It is not a necessary proposition, which could be known *a priori*, but a contingent proposition about the constitution of the actual world. The only ground for believing such a proposition would be *inductive*. Now, as we have seen, induction can accomplish nothing on Keynesian lines unless the proposition to be proved has a *finite* probability *antecedent to* all attempts to verify it by specific observations. So the ultimate question for Keynes is this. Is it intelligible to say that the Principle of Limited Variety has a finite antecedent probability? And, if so, have we any reason for assigning such a probability to it? To these questions he supplies no answer.

The great merit of Keynes's discussion lies, not in any answers that it gives, but in the light which it throws on the nature of the questions at issue. It shows us, I think, that a certain line of approach, which seemed promising so long as it lay in partial obscurity, turns out to be a *cul de sac* when the mists are blown away.

The last of our logicians is Frank Plumpton Ramsey, who was born in 1903 and died in 1930. He was a brilliant mathematician, and his professional work was done as lecturer in mathematics in the University and as director of studies in that subject in King's College, Cambridge, of which he became a Fellow at a very early age.

A volume, containing the most important of his philosophical writings, was published by his friend and colleague Mr. Braithwaite in 1931 under the title *The Foundation of Mathematics*. This collection does not include his two contributions to mathematical economics. One of these, *A Mathematical Theory of Saving*, was described by Lord Keynes as 'one of the most remarkable contributions to mathematical economics ever made'. Ramsey was from his early days interested in the work of Wittgenstein; he helped with the English translation of *Tractatus Logico-Philosopicus*; and on its appearance he wrote a long and able critical notice of it in *Mind*. It is worth noting that he was in his twentieth year when he so successfully undertook this important bit of work at the invitation of the editor of *Mind*.

Ramsey was steeped in the work of Whitehead and Russell on the philosophy of mathematics, and his first and most important work was a long essay entitled *The Foundations of Mathematics*. In this he discussed with great originality and subtlety the theory of logical types and the various paradoxes in view of which that theory had been put forward by Russell. His most important achievement here was to distinguish between semantical and genuinely logical paradoxes. He claimed to show that the former can be obviated without the theory of types, and that the latter require only a much simpler theory of types than that put forward by Whitehead and Russell.

Later Ramsey became interested in the philosophy of probability. He rejected Keynes's view that probability is concerned with a logical relation between supposal and proposal analogous to, but weaker than, the relation of entailment between the premisses and the conclusion of a demonstrative argument. As regards the frequency-theory, he recognized that it provides a consistent interpretation of the accepted axioms of the calculus of probability, and he admitted that this interpretation may be the one that is of most importance in scientific applications of probability. But he insists that in a vast number of cases probability is concerned, as de Morgan and many others had held, with *partial belief.*

He then proceeded to do what hardly anyone else had attempted, viz. to explain how degrees of belief may be estimated. He does this in terms of the notion of the sums which a person would be prepared to wager on the various alternatives, under certain assumptions which he enumerates. Taking this method of measurement, he proceeds to work out the axioms of probability as the principles for ensuring the internal consistency of a system of partial beliefs. Finally, in terms of this, he works out a theory of the logic of induction. Ramsey was in process of developing and modifying this theory up to the time of his death. Among his fragmentary papers are most interesting and suggestive reflections on the nature of theories and on the nature of general propositions and of causal laws.

Newton said of his pupil Roger Cotes, who died in 1716 at the age of thirty-four, 'if Cotes had lived, we might have known something'. Surely we can say no less of Ramsey, who had achieved so much in his short life, and whose powers were still developing at the time of his death.

(2) *The Psychologist-Philosophers.* I pass now to our two psychologist-philosophers, Ward and Stout.

James Ward was born in 1843 and died in 1925. He entered unusually late on his academic career. Brought up in an extremely evangelical home, he had studied for the nonconformist ministry at a theological college in Birmingham, and had then lost his faith in Christian orthodoxy during a year's intensive philosophical study in Germany. In 1871 he had accepted the office of minister to a Unitarian church in Cambridge, but in the following year he felt obliged to resign. It was not until 1873, at the age of thirty, that he entered Trinity College, Cambridge, where he had won a scholarship in moral science. He was elected to a Fellowship of the College in 1875, and became lecturer in moral science in 1880. In 1897, on the founding of the Professorship of Logic and Mental Philosophy, he was appointed to that chair, and he held it until his death in 1925. Throughout his life he remained a convinced theist and a stern puritan. A sincerely good and deeply religious man, with a melancholy disposition, a dyspeptic stomach, and a sharp tongue, he had all those virtues which have tended to make virtue so unpopular. He was already sixty-five when I began to study moral science. He always treated me with great kindness when we met, but I cannot say that I profited greatly from his lectures or that I ever came to feel quite at ease with him.

Like so many Cambridge philosophers, Ward approached philosophy from the side of natural science, but, unlike most of them, his scientific background was physiology and natural history. Soon after gaining his Fellowship he spent a second year in Germany, this time working at experimental physiology in Professor Ludwig's laboratory at Leipzig. After his return to Cambridge he experimented on crayfish in Michael Foster's laboratory. Throughout his life he was a keen naturalist, and in particular a patient and accurate watcher of wild birds. Another important part of his mental equipment was a profound knowledge of German philosophical and psychological literature. In this he resembled his antagonist in many controversies, the great Oxford philosopher F. H. Bradley.

Ward's most important contribution to psychology was the article under that heading which he contributed to the *Encyclopaedia Britannica* in 1886. This at once created a revolution in English psychology. No serious student of the subject could neglect to read it, and it remained available only in this inconvenient form for thirty-two years. Then in 1918 Ward published his *Psychological Principles*, which embodies the article with many modifications and additions, and must be regarded as expressing Ward's final views on psychology.

Ward had considered carefully, and he rejected deliberately as quite inadequate to the empirical facts, any attempt to reduce the human mind to a system of interconnected presentations which interact with each other in accordance with laws analogous to those of mechanics or physics or chemistry. He took it as axiomatic for psychology that every experience is had by some one *subject*, and that a subject which *has* experiences cannot intelligibly be supposed to be itself either an experience or any set of experiences, however elaborately interconnected. He took it to be obvious that nothing can intelligibly be described as a 'presentation' except in so far as it is presented to some subject, and is thus the object of an act of awareness which is an experience belonging to that subject. He was, however, careful not to identify the psychological category of *subject* with the ontological category of *soul*. The question of the relation or lack of relation between these two concepts is one for philosophers, not for psychologists as such. To the psychological subject he ascribed two and only two fundamental faculties, viz. (i) that of being aware of presentations and attending selectively to them, and (ii) that of feeling pleasure or displeasure. These feelings are called forth in the subject by the details of the presentations of which it is aware, and they in turn determine the distribution of the subject's attention over the sumtotal of its presentations at any time. As regards the presentations of which any particular subject is aware in the course of its experience, they constitute a *continuum*, both at each moment and from one moment to another. In this continuum there are objective differentiations, and certain items are discriminated by the selective attention of the subject under the stimulus of its feelings of pleasure and displeasure.

This view of the fundamental presuppositions of psychology is, I take it, highly unpopular at present, at any rate in England and the U.S.A. I should imagine that Ward's book is unread and his arguments completely ignored by most contemporary writers on the philosophy of mind. This does not alter the fact that Ward had an immense influence on the psychological thinking of men like Johnson and Stout, who in turn influenced many others. Nor does it, to my mind, preclude the possibility that Ward may be substantially right, and the contemporary fashionable opinion fundamentally mistaken, on these matters. After all, there are no new relevant *facts* available. And Ward's detailed knowledge of, and familiarity with, the relevant facts was considerably greater than that of most present-day writers; whilst his intellectual powers, and the extent to which he devoted them to reflection on these problems, were at least as great.

In 1899 there appeared Ward's first large-scale contribution to philosophy in general, as distinct from psychology. This was his Gifford Lectures, entitled *Naturalism and Agnosticism*. When these lectures were composed the name of Herbert Spencer was still one to conjure with in enlightened circles both in England and abroad, though the ethical and political parts of his system were already beginning to acquire the *patina* of a museum-piece. Ward's Gifford Lectures may fairly be said to have administered the *coup de grâce* to Spencer's claims to be taken seriously as a philosopher.

Ward takes naturalism to be the attempts at philosophic synthesis made by persons who regard the methods of natural science as the only available ways of getting knowledge about matters of fact, and who treat the concepts used by scientists and the laws discovered by them as exact and literal transcriptions of purely objective facts. He had little difficulty in showing in detail that such thinkers are reifying abstractions and idealizations which scientists have had to make in order to deal approximately with the complexities of nature, and that they have failed to see how much there is of the human and the subjective in the concepts of science. In general, he argues, the great fault of naturalistic philosophers is to ignore the problems of epistemology. As a result, they have ended with a theory about the nature of the external world and of the individual mind and of the relations between the two which makes it impossible to understand how men could have acquired the scientific knowledge on which the naturalistic synthesis is based. The nemesis of this, in the case of the more intelligent and reflective of them, is agnosticism or scepticism; and this cannot be confined, as they would wish, to the objects of religious belief or the dogmas of theology.

It was not until he was an old man that Ward put together and published the positive results of his epistemological and ontological thinking. He had the unusual honour to be invited for a second time to give the Gifford Lectures, and he published these lectures in 1911 under the title: *The Realm of Ends: — Pluralism and Theism*. The theory here set forth is a form of pan-psychic pluralism, reminiscent of Leibniz's doctrine, but without the embarrassments due to Leibniz's denial of interaction between monads. What appears to a human being as a material thing is in fact, according to Ward, a complex composed of entities, each of which is of fundamentally the same nature as a human mind, but indefinitely simpler and less intelligent, and utterly hide-bound by habit. Individually they cannot be perceived by us; and a complex of them, which appears to us as a bit of matter, would appear in characteristically different ways to observers of different kinds and grades.

According to Ward, the laws of physics are *statistical* laws about the average or the collective behaviour of vast numbers of such low-grade habit-bound minds. He held that the particular laws which now hold in nature are the products of slow evolution, and that they are destined slowly to change in the course of further evolution. The general principle governing such secular changes is that behaviour, which was originally spontaneous and consciously initiated and controlled, tends by repetition to become habitual and automatic. Ward, like Lloyd Morgan and Alexander, postulated the emergence in the course of history of genuinely new features, which are not even in theory predictable from the fullest possible knowledge of antecedent facts and laws.

On Ward's view, the reality which appears to human percipients as a person's body is, like any other material thing, a certain complex of low-grade minds. Such a complex may be called a person's 'organism'. A human mind stands in specially intimate telepathic *rapport* with those low-grade minds which together constitute its organism. By this means it gains indirect knowledge of things outside its organism and it can indirectly control and modify them.

Ward thought that the pluralistic and panpsychic features in his system are practically forced upon anyone who, from the basis of an adequate epistemology, tries to take a synoptic view of all the facts of physics, biology, physiology and psychology. He thinks that it is quite open for a reasonable man to stop at that point. But, *if* such a person should raise questions about the origin and the destiny of this pluralistic panpsychic universe, then Ward holds that he will find the most satisfactory answer available to his question in a certain form of *theism*. This theory postulates a single creative person, on whose existence that of all the monads one-sidedly depends; and it postulates unending future existence, at any rate for all monads at or above the human level. Ward does not claim that this superstructure to his panpsychic pluralism can be proved. These propositions are at most ventures of faith, and the only available test for them is whether or not such over-beliefs have been and will always remain indispensable factors in the evolution of individuals and societies.

Ward left no disciples among later teachers of philosophy in Cambridge. But he had a profound influence on one eminent Cambridge philosophic theologian. Dr. F. R. Tennant's great work, *Philosophical Theology*, published in 1928 and 1930, is plainly inspired by and permeated with Ward's psychological and philosophical theories. Without prejudice to its own importance and originality, it may be said to contain the best statement of Ward's psychological and epistemological principles which is to be found outside his own writings.

I pass now to our other psychologist-philosopher, George Frederic Stout. I could not omit him from my list, for he was a distinguished student of philosophy in Cambridge and was for a time Fellow of St. John's College and lecturer in moral science here. And I certainly would not wish to omit him; for I was deeply indebted to him both for personal kindness and for invaluable philosophical stimulus when I was beginning my professional career, and I regard him as one of the ablest all-round English philosophers of the last fifty years. But, although he held a Fellowship at St. John's College, Cambridge, from 1884 to 1896, he was a lecturer in the University only for the last two years of that period, and all the rest of his long life was spent away from Cambridge. It would therefore be unfitting here to devote to him the space which the importance of his contributions to philosophy deserves.

Stout was born in 1860 and died in 1944. Before taking up the study of moral science he won brilliant academic success in classics with special distinction in ancient philosophy. His achievement in moral science was no less outstanding, for here he obtained special distinction in metaphysics. In 1892 he became editor of *Mind*. He held that difficult post with great success until 1922, when he resigned and was succeeded by Professor Moore. He left Cambridge in 1896 to become Lecturer in Comparative Psychology at Aberdeen University. Three years later he left Aberdeen to become the first holder of the Wilde Readership in Mental Philosophy at Oxford. He stayed there until 1903, when he became Professor of Logic at St. Andrew's University in Scotland. He held that chair for the next thirty-five years. In 1939, in his eightieth year, he left England and went to live in Sydney, Australia, where his son Alan was and still is professor. There he spent the remaining five years of his life. He kept the full vigour of his intellect up to the end, and played an important part in philosophical discussions in his new home.

Stout published two books on psychology which at once became, and have ever since remained, standard works These were his *Analytic Psychology*, published in 1896, and his *Manual of Psychology*, first published in 1899. The latter, in spite of its repulsive colour and inconvenient format, at once became a standard textbook, though it is very much more than a text-book. It was repeatedly revised and re-published, latterly in collaboration with distinguished younger psychologists, such as Professor Mace and Dr. Thouless. The fifth and last edition, revised in collaboration with the former and provided with an appendix on the *Gestalt Theory* by the latter, appeared in 1938, and has already been thrice re-printed since then.

Throughout his life Stout took an active part in the psychological, epistemological and metaphysical developments which made that period so exciting a one in the history of English philosophy. He never lost his interest in new ideas or points of view, or his power to understand them and to appraise them critically but fairly. But he was a highly independent thinker, and by late middle life he had achieved a system of his own which he never afterwards saw reason to modify in principle. The most important of the numerous papers which he had published up to 1921 were collected and published in 1930 under the title *Studies in Philosophy and Psychology*. At least three of these papers, viz. 'Real Being and Being for Thought', 'Some Fundamental Points in the Theory of Knowledge' and 'The Nature of Universals and Propositions', are among the most important and original contributions made in England to philosophy during the period. Of the remaining fourteen papers none falls below a very high standard. Stout had been a pupil of Ward, and had a great affection and admiration for him. The paper entitled 'Ward as a Psychologist', with its appendix 'James Ward on Sense and Thought', is the best account that exists of the fundamental principles of Ward's psychology. It is highly critical, but it is the criticism of a man who understands and can sympathize and appreciate. In other essays in this collection Stout criticizes acutely certain important doctrines in the philosophy of Bradley and in that of Russell, and in so doing defines and defends his own characteristic views on a number of fundamental points.

Stout was Gifford Lecturer from 1919 to 1921. One volume based on these lectures and entitled *Mind and Matter* appeared in 1931. A second volume, based on the rest of the lectures, was promised at the time, but it did not appear until twenty-one years later. In 1952 it was published, under the title *God and Nature*, by Stout's son Alan, who compiled it from his father's notes.

In these two volumes is to be found the philosophic system which was the permanent background of Stout's many essays on particular problems, together with his reasons for holding it. I cannot attempt here to give more than the most sketchy account of this. It must suffice to say that Stout's conclusions are based on a highly original analysis of the problem of sense-perception and the existential status of sense-data, of the nature of activity and of causation, of the unity of the self, and of the mind-body relationship in a human individual. He rejects as inadequate the regularity-analysis of causation, and as unnecessary and unintelligible the doctrine of a pure ego, and he denies the possibility of a disembodied finite mind. He holds that sense-data are neither mental nor material. He asserts that they are fragments of an objective continuum of sensibilia, and that material things are in some way composed of sensibilia in this continuum. Finally, he holds that this objective continuum of sensibilia is existentially dependent on a single non-finite mind which, unlike any finite mind, is aware of it as a whole and not merely of selections from it. His doctrine is thus a very subtle and highly elaborate blend of realistic and idealistic elements, culminating in a peculiar form of philosophic theism.

(3) *Pure Metaphysicians.* The one pure metaphysician in our list is John McTaggart Ellis McTaggart, who was born in 1866 and died in 1925. He became Fellow of Trinity College, Cambridge, in 1891, and lecturer in moral science in 1897. He had only just retired from that office at the time of his sudden and unexpected death.

McTaggart's intellectual background was extremely unlike that of most of the philosophers under consideration. He was from the beginning a pure metaphysician, with very little knowledge of, or interest in, either mathematics or any of the natural sciences. Even within the philosophical sphere he practically ignored psychology and epistemology. Though not interested or expert in formal logic, he had an amazing power of detecting logical fallacies and of constructing, without symbolism, complicated chains of deductive reasoning, which were in the main logically impeccable. In this respect, it seems to me, he had the intellect of a lawyer of genius in the highest and most abstract branches of the law. He was a mystic, and at the same time a *bon vivant* and a man of admirable wit. He had, and assiduously cultivated, a number of strong prejudices; he combined opinions which are seldom held together; and, when he defended in public an opinion which he happened to share with others, he was liable to do so by arguments which acutely embarrassed them.

I was McTaggart's pupil from the time when I began to study philosophy, though never in any sense his disciple, and I succeeded him in his lectureship when he retired. I am deeply indebted to him both as a teacher and as a most faithful and helpful elder friend. He did me the honour to make me a co-trustee under

his will and his sole literary executor. In the latter capacity it fell
to my lot to see through the press the second volume of his great
work, *The Nature of Existence*, which was fortunately complete in
typescript at the time of his death, though it lacked his final cor-
rections. Some years later I wrote and published an elaborate
critical commentary on his whole system, under the title of *Examination of McTaggart's Philosophy*.

Except for his semi-popular book, *Some Dogmas of Religion*,
which came out in 1906, all McTaggart's earlier published work
was concerned with the philosophy of Hegel. Absolute idealism,
deriving from Hegel, may fairly be said to have been for many
years the orthodox philosophy in British universities outside
of Cambridge in McTaggart's youth and middle age. Its most
distinguished representatives at the time were Bradley and Bosanquet. McTaggart was the only absolute idealist among the
Cambridge philosophers; and his interpretation of Hegel was quite
peculiar to himself, though it was based on a profound study of
the text and supported by extremely ingenious exegesis of the
master's often unintelligible sentences. In the first of these books,
Studies in Hegelian Dialectic, published in 1896, McTaggart endeavoured to explain and to defend the peculiar Hegelian method of
argument by thesis, antithesis and synthesis. In the second of
them, *Studies in Hegelian Cosmology*, published in 1901, he expounded and defended *inter alia* his own highly original and unorthodox interpretation of the highest category in Hegel's *Logic*,
viz. the Absolute Idea. In the last of them, *A Commentary to
Hegel's Logic*, published in 1910, he investigated in detail, category by category, the actual course of Hegel's dialectical argument
from Pure Being to the Absolute Idea, and pronounced on the
validity or invalidity of each step.

The upshot of the positive argument in *Studies in Hegelian Cosmology* may be stated as follows. Whatever Hegel himself may
have held, his general principles, when fully worked out, imply
that the universe, as it really is, is not a *person* but a perfect *society*
of perfect and eternal persons, each of whom is in love with one or
more of the rest. Moreover, it is highly probable that each human
mind, as it really is, is identical with one of these persons. If so,

each of us is in reality *eternal*, and our eternity will probably appear *sub specie temporis* as persistence throughout the whole of past and future time.

From this conclusion McTaggart never departed, though he came to doubt the validity of the efficacy of the Hegelian dialectic as a means of proving it. In a chapter of *Some Dogmas of Religion*, entitled 'Human Immortality and Pre-existence', he argues that the antecedent objections to human survival of bodily death, drawn from common-sense and natural science, are quite worthless. He thereupon takes, purely as a hypothesis for the present, the doctrine that each of us *sub specie temporis* persists throughout the whole of past and future time, and that this existence is split up into a sequence of many successive lives, each beginning with a birth and ending with a death. He defends this hypothesis against obvious *prima facie* objections, and he claims that it is compatible with the facts of heredity. He claims also that it would provide a neat explanation for certain other facts, e.g. for love at first sight, and for the rapidity with which some men acquire certain skills which others attain (if at all) only after years of practice. He tries to show that loss of memory of one's previous lives does not make this hypothesis meaningless or this kind of survival practically worthless, and that it has the merit of ridding us of a burden which would become unendurable.

From about 1912 onwards McTaggart was engaged in working out his own system of ontology. Abandoning the dialectical method, he claimed to prove, by straightforward deduction from a few allegedly self-evident premisses and a very few universally admitted empirical facts, that the structure and contents of the universe must be such as they would be on his interpretation of Hegel's category of the Absolute Idea. I cannot attempt here even to sketch the outlines of this extraordinarily complex, subtle, comprehensive and closely interlocking skein of argument. It is the less needful to do so, as McTaggart, who had an unrivalled capacity for lucid and succinct statement, has himself given an admirable synopsis in his contribution to *Contemporary British Philosophy*, Vol. I.

If McTaggart's conclusions be correct, it is plain that each of us must radically misperceive, not only all that he ostensibly perceives by his senses, but also himself and his own mental processes. For, apart from all more specific illusions, we perceive everything as *temporal*, and McTaggart claimed to prove by an extremely interesting and original argument that temporal characteristics are self-contradictory and therefore cannot really belong to anything. McTaggart was thus faced with the two fundamental problems which confront all systems of absolute idealism. How can that which is really timeless appear to that which is really timeless as enduring and changing? And how can the perfect parts of a perfect whole misperceive it and themselves and each other in the numerous and fundamental ways in which they in fact do? Perhaps the most impressive part of McTaggart's system is his attempt to solve in detail this fundamental problem, which all other absolute idealists have shirked or concealed under a rhetorical smoke-screen of metaphor and generality. All that I can say here of McTaggart's constructive theory is this. He argues that all other misperceptions depend on the fundamental illusion of misperceiving what is really timeless as temporal. He therefore set himself to determine the real nature of those timeless series of timeless terms which appear to us as temporal sequences of transitory things and of events. I cannot attempt here to expound the very ingenious and elaborate solution which he proposed for this problem.

I do not suppose that McTaggart made a single disciple. But he certainly exercised a most salutary influence on his pupils by his logical subtlety, his combination of rigid intellectual honesty with deep feeling, and the exquisite clarity with which he expressed his most complex thoughts. For my part I would say without hesitation that the two volumes of the *Nature of Existence*, in which he expounded and tried to demonstrate his system, are a quite unique contribution to Western philosophy. The only works with which they can fittingly be compared are the *Enneads* of Plotinus, the *Ethics* of Spinoza and the *Encyclopaedia* of Hegel. Unlike those classics of speculative philosophy, they are written in a pellucid style, which eschews vagueness and metaphor, and makes reading a pleasure for those who can appreciate this difficult kind of excellence.

(4) *The Moralist-Philosophers.* I turn now to our two moralists, and I begin with Sidgwick. Henry Sidgwick was born in 1838 and died in 1900. After a very distinguished academic course in classics, and a highly respectable one in mathematics, he became Fellow of Trinity College, Cambridge, in 1859, and lecturer in moral science in 1867. At that time a holder of a college fellowship had to express formally his assent to the doctrines of the Church of England. This obligation was not usually taken very seriously; but Sidgwick was an exceptionally conscientious man, and by 1869 he had reached a theological position which, he felt, obliged him to resign an office held under those conditions. The College understood and appreciated Sidgwick's motives and enabled him to continue to teach for it, though inevitably with diminished income and amenities. As soon as an alteration in the law enabled it to do so, it elected him to an honorary Fellowship. He became Knightbridge Professor of Moral Philosophy in 1883, and he held the chair until shortly before his death in 1900. Apart from his philosophic activities, he played a very important rôle in the transformation of the University from its ancient to its modern organization, and in its day-to-day policy and administration. Together with his wife, who was sister to the Conservative statesman and philosopher Arthur James Balfour and was one of the ablest persons in England throughout her long lifetime, he had much to do with the gradual opening of Cambridge University to women students, and in particular with the founding and initial development of Newnham College for women.

Sidgwick's most important contribution to moral philosophy is his *Methods of Ethics,* which was first published in 1874. It went into many editions and assumed its final form in the sixth edition, published in 1901, the year after the author's death. Other works which he published in his lifetime were *Principles of Political Economy* (1883), *Outlines of the History of Ethics* (1886), and *Elements of Politics* (1891). Shortly after his death the following works, embodying courses of lectures by him, were published, viz. *Philosophy, its Scope and Relations* (1902), *The Ethics of Green, Spencer, and Martineau* (1902), *Development of European Polity* (1903), and *The Philosophy of Kant* (1905). I shall confine my attention to Sidgwick's ethical doctrines and to the attitude which they led him to take up towards human immortality and towards theism.

Sidgwick regards the notion of moral obligation as unique and unanalysable, but perfectly familiar to every sane adult human being. It is not clear to me, from his very elaborate and subtle discussion of the notion of goodness, whether he did or did not take the same view about moral good and evil, but I suspect that he did.

Sidgwick distinguished carefully, perhaps for the first time, between what he calls 'psychological hedonism' and what he calls 'ethical hedonism'. The former is the doctrine that the only ultimate human motive is desire to get and to prolong pleasant experiences and to avoid and to cut short unpleasant ones. This Sidgwick rejects as false, after careful discussion. The latter is the doctrine that nothing is intrinsically good or bad except experiences, and that the only characteristic of an experience which makes it intrinsically good or bad is its pleasantness or its unpleasantness respectively. Sidgwick holds that, when all the numerous sources of confusion have been envisaged and removed, this proposition can be seen on inspection to be necessarily true.

Now it is generally admitted that each of us is *inter alia* under a moral obligation to try to conserve and increase the amount of good in the world and to try to diminish and to avert evil. But it also seems *prima facie* obvious to common sense that a person is under many other moral obligations, which are as self-evidently binding as this one, and are not derived or derivable from it. Plausible examples are the obligation to keep one's promises, to answer questions truly, and so on. Sidgwick undertook an extraordinarily careful and subtle critical analysis of the morality of common sense in the Western hemisphere in historical times, with the following object in view. He wanted to find out whether it could be reduced to a set of propositions, severally self-evident and collectively consistent, of the form: 'Such and such conduct is unconditionally obligatory in such and such circumstances.' He found himself compelled to give a negative answer to this question. According to him, there remains only one proposition, asserting an unconditional obligation, which continues, after this process of analysis, to appear necessarily true on inspection. It is this. The one and only ultimate obligation is to act on each occasion in such a way as will tend, under the circumstances, to conserve or increase the amount of good or diminish the amount of evil in the universe. If we add to this Sidgwick's principle of ethical hedonism, we can substitute for the word 'good' the phrase 'pleasant experience', and for the word 'evil' the phrase 'unpleasant experience', in the above statement of our one ultimate obligation.

Sidgwick then reconsiders the morality of common sense, in the light of this principle of hedonistic utilitarianism. He tries to show in detail that the special obligations, which common sense regards as self-evident in special kinds of situation, do in fact accord with those which would follow in such situations from that principle and from the psychological and social properties of human nature. He tries to show that, in marginal cases where two or more principles of common-sense morality conflict, common sense itself appeals to this principle as arbiter. Lastly, he shows that, on the utilitarian principle itself, it is most undesirable that plain men, in the ordinary recurrent situations of their daily life, should directly appeal to that principle in determining what they ought to do.

So far Sidgwick seemed to himself to have brought coherence into the theory of morals. But there remained for him the following difficulty. The utilitarian principle needs to be supplemented by some principle about the right way of distributing one's beneficient activities as between oneself and others, and as between the various individuals other than oneself whom one can affect by one's actions. The principle of distribution naturally associated with utilitarianism is that of complete impartiality between self and others and between all others, except in so far as departure from it will produce more happiness or less unhappiness on the whole and in the long run. Sidgwick accepted this neutralistic principle of distribution as self-evident. But he *also* found self-evident another principle, which Butler had formulated in a famous concessive sentence, viz. that a person is *not* justified in undertaking any course of action unless he is convinced that it will either be conducive to *his own* happiness or at any rate not detrimental to it. It seemed, then, to Sidgwick that *both* the neutralistic principle of distribution and this egoistic principle are self-evident. And it was plain to him that they are inconsistent with each other. Now Sidgwick had no remedy to offer for this *theoretic* incoherence at the heart of morality. What he did carefully consider is the factual conditions which must be postulated if no conflict is ever to arise in *practice*. He was quite certain that within this life such practical conflicts can and do arise. Conduct which would be permitted or enjoined by the neutralistic principle would in certain cases be forbidden by the egoistic principle, or conversely. A *necessary* condition for the avoidance of such conflicts in the long run would be that human beings should survive the death of their present bodies. But this condition would be by no means sufficient. An equally necessary condition is that the course of nature in this life and the next should have a special teleological character, such that sacrifices of one's own happiness for that of others in this life will be compensated in the life to come. The most familiar form of this postulate in the Western world is theism.

As regards the postulate of human survival, Sidgwick thought it conceivable that empirical evidence might become available. This possibility was one motive at the back of his life-long active and critical interest in psychical research. He and his wife were largely responsible for making this a serious and respectable scientific subject in England, through the foundation of the Society for Psychical Research in 1882 and the care which they took to set it in the straight and narrow path of science from the outset. As regards theism, Sidgwick saw no prospect of its ever becoming more than a practical postulate. In that respect it seemed to him to be neither better nor worse off than the presuppositions about nature which lie at the back of the inductive procedures of natural science.

Sidgwick's perfect balance and calm good sense, his obvious devotion to truth, and his method of doing philosophy, if not the conclusions which he reached, had an immense influence on the next generation of Cambridge philosophers, such as Johnson, Stout, McTaggart and Moore, who were his pupils.

I shall do no more than mention William Robert Sorley, who succeeded Sidgwick as Knightbridge Professor in 1900, held the

D

chair until 1933, and died two years later at the age of eighty. He was an able philosopher, as his Gifford Lectures, entitled *Moral Values and the Idea of God*, published in 1918 abundantly testify. He was also a learned and accurate historian of philosophy, and his *History of English Philosophy*, published in 1920, is a standard work. But I am sure that I do his memory no injustice in saying that he stood outside the main stream of Cambridge philosophy and has exerted little influence upon it.

(5) *Professor G. E. Moore*. Professor Moore, whom I treat as in a class by himself, has undoubtedly had a greater influence than any one other man on English philosophy in general and Cambridge philosophy in particular during the last fifty years.

George Edward Moore was born in 1873. He had a distinguished undergraduate career as a student of classics before taking to moral science. He became Fellow of Trinity College, Cambridge, in 1898. He left Cambridge in 1904 and held no teaching post until he returned in 1911 to become a university lecturer in moral science in succession to the elder Keynes, who had become Registrary. He took over the editorship of *Mind* from Stout in 1920, and continued to hold it until 1947, when he relinquished it to the present editor, Professor Ryle of Oxford. In 1925, on the death of Ward, he became Professor of Philosophy in Cambridge, and he held that chair until 1939, when he retired on reaching the present statutory age-limit of sixty-five. During the war he was lecturing in the U.S.A. He returned to Cambridge in 1944. He was honoured with the Order of Merit in 1951.

Moore has not been a prolific writer, though the aggregate of his published papers is quite considerable. The immense influence which he has exercised arises partly from the fact that several of his publications have given a quite new turn to philosophical discussion, and that all of them have been models of acute, subtle and profound thinking on absolutely fundamental topics, expressed in clear, simple English. Then, again, Moore has greatly influenced generations of Cambridge students and teachers of philosophy by courses of lectures which he has never published, e.g. on philosophical psychology, by discussion-classes, and by his interventions in philosophical debate. He has been a regular attendant at meetings of philosophical societies, and his contributions to the discussion of other men's papers have always gone to the root of the matter and have often been the most important event of the occasion.

Moore is essentially a critical and analytic, and not directly a constructive, philosopher. But he is the very opposite of a philosophic sceptic. What is almost unique about him — though this quality was shared by his eminent Oxford contemporary Prichard — is a combination of simplicity and directness and what looks superficially almost like naivety, with the most remarkable powers of analysis and criticism. Often this has had the devastating effect of the child in the fable, who horrified the courtiers by piping out that the emperor was in fact naked. One other general feature of Moore's work should be noted. He has confined his attention, on the one hand, to the beliefs — or, as he would say, to the *knowledge* — of common sense, and, on the other hand, to the theories of philosophers. He has not, like so many of his contemporaries, e.g. Whitehead and Russell, concerned himself with the methods or the results of mathematics or of natural science. This is not, I am sure, because he underrates their philosophic interest and importance. He would say, I think, that he lacks the technical knowledge and training needed for contributing directly anything of value here, and that there is enough for him to do in fields where no such background is needed.

Moore's earliest work was in ethics. His *Principia Ethica*, published in 1903, marked the beginning of a new and very fruitful phase in English moral philosophy. This lasted until the development of the now fashionable view that moral sentences in the indicative do not really express *judgments*, in which a predicate is asserted or denied of a subject, but serve merely to evince certain emotions in the speaker or evoke them in the hearer, or are disguised expressions of commands.

Assuming without question that such sentences *do* express judgments, Moore argued that moral predicates, and in particular goodness, are not only unanalysable, but are qualities of a unique and peculiar *kind*, which he calls 'non-natural'. Those who thought

otherwise had, according to Moore, failed to distinguish between
goodness itself and some natural characteristic which they believed
(rightly or wrongly) to be necessary and sufficient to confer goodness on anything that possesses it. This confusion Moore labelled
'the naturalistic fallacy'. He reverted to this topic in an essay entitled 'The Conception of Intrinsic Value', published in his *Philosophical Studies* (1922). His latest published pronouncement on it,
made in view of criticisms by supporters of the emotive or im-
perative analysis of moral indicatives, is to be found in the terminal
essay which he contributed to the collective volume entitled *The
Philosophy of G. E. Moore* (1942). Moore's other published contributions to ethics are an essay in the *Philosophical Studies* entitled
'The Nature of Moral Philosophy', and a small book called *Ethics*,
published in 1912. In the latter he develops with his usual meticu-
lous care a utilitarian, but non-hedonistic, account of what makes
right acts right.

In the year which saw the publication of *Principia Ethica* Moore
contributed to *Mind* an article entitled 'Refutation of Idealism',
which was in its way no less a landmark in English philosophy. It
started afresh, and from a new angle, that intensive discussion of
the nature and validity of sense-perception which has been going
on here ever since. To this Moore has made several later contributions of fundamental importance. These are the essays entitled 'The
Nature and Reality of Objects of Perception', 'The Status of Sense-
data', and 'Some Judgments of Perception', all of which are re-printed in his *Philosophical Studies*. Another essay in this collection,
which deals with a very different topic, is the one entitled 'External
and Internal Relations'. This is a penetrating analysis of a confused
notion which has played an important part in the arguments of
many absolute idealists. It is here that Moore makes clear the
vital distinction between what he calls 'entailment', which is the
kind of logical relation that subsists between the premises and the
conclusion of a valid demonstrative argument, and the notions
which Russell describes as 'material implication' and 'formal implication'.

In 1925 Moore started a new hare, which is still being vigorously hunted by the keenest philosophical hounds on both sides of

the Atlantic. This was the essay, entitled 'A Defence of Common Sense', which was his contribution to Vol. II of the collective work *Contemporary British Philosophy*.

The essential point of this may be stated roughly as follows. Moore mentions a number of typical propositions, some physical and some psychological, which may fairly be called 'common-sense' propositions. Among the former are the propositions that his own body has existed for many years, and that there are and have been other living human bodies. Among the latter are the propositions that he himself has had experiences of various kinds, and that those other living human bodies have been the bodies of *persons*, each of whom has had experiences of various kinds. Now Moore makes, in regard to such propositions, two claims to *knowledge* in the strictest sense. One may be described as a claim to 'first-order' knowledge, and the other as a claim to 'second-order' knowledge. (i) He claims to *know* many propositions of each of the kinds which I have mentioned. This is the first-order claim. (ii) He claims to *know*, with regard to the other persons whom he knows to be the owners of the other living human bodies which he knows to exist, that each of *them* knows many propositions of each of the kinds which I have mentioned. This is the second-order claim, since it is a claim to knowledge about knowledge.

Now it is essential to notice that Moore holds that each of the sentences which he has used in giving examples of common-sense propositions is completely *unambiguous* and completely *intelligible*. Each such English sentence, according to him, has one and only one literal meaning, and everyone who knows English understands any such sentence in precisely the same sense. Thus Moore would not be content with the admission that we all know that such propositions are true in some sense or to some degree. He insists that we all know them to be true *without qualification* in the *one sense* in which we all understand them.

Moore distinguishes sharply between *what* a sentence means and the *analysis* of what it means. According to him, as we have seen, there is no kind of doubt as to what such sentences mean, and no kind of doubt in many cases that what such a sentence means is true. But he holds that there is no certainty as to the *correct analysis* of what such sentences mean. His view is that the business of philosophers with these common-sense propositions is, not to discuss their truth or falsity, but to try to find the right analysis of them. In view of later developments it is worth while to note the following two points. Moore never alleged that this is the *only* legitimate business of philosophers. And he never committed the absurdity of insisting that the philosophic analysis of common-sense propositions must be stated entirely in common-sense language.

It is natural that this programme should have raised much philosophical dust. Moore merely states that there is a fundamental distinction between meaning and analysis, and merely asserts that the former is agreed upon, and in many cases known to be true, by everyone, whilst the latter is open to doubt and controversy. He does not attempt to define 'analysis' or 'meaning', or to offer any criterion for judging whether a proposed analysis of the meaning of a sentence is correct or not. So English and American philosophers, ever since 1926, have been involved in endless discussions about the 'meaning of analysis', 'the analysis of meaning', the 'meaning of meaning' and the 'analysis of analysis', and the straw has been chopped very fine indeed.

(6) *Logico-mathematical Philosophers.* The last class in my list consists of Whitehead, Earl Russell and Wittgenstein. I shall take Wittgenstein first, and thus out of his chronological order. I shall devote only a few lines to him, because several of my younger colleagues, who will be lecturing in this course, have attended his lectures and discussion-classes and have been profoundly influenced by him, whilst I have neither done the former nor suffered the latter.

Ludwig Josef Johann Wittgenstein was born in Austria in 1889. He came to England some years before the first world war and studied engineering at the University of Manchester. This aroused his interest first in pure mathematics and then in the philosophy of mathematics. This in turn led him to make the acquaintance of Russell, who was then in Cambridge; and he came here to work with him on mathematical logic and the philosophical problems that arise in connection with it. He fought in the first world war as an artillery officer in the Austrian army and was captured by the Italians. Soon after the armistice he was released, and by that time he had completed the manuscript of the only book that was published in his life-time. This appeared, in German with an English translation on alternate pages, in England in 1922 under the title of *Tractatus Logico-philosophicus*. It was immediately hailed as a work of first-rate importance and originality, and it has had immense influence. Some time later, largely owing to the good offices of Lord Keynes and of Ramsey, Wittgenstein returned to Cambridge. In 1930, Trinity College, which had in the meanwhile been helping him with grants, elected him to a special kind of Fellowship in order to enable him to devote himself without interruption to his philosophical work. In 1939 he succeeded Moore as Professor of Philosophy. He retired, at his own request, in 1947 in order to give his whole time to his researches. He died in 1951, leaving behind him the completed manuscript of at least one important book. Wittgenstein's influence was exerted by discussion and by 'thinking aloud' rather than by formal lecturing or published writings. It has been greater than that of any other Cambridge philosopher of our period except Professor Moore and perhaps Lord Russell. Wittgenstein exercised an almost hypnotic effect on many of his pupils, which, as he freely admitted, was not always to the good of the weaker brethren and sisters.

I turn finally to Whitehead and Russell. I owe very much to their teaching, and I am happy and proud to have been honoured with their friendship as a young man.

Alfred North Whitehead was born in 1861 and died in 1947. He was a very distinguished pure mathematician, and from 1884, when he became Fellow of Trinity College, Cambridge, to 1911, when he left Cambridge for London, his work and his teaching were almost wholly mathematical. His interest in general philosophy, as distinct from mathematical logic, grew rapidly during the period from 1914 to 1923, when he was Professor of Mathematics at the Imperial College of Science in the University of London. In 1924, at the age of sixty-three, he accepted an invitation to become a professor of philosophy at Harvard University, and the rest of his long life was spent in America and devoted to philosophy. The work which he did there, however important it may be, does not concern us, for it had little affinity with, and no appreciable influence upon, philosophy in Cambridge. What concerns us here is the three books on the philosophy of mathematical physics which he published between 1918 and 1923, and his earlier collaboration with Russell in the production of *Principia Mathematica*. The latter will be most conveniently dealt with when we come to Russell.

The three books in question are *The Principles of Natural Knowledge* (1919), *The Concept of Nature* (1920), and *The Principle of Relativity* (1922). They were written at a time when the theory of relativity had stirred the waters to their depths, and slightly before the impact of the quantum theory had been generally felt. In the first two of them Whitehead was mainly concerned with the following three problems. (i) To overcome the familiar dualism between a world of scientific objects, supposed to be knowable only as the remote causal ancestors of our sensations, and a world of sense-data, supposed to be private to individual percipients. (ii) To show in detail the connection between the crude data of sense-perception and such refined mathematical concepts as those of point, instant, particle, instantaneous velocity and so on. (iii) To deduce the transformation-equations of the special theory of relativity from extremely general features of our spatio-temporal experience, without reference to such concrete and contingent matters as the synchronization of clocks by means of light-signals and the measurement of lengths by means of measuring-rods. Whitehead claimed to solve the second of these problems by means of what he called the 'Principle of Extensive Abstraction'. An instance of the use of this principle is the definition of a 'point' as the logical sum of the class of all those series of volumes such that *each* series would commonly be said to 'converge to a point' and *all* the series would commonly be said to 'converge to the same point'. The essence of the method is, of course, to translate these phrases into others, in which the word 'point' and its equivalents do not occur, and in which nothing is mentioned except *volumes* and certain perceptible relations between volumes.

In *The Principle of Relativity* Whitehead dealt, in a highly original way, with the general theory of relativity. The mixture of philosophical or epistemological considerations with purely mathematical deductions, which is characteristic of the book, made it distasteful to both philosophers and mathematicians, and, to use Hume's phrase, it 'fell still-born from the press'.

Last but not least in my list of Cambridge philosophers is Bertrand Arthur William, third Earl Russell. He was born in 1872, and became a Fellow of Trinity College, Cambridge, in 1895. He was College lecturer from 1910 to 1916. Since then he has mainly lived out of Cambridge. He was awarded the Order of Merit in 1951; the same high honour had been awarded to Whitehead six years earlier. Like Whitehead, he began his career as a pure mathematician. When he first turned to philosophy he was much influenced by the absolute idealists Bradley and Bosanquet. His first book, *The Foundations of Geometry* (1897), which treats space as a form of intuition, bears witness to this influence, which was but transient.

The next phase in Russell's development was reached under the influence of Moore. He now rejected absolute idealism and the logic associated with it, and became a realist in the Scholastic sense of the word. At this time he had occasion to make an intensive study of the works of Leibniz. The result of this was expressed in his book *The Philosophy of Leibniz* (1900). Russell argued that all the most characteristic doctrines of Leibniz's philosophy, however paradoxical they may seem, are necessary consequences of the commonly accepted view that every true proposition ascribes to a subject, which is a substance, a predicate which corresponds to a state of that substance. Russell's interpretation received considerable support very soon afterwards from the hitherto unpublished papers of Leibniz which Couturat discovered at Hanover and published in 1903.

Meanwhile Russell was becoming more and more interested in the philosophy of mathematics. In 1900 he first came to appreciate the importance of the symbolic logic of Peano and the work of Frege on arithmetic. The results of his new insights were embodied in his *Principles of Mathematics* (Vol. I), which appeared in 1903. The essential theme of this book is that pure mathematics has no concepts which cannot be defined in terms of those of logic, and no special methods of reasoning other than those recognized in any reasonably complete system of formal logic. The book contains a great deal of interesting and important matter beside this, e.g. an examination of the principles of dynamics, and a reasoned acceptance of the philosophically unpopular theories of absolute space, time and motion. It presents Russell in the most realistic phase of his philosophical development.

There was to have been a second volume of the *Principles of Mathematics*. It was never written because Russell had begun to collaborate with Whitehead in the detailed carrying out of the programme outlined in the first volume. The result of this collaboration was one of the great philosophical works of the century, *Principia Mathematica*. The first volume of this appeared in 1910, the second in 1912, and the third in 1913. There was to have been a fourth volume, wholly by Whitehead, on geometry, but this unfortunately was never completed. The two collaborators each contributed very importantly to the contents of all the published volumes, and they deserve an equal share in the honour due to the work.

In the course of his work on mathematical logic Russell came upon the famous contradiction about the class of all classes which are not members of themselves. His attempt to deal with this, and with other paradoxes of a similar kind, by the notion of a hierarchy of logical types, has been the occasion of some of the deepest and most fruitful work that has been done on philosophical logic in our time.

Gradually Russell became dissatisfied with the somewhat naive logical realism which had hitherto been the philosophical basis of his work in logic. This dissatisfaction was perhaps quickened by the excesses to which that doctrine is carried in the works of Meinong, which Russell admired and had carefully studied. The first outcome of this new tendency was his theory of descriptions, i.e. his analysis of propositions expressed by sentences of the form 'The so-and-so is such-and-such', and his account of their existential import. Closely connected with this in Russell's mind was the epistemological distinction which he drew between what he called 'knowledge by acquaintance' and 'knowledge by description', and the epistemological principle, which he asserted, that in order to understand a description one must be acquainted with all the terms in the analysis of it. This part of Russell's work has helped to clear up a number of confusions and to solve a number of long-standing problems.

The next phase to be noted in the development of Russell's ideas is the notion of what he calls 'logical constructions', and its application to the problem of sense-perception and the nature of material things and of minds. There had been plenty of particular applications of this notion within pure mathematics, and plenty more in *Principia Mathematica*. An example is the definition of $\sqrt{2}$ as the class of all rational fractions whose squares are less than 2. Russell now applied the notion to the problem of the relation between the material things which we perceive and the sensations by which we perceive them. The older view, which Russell himself had taken in his little book *The Problems of Philosophy* (1912), may be stated roughly as follows. Material things and sense-data are of the same logical type, viz. particular existents, but of fundamentally different ontological kinds, and the relation between them is *causal*. Certain events in material things are the causal ancestors of the sensations by which those things are preceived. Russell proposed to substitute for this the doctrine that a material thing is a logical construction out of sense-data. What this comes to is roughly the following. A material thing is not a particular existent. It is a *class* of sense-data and unsensed sensibilia inter-related in certain assignable ways, viz. the class of all those sense-data and sensibilia which would commonly be called 'appearances of' one and the same thing from various points of view and under various conditions. Russell was vigorously engaged in this line of work round about 1914. His slogan was: 'Replace entities inferred as causes, by logical constructions out of the entities commonly taken as their effects!'

Russell was now coming much under the influence of the behaviouristic developments in psychology and of the theories of the psycho-analysts. One of the most exciting books that he ever wrote, *The Analysis of Mind* (1921), shows strong traces of these influences. But the most interesting strand in it is the attempt to treat a mind as a logical construction out of elements of the same kind as those which enter into those other logical constructions which are material things. Russell thus tried to develop a system of neutral monism, in which the ultimate stuff of the world is sensibilia and images, whilst minds and material things are collections of such entities organized on two fundamentally different principles.

Unlike Moore, Russell has always been greatly concerned with the philosophical implications of physical science. His next important book, *Analysis of Matter* (1927), was an elaborate and detailed attempt to make a synthesis of his earlier accounts of mind and of matter, at the level of ordinary sense-perception, with the story related by relativistic and quantum physics about the external world.

In his later years Russell has become greatly interested in the problem of induction and scientific inference. His latest important contribution to philosophy up to date is the book *Human Knowledge, its Scope and Limits*, which appeared in 1948. The main problem which he sets himself here may be described very roughly as follows. Let us grant that what the mathematical physicists tell us about the external world is substantially true, and let us grant also that what the physiologists, anatomists and psychologists tell us about the causal conditions of sensation and of sense-perception and habit and action is substantially true. What are the minimal assumptions that must be made about the structure and the routine of the world, in order to account for the fact that persons in our situation have been able to acquire knowledge of the kind which we have acquired? A typically Kantian problem, though Russell would probably not welcome the parallel!

A man who has written so much and who wields so fluent a pen as Russell inevitably makes slips, has his weaker moments, and in general exposes himself to criticisms which more cautious or more costive philosophers escape. And a man who continues to philosophize and to publish his thoughts up to a very advanced age will almost certainly fall foul of the prevailing fashions, and find his latest writings treated with neglect, condescension or insolence by his juniors. To some extent this has happened to Russell. I will therefore take this opportunity to say, in conclusion, that Russell's contributions to philosophy during the last fifty years have been of inestimable importance. We all stand on his shoulders, and those who are now inclined to decry his work or to damn it with faint praise will be fortunate indeed if they can accomplish in their prime anything comparable in value with some things that he has written in his old age.

A. C. EWING

Recent Developments
in
British Ethical Thought

ALFRED CYRIL EWING, D.PHIL. (Oxon), LITT.D. (Cantab.): born 1899; educated at Wyggeston Grammar School, Leicester, and University College, Oxford; Reader in Philosophy at Cambridge University since 1954; Fellow of Jesus College, Cambridge, since 1962; held lectureships in Philosophy at University College, Swansea, 1927-31, and Cambridge University, 1931-54; Visiting Professor at Princeton and Northwestern Universities, 1949; Fellow of British Academy since 1941.

Chief publications: *The Morality of Punishment (with some Suggestions for a General Theory of Ethics)*, 1929. *Idealism*, 1934. *A Short Commentary on Kant's Critique of Pure Reason*, 1939. *The Individual, the State and World Government*, 1947. *The Definition of Good*, 1947. *The Fundamental Questions of Philosophy*, 1951. *Ethics* (in the Teach-Yourself Series), 1953. *The Idealist Tradition*, 1957 (Ed). *Second Thoughts in Moral Philosophy*, 1959. 'The Work of G. E. Moore', *Indian Journal of Philosophy*, Vol. I, 1959. Various contributions to *The Proceedings of the Aristotelian Society* and to philosophical journals.

A. C. EWING

RECENT DEVELOPMENTS
IN
BRITISH ETHICAL THOUGHT

I. THE GOOD AND THE RIGHT

THAT 'ethics' in the sense in which it is a subject of study by philosophers, or, to use an equivalent term, 'moral philosophy', should aim at being a rigorous science, or at least one as rigorous as the nature of the subject will permit, and not primarily a branch of literature or an attempt to persuade people to do what is right or to express one's sense of emotional frustration or crisis, is an ideal that almost all British philosophers have set before themselves since the time of Hume. The methods of ethics have been generally held to be very different from those of the natural sciences, and few British philosophers would try to whittle down this difference, but they would hold that it aims at truth as its primary object as much as does any natural science. Even those who deny the objective truth of ethical judgments still usually think of moral philosophy as a means to finding out the truth, at any rate about the nature of our so-called ethical judgments or reactions. Thus what I have said holds just as much of Ayer as of Moore. Ayer indeed maintained in *Language, Truth and Logic* that our ordinary so-called ethical judgments are not assertions of what is true but expressions of emotion or practical exhortations, but he certainly held also that in saying this very thing about the nature of our ordinary ethical judgments philosophical ethics is propounding a truth. Our ethical judgments really are, on his view, of such a nature, and the statement that they are expressions of emotion and practical exhortations is not itself an expression of emotion or a practical exhortation any more than are the statements of physical science. That ethical judgments are not objectively true is a judgment that itself claims objective truth and theoretical, not practical, justification. It is vindicated, if at all, by the standards of truth, and not by rhetoric or congruity with one's emotional needs, and to its truth practical utility is irrelevant. It no doubt is more important that people should do what is right than that they should have a true idea of the nature of their ethical judgments, but the latter has some importance at least, and this is the aim of philosophical ethics, for what it is worth. I do not know if there are many continental philosophers who would disagree with these statements, but I make them because I certainly fancy that the ideal of ethics as an exclusively theoretical science in abstraction from literary expression or practical ends is operative in England to an extent which differentiates it from philosophical ethics in many other countries.

In trying to find out the truths of ethics it is taken for granted that its methods should be as rigorous, as scientific in a broad sense, as those of any natural science; but it is also generally recognized that they have from the nature of the case to be very different from the methods of what are usually called 'sciences'. While the latter proceed by induction based on observations, philosophical ethics proceeds largely by analysis of concepts and of propositions, and the kind of discoveries it makes are so different that most British philosophers would hesitate to call them new discoveries in the sense in which scientific discoveries are new. They are regarded as disclosing what in a sense we know already and as doing so by analysing the propositions of common sense, that is, analysing what we mean by our ordinary ethical statements and terms. Yet what they do seek to tell us is the truth, if only the truth about the workings of our own minds.

Anyone who looks to British moral philosophy for eloquent appeals to lead the good life or for emotional literary expressions of the perplexities of life will be very disappointed indeed. The former is the job of the preacher, the latter of the novelist or poet, neither is regarded as the job of the philosopher. It is the sharp separation between the theoretical and the practical or the emotional problem which as much as anything perhaps marks the difference between a good deal of contintental and British philosophy today. Hardly any British professional philosophers have been importantly affected by 'Existentialism', and although there is a widespread feeling among British writers on ethics that the subject should be more practical than it is, this has not as yet realized itself in their works in direct suggestions for dealing with practical ethical problems of life. Certainly in order to understand these philosophers we need to avoid having in our minds all the time the question — What is the practical use of their discussions? Ethics is, according to British philosophers in general, a kind of science in which the main method is analysis, and a science moreover which stands on its own feet without appealing to the support of metaphysics (though the latter view would no doubt be opposed by a great many theologians in this country as in others). Its study may have good practical results and may even make one better qualified to decide particular ethical questions in politics and daily life, though there is a tendency rather to minimize the extent to which this is so, but primarily it aspires to be a sort of science and aims at truth as a science.

Now modern British philosophical ethics may well be said to have begun with the publication of Moore's *Principia Ethica* in 1903, although Sidgwick's *Methods of Ethics* (1874) without having anything like the influence of the above-mentioned work anticipated it in its careful analytic method. Moore laid down the principle that good is a simple indefinable quality and based all obligation on the amount of good produced so that the right act for him was always the act which produced the greatest good or, to be more accurate, the greatest balance possible under the circumstances of good over evil. These are the two leading doctrines of Moore's ethical system, held also incidentally by Sidgwick, who, however, unlike Moore was a hedonist. They aroused two very prolonged controversies, with which I shall be dealing almost exclusively in my two lectures, and in this one I shall deal with the second. Moore was not a utilitarian like Sidgwick in the sense of believing that pleasures was the only good, but he was one in the sense of believing that the rightness of an action depended solely on its producing good results in the widest sense of that phrase. Consequently the only ultimate criterion for him whether an action was right lay in its consequences, but empirical inductive evidence as to what the consequences of an action are likely to be is not enough for ethics, we require also a knowledge as to whether such consequences would be good or bad in themselves. From his view that good is indefinable Moore concluded that the proposition that something was good or bad in itself was a synthetic proposition and could only be known by intuition. Moore makes no attempt to support his intuition as to what is good or bad by argument except in one respect, and it may be said that even this is not so much an argument as a help towards seeing the goodness or badness of something intuitively. I am referring to the use he makes of the device of asking us to imagine something in isolation which is in practice always accompanied by other things. This method of ideal isolation is used with effect by Moore against hedonism, when he asks whether 'if we *could* get as much pleasure in the world, without needing to have any knowledge or moral qualities, or any sense of beauty, as we can get *with* them, then all these things would be entirely superfluous',[1] and pleasure still seem the only good. And certainly, if we can intuit goodness at all, it is plain that we are in a better position to be aware of the intrinsic goodness of something when we imagine it by itself apart from the other things with which it is usually tied up in practice. But the advice to imagine it like this does not enable you to *prove* that good is where you think you intuit it.

In another respect, however, Moore was by no means an intuitionist. An 'intuitionist' in ethics commonly means someone who holds that we can intuitively see certain actions to be right or wrong, and Moore thought on the contrary that this could only be established by inference. The inference must take the form of arguing on inductive evidence to the likely consequences of an action and comparing those with the likely consequences of alternative actions. As I have said, such arguments could not have ethical significance unless they were supplemented by an intuition of the good or evil in these anticipated consequences, but the *argument* is necessary.

[1] *Ethics*, p. 147.

Moore's view that one's duty or the right act to do is always that act which is most conducive to the production of good and that a consideration of the goodness or badness of the consequences it will produce provides the sole ultimate criterion for deciding whether we ought to perform an act or not is commonly known as 'utilitarianism', but to distinguish them from hedonistic utilitarians the thinkers who hold this view but do not hold that pleasure is the only good have been called 'ideal utilitarians'. The best expositions of this type of view in English are Moore's *Principia Ethica* and *Ethics* and Rashdall's *Theory of Good and Evil*. The plausibility of the doctrine is obvious. It is very hard to believe that it could ever be one's duty deliberately to produce less good than one could or more evil than one need, and still harder to believe that it would be right to be satisfied with a world which, however much pleasure it contained, should contain none of the other things we are inclined to account intrinsically valuable. And to say that it will do good or at least more good or less harm than its alternatives seems to provide a rational ground in a way in which nothing else could for saying that an action is our duty or right. The theory gives a highly plausible explanation why we should do some things and not do others and a workable (though not easy) criterion for deciding cases of difficulty.

It indeed seems a serious objection to the view as formulated by Moore that we can never be certain whether a particular action will produce the best possible consequences, and that therefore it might well happen that an act which the agent had very good reason for thinking right turned out to be very wrong because it by a stroke of ill luck led to very bad consequences; but the objection might be met by saying that the right act in a given situation is not the act which would in fact produce the best possible consequences, but the act which it would be rational to choose taking into account only the goodness or badness of the likely consequences and the degree of probability of these consequences. This is much more in accord with the ordinary usage of the terms *right* and *duty*. If we say like Moore that the right act or the act which it is one's duty to do is the one which will in fact produce the best possible consequences, we shall have to admit that it is improbable that any human being has ever acted rightly, for whatever one does a being who forecasted consequences perfectly could surely always suggest an action the results of which would be still better. We do not ordinarily say that a person has acted wrongly because the consequences of his action turn out bad on account of some circumstances that he could not possibly be expected to have foreseen. And the reformulation would enable a utilitarian to maintain that we could know with certainty what we ought to do in very many cases despite the uncertainty of predictions, because we can know at least that it is probable that the results will be better if we do A than if we abstain from doing it or vice versa. Thus, if you will excuse my saying so, I cannot *know* that it would not do more good than harm to shoot one of you on the spot. I cannot possibly know all the indirect consequences of shooting you, and it might happen that through some accident the consequences turned out beneficial, but if we accept the second formulation of utilitarianism this need not prevent my saying that I know such an action to be wrong, since I have good reasons for thinking that to kill you would do harm and no probable reasons for thinking it would do good, and I can know that it would be wrong of me to choose what I had good reasons for thinking probably harmful on the whole and none for thinking beneficial.

But Moore's utilitarianism has been strongly attacked on other grounds of a more fundamental nature. The first blow in a very long controversy was struck by Prichard in an article in *Mind*, 1912, posthumously republished with other articles by the author in Prichard, *Moral Obligation* (1949). The article bears the striking title, 'Does Moral Philosophy rest on a mistake?', and is noteworthy as a philosophical defence of extreme intuitionism in ethics. The defence is conducted by trying to prove that, though we may know quite well what our duty is, no reason can ever be given to *show* that something is our duty, and Prichard urges that the utilitarian makes an unjustifiable jump from the good to the ought. You can only derive an ought, he contends, from another ought, and he denies that the fact that something that one could do will produce good results is itself any reason why one ought to do it. I cannot help believing that he is here in sharp conflict with the moral consciousness of most people. This, I think, is still more clearly brought out if we substitute 'evil' for 'good' and 'ought not' for 'ought'. It is surely completely self-evident that the fact that an action which I propose to do would inflict a great deal of harm on somebody else is a strong reason why I ought not to do it. Prichard has in fact not been followed to the full extent of his revulsion against utilitarianism, but he has stronger objections to full utilitarianism than the one I have mentioned, even if they do not lead to the conclusion that we can know what is right quite irrespective of the good or evil liable to be produced by a proposed action. Thus he argues that, if utilitarianism were true, it would be as morally wrong to hurt oneself as to hurt others, whereas it is not morally wrong at all but only foolish. And he points to the fact that our consciousness of the obligation to pay our debts or tell the truth is normally not preceded by a recognition of the good done by this, still less by a reflection that our fulfilment of the obligation will produce better consequences than any other alternative at our disposal. Prichard himself of course had to bring in consequences somehow as relevant, and he did it by maintaining that, while we cannot *infer* that an action is right or wrong from the good or evil it does or is expected to do, we must before we can see whether an act is right know its nature and, since an act cannot be altogether separated from its consequences, we can only do that if we have some knowledge of the consequences it tends to produce. Thus we could not know that it was our duty to send money to A in payment of a debt if we had no reason to anticipate it would reach A. However, he stresses rather the relations of an act to the past than to its consequences, i.e. in this case its relation to a previous act of incurring a debt to A, and he insists that, even if we can only see whether an act is our duty after coming to know something about the consequences to be expected from it, the judgment that it is our duty is in no wise an *inference* from the *goodness* of its consequences, or from the goodness of the act itself for that matter. The function of moral philosophy, he holds, is not to give arguments to help us to decide what we ought to do, but to remove errors and confusions which lead us to distrust our intuitive knowledge and prevent us from seeing acts and situations as they really are in their moral significance.

It would be hard to find a living British philosopher who goes as far towards a purely intuitionist view as did Prichard. The nearest approach is made by E. F. Carritt (v. *The Theory of Morals*, 1928), but within the field of ethical theories which are non-naturalistic and admit objectivity the chief opponent of utilitarianism has been the theory developed by Sir David Ross in *The Right and the Good* (1930) and *Foundations of Ethics* (1939). (C. D. Broad, the retiring Professor of Moral Philosophy at Cambridge, has shown some inclination towards a similar theory (v. *Five Types of Ethical Theory*, 1930), but I could not say that he holds it. He has also shown some inclination to break with objectivism). Ross introduced the concept of *prima facie* duty, by which he means an obligation which is not absolute but holds only in the absence of a stronger obligation.[1] Thus we always have a *prima facie* duty not to lie, but this obligation may in exceptional circumstances be overruled by another, e.g. the obligation to save life. Some of our *prima facie* obligations owe their validity, Ross admits, to the good done by their fulfilment, and in so far he is a utilitarian, but others depend not on this but on certain relations to other people in which we have placed ourselves or been placed. The fulfilment of even the latter class of obligations indeed always produces some good, but they remain at least *prima facie* and sometimes absolute obligations even in cases where a greater good could be attained by violating them. Thus, if I have promised to pay A a sum of money, I am not dispensed from the obligation by the mere fact that I could do more good with the money in some other way. When one *prima facie* duty conflicts with others, including those based on the goodness of their effects, Ross thinks no general rules can be provided for the solution of the conflict, we have just to judge what is right in each case on its merits after considering the particular circumstances involved. Thus a promise ought not

---

[1] This must not be confused with what one would naturally expect to be the meaning of the words *prima facie* obligation, i.e. something which seems to be but may not really be an obligation. *Prima facie* obligations in Ross's sense are always real obligations, though not absolute ones.

necessarily to be broken because it will do more harm to keep it, but the harm done is in some relatively rare cases sufficiently great to make breaking the promise absolutely obligatory. Whether it is or not in a given case is a matter for individual judgment or intuition. Yet even in cases where it ought not to be fulfilled keeping a promise remains a *prima facie* duty: a promise really has a feature about it which in itself calls for action in a certain direction, though this feature is occasionally outweighed by others. This is supported by the fact that, if he does feel it his duty to break a promise, a good man will still deplore this feature of his action and will feel himself under a *prima facie* obligation to make up for it later on to the man to whom he has made the promise. The utilitarian would explain the duty of keeping promises by saying that it is a rule the fulfilment of which generally leads to the greatest good, but our attitude to exceptions, it has been urged, is quite different from what we should expect on such a supposition. Breaches of promise are not merely unorthodox methods of producing the greatest good occasionally justified, if so there would be nothing regrettable about them provided they did good any more than there would be about giving a patient a drug which normally did harm but would do good in his particular case, but this is not how the good man feels about them at all: they are in themselves regrettable even when justified. Ross complained that the utilitarians took too narrow a view of persons in that they regarded them simply as receptacles into which as much good as possible was to be poured and did not do justice to the numerous personal relations which hold between men: as debtor to creditor, child to parent, etc.

There can be little doubt that Ross has given a very good account of the ways in which we think in making our ordinary ethical judgments, but it is widely felt that a theory of moral philosophy calls for much more in the way of systematization and explanation than he provides. Philosophers are not in general content to be left with a chaos of unrelated *prima facie* duties, but have felt that the required explanation would be provided by a utilitarian doctrine which gave as the reason for all our duties the fact that their fulfilment would produce the greatest good. I shall not go over the attempts to bring *prima facie* duties such as that of fulfilment of promises under the utilitarian schema by pointing to their indirect effects, e.g. on general confidence. For even if such attempts fail, the utilitarian still has another resource which will enable him to escape refutation by Ross and to do so without clashing sharply with common-sense ethics. He may say that, e.g. the keeping of promises is intrinsically good or, perhaps more plausibly, that the breaking of them is intrinsically bad, and that this intrinsic goodness or badness should be taken into account as well as the consequences of the action. Obviously it is right to include in the total good or evil produced by an action besides the good or evil belonging to its consequences any which is present in the action itself, and the addition of this to the sum may account for our sometimes arriving at different decisions from those we should have reached if we had considered only the effects and ignored the intrinsic character of the actions. Thus the intrinsic evil of breaking a promise would have to be set against any bad consequences of keeping it and might outweigh the latter so that keeping the promise was rendered right when otherwise it would have been wrong. Neither the utilitarian nor Ross would say that promise-keeping was always obligatory whatever the harm done, but even in a case where the intrinsic badness of breaking a promise was outweighed by the harm which keeping it would do, this would not prevent the breach of the promise being itself bad. Only, because it then consisted in the choice of a lesser evil rather than a greater, it would be no longer wrong, though intrinsically bad. Again the utilitarian may defend the common view that it is right and praiseworthy to sacrifice a good of one's own in order to confer a slightly lesser good on somebody else by saying that we must add to the good produced the intrinsic goodness of acts of benevolence. He may also invoke the principle of organic wholes laid down by Moore,[1] according to which a whole may depend for its value not only on its constituent elements but on the relations between them, and say that, even where good A is less than good B, the organic whole, good A produced by my

---

[1] *Principia Ethica*, chap. I, sect. D.

keeping my promise, may be better than the organic whole, good
B produced by breaking the promise, or the organic whole, good
A produced by self-sacrifice for another, better than good B
produced by myself for myself. If he adopts such a line I do not
see how an advocate of Ross's view can refute him. At least this
is so as long as the discussion remains at the level at which it has
been conducted so far, it being assumed that both 'good' and
'right' have a meaning independently of each other.

But have they? Here my own theory comes in.[1] There is a type
of definition of good, which has appeared in a number of works
by other philosophers, that is not naturalistic or metaphysical and
that would therefore not destroy the autonomy of ethics, and yet
would remove good from its position as the fundamental ethical
term. Thus 'better' has been defined as 'worthy of preference', and
'good' as 'worthy of love', of 'desire', or 'admiration'. Putting
these various psychological terms together under the heading of
'pro-attitudes' (incidentally a term I borrowed from Ross) I have
suggested that 'good' might be defined as 'such that we ought to
have a pro-attitude towards it', or as 'fitting[2] object of a pro-
attitude', which I regard as an equivalent phrase. This allows for
varying subordinate definitions of 'good' according to the pro-
attitude chosen and so would account largely for the variations
between the different senses of 'good'. It has sometimes been used
as standing for 'fitting object of approval as means', sometimes for
'fitting object of desire for its own sake', sometimes for 'fitting
object of moral admiration'. Now of course Moore has argued that
good is indefinable, but whatever the merits of his arguments they
could not overthrow the definition proposed. For what Moore is
concerned to refute are views which reduce good to something
not specifically ethical but psychological, or for that matter
metaphysical. But my definition of good is one in terms of another
ethical concept, not itself regarded as definable, and therefore it
cannot be argued that it reduces ethics to something non-ethical.
Moore rules out naturalistic definitions of 'good', by which he
meant, roughly, definitions of 'good' in terms wholly of concepts

[1] In *The Definition of Good* (Routledge & Kegan Paul), 1947.
[2] This use of the concept of fittingness in ethics was perhaps originally suggested by
Broad, *Five Types of Ethical Theory*, p. 164.

of a natural science. The definition of good proposed does indeed include a concept of the natural science of psychology, the concept of pro-attitude, but it cannot possibly be said to be wholly naturalistic since it also includes an ethical concept, 'right' or 'fitting', and I should be strongly opposed to any theories which tried to analyse this concept naturalistically.

Now, if my definition be accepted, what is the pro-attitude which is primarily relevant to 'good' as understood in the discussion between the utilitarians and Ross? Surely in the context of this dispute we are considering good as the object of action, so the pro-attitude in question will be that of choosing or setting oneself to produce. 'A is intrinsically good' will then become 'A is something which one ought to choose or set oneself to produce for its own sake'. But this is just what is meant by saying 'it is a *prima facie* duty to produce A'. So the two views, that of the utilitarians and that of Ross, become on this definition indistinguishable. 'The best' in a given situation will become 'what we ought to seek in that situation', and therefore it must always be our duty to seek to produce the greatest good.[1]

My definition would of course be disputed by other philosophers, but even if you do not feel at all inclined to agree with it, you may note that it at least serves as an illustration of the way in which the solution of a problem may depend on a question of analysis. If we are intelligently to maintain the view that the rightness of an act depends on its productivity of good, and wish to escape a vicious circle, we ought first to make up our mind that good is not itself to be defined in terms of right. If it is, the whole setting of the question will be altered, and the particular issue disappear. And this is the usual reason for which analysis is important in philosophy. It is not that we want to find out as an end in itself what people mean by certain words. Under what conditions human beings will make certain noises is not as such a question of philosophy at all. But, when we are confronted with a philosophical problem, it is certainly our philosophical duty to

---

[1] 'Ought' or 'duty' is also used in such a sense that we always 'ought' to do and it is always 'our duty' to do what we think we ought, but that sense is not directly relevant to the question of deciding what we objectively ought to do in a given case, the question about which the controversy with utilitarianism arose.

analyse as far as possible the meaning of the terms involved. We shall then often find that the question has various meanings which it is essential to separate before it can be answered, and when this analysis and separation has been affected the problem may solve itself.[1] And since, whatever sort of philosophy we do, we shall have to employ common-sense terms, it is important to make up our mind what these terms mean and how, if at all, the philosophical sense in which we are using them varies from the common-sense sense. My colleagues will no doubt have informed you sufficiently of the errors in philosophy which arise through a neglect of these precautions. I myself am not regarded as a member of the modern analytic school of philosophy, rather perhaps as a reactionary opponent, but I certainly too would exalt the importance of analysis, though I feel that some contemporary British philosophers give the impression of pursuing it as an end-in-itself and devoting most of their time to sharpening a philosophical knife which they rarely use to cut anything. And since, as was said at a meeting of the body which organized this school, it is desirable that you should not merely hear about analysis but witness particular pieces of analysis being done, I commend this one to your attention.

It is difficult or perhaps impossible to prove any particular analysis true. For, if we analyse A as BC, it seems the most we can ever prove is that the extension of A and BC coincide, not their intension. It will always be possible for an opponent to maintain that A is really distinct from BC, though it always accompanies BC, and therefore that BC is not a correct analysis of A. Thus in the present case it seems clearly true of everything good that it is a fitting object of a pro-attitude and of everything which is a fitting object of a pro-attitude that it is good, but it does not necessarily follow that the two coincide in meaning. It may still be held that there is an indefinable quality of goodness distinct from the complex property I suggested as the definition of good, though it always accompanies the latter. All I can say is that

[1] 'It appears to me that in Ethics, as in all other philosophical studies, the difficulties and disagreements, of which its history is full, are mainly due to a very simple cause: namely to the attempt to answer questions, without first discovering *precisely* what question it is which you desire to answer' (Moore, *Principia Ethica*, opening sentence of preface).

I cannot discern such a quality, a disability which I share with the majority of other philosophers, and my analysis I think may claim to be in some measure confirmed by its success in dealing with ethical problems. If it can be claimed that it settles the dispute between Ross and the ideal Utilitarians, and solves other ethical problems which I have not space to mention now, that is of itself an argument in its favour.

It has been a common criticism of Ross's view, which I have already mentioned, that it leaves us with a chaos of unrelated and unexplained *prima facie* duties, and the same criticism might be urged against me. It still seems as if the utilitarians did something in the way of explaining man's actual duties systematically and we did not. The utilitarian cannot indeed carry the explanation a stage further back and say why certain kinds of thing and not others are good-in-themselves, but can only say that he sees them to be so, still to say that an action produces good or averts evil does seem to be giving an ultimate reason for it and explaining its obligatoriness in a way in which to say that it is an instance of a *prima facie* duty does not.

Now it certainly seems to me that there is not enough in the way of rational explanation or justification in Ross's theory, but in general something can be rationally justified in two ways at least. One proceeds by referring what is to be explained to a set of ultimate axioms, each held to be completely self-evident in its own right, such as the proposition that pain is intrinsically evil or kindness intrinsically good. But there is also such a thing as explanation within a coherent system in which the different parts confirm and support each other, and there may be a scope for a rational explanation of this kind without utilitarianism in the ordinary sense of an explanation of the right by the good. My own view is that there are two criteria in ethics, self-evidence and coherence. On the one hand we cannot deduce our ethics by pure logic or by the methods of the natural sciences without having recourse anywhere to ethical propositions accepted on the strength of intuition. Yet what presents itself to us as intuitively self-evident is not therefore necessarily certain; we may be deceived. So our intuitions are the better for confirmation, and this confirmation can be provided by their mutual coherence, while coherence may of course also be used as a criterion to decide in cases of actual conflict between intuitions or apparent intuitions. There will be a stronger case for accepting the one which coheres better with other ostensible intuitions. I do not say that this criterion of coherence is needed in all cases to confirm and can in all cases override subjective certainty, but certainly both coherence and intuitive self-evidence are needed as criteria in ethics. Now even if the *prima facie* duties cannot be deduced from some more ultimate good, they may be seen to confirm each other by examining the way in which they fit together into a system so that to fulfil one tends to fulfil others and to violate one tends to bring a man into a position in which he has to violate others. Clashes between different *prima facie* duties of course are frequent, but they can mostly (though not always) be traced to wrongdoing on the part of somebody. Now if they constitute a coherent system, it is just what one would expect that a violation of one would tend to lead to situations in which they clashed, so that whatever you did you had to violate others, as when you deny one proposition in a logical or mathematical system and then proceed consistently, you have to deny others. It is proverbial that one lie leads to other lies if the man who told it is not to sacrifice the good he hoped to produce by telling the first: a man who has deceived other people by making incompatible promises must break at least one promise. Therefore the clashes rather confirm than refute the view that the valid *prima facie* duties constitute a coherent system supporting each other; and I think we can see of each valid *prima facie* duty that it also belongs to its intrinsic nature to tend to fulfil and further the fulfilment of other valid *prima facie* duties, even if this tendency is not realized in all cases owing to accident. We can almost always give several reasons and not just one why we ought to act in a particular way, and to give an ethical reason is to say that it fulfils a general *prima facie* duty.

It has also been objected plausibly that the concept of *prima facie* duties is essentially secondary, presupposing the concept of absolute duty, and therefore cannot be regarded as an ultimate concept of ethics, and Ross rather plays into the hands of his critics by suggesting that they are to be regarded as *tendencies* towards being absolute duties.[1] A tendency concept would seem to be definable in terms of that towards which it is a tendency and therefore as less ultimate than the latter. But it seems to me that to say of an act that it is a *prima facie* duty in Ross's sense is really to say something more than that there is a tendency for it to be one's absolute duty: it is to say positively that we ought to adopt a pro-attitude towards it, not necessarily the pro-attitude involved in doing it, but at any rate the attitude of approving the proposed act in the respect under consideration (even if it would be wrong on the whole). Even in the exceptional cases where it is our duty to break a promise, we shall never, if we act rightly, let our attitude and hardly ever our behaviour be uninfluenced by the fact that we have promised. We shall at least regret our breach of faith: we shall, if possible, explain ourselves to the promisee and make it up to him in other ways. The only exceptions to this seem to be with promises of such a kind, e.g. those extracted by violence or fraud, that it is doubtful whether there is even a *prima facie* duty to keep them. I therefore think that the concept of *prima facie* duty is a very important contribution developed in this country in recent ethical controversy. Absolute rightness, as applied to acts, must, I think, be regarded not exactly as the sum but as the resultant of a number of features in acts which do not themselves all severally carry with them absolute rightness but contribute in that direction. The primary ethical intuition is not that an action is fitting or unfitting as a whole, but that it is fitting or unfitting in certain respects, though of course if, as often, we see it to be fitting in one respect and unfitting in none or vice versa, we shall conclude it at once to be absolutely right or wrong.

Even if my view be accepted, I should not wish it to be concluded that the whole controversy between the utilitarians and holders of the conception of *prima facie* duties was of little importance. Even if it turn out that, when good is rightly analysed, the main proposition in dispute becomes a tautology, it does not follow that they were getting excited about a mere tautology. To say that, if a proposition is analysed in a certain way, it becomes a tautology, is not the same as to say that the proposition that it is to

[1] *The Right and the Good*, pp. 28-9; *Foundations of Ethics*, p. 86.

be analysed in this way is itself a tautology. It is in itself an important and not merely a verbal question about the concepts of ethics whether they are so related that the propositions connecting them turn into tautologies. Further, while the rival parties become assimilated if the utilitarians adopt the expedient of regarding, e.g. breaches of promise as bad in themselves, in practice the utilitarians have tended to stress consequences much more and ignore the goodness or badness of acts in themselves. In that case the controversy becomes very important and has great practical bearing. For the question often arises whether we ought to seek, if it seems necessary, to further a good end by evil means such as deceit, violence or injustice, and while it seems to most philosophers unreasonable to rule out the employment of such means under all conditions however good the end, it is a very important question whether the matter ought to be settled simply by reference to the consequences, direct or indirect, or whether we are to consider the means as *prima facie* open to objection even apart from any consequences they may have. The controversy is also linked up with the difference between the Hebraic or Kantian view according to which ethical action is primarily the fulfilling of a law and the Greek view according to which it is primarily the realization of various concrete ends. I certainly prefer the latter view as more rational, in spite of my analysis of good in terms of ought and my rejection of a utilitarianism which decides everything ultimately in terms of consequences beyond the act.

I do not of course mean to give the impression that my view is generally accepted in Great Britain — far from it. Some people would reply to me that we ought to adopt a pro-attitude towards something A only because A is first seen to be good; and all the views I have mentioned in this lecture are subject to attacks from another quarter which I shall discuss in the next lecture. A large proportion of philosophers in this country would positively reject or very much hesitate to accept any view which like Moore's, Prichard's, Ross's and mine, maintains that ethical concepts are not analysable in terms of psychology and that ethical judgments are yet objectively true as are those of a factual science. Of these philosophers I shall speak in the next section.

2. THE NATURE OF ETHICAL JUDGMENTS

We shall turn now to Moore's other doctrine, the doctrine that the fundamental concept of ethics is indefinable and 'non-natural',[1] and to the long controversy which arose from this and still continues. This controversy is largely independent of the question which term we select as fundamental in ethics. Moore held the view that good was the fundamental term and he therefore made good indefinable, but almost everything that could be said in favour of his view of good can be said in favour of a similar view about right or ought if we take one of these closely related concepts as fundamental. As a matter of fact he seems in his later work, *Ethics* (1912), to have changed his view and to be holding that both good and duty are indefinable. Thus, while in *Principia Ethica* he says that 'duty' applied to an action just *means* that 'it together with its consequences presents a greater sum of intrinsic value than any possible alternative',[2] and that the same may be said about the phrases 'it is right to do this' or 'this ought to be done', in *Ethics* he holds indeed that 'it must always be our duty to do what will produce the best effects upon the whole', but while insisting that this is 'quite self-evident',[3] admits that it cannot be proved and is therefore presumably not something that follows analytically from the definition of duty. In his latest statement on ethical concepts he definitely rejects both the view that 'intrinsically good' can be defined in terms of 'ought' and the view that 'ought' can be defined in terms of 'intrinsically good'.[4] But the question I am discussing today is not which ethical term is indefinable but whether any are, and on this I agree with Moore.

We must of course realize that Moore is not claiming 'good' to be indefinable in every sense in which the term is used. He realized well enough that 'good' has a number of different usages and asserted only in regard to one that the term was indefinable, namely that one in which it stands for 'good as an end in itself'. He did, however, hold that this indefinable sense of 'good' was the fundamental one. Again, he did not deny that there were senses of 'de-

[1] Vide *Principia Ethica*, chap. I, sect. B.
[2] Ibid., pp. 24-5.   [3] p. 143.
[4] *The Philosophy of G. E. Moore* (1942), pp. 610-11.

finition' in which even this sense of 'good' was definable: what he maintained was only that in one sense of 'definition', that of 'analysis', it was indefinable. To give a definition of something may mean merely to name a quality or relation by which the subject of the definition is always accompanied, and in that sense of 'definition' Moore neither affirmed nor denied that 'good' was definable. What he said was that 'good' could not be defined in the sense of being analysed in terms of something else. We may bring out the distinction between the two senses of 'definition' by taking the case of colour, which Moore himself cites as analogous. It is quite proper for a physicist to define a colour, say yellow, in terms of the wave-lengths which accompany it, but it would be most silly to identify these waves with the seen colour. The latter cannot be analysed in terms of anything else, otherwise a person who had never seen the actual colour might know what yellow looked like, which is certainly not the case. Similarly, even if goodness were always accompanied by one characteristic, it would not follow that this characteristic constituted the definition of goodness in Moore's sense unless goodness could be actually identified with the characteristic. It seems to me that many of the writers prior and some subsequent to Moore's *Principia Ethica* who gave what purported to be a definition of 'good' were not using 'definition' in Moore's sense or had confusedly mixed up some other sense of definition with Moore's one.

The importance of Moore's contention that good is indefinable lay mainly in its assertion of what Kant called the autonomy of ethics. For a moral philosopher to take as his central doctrine the principle that the main concept of ethics is indefinable seems at first sight a singularly bleak and unfruitful line of approach, and there has certainly been a strong reaction against it because of its negative character. But in philosophy it is often even more important to assert what something is not, than what it is, in order to eliminate mistakes. And we must remember that to say that good is indefinable is not to say that it is unknowable or that we can say nothing more about it. It is only to deny that it can be reduced *in toto* to something other than itself. We can still know very well what good is, Moore claims, just as, though we cannot define yellow, a man who is not colour-blind can know very well what yellow is. He can know this because he has the experience of seeing it, and we can on Moore's view experience goodness just as directly as we can experience colour, though in a very different way, one which is not a matter of the physical senses or even of ordinary psychological introspection. This is the main point of what he meant, I suppose, when he called good a 'non-natural quality'. He had certainly not the least wish to introduce the idea of the 'supernatural' in any ordinary sense into his ethics. He did not accept any theological assumptions, still less think them needed for ethics. The main importance of his contention lay in ruling out the views of all philosophers who, whether confusedly or with a full consciousness of what they were doing, explained away the distinctive character of ethics and reduced it to a branch of some natural science, usually psychology, as you do if you analyse the fundamental concepts of ethics in terms of the concepts of that science. Like Kant, Moore insisted that ethics was autonomous, a branch of study with its own distinctive laws, not needing to apply for authority elsewhere, as against both those who tried to make it a branch of a natural science (the 'naturalistic' fallacy) and those who sought to base it on metaphysics. Like Kant he rejected sharply the attempts to analyse good either in terms of pleasure or desire or in terms of the will of God. Moore indeed accuses Kant of having failed in his object and really made ethics heteronomous in character by identifying 'this ought to be done' with 'this is willed by a free will', a metaphysical proposition,[1] but we need not here go into the question whether this accusation is justified or not. The *aims* of the philosophers were in the respects I have mentioned undoubtedly similar in character, whether they carried them out consistently or not. Of course there is an enormous difference between the ethical systems they produced. Moore differed from Kant, I think, especially in taking good as the fundamental concept of ethics rather than ought,[2] but Moore's arguments against defining good seem to be intended to show not that good is the fundamental concept of ethics, which seems to be rather taken for granted, but that the

[1] *Principia Ethica*, pp. 126-8.
[2] On this point of Kantian interpretation I am in disagreement with Prof. Paton.

fundamental concept of ethics, whatever it is, cannot be reduced to anything non-ethical.

Moore's criticisms were directed primarily against naturalistic definitions of good, that is, those definitions which made it an empirical concept falling within a natural science, usually psychology. His arguments against such definitions as stated in *Principia Ethica* would not now be defended by anyone, least of all Moore himself, though this is not the case with the main principle at the basis of most of them, which is at least highly plausible. With the reasons why people are tempted to give such definitions you will be very familiar, but there remains the unbridgeable gulf between fact and value, between the is and the ought, and in this country at least few philosophers, even among Moore's opponents, have carried naturalism to its bitter end and made ethics into just a natural science. Few would-be naturalists — Hume in some moods at least is an exception — would be prepared to maintain that all ethical propositions could be conclusively proved or disproved by inductive empirical generalizations. Yet this is the conclusion which follows logically from naturalism. If 'right' just meant 'what most people approve' or 'good' just meant 'what most people desire', we could on principle settle what is right or good simply by arriving at statistics about men's feelings of approval and desires. As Professor Broad has pointed out, the logical consequence of a view which defines ethical concepts in psychological terms 'is not that in disputes on moral questions there comes a point beyond which we can only say "de gustibus non est disputandum". On the contrary the logical consequence of the theory is that all such disputes *could* be settled, and that the way to settle them is to collect statistics of how people in fact do feel. And to me this kind of answer seems utterly irrelevant to this kind of question'.[1] That it leads logically to this conclusion seems to me a very strong argument against naturalism. The naturalist would indeed have to go even further than Professor Broad suggested: he would have to say not merely that all ethical propositions are capable of being settled by adducing statistics, he would have to say that they simply are vague propositions about statistics. That is what it comes to if we

[1] *Five Types of Ethical Theory*, p. 115.

say, for instance, that 'good' just means 'what most people approve' or 'what most people desire'. For the difference between vagueness and definiteness is the only difference between saying 'most' and saying, e.g. 84.65 per cent. And, whatever ethical propositions are, it is surely evident that they are not vague propositions about statistics, whether about most human beings, or about the speaker, as in the more subjective forms of naturalism where good is equated with that towards which the individual who makes the judgment usually has feelings of approval ('tends to have' must mean here 'usually has') or with what will usually in the long run satisfy him. Still less are they statements merely about the momentary feelings of the speaker or about what will satisfy him at the moment. Naturalistic definitions of ethical terms make ethical propositions a merely factual account of what is, but, as Kant long ago insisted, what ought to be cannot be reduced to what is. A very neat refutation of naturalism is given by Hare.[1] If a naturalist defines 'good' as C we have to ask whether he 'ever wishes to commend anything for being C. If he says that he does, we have only to point out to him that his definition makes this impossible'. (For to commend it for being C would then be just to say it is C because it is C.) 'And clearly he cannot say that he never wishes to commend anything for being C, for to commend things for being C is the whole object of his theory.'

But most naturalistically inclined philosophers, in Britain and the United States at least, have now shifted their ground. They would admit that a naturalistic analysis does not yield an exact equivalent of ethical judgments. But this, they insist, is not because there is something else asserted in our ethical judgments, something about a non-natural quality or relation, but because the naturalistic analysis conveys only at most the dry factual content and not the emotional flavour or practical significance of our ethical judgments. Ethical judgments are looked on as not assertive at all, or as emotive and practical rather than assertive. They do not indeed *say* that the speaker has a certain emotion or attitude, in which case they would be empirical introspective judgments of psychology, but they *express* the emotion or attitude as an ex-

[1] R. M. Hare, *The Language of Morals*, p. 93.

clamatory phrase or an emotional appeal might. They do not affirm as a truth that somebody ought to do so-and-so, but they urge him to do it. Or, in so far as they do make assertions at all, this is regarded as only a minor part of their function and not the specifically ethical part. They are regarded either as not telling one anything at all that could be true or false and therefore as not strictly judgments,[1] but rather something analogous to exclamations, exhortations, commands, or as empirical judgments with an exclamation or exhortation attached. On the former view they just have no cognitive or informative function; on the latter 'this is wrong' becomes, e.g. 'this is to refuse to do what you had promised' (a strictly empirical proposition) 'down with you!' or 'this hurts somebody — don't do it'; 'this is good', becomes, e.g. 'you thought of the happiness of your friend before your own — hurrah! go on doing it'.

The best-known lengthy exposition of this type of view is in the book *Ethics and Language* (1944) by C. L. Stevenson, an American, but besides being put forward in a chapter of Ayer's *Language, Truth and Logic*, it has also inspired a great many articles in the periodicals of this country. Stevenson and those who think like him hold that Moore and the defenders of the 'objectivity' of ethical judgments have erred in taking a much too intellectualistic view of the latter and in ignoring their practical and emotive sides. These criticisms find expression in the complaint that, if good were just a simple non-natural quality, there would be no reason why we should pursue what has that quality. This objection does not indeed impress me much personally. Moore can reply that, if 'should' here means 'ought', it is self-evident that we ought to pursue what is good, and that if on the other hand it means 'psychologically could', this requires no explanation any more than the fact that we can pursue what attracts us sensually. We could not indeed pursue the good unless we had some desire for it, at least in a dispositional sense,[2] but that human beings desire some ends in preference to others is not something which is susceptible of an

---

[1] I shall, however, still continue to use the term 'judgments' of them, in the absence of another suitable one, even when talking of such views, although it is strictly speaking a divergence from the proper meaning of the word.

[2] I am not sure whether this is or is not a tautology.

a priori explanation,[1] as empirically inclined naturalists surely
know, and therefore it may just as well be an ultimate fact about
our nature that we desire what is good as that we dislike being
burnt. But I think the argument has somehow had a good deal of
influence. And certainly Moore, Ross and I myself have not said
much about the practical emotive function of ethical judgments,
but talked as if they were as much an intellectual matter as judgments about matters of fact. This is not because we did not think
they had a practical emotive function — nobody in their senses
could fail to know that — but because, in my case at least and I should
fancy in that of the others, we thought it too obvious to need
stressing. We were after all concerned with answering the question
how one is to decide what is really right, and not how people are
to be psychologically induced to do what is right. Yet for a complete account what there is to say about the intellectual side of
ethical judgments no doubt requires to be supplemented by an
account of their emotive and practical character. Still an intellectual side there surely is, and to that side I am convinced this modern
tendency has not done justice. Here it shows a similarity to other
strong anti-intellectualist currents of the present day, for instance,
existentialism.

How are we to decide between, e.g. Stevenson and myself? It is
usual in this country to regard the controversy as one about the
analysis of ethical judgments, i.e. the analysis of what we really
mean in our ordinary ethical discourse. That philosophical controversies in England have for long taken this form is due to Moore's
approach to the subject. As you are no doubt well aware, Moore
started with the assumption that we *know* common-sense propositions to be true, and moreover know them without requiring any
philosophical proof. This assumption has commonly been retained
by British philosophers as regards the factual propositions of daily
life, but the very philosophers who retained it have often proceeded
to put forward modes of analysis of the propositions in question
which certainly do not appeal to common sense. A similar course
has been adopted as regard ethical judgments. The naturalist or

---

[1] At least by us. I should not myself want to say that causal laws are not ultimately
explicable *a priori* by a mind of sufficient insight, but we certainly do not possess the
insight.

the Stevensonian is not an ethical sceptic in the sense of denying the validity of our ordinary ethical judgments: what he claims to do is not to contradict but to analyse them. The method of analysis seems indeed to be valued by such thinkers just as providing the way of escaping from an ethical scepticism that would otherwise be inevitable. Their philosophical and epistemological background is such that they could not accept any ethical judgments interpreted non-naturalistically as significant and true, therefore they have to choose between rejecting all ethical judgments and interpreting these in a way consistent with their epistemology. Now it is hardly possible really to believe that all ethical judgments are false, therefore the only course left open to these thinkers is to give an analysis of ethical judgments which will make their character such that they can be accepted as valid even by a philosopher who is so much of an empiricist as not to be prepared to admit any truths outside the realm of natural science. And there are two ways of doing this. One is to maintain that ethical judgments are true but of such a character as to fall within natural science. This is the course adopted by those who analyse them 'naturalistically', as merely ascribing psychological predicates such as 'desired'. The other course is to maintain that it is not the function of ethical judgments to be true, because they do not assert anything but only express feelings or urge people to action. If so it is not indeed the case that they are true, but this is not because they are false, but because they are not the sort of thing which could be either true or false. They resemble in this respect exclamations or commands, which we could not possibly say are true but need not therefore stigmatize as being false. They do not assert anything, and what does not assert anything cannot be either true or false. Strictly speaking, they are not judgments at all. They have the verbal form of judgments but are really commands or exhortations, or something which is much more like these than like the ordinary judgments of natural science. These philosophers can then admit that 'ethical judgments' fulfil their own characteristic function without admitting them to be true. They need not be ethical sceptics in the sense of saying that it is a mistake to hold that it is wrong, e.g. to torture people. They can say like anybody else that it is wrong and claim to be saying so in the sense in which people generally do, but this is not supposed to be a judgment or assertion but something of the nature of an exhortation or exclamation. It does what it is intended to do and is therefore to be approved, but it is not a true judgment because it does not aim at truth.

Now the arguments of opponents of such theories have been directed to showing that the modes of analysis proposed grossly misrepresented what we actually mean when we make ethical judgments. It has been pointed out, for instance, that when we call something wrong, we intend to contradict what is said by somebody else who calls it right in the sense in which one statement of fact contradicts another. I have not space here to go into the numerous objections that have been brought against the various forms of naturalism and subjectivism, but I do not see how anybody can reasonably doubt that these arguments show at any rate that such modes of analysis fail to give anything like an adequate account of what we mean in the ordinary straightforward sense of 'meaning' when we make what we call 'ethical judgments' in our daily practical life. We do mean to say something true and what we mean to say is not merely what we or other human beings desire or feel as a matter of actual fact. Our opponent can thus only save himself by admitting that he is not using 'mean' in its ordinary straightforward sense but in some other sense, although a clear definition of this other sense he has so far failed to provide. But to admit this is to admit that his theory as an attempt to reconcile a naturalistic or Stevensonian view with our ordinary ethics has broken down, though this, strangely enough, does not seem to have been usually realized. For, if it is once admitted that the only sense in which ethical judgments can be accepted is not the one in which they are meant by common sense, then the attempt to maintain that the ethical view in question is reconcilable with the acceptance of our common-sense ethical judgments has been abandoned in effect. I am not really accepting the belief in dragons if I say that there are dragons but define 'dragons' as 'elephants'. It will then have to be admitted that what we actually believe and intend to say when we are making ethical judgments is mistaken. This admission is not avoided by giving our words a new sense in which they do mean something acceptable to the naturalist or Stevensonian, provided it is not the sense in which we actually use the words in question. You can make any sentence true by altering its meaning. My opponent may of course say that the common-sense view is muddled, and that he is giving the nearest view to it which can be intelligibly and consistently stated, but this is not to say what we ordinarily mean in our ethical judgments but to correct it.

Of course to show that a view of ethics is inconsistent with our ordinary common-sense ethical beliefs is not necessarily to refute it. It may be replied — 'So much the worse for common-sense ethics.' But, while I certainly should not wish to claim infallibility for common sense, it would be hard indeed to hold that all our ethical judgments, even the apparently most evident, are fundamentally mistaken, as we should have to hold if nothing is right or wrong in the sense in which we in our ordinary ethical life believe it to be so. Common-sense ethics may indeed legitimately be amended, but cannot surely be completely repudiated. All our ethical judgments cannot be wrong in the most fundamental ethical point as they would be if what we ordinarily mean by 'good' and 'right' had no application. Surely in regard to our more certain ethical judgments the *onus probandi* is on the sceptic, and we should only be justified in this ethical scepticism if the most rigorous arguments were available to establish it. Now there may be difficulties about an objective non-naturalistic view, e.g. those connected with differences of opinion in ethics, but there is certainly nothing like a rigorous disproof of it available. (I think myself that the differences of ethical opinion can easily be explained on such a view, but I have not space to discuss this now.) No doubt the principle that all ethical concepts are to be reduced to empirical concepts of psychology is one which fits in well with many people's philosophy today, but this is no proof, and the opposite fits in better with many other people's philosophy. And it does seem to me very decidedly on reading naturalists and Stevensonians that their account of ethical judgments is derived rather from their general epistemological assumptions than from a direct study of our first-hand experience in making ethical judgments. But, be that as it may, the tendency is certainly now, even among holders of the views I have criticized, to admit that their views cannot be proved even in a loose sense of proof but to defend them merely on the ground that the further supposition of 'a non-natural ethical property' or 'properties' (reverting to Moore's rather unsatisfactory terminology) is unnecessary. It may be answered that it is not indeed logically necessary, but necessary if we are to accept some of the things we most certainly know, i.e. our best authenticated ethical propositions, though it must be remembered that it is one thing to say this and another to commit oneself as to the precise form which will be taken by this additional element going beyond the sphere of natural science.

The views of ethics which I have contrasted may seem to be in almost the sharpest possible opposition, and so I felt till very recently, but I think now that British ethical thought is moving strongly in the direction of a compromise solution which would tend to make the difference between myself and the thinkers influenced by Stevenson more a matter of degree and emphasis than of kind. In recent years there has been a marked tendency in several quarters to take a view according to which 'ethical judgments' are regarded neither as judgments in the strict sense which could be either true or false nor as commands or exclamations, but as something *sui generis* in between the two.[1] Further, it is now suggested that, although ethical judgments cannot be shown to be true by reasoning and, since they are not propositions capable of being true (or false), cannot even be supported by reasoning in the way in which a proposition can be, yet it does not follow that therefore there cannot be good or bad reasons for action. One kind of action can still really be preferable to another, and one can give reasons for one's preference that not merely in fact do appeal but ought to appeal to other men. It is a very serious defect of Stevenson's doctrine that he is obliged to put on the same level without distinction all means of inducing people to perform an action or to take up a favourable ethical attitude to the action. For since in making what

---

[1] S. E. Toulmin, *The Place of Reason in Ethics* (1950); R. M. Hare, *The Language of Morals* (1952), also articles by W. H. F. Barnes in *Proceedings of Aristotelian Society*, Supplementary Volume XXII and M. Macdonald in *Philosophical Analysis*, ed. M. Black. The tendency is also in accord with the views of Professor Wisdom, but there is no published writing by the latter on ethics which I can cite.

we call moral judgments we do not according to him affirm propositions, he admits that we cannot have arguments that establish or even logically support ethical conclusions. Ethical argument consists, for him, not in establishing or supporting any conclusion, but in saying things which are thought likely to make a person change his attitude in fact. Now changes in attitude may be effected by a number of means including for instance those which have been used by the Russian secret police as well as those more in favour with moral philosophers, and on a Stevensonian view it seems as if there can be no ground for adopting any one effective method rather than any other except an arbitrary individual preference. The test is whether the attitude is really changed, not whether the change is reasonable. The theory indeed leaves no room for any significant distinction between changes of attitude which are reasonable and changes which are unreasonable.

If there are objectively true ethical judgments, then an argument which really shows one to be true or makes it reasonable to hold that it is true is better than an argument which does not but merely persuades people that it is true. This distinction it is not possible for a thorough Stevensonian to make, but it is possible for the newer type of ethical theory to which I have just referred. For according to this theory ethical judgments, though not strictly true or false, can be really better or worse, and reasons for them can be really valid (or invalid) and not merely persuasive. A person who holds such a view need not, like Stevenson, put all reasons in ethics on a level except as regards effectiveness in persuasion and all ethical judgments on a level except as regards the number of people to whom they appeal. Sometimes indeed holders of the view seem to fall back on defining 'valid' or 'invalid' in terms of people's actual sentiments, and in so far as they do this they have really reverted to the naturalistic doctrine, but this is not always their intention, and if not, a new view has emerged much more like an objective theory of ethics. The new view still indeed denies the title of true (or false) to value judgments, but this seems to be mainly because they are of a very different type from the judgments of natural science. This a non-naturalist would be the last person to wish to deny, though he would think it more appropriately expressed by saying that they are true of a very different kind of subject-matter than by saying they are not true at all. And perhaps the new school is an improvement on the non-naturalists in that its members connect ethical judgments more essentially with emotional expression and practical action. In fairness to myself I must, however, point out that my own view, according to which good is not regarded as a simple quality but is analysed as that which is a right object of a pro-attitude, agrees with them in so far as I have incorporated a reference to these emotional and practical attitudes in the very definition of 'good'. And I am not satisfied that all the people who have suggested a view like the one just outlined have really emerged from naturalism and Stevensonianism or realize that, if you admit you can give good reasons for ethical actions, you must at some stage or other fall back on an intuition as to what reasons are ultimately good, though if we used the term 'practical reason' or 'practical judgment' instead of intuition they might be less inclined to object. (To say that we sometimes see by 'intuition' what constitutes a good or bad reason in ethics is only to say that we can sometimes know what is a good reason without having to give another reason why it is a good reason, a not very extravagant suggestion.) But in any case I assuredly welcome the change, and it opens up the possibility of something approaching a general agreement between the rival schools as to what ethics is (with of course differences of detail and emphasis). For an objectivist cannot maintain that ethical judgments are just like those of natural science or any other branch of objective study, and his opponent cannot reasonably maintain that they are just commands or exclamations, so that we must in any case put them somewhere in between the two, though no doubt some people will emphasize the analogies between them and either extreme more than others do. The most important point, without the concession of which there can be nothing but extreme opposition, is that the rightness of an ethical judgment does not consist merely in its conformity with the actual attitudes of men. Once this is granted ethical judgments become something *sui generis*, not reducible to any other kind but only discussable by analogies with other kinds, and we may then recognize that each theory, even if one-sided, has a certain value in bringing out one or other of the analogies.[1] On such lines we could have, if not complete agreement in ethics, at any rate agreement to differ, and if this is achieved we may hope that British moral philosophers, no longer feeling the need, as they do at present, to expend most of their energy in determining what ethics is in general, will have the leisure to turn their attention again to concrete problems within the field of ethics.

[1] I owe this suggestion of a compromise mainly to Professor Wisdom.

POSTSCRIPT

SINCE I wrote these papers, I have definitely abandoned the view that the existence of any 'non-natural' quality or relation is required if moral and evaluative judgments are to be objectively true. This view shared with naturalism itself the implicit assumption that such judgments did the same sort of thing as empirical or scientific judgments, for it is this assumption which implies that their truth must consist in, or depend on, 'correspondence' to actually existing qualities or relations, whether we call these 'natural' or 'non-natural'. The assumption does not hold if, as seems to be the case, their function is not to describe what exists but to do something quite different. I think now that they express primarily the conative or practical rather than the cognitive side of our nature, but that they can still be true in so far as they do not merely express this but also claim or imply that the practical attitude expressed is justified. It is this claim to objective justification that differentiates my view from Stevenson's, but it should not be understood as a claim that such judgments *describe* the facts correctly in terms of 'natural' or 'non-natural' properties or relations. To describe something is not the same as commending or condemning it, still less it is the same as saying what we ought to do about it. It depends on the empirical situation what we ought to do and on the empirical nature of something whether we ought to commend or condemn it, but this is not the same as to say that what we ought to do is just to state the empirical facts: it is rather to adopt an attitude which we regard as justified towards them.

This and other changes in my view since 1953 are expounded and defended in my *Second Thoughts in Moral Philosophy*.

A. C. EWING

C. A. MACE

Some Trends
in the
Philosophy of Mind

CECIL ALEC MACE, M.A. (Cantab.), D.LIT. (Lond.): born Norwich, July 22nd, 1894; educated at King Edward VI Middle School, City of Norwich School and Queen's College, Cambridge; Lecturer in Philosophy and Psychology, University College, Nottingham, 1922–25; University of St. Andrews, 1925–32; Reader in Psychology, Bedford College, University of London, 1932–44; Tarner Lecturer, Trinity College, Cambridge, 1940–41; President, Aristotelian Society, 1948–49; President, British Psychological Society, 1952–53; Hon. Fellow of the Society since 1965, Professor of Psychology, Birkbeck College, University of London, 1944–61, and Hon. Fellow of that College since 1963.

Chief publications: (with G. F. Stout) Article on 'Psychology' in *Encyclopaedia Britannica*, 14th edition. *The Psychology of Study*, 1929. *The Principles of Logic*, 1933. Various articles and papers in *The Proceedings of the Aristotelian Society*, *Mind*, *The British Journal of Psychology* and other journals of philosophy and psychology. *The Psychology of Study*, 1932. (Pelican edition, revised) 1962. *The Principles of Logic*, 1933. Various contributions to *Encyclopaedia Britannica*, *Chambers*, and *The Encyclopaedia of Philosophy*) together with papers in *The Proceedings of the Aristotelian Society*, and in journals of philosophy and psychology. A comprehensive bibliography (up to 1961) together with commentaries by past colleagues and students are contained in a Festschrift entitled *C. A. Mace: A Symposium* (London, 1962).

C. A. MACE

SOME TRENDS
IN THE
PHILOSOPHY OF MIND

EVERY age, it has been said, is an 'age of transition'. So too, it might be said, is every age, in the history of the philosophy of mind at least, an age of revolt. Indeed this is almost a logical necessity. One who enters the pages of this history does so only by raising some banner of revolt; and the more faithful his disciples the sooner they are forgotten. It is upon the unfaithful disciple that the mantle always falls. Though this be so in general the present century has been to a quite unusual degree a period of great revolutions in the philosophy of mind.

At the beginning of the present century there was, in psychology, an all-but-established order with an all-but-completed programme. This order had five characteristic features. It was, to use conventional labels, dualistic, intellectualistic, sensationistic, atomistic and associationistic. The theory was, that is to say, that Nature is divided into two realms, the realm of matter and the realm of mind. It is the business of physics, chemistry, biology, etc., to explain all that is the case and all that happens in the realm of matter, and it does so in terms of a small number of elements of matter, atomic in form, and in terms of a small number of principles or laws. So, too, is it with the science of the realm of mind. There are, it was thought, at most three sorts of mental elements — cognitions, feelings and conations; and these can almost certainly be reduced to two, and very probably to only one. This basic 'element' is of the cognitive type — of which sensations and images are the obvious if not the only examples. Moreover, perceptions and ideas (the only other things to be considered) are the molecules of which sensations and images are the atomic components. The law of association is the basic principle in accordance with which the atoms are combined into complex wholes. So the programme of psychology is just this: to analyse experience into atomic elements and to explain how every complex percept, every 'ideal construction', and every train of thought comes into being in consequence of associative combinations.

So very widely was this methodological theory accepted that even James Ward, himself a leader of formidable revolts, could write in the following way:

'Try, if you choose, for yourselves and see if you do not find that the material of all that is presented to our mind is reducible to sensations and movements, just as the material of all the vast variety of substances on the earth is reducible to some one or more of the chemical elements. The greatest part of our work is, it is clear, in both cases to study the compounds. The inquiry of chief interest in psychology is, then, that concerning the formation of complex ideas out of simple ones, of perception out of sensation, of thought out of perception.'[1]

This programme, this 'inquiry of chief interest to psychology', was in fact almost completed. The job was nearly done. Most of the 'compounds' had been anlaysed, and only a few pockets of resistance remained to be dealt with. The 'feeling of pleasure' is a little puzzling, but someone had suggested that it was a sort of sensation of 'tickle', and no doubt that is what it would turn out to be. Willing, and 'conation' generally, is another tricky case, but that might well be shown to be some variant of the 'feeling of effort', i.e. a sort of kinaesthetic sensation. 'Feelings' and 'conations' having been 'reduced' there would remain a few puzzles about the facts of memory which are not obviously explained in terms of reproductive association, and a few more puzzles about creative thought. Nevertheless the representatives of the established order knew in principle how these pockets of resistance could be liqui-

[1] Psychology Applied to Education, pp. 22-3. This work was published in 1926. It should, however, be noted that the passage occurs in a lecture first delivered in 1880, six years before the revolutionary article in the Encyclopaedia Britannica.

dated. It is in fact a little curious that they showed so little anxiety about the security of their jobs when everything was so very nearly explained. However, there were no grounds for anxiety on this score because the whole system collapsed, and psychology had virtually to begin all over again.[1] The system collapsed almost simultaneously in all its parts. Upstarts like Sigmund Freud appeared suggesting that the inquiry of chief interest to psychology is *not* that concerning the formation of complex ideas out of simple ones but an inquiry of quite another kind. But even ignoring onslaughts from without, in the citadel itself there was trouble enough arising from insurrections on the part of those who were in the main concerned with the traditional problems of traditional psychology.

Now that the fury is abating and the dust beginning to settle we can ask with greater prospect of enlightenment, what the trouble was all about. What, in particular, was wrong about this doctrine of the two realms? Was it really quite as silly as it now seems?

But first, we may ask, what exactly is the doctrine that has been called in question? What precisely is it that is being denied? Those who attack the system do not always define with clarity the system they are attacking. To answer this prior question, we need not go all the way back to Descartes. For a naive but fairly clear expression of the dualistic hypothesis we cannot do better than take one that belongs to the middle of the period under review. In the year 1926 Charles Spearman wrote as follows:

'This cosmos of ours would appear to be constructed upon a peculiar plan. The bottommost layer of it consists of metaphysical "substances" partly psychic as one's own self and other selves and partly physical as the stocks and stones around us. Upon these are superposed attributes and of two kinds. The one kind inheres in the substances and may be called their "characters": thus "happy" is a character of a person as extension is of a tree. The other kind

---

[1] This highly condensed description of the all-but-established-order is of course a gross oversimplification. No actual psychologist conforms to the description. The 'traditional psychologist', like the 'economic man' and Ward's 'psychological individual' must be regarded as an 'ideal type' by reference to which the actual deviants from the type can be easily described.

mediates between two or more substances and consists of . . . "relation", as when one person thinks of another, or two trees stand side by side.'[1]

Now why exactly has this account of the world come in recent years to seem so curious? And so wrong?

Of course there is a sheer logical blunder in the suggestion that two sorts of 'substances' can be distinguished after distinguishing substances as such from their attributes — the only things by references to which one substance can be distinguished from another. This blunder can be corrected. What then remains is the suggestion that there are two kinds of 'attributes': the non-relational 'characters' which can inhere in a single substance, and the 'relations' which mediate between two or more substances, and that each of these kinds of attributes may be further subdivided into two sorts, the physical and the mental. 'Being extended' and 'standing side by side' are examples of physical attributes and 'being happy' and 'thinking of' examples of the mental. Now is there anything very silly in that?

Surely not. We can see what Spearman means, and we can see that the world could have been like that. But then a few steps are taken by way of elucidation and out come the hoots of derisive laughter, and lots of jokes about the ghost in the machine. This consequence ensues from the implicit assumption that the two sorts of attributes are mutually incompatible. Just as no one thing can be both a cube and a sphere, no one thing can be both wholly red and wholly green, so one and the same thing cannot be both happy and extended. Nor, too, can a couple of trees standing side by side think of one another. The doctrine of the two realms and the doctrine that one human being is composed of two things, a body and a mind, depend upon, and follow from, this assumption of the incompatibility of physical and mental predicates.

We then consider a simple human situation. Guy and Pauline are sitting side by side on a seat in the park thinking of and adoring each other. Are we then to say: 'There are four things on this seat in the park, two palpitating bodies and two ecstatic

[1] *The Nature of Intelligence*, p. 66.

souls?' Must we say without regard either to romance or good sense — 'two ghosts in two machines'?

Of course, Gilbert Ryle's quip about the 'ghost in the machine' has been taken much more seriously than perhaps was ever intended. A ghost, it might be demurred, is a very different thing from what Descartes or Spearman or anyone else has ever meant by a soul or mind. Roughly, a ghost is something which has some of the sensory or phenomenal properties of a material thing, but differs from a material thing in respect of the most important causal or dispositional properties. A mind on many accounts would seem to lack all sensory or phenomenal properties but to have some of the causal properties of a material thing. It has been alleged to move the pineal gland or to influence the course of neuro-physiological processes. We may disbelieve in ghosts, but the hypothesis that such things can be is quite intelligible, and could in principle be verified. We can describe what it would be like if a ghost were really there, and we can say what it would be like for oneself to be a ghost in or out of a machine. To say that this hypothesis lacks sufficient validation is to make a trivial observation. With 'mind', as so often conceived, the case is much more serious. If minds lack 'phenomenal properties' it is not so easy to say what it would be like either to be, or be presented with, a mind. It was, however, only in recent history and by steps and stages that the concept of mind became divested of content. To begin with Descartes, a mind was the most observable of things in the world. On his account it, and it alone, really possessed all the phenomenal properties that anything whatever might appear to possess. These phenomenal properties were by him divided into three classes; those that really belonged to the soul but appear to belong to objects external to the body, those that really belonged to the soul but appeared to belong to the body, and those that both really belonged to the soul and appeared to do so.

In the history of philosophy and science these phenomenal properties have been hustled around in the most extraordinary way. Benighted common sense is content to let them belong just where they seem to belong, despite the awkward puzzle that arises in so doing. Galileo and the physicists peeled them off from material objects without caring much what became of them. Descartes salvaged the discarded peel. Phenomenal properties were given a new standing in the world as 'states' of the soul. The position again became unsettled when Locke redescribed them as ideas in or before the mind, rather than as states of the mind that 'had' these ideas. This was the first step in their expulsion from the mind altogether, and in their passage to yet another curious status — that of attributes of a 'neutral stuff' from which both mind and matter were said to be 'constructed'.

These migrations of the sensible properties have been attended by puzzling changes in the categorial form of the concept of mind. Some of these changes may have been unwitting 'category mistakes', whilst others were deliberate and intentional.

The idea of a 'category' is vague, slippery and ill-defined. We know, more or less, where we are with the categories of Aristotle; and we know, more or less, where we are with the categories of Kant. Today, the word is used in a more free and easy way. The distinctions between 'things', 'qualities' and 'relations' may be described as categorial distinctions. So too may the distinctions between 'facts' and 'events', between 'elements' and 'constructs', between dispositions and their actualizations. It is a categorial mistake to confuse a 'fact' with an 'event' or to treat a dispositional property as though it were an occurrent actualization or a persistent manifestation of the disposition in question. We must distinguish, however, category blunders from deliberate categorial revolutions. The history of the philosophy of mind is very largely the history of such revolutions. The different accounts of consciousness, of mental life, or of 'mental phenomena', that compose different philosophies of mind do not differ about what is observed. They differ in respect of the general concepts, the categories, in terms of which what is observed is described. Every transition from one philosophy of mind to another is a sort of categorial revolution; and each reformer could claim to be correcting a category mistake. It was a categorial revolution, when thought was first described as a 'state' of the soul. It was a categorial revolution when Locke introduced his new way of ideas describing these as 'objects presented to the understanding'.

It was a categorial revolution when Hume redescribed them as 'loose and separate particulars' and it was another categorial revolution when James described them as composing a 'stream' and again when Titchener called them 'processes'. The difficulty in settling the categorial issue was perhaps responsible for the vogue, especially in the works of nineteenth-century philosophers, of the word 'phenomenon'. 'Phenomena' would seem to enjoy a measure of categorial neutrality. Psychology, it was said, is the science of mental phenomena, and 'a phenomenon', as the word was used, could be almost anything anyone cared to make it — an appearance or a reality, a fact, an event, a disposition or an actualization. But categorial neutrality cannot be maintained, categorial decisions must be made. Assumptions will out.

If there can be no categorial neutrality there can, nevertheless, be categorial tolerance. The continuous process of redescription which makes up the history of the philosophy of mind may itself be redescribed in terms of the currently employed idea of a 'model'. Descartes, we might say, described the mind in terms of the model of 'the substance and its states'. For Locke the model was 'the container and its contents'. G. F. Stout once remarked that Ward talks about the 'I' as though it were an 'Eye'; but what we may call the Model of the Looking Eye goes back at least as far as Locke, whose container seemed to contain an eye looking at all the other contents. Ward's contribution was to invent the 'scanning eye' with the power of changing the plastic continuum that it scanned. Within the framework of these models other models are built in — the model of Molecule and the Atom, the model of the Flowing Stream, and the model of the Elastic Jelly. The model of the container and its contents can be developed into the model of the brightly illuminated chamber standing over a dark and mysterious cellar — this is the model of theories of the conscious and the unconscious mind. All these models tend to be visual and when we visualize them clearly they all look absurd. But not one of them is entirely absurd. Each draws attention to something of interest and importance. Absurdity results when some irrelevant features in the model are attributed to whatever is modelled.

As we pass through this succession of philosophies of mind in the seventeenth, eighteenth and nineteenth centuries it is not immediately obvious whether illumination was increasing or whether things were going from bad to worse. In any case the great transition in the present century did not come about by the suggestion of yet another model for the description of the mind. It came about in quite a different way — through the emergence of and the successive transformations of the doctrine of Behaviourism. Behaviourism was the child of very humble parents, but it was blessed with noble patronage. What was certainly in its earliest form a rather silly theory attracted the interest, for good reasons, of the ascendent schools of philosophy, phenomenalists, positivists and those who said that the business of philosophy is to 'analyse'.

The situation in the 1920s, it will be recalled, was this. Dominant at the time, in the philosophy of mind, was a peculiar hybrid 'model' — a combination of the model of the Container and its Contents and the model of the Agent and his Acts. Two very powerful trends had combined to neutralize the 'objective contents' of the mind — Stout had followed Brentano in making 'acts' or 'modes of reference' the essential and characteristic ingredients in whatever is 'mental'. The Mill-Mach-James-Russell variants of phenomenalism had progressively reduced sensation and images to the status of primordial 'neutral stuff'. The ghost in the machine had indeed become ghostly — an invisible actor performs diaphanous acts. After G. E. Moore had introduced this adjective 'diaphanous' it became impossible longer to blink the fact that 'the mind' has no phenomenal properties at all. Phenomenalists who wished to maintain a belief in the mind were clearly in a very awkward predicament, and to them in their plight Behaviourism was a veritable godsend. Why should we not say, they said, that the act of perception, the act of recall, the acts of believing, liking, wanting, etc., are all acts in the simplest and obvious sense — just bits of bodily behaviour. This we may call *Naive Behaviourism*. Preposterous as the suggestion seemed at first, the proposal did not work out too badly. It worked rather surprisingly well, but on the other hand the fact that it worked well was not in every way surprising. Traditional theories accepted some form of parallelism between mental facts and their bodily conditions and expressions. Characteristic forms of behaviour were admitted to be what might be described in the old-fashioned text-books of logic, as the 'propria' of mental phenomena — a proprium being an invariable accompaniment of an 'essential' property without itself being itself an essential property. Now it is a well tried and well established methodological device to change a proprium into a definition. Physicists had used this device in dealing with sound, and heat, and light. Hobbes had, in fact, already in another way used the same procedure in dealing with the facts of mind. And so it seemed we were able to give a 'behaviouristic definition' of every kind of mental act.

But Naive Behaviourism will not quite do. It is, for example, most unplausible to suggest that a man is actually behaving in a distinctive way in regard to everything he perceives, remembers, imagines, desires or believes. However, the objection can be met by a simple amendment of the analysis. To perceive something is not actually to behave in a characteristic way in regard to what is perceived, but to be *disposed* to behave in a characteristic way in regard to it. Generalized, the idea issues in what might be called *Dispositional Behaviourism*. This will clearly take care of all the various types of 'attitudes' and modes of reference of a mind to its objects. In fact at this point Behaviourism assimilates the old psychology of the 'conscious attitudes' into the new psychology of attitudes conceived in terms of 'set', 'einstellung' or 'organic states of readiness'.

Still further generalized, the theory may be described as '*Analytic Behaviourism*'. Behaviourism had begun as a rather vulgar iconoclastic revolution. There are, it was baldly said, no minds, no thoughts, no mental images, no dreams or nightmares, no feelings, no desires. There is nothing, nothing, nothing but bodies and their responses to stimulation. Receiving the aristocratic embrace of analytic philosophers, this revolutionary movement was remodelled and transformed into a genteel instrument of logical analysis. The central plank in the platform of the analysts was that we often know the truth of a statement without knowing its analysis. We know that we have two hands, and so know that material things exist. What we do not know is the analysis of these statements. Clearly, what is sauce for the goose is sauce for the gander, and in this case sauce for the ghost in the machine. We know we have thoughts, and feelings, dreams and desires, and so we know that we have minds. What we do not know with the same assurance is the correct 'analysis' of these statements.

Hence many ideas that the naive behaviourists and dispositionalists were anxious to extrude from the 'philosophy of mind' are rehabilitated – including the introspective act. The suggestion is now that it too can be analysed in a behaviouristic way. Several alternatives are open. To perceive that one is perceiving, for example, is an introspection. If then we say that to perceive a lamp-post is to react in a certain way to the lamp-post, then to perceive a perception is to react to a reaction. If we prefer to say that to perceive a lamp-post is to be disposed to react to the lamp-post, then the corresponding state of introspection is a disposition to react to a disposition. So far, so good, but this is still not quite good enough. It remains very paradoxical to say that to believe that it is going to rain is just to be disposed to do this or that sort of thing. This suggests that as we have to wait to see which way the cat jumps in order to know what the cat wants to do, so we have each to wait to see how we are going to behave before we know what we believe, hope or fear. This is clearly not the case. We have to distinguish 'felt' dispositions from dispositions which can exist without being felt at all. An 'inclination' to sneeze is very different from a tendency to walk round in a circle when lost in a wood. For Guy to verify his suspicion that Pauline has a cold and a dispostion to sneeze he must await the occurrences of behaviour of a snuffling or sneeze-like character. But for Guy to verify his suspicion that he himself has a disposition to sneeze he has not to wait for anything more to happen. He has only to note the presences of phenomenal data of a certain quality and pattern. The distinction is not peculiar to the class of disposition disclosed by introspection or self-observation. There are dispositional properties in material things, the possession of which at a given time can be asserted only on the basis of observing what happened before or what happens after the time in question. There are, however, dipositional properties which we attribute to material things in part upon the basis of observing the presence of phenomenal characters *at* the time in question. Glass can *look* as well as *be* fragile. Bishops and knights, in chess as in real history, are 'essentially' beings with certain potentialities and other dispositional properties, but we identify them by phenomenal characteristics. Human beings can *look* as well as *be* timid, aggressive, sanguine or melancholic. There is no mystery in this, nor need there be a category confusion. It is simply that characters of differing categorial types often occur in association. The phenomenal basis for the assertion of dispositional properties could be set out in tedious detail. For the purposes of physics there is little use in doing so, but for psychology these associations are of interest and importance. The fact would seem to be that the states, the acts and the dispositions of a person are presented to that person in very considerable detail and in a quite distinctive way. The phenomenology of a person as that person is presented to himself is vastly more complicated than the phenomenology of a person as he is presented to someone else. This is due in part to the fact that he can use more of his senses in observing himself than can the other person in observing him. In most of the natural sciences, and most of all in physics, there are good and sufficient reasons for being parsimonious in the use of the senses. We may if we like say that a rainbow is 'really' an affair of electromagnetic events which 'appear' to the observer as a band of spectral colours. So, too, we may, if we like, say that a person is 'really' an affair of biochemical events which appear to that person as a complicated tissue of experience in various modalities of sense.

This tissue is very complicated indeed. There are somatic and kinaesthetic sensations which form the substance of the 'body schema'. But there is more than that. There are not only pains in the neck, there are pains in the heart as well. There are waves of emotion, felt inclinations, and there are trains of thought to be observed.

In short, there is a ghost in the machine after all. The ghost in the machine is, we may say, the machine itself as it appears to itself; and it can appear to itself as an extremely spiritual sort of thing — even as a 'disembodied mind'. We can at least say, in phenomenological terms, what it would be like to be a 'disembodied mind'. Novelists have done so. In general they describe it as something talking to itself — asking question, posing suppositions and making assertions. William James was very nearly right in making the suggestion that the quintessence of the awareness of the self resided in the sensory content of the passage of the breath through the epiglottis. What he failed to notice was that the most characteristic experience was not that of panting, but the experience of uttering words in subvocal statements. The ancients were rather near the truth in their doctrine of the spirit as the *Logos*. The 'introspected self' is thus a bodily self, not as someone else's body appears to and is described by the professional anatomist in his laboratory, but as the anatomist's own body appears to the anatomist himself. It is ghostlike in the sense that it has the phenomenal properties of a material thing but differs from a material thing in its causal properties. It is 'epiphenomenal'. This is true and important not only in regard to the body itself and its organs but also of the 'behaviour' of the body and its organs. The behaviour as well as that which behaves can also be described in a phenomenological way.

There would then appear to be a certain convergence between these trends in the philosophy of mind and certain trends in 'empirical psychology. This cosmos of ours, it seems to be agreed, is *not* constructed on Spearman's 'curious plan'. It is not composed of two sorts of 'substances', bodies and minds. The sharpest dichotomy in science is that between inanimate matter and living things (though this perhaps is not so very fundamental), and psychology is just one of the natural sciences concerned with things that are alive. But there is another dichotomy in consequence of which psychology is, and must remain, just a little peculiar — that between physics and phenomenology. In empirical psychology at the present time there are in the main two vigorous growing points, 'ethology' and the theory of perception. Ethology is, roughly speaking, behaviourism without metaphysical strings. It is the generalized study of behaviour of living things, and as such is in the behaviouristic tradition. In the study of perception, on the other hand, there is a great revival of interest in the ways in which things appear. Contrasted and unrelated as these two lines of development might seem to be, they are connected in an interesting way, since the sort of 'explanation' that is sought of the ways in which things appear is one that can be given in terms of the concepts required for the explanation of the ways in which organisms behave.

'The inquiry of chief interest' today is not that concerning the formation of complex ideas out of simple ones, but the explanation of behaviour. It is clear now that behaviour is not to be explained merely by reference to 'stimuli' (described entirely in physicalistic terms). Output is not wholly explained by references to 'input' but requires a detailed analysis of the total through-put. Hence a concentration of interest in the neurophysiology of the central nervous system. The chief interest in the facts regarding the ways in which things appear arises from the light that is thrown by phenomenology upon the events that intervene between stimulus and reaction. The psychologist's concern with phenomenology — the ways in which things appear to persons and the ways in which persons appear to themselves — is not a concern with phenomenology for its own sake, but only for the light that it may throw on the 'underlying' neural processes.

This interest is not, in principle, a new development. The physicist has, for example, for long been concerned with the phenomenology of the visible spectrum in so far as the phenomenal facts may afford data for constructing and testing theories concerning the nature of light. Physiologists have for long been interested in the same facts in so far as they may afford data for constructing and testing theories of 'colour vision'. What is new is the extension of this interest to all the more complex facts of perceptual experience — the 'constancies', the phenomenon of figural after effect and all the phenomena of 'perceptual organization'.

Dualism is dead — for the present. In its Cartesian form it is no doubt dead for ever. But casting out devils is proverbially a tricky operation. So is exorcising ghosts. A dualism remains. There are still two ways of picturing and describing the world, the way of physics and the way of 'common sense'. Physics has its say, but the rainbow remains in the sky. The rainbow is a sort of ghost. The rainbow we see *is*, we may say, the physical rainbow as it appears. Or we may say, if we prefer to do so, that the physical rainbow is the ghost — just a sophisticated way of thinking and talking about the real rainbow that we really see.

The Body-Mind complex is very like the rainbow. What shall we say here? We may say, if we like, that the introspected mind is just a body and its goings on as they appear to the body in question and not to anybody else. Or, if we prefer it, we may say the physical body as it is described by the anatomist is the more ghostly thing, a phantasy of cells and cell assemblies, a convenient way of talking about ourselves, and that we *really* are more or less what we feel ourselves to be.

Though this dualism remains, something has been gained. We are left with one dualism, not two. Classical dualism added to this dualism of 'primary' and 'secondary' qualities, the dualism of the physical and the mental. The 'philosophy of science' which would seem to be implicit in the writings of most contemporary psychologists, and fairly explicit in some, is one in which the second dualism has been 'reduced' to the first. The dualism that remains is one that is common to all the natural sciences, and the 'philosophy of mind' thus becomes incidental to a more generalized 'philosophy of nature'.

POSTSCRIPT

FURTHER reflections of the author on trends in the philosophy of mind since 1956 are contained in a paper on *Causal Explanations in Psychology* contributed to a Festschrift presented to Sir Cyril Burt (London 1965) and in the Manson Lecture to the Royal Society of Philosophy under the title '*The Body-Mind Problem*' in *Philosophy, Psychology and Medicine* (1965) published in *Philosophy* in 1966.

S. KÖRNER

Some Types
of
Philosophical Thinking

STEPHAN KÖRNER, JUR. DR., M.A., PH.D.: born in Czechoslovakia, September 26th, 1913; educated at a classical gymnasium, Charles University, Prague, and Trinity Hall, Cambridge; appointed Lecturer in Philosophy, 1946, and Professor, 1952, both at the University of Bristol. Visiting Professor at Brown and Yale Universities (1957, 1960), Editor of *Ratio* since 1961.

Chief publications: *Kant* (Pelican Series), 1955. *Conceptual Thinking*, 1955. *The Philosophy of Mathematics*, 1960. Various papers in *Mind*, *The Proceedings of the Aristotelian Society* and other philosophical journals.

S. KÖRNER

SOME TYPES
OF
PHILOSOPHICAL THINKING

IN this essay[1] I shall try to characterize some types of thinking which, in varying degrees, are involved in all philosophizing and are peculiar to it. For this purpose I propose to consider various species of philosophical thinking in their relation to each other and to other theoretical inquiries, and to compare philosophical thinking with other and more familiar procedures. I shall then briefly consider the allegations against philosophy that it is subjective in some odious sense of the term and that it is incapable of progress, and I shall conclude with a few words on the practical problem of teaching philosophy.

Unavoidably, my argument will have to be sketchy and schematic. Examples and illustration will often have to take the place of systematic exposition and finer points and qualifications will have to be disregarded.

I

(1) There can be little doubt that a large part of everybody's life is devoted to the interpretation of his environment. Whatever his occupations and purposes, the individual is faced at every moment with something given to him which calls for his interpretation if his purpose is to be achieved and his action successful. The distinction between what is given and what is interpretation pervades all thinking. It finds expression in such familiar oppositions as that between data and explanation or facts and theory.

[1] Except for some omissions the essay is based on an Inaugural Lecture in the University of Bristol which was intended for an audience of intelligent laymen.

The border-line between what is considered to be given and what is regarded as interpretation is not fixed and depends mainly on the purpose in hand. A soldier in the field will be careful to distinguish clearly between what appears to be a moving branch and his interpretation of it as an actual moving branch. A lawyer will have to distinguish carefully between observed behaviour and the interpretation of it as intentional, unintentional or negligent. Again any experimenter or scientific observer will labour to avoid habitual interpretations obscuring his observations in a manner to defeat his special purpose. What by one person or at one time is taken to be brute fact is often recognizable by some other person or at another time as a more or less articulate combination of facts and superimposed interpretations.

Now many of our interpretations are so habitual, familiar and reliable for predictions that we tend to overlook that they are interpretations. Thus we say, and who will blame us, that we perceive physical objects when in fact we only interpret certain appearances as belonging to physical objects; or that we perceive persons when in fact we are only interpreting certain appearances as belonging to persons. Indeed a physical object or a person is on any view a highly complex unity of an unlimited number of different aspects which cannot conceivably be given to any one observer at one and the same time. When I say that I see a table I am referring to a visual appearance, but I imply, among many other things, that this visual appearance is related to other actual and possible visual appearances, to actual or possible tactual appearances, to possibilities and impossibilities of manipulation. To unfold what, apart from a reference to a visual appearance, is involved in the statement that I see a table would take a long time. To unfold the meaning of the statement that I see a person would take much longer.

My object in drawing attention to this rather obvious state of affairs is to show that the distinction between what is given and what is interpretation can be pushed further than is done, and, for that matter, further than reasonably *need* be done, in the laboratory, the law-court or the ordinary business of life. The attempt to describe what is given with the minimum possible admixture of interpretation is often called 'phenomenological description' or 'phenomenology' (i.e. the theoretical concern with uninterpreted phenomena). It has, as a matter of fact, been practised by most philosophers and is to be found in the works of thinkers as different as Plato and Aristotle, Descartes and Hume, the impassioned existentialists and the level-headed logical positivists.

The purpose of phenomenological description is frequently misunderstood. The philosopher who distinguishes between a visual appearance and the interpretation of it as something belonging to a physical object is often taken to be denying thereby the existence of the external world, or at least to be doubting it. He is doing nothing of the kind. He is not concerned either with undermining *or* confirming the belief in the existence of external objects, of persons, or, I may add, of moral or immoral actions, beautiful or ugly things, numbers or atoms, but merely with the clarification of these beliefs, with their logical interrelations, their similarities and differences. His question is not whether we are right or wrong in holding these beliefs, but with *what* precisely we are holding when we hold them. He is concerned not with their truth or falsehood, but with their meaning. And it is for the purpose of making this meaning explicit that he finds himself forced to distinguish, in these beliefs, as rigorously as possible, and certainly more strictly than is usual, between the given and the interpretative elements.

Phenomenological description is involved in philosophical thinking long before it arrives at those cross-roads whose uninformative sign-posts are inscribed 'materialism', 'realism', 'idealism' (absolute and subjective), 'pragmatism' or something-or-other-ism. Anybody who cares to study the phenomenological descriptions, say of perception or of remembering by philosophers of mutually opposed schools, will be struck, and possibly disappointed, by the large extent of their agreement.

Here then is a procedure which is peculiar to philosophy and whose principles are easily understood: for phenomenological description differs from more familiar types of description only in that it requires a more radical separation between that which is given and that which is interpretation. Although it mainly serves

the purpose of preparing the ground for tackling purely philoso
phical problems it is not without relevance to non-philosophical
inquiries.

The success of many scientific theories depends, at least in
part, on happy simplifications, on neglecting such features of
experience as can be safely and profitably ignored in the context
of the theory. If, as is quite natural, we transfer the explanatory
apparatus which has been useful in one field of inquiry to another
we may find that its simplifications have ceased to be harmless, in
which event the practice of phenomenological description has its
relevance as a safeguard against confusing our models of experience with this experience itself.

For example, it is useful in dealing with limited tracts of human
behaviour to ignore the power of some motives. If we are concerned with man as a selling and buying animal it is helpful to
assume that the only effective human motive is self-interest. In
terms of this simplified picture of human motivation we can
explain and predict a great many actions. As a result the temptation arises to explain all human behaviour in this way. A phenomenological description of how we make up our minds in various
types of situation will reveal 'economic' man as a simplification
really useful only in a limited field of inquiry.

Again, it is very helpful in the natural sciences to picture
change, movement and consequently time by means of a directed
line each of whose segments consists of an infinite number of
unextended points. If we regard this idealized picture as describing
our actual experience of a process in time we are heading straight
for Zeno's antinomy of the moving arrow which cannot conceivably move. The source of this antinomy, as is rightly pointed
out by Hilbert and Bernays (*Grundlagen der Mathematik*, Vol. I,
p. 16), lies not in any failure to apply the mathematical theory of
convergent series but in the assumption 'that an infinite succession
whose completion cannot be achieved in fact or principle is
regarded as given completed'. It lies in mistaking a highly complex idealization for a phenomenological description.

I trust the reference to Zeno will not suggest that phenomenology is of no use for modern problems which arise on the borders

of mathematics. This, I believe, is far from being the case. True, the problems and antinomies surrounding the idea of infinity no longer, today, concern the infinitely small. Since the middle of the nineteenth century they have concerned the notion of actually given complete totalities; e.g. the set of all integers or the set of all real numbers. The new antinomies are at least as serious as those pointed out by Zeno and they are far as yet from being resolved in a manner to satisfy all contemporary mathematicians and logicians working in this field. Even in their general approach to the problem these thinkers differ greatly. Some of them would discard the notion of the actual infinite altogether even if it means sacrificing large parts of mathematics. Others, somewhat shamefacedly, are content to 'adopt a smooth running technique which does not appear to be inconsistent'.

It seems to me that one cannot hope to tackle successfully the problems and paradoxes connected with the various notions of infinity without showing how they arise out of a gradual process of idealization from other notions, especially that of a finite collection which describe, but do not in any way idealize, experience. Leading mathematicians like Brouwer, Hilbert and Weyl implicitly recognize the necessity of this task and its relevance to mathematics in their works. It is a task which clearly presupposes the philosophical procedure of phenomenological description.

(2) Just as no difference in kind separates phenomenological description from other more commonly practised descriptions so none separates philosophical analysis from the analysis of concepts which occurs in other theoretical fields.

The situations which call for such analysis are familiar to most of us. When concepts which have been applied smoothly and efficiently in the early stages of an inquiry begin to lead to contradiction, confusion and deadlock, it becomes necessary to stop using these intellectual tools for a while and subject them to examination. This is what in fact happened to the notions of infinitesimals, of Newtonian space and time, and of causality in its Aristotelian usage.

As distinct from a scientist, a historian or a literary critic who, as a rule, will feel the need of analysis in reference to the categories which he uses in his special field, the analytical philosopher will concern himself rather with categories which like 'cause', 'number', 'purpose', 'existence' are common to many or all other theoretical inquiries. He will also examine such concepts as 'moral obligation' or 'beauty', concepts not used in any technical inquiries except, of course, philosophical ones. The difference between philosophical and other types of analysis lies not so much in the procedure as in the concepts subjected to it.

Consider an illustration from the time when analytical philosophy first began to be regarded as an autonomous and self-sufficient way of philosophizing. It should be noted how closely related it is to important problems of which the possibility of proving or, for that matter, of disproving the existence of God is one. Consider the assertion that unicorns do not exist. Here, if we regard 'existence' and 'non-existence' as properties, our assertion attributes to unicorns the property of non-existence. If, however, a property is attributed to anything then that to which it is attributed must, in some sense, exist. Consequently by asserting that unicorns do not exist we should be implying that unicorns exist in the same manner as lions or elephants.

If this situation seems unsatisfactory then the need arises for 'analysing' existential statements and their negations. Russell has suggested, quite roughly speaking, the following analysis: When we say that unicorns do not exist, we 'really' mean (or ought to mean) that the statement 'This is a unicorn' is never true. Similarly when we say that lions do exist, we 'really' mean (or ought to mean) that the statement 'This is a lion' is sometimes true.

Russell has in fact analysed the notion of existence in terms of a notion of truth. If we accept his analysis our assertion that unicorns do not exist no longer implies the belief in a realm where unicorns, round squares and similar beings, or rather non-beings, lead a happy if shadowy existence. On the other hand our harmless talk about unicorns and in general about that which does not exist is in no way restricted. Russell's analysis is in a manner of speaking a surgical operation which has removed from existential statements certain unwanted metaphysical implications while leav-

ing them in other respects sound and healthy. Many other examples could be given, some of which like the analyses of logical
deducibility, of probability, of teleological explanation have
proved relevant to theories far removed from philosophy.

What, now, is the nature of philosophical analysis? In order to
understand this we must, to begin with, be prepared to distinguish
between what the analytical philosophers believe themselves to be
doing and what in fact they are doing. Analytical philosophers
have often regarded the difference between a normal consideration
of concepts and their philosophical analysis as quite similar to the
difference between the normal and a particularly careful observation of physical objects as a result of which the objects are not
changed but merely reveal their outlines and important features
more clearly. Thus in the fairly representative words of the late
Professor Stebbing philosophical analysis consists 'in discerning
relations and characteristics which are in no way altered by the
process of analysis'.

Now if we look at the practice of analytical philosophers we
shall find it difficult to accept this account of what they are doing.
Thus, as we have seen, Russell's analysis of existential propositions
does not consist in discerning the meaning of the notion of existence, but in replacing one notion of existence which implies unwanted or undesirable metaphysical beliefs by another notion
which does not.

The general character of philosophical analysis stands out if we
take note of two types of requirement which analytical philosophers adopt for their procedure even if they are not clearly aware
of this. It is required first that the notion to be analysed must in
some way be defective, e.g. self-contradictory, too vague, con-
taminated by an unacceptable metaphysics, or otherwise unsuit-
able as an intellectual tool for an intended task; while the analysing
notion must be free from these defects. Secondly, it is required
that the analysed and the analysing notion must stand in a certain
relation to each other which justifies the replacement of the former
by the latter when necessary. We might call such a relation a 'replacement-relation'.

Some consequences of this characterization of philosophical

analysis as the replacement of defective by non-defective notions are worth noting. First of all, all philosophical analyses fall into various types on the one hand according to the replacement-relations which the analysing philosopher sees fit to adopt, on the other according to the criteria by which he determines whether a notion is defective or sound. Replacement-relations range from the synonymity between two concepts over various types of logical equivalence to more or less qualified resemblance. The variation of the criteria of defectiveness, of which I have given examples, seems almost unlimited.

A more important consequence of our account of philosophical analysis is seriously to qualify that self-sufficiency and autonomy which by most of its practitioners analysis is supposed to possess: for clearly the choice of one replacement-relation or of one criterion of defectiveness rather than another is not a result of philosophical analysis but a pre-condition of it. The arguments by which an analytical philosopher, if pressed hard enough, would justify his choice of replacement-relations and defend his criteria of sound notions, would be philosophical arguments, but they would not fall within analytical philosophy. In other words it is not true that all philosophy is analytical philosophy or even that analytical philosophy is independent of other types of philosophical thinking.

(3) If philosophical analysis is not autonomous, the standards of its adequacy being taken from elsewhere, we must next ask what the logical status of these standards is. Two suggestions are possible and are often made: according to the first these standards are embodied in the common sense of the ordinary man, or, as it is nowadays often put, in his habits of speech. But this appeal to the man in the street must, I believe, fail because there are so many different men and so many different streets and because there is no reason why one of these streets should be preferred even if it should turn out that it leads through the centre of Oxford and the outskirts of Cambridge. The second answer is that the standards by which the adequacy of philosophical analysis is judged are metaphysical propositions. To be of any use, however, this answer requires a definition of metaphysical propositions.

Now I cannot in the time at my disposal systematically explain my position in this matter. Instead, I propose to try to illustrate it by considering one of the many metaphysical disputes which arise within all fields of theoretical thinking and consequently within the domains of both the faculty of arts and the faculty of science. I could take as an example a metaphysical dispute between two historians or two literary critics because I am under the impression that while members of the faculty of arts are as a rule much too ready to take the existence of metaphysics for granted, scientists are often unreasonably reluctant to admit even its possibility.

My illustration is taken from the correspondence between Einstein and Born as published in the latter's book *Natural Philosophy of Cause and Chance*. Einstein writes: 'You believe in the dice-playing god, and I in the perfect rule of law in a world of something objectively existing which I try to catch in a widely speculative way . . . The great initial success of quantum theory cannot convert me to believe in that fundamental game of dice . . . I am absolutely convinced that one will eventually arrive at a theory in which the objects connected by laws are not probabilities, but conceived facts, as one took for granted only a short time ago. However, I cannot provide logical arguments for my convictions . . . .'

Einstein's belief here is a fair example of what I have ventured to call a 'metaphysical directive'. His belief cannot be expressed either by a logico-mathematical proposition or an empirical one. In particular, it is not a physical theory although it is relevant *to* physics. The difference in the belief of Einstein and that of Born can be roughly expressed by saying that the former accepts while the latter rejects a rule to the effect that the notion of a law of nature, which is to be used in the construction of physical and other theories, should not be a relation between probabilities. I call such rules to the effect that in the construction of theories some categories rather than others should be used, metaphysical 'directives', in order to distinguish them from other types of metaphysical proposition.

This is not the time to defend the view that some metaphysical propositions are metaphysical directives, or to discuss in detail the relations between these directives on the one hand and logical or empirical propositions on the other. If, however, my view is correct, it follows that some metaphysical propositions at least are meaningful in the same straightforward sense in which rules in general are meaningful.

It follows further that a person's metaphysical beliefs may be much more than a collection of irrelevant ornaments and in particular that his acceptance of metaphysical directives may indeed give direction to his whole theoretical endeavour. Thus a physicist who shares Einstein's metaphysical belief will persevere in his attempts to find a physical theory which will, roughly speaking, fit both the facts and his metaphysics, while one with Born's metaphysical beliefs will give preference to other paths of inquiry.

Our account of philosophical analysis has led us to consider the nature and function of metaphysical directives since these latter, whatever more they may do, at least constitute the standards by which the success or failure of a philosophical analysis is judged. We must now turn to philosophical inquiries whose task it is to discover such metaphysical directives and, if necessary, to modify them.

The inquiry which aims at the discovery of the metaphysical directives which are accepted by any group of thinkers is, like every inquiry which aims at the discovery of accepted rules, empirical or, more precisely, anthropological. It is easily described but not always easy to pursue with success: the philosopher who undertakes it has to meet many difficulties. Thus a thinker who accepts certain metaphysical directives may often not be aware of this fact, may be unable to formulate those he accepts and may, indeed, believe that he has accepted some which in fact he has not accepted.

A large part of Kant's philosophical work can be regarded in this light. It is an attempt to make explicit the hidden metaphysical directives to which, as he put it, *all rational beings* are committed. He understood by a rational being anyone who implicitly accepts on the one hand the theoretical principles of Aristotelian logic, Euclidean geometry and Newtonian physics and who on the other hand accepts a moral principle embodied in the notion of duty.

What he calls 'the critique of pure reason' is largely an inquiry into the metaphysical directives which are associated with these theoretical and practical principles. It is true, of course, that Aristotelian logic, Euclidean geometry and Newtonian physics have been replaced or supplemented by other theories and that Kant's account of metaphysical propositions is, as a result of the development of modern logic, no longer tenable. Yet, in spite of these qualifications Kant's critical philosophy is, among many other things, one of the most impressive examples of that philosophical procedure which drags to the light of day the metaphysical directives which are implicit in mathematics, the natural sciences and other fields of inquiry.

Once the metaphysical directives which are implicitly accepted by a group of thinkers, usually a very large group, are made explicit a new kind of philosophical problem arises. It may be that the system of these directives is inconsistent, vague, incomplete or that it is adequate to some non-philosophical theories only. In short, when the critical task is fulfilled and the implicitly accepted directives are made explicit there often arises the new task of reconstructing the system of these directives.

An example will again have to take the place of detailed explanation. Many philosophers who have tried to exhibit clearly the metaphysical directives which they implicitly obey in their thought about matters of fact and questions of value have found that the principles which they accept in making factual judgments are or seem to be incompatible with the principles which they accept in passing value judgments, especially moral ones. It appears, in particular, that the categories which are applied in scientific inquiries are inconsistent with the categories which are applied in moral thinking. This real or apparent clash can be made quite clear, if we imagine a judge, who happens to be also a scientist concerned with developing a scientific theory of human behaviour. We may imagine that he divides his daily work evenly between the courtroom and the laboratory. In the morning he will assume that the persons whom he sends to prison for having committed a crime were free to do otherwise and are therefore responsible for their actions. In the afternoon, in the laboratory, he will try to explain the behaviour of his subjects, and indeed all human behaviour, on the assumption that anybody who performs any action is not free to do otherwise and in this sense not responsible.

This particular clash of principles is often, and much too neatly, labelled as the conflict between free will and determinism. Whether real or apparent, it calls for a harmonization of the metaphysical principles governing theoretical thinking with those governing moral valuation. It calls in other words for metaphysical reconstruction. Even apart from the reasons adduced in their support, some suggestions towards such reconstruction may perhaps be worth indicating. The thinker may come down on the side of the scientist and regard responsibility and moral freedom as fictitious categories of a merely pragmatic significance. He may defer to the claims of his moral experience and regard those scientific categories which are incompatible with moral responsibility as, at the most, useful accessories in a fairly recent, highly ingenious, and rather superficial intellectual adventure. He may seek a solution in a mystical coincidence of opposites, in an illusion produced by the grammar of our language, or indeed in many other directions. The point here is that in looking for a solution at all we should be engaged in a task of metaphysical construction. We should also be facing a theoretical problem which is vaguely felt even by very busy people who are quite happy to forget it as quickly as possible.

Metaphysical directives are not all of equal importance to the person or group accepting them. This will be seen most clearly if we consider the manner in which metaphysical beliefs are justified. For example, a mechanist might argue against a vitalist that theories which conform to mechanistic metaphysical directives are on the whole more successful as instruments of prediction. He will, in other words, justify metaphysical mechanism by appealing to the principle of verification. This principle, which has dominated European thought for at least three centuries, is as clear an example of a metaphysical directive as any; and its acceptance does not mean, therefore, the end of metaphysics as has been believed by some logical positivists. It is perhaps the one metaphysical directive of which scientists are most clearly aware, though it is not the only one which they adopt. That they ought to adopt no

TYPES OF PHILOSOPHICAL THINKING 127

other is a philosophical doctrine rather than the principle of scientific method.

In discussing the relation between metaphysical directives and theories conforming to them I have implied nothing about the order of their appearance. It seems to me that at some periods, e.g. in the seventeenth century, the formulation of metaphysical directives on the whole preceded the construction of theories which conform to them, but at other times, e.g. in the eighteenth century, the order is reversed. This whole question, however, is no longer a philosophical but a historical one. It is similarly the task of the historian to ascertain the causes which favour the acceptance of a metaphysical system. It may be that the success of a theory or group of theories which conform to certain metaphysical directives leads to the adoption of the latter in all theorizing. Even such external factors as the attitude of governments to what is useful, valuable or ought to be believed, may work for or against the spreading of particular metaphyscial doctrines.

An important question arises as to whether there are any metaphysical directives whose acceptance is necessary in the sense that no theory which contravened them could conceivably be constructed. The search for such metaphysical directives would lead us into the field of logic. Even there we should, however, find that many so-called laws of thought, e.g. the law of excluded middle, need not be, and in fact are not, generally adopted. If we wished to discover a hard core of common logic which did not admit of alternatives, we should have to look for rules governing the use of concepts which, as a matter of anthropological fact, are employed by all human beings who are at all capable of conceptual thinking.

Phenomenological description, philosophical analysis, the philosophical inquiry into accepted metaphysical directives and their reconstruction are according to the preceding account all closely related to each other. As inquiries, moreover, they sufficiently resemble non-philosophical inquiries to admit of border-line cases. Between philosophical and other theoretical procedures there are such border-line cases; and this is relevant to our present topic in at least two ways. It implies on the one hand that the nature of the philosophical procedures with which we have been dealing is not more difficult to grasp than that of other and more usual types of thinking. It implies on the other hand that beyond the border-country we find theoretical procedures which are peculiar to philosophy.

(4) So far I have said nothing about synoptic philosophy, which to many philosophers from Plato to Samuel Alexander and A. N. Whitehead has appeared as the ultimate aim of all philosophical thinking. Plato in a famous passage in the Republic (VII, 537c) defines the philosopher as the synoptic man, i.e. the man who unlike the specialist is capable of seeing things together. This definition, which has since often been repeated, says too little about what is involved in philosophical synopsis as distinct from other ways of gathering different special fields of experience into a wider system. To recognize a piece of philosophical writing as an example of synoptic philosophy is not difficult. It is very difficult indeed to describe synoptic philosophy on the lines on which I have been describing other philosophical procedures. This would involve discussing the relation which synoptic philosophy bears to other types of philosophical and non-philosophical thinking; it would involve answering the question whether, and if so in what sense, a work of synoptic philosophy could be called adequate or inadequate; and also the question why synoptic philosophy seems more akin to religion and poetry than it is to science. While, at least at present, I have no answer to offer, I would make two observations which unfortunately are not as little needed as I could have wished them to be: namely, that the great synoptic philosophers of the past have all been masters also in the other fields of philosophical thinking; and secondly that to be a tyro in philosophical analysis and to be ignorant of science and mathematics is not sufficient to invoke one into an example of Plato's synoptic man.

II

Philosophy, like the natural sciences, and like mathematics, has no infallible recipe for discovery. Like other disciplines it depends on ingenuity, critical ability and imagination and has its creative geniuses and its more or less competent practitioners. Philosophy, however, is often blamed in that, unlike the sciences and mathematics, it lacks any generally agreed method for deciding the acceptability or otherwise of its results. In order to see how far this accusation is justified, let me try to describe in a very general manner the life of philosophical problems from their inception to their natural or violent death.

A philosophical problem starts with what Aristotle called wonder and what, not less appropriately, some contemporary philosophers have called philosophical puzzlement or perplexity. It does not always end there. Often it is possible to express one's perplexity in terms of a problem which is more or less determinate, that is to say, a problem the solution of which would have to satisfy certain requirements. It may happen that once these requirements are clearly stated they are found self-contradictory, so that what seemed to be a problem turns out to be merely a perplexing confusion. Again, once the requirements are formulated it may happen that the problem is dropped because it has revealed itself as trivial. If the requirements for the solution of a philosophical problem are seen to be neither self-contradictory nor trivial, we can do nothing but attempt its solution.

In philosophy as elsewhere the requirements which the solution of a problem must fulfil constitute the definition of it. The acceptability of a solution depends thus on the one hand on the extent to which these requirements are recognized, and on the other hand on the degree of precision with which they are formulated. In both these respects philosophical problems vary greatly. At one extreme we find problems of logic which are defined in terms of requirements which are at least as widely accepted and at least as precisely formulated as is the case with problems of mathematics. At the other extreme we find philosophico-religious problems defined by requirements which are accepted only by comparatively small groups of thinkers and which admit of very much less clear-cut formulation. The accusation that philosophy is 'subjective' in the sense of lacking a general agreed method for deciding the acceptability of its results tends to lose force as we move from the problems of *Weltanschauung* towards problems of logic.

It would, I believe, be a misfortune if philosophers ceased to pay attention to philosophical problems and solutions peculiar to certain limited groups of past or present thinkers. To do this is to neglect an important means of understanding human actions and history: for whatever may be the nature of historical causality the explicit and implicit philosophical beliefs of men often help us to understand what they have done and what they are likely to do. I do not for a moment wish to imply that the philosopher should give up his proper task and become a historian of philosophical ideas; but I do think that the historian of ideas should have some first-hand knowledge of dealing with philosophical problems.

If what I have said about the various types of philosophical thinking and about the life and death of philosophical problems is correct, it should be possible to meet the allegation that philosophy makes no progress and is indeed incapable of it. In so far as it is concerned with the analysis of concepts and the discovery and reconstruction of metaphysical directives relevant to other inquiries, philosophy progresses with the progress of these by receiving problems from them and by setting them problems in turn. Thus the philosophical problems of probability, induction and the logic of confirmation arise from the natural sciences, whereas a metaphysical view, for example that of Einstein which I instanced earlier, sets, or at least modifies, scientific problems.

Again, in so far as philosophical thinking is successful in its attempt at the clear formulation of requirements for the solution of its problems it may give birth to special sciences with their own problems and methods. Many sciences have in this way arisen from philosophy and proved their vigour by ungratefully disclaiming their parentage. Even fairly recently philosophy has in this manner been, at any rate partly, responsible for experimental psychology, many of whose first laboratories were protected and nurtured by philosophers. It may well be that soon a new science of linguistics will turn its back on philosophy, who will part with this, her latest offspring, with mingled feelings of pride and relief. That philosophy progresses in still other ways from bewilderment towards clarity could be easily demonstrated to those who spend their days doing philosophy. But then, they know this anyhow.

The present occasion seems to demand that I should say something of my attitude to the problems of teaching philosophy. I believe with Kant that the duty of the teacher is to teach the student not philosophy (in the sense of a body of doctrines), but how to philosophize. This he can do only by showing how various philosophers, including himself, are tackling philosophical problems. Since, as I have tried to show, philosophy and the other fields of inquiry are closely interrelated, philosophy should not, I believe, be taught in entire isolation from other subjects, but is best taught to those who either have some knowledge or are in the process of acquiring some knowledge of other fields.

One cannot nowadays discuss the teaching of philosophy without considering the vexed question of symbolic logic. On the one hand many philosophers ignore the great advances which logic has made in the last hundred years and some are even inclined to think symbolic logic a danger to philosophy and would keep it out of the curriculum. Their, often unfounded, objections remind us of those which Aristotle raised against Plato and his followers. He too feared that philosophy was in danger of being swamped by mathematical techniques. There are, on the other hand, philosophers who believe that logic (or semantics) is destined to replace philosophy and whose confidence in symbolic formulations is often, to say the least, astonishing. My own view is that the elements of symbolic logic should be taught in university courses because a great deal of modern philosophy can hardly be understood without it; because its methods and results give rise to important and far-reaching philosophical problems; and because the teaching of modern logic is a good antidote to a frequent tendency in average students to replace systematic thought by feeble inspirations.

I have no more to say on the matter of teaching, except to express my personal conviction that philosophy can, like almost no other subject, create and fortify the habits of intellectual curiosity, honesty and modesty, and thereby well serve the ideals of a true university and a humane civilization.

POSTSCRIPT. For my fuller views on philosophical method see 'Some remarks on Philosophical Analysis (J. Philos. LIV. 18, 1957) and The Philosophy of C. D. Broad Ch. 2 (Schillp ed., N.Y. 1959).

R. B. BRAITHWAITE

Probability and Induction

RICHARD BEVAN BRAITHWAITE, M.A. (Cantab.), F.B.A.: born Banbury, January 15th, 1900; educated at Sidcot School, Somerset, Bootham School, York, and King's College, Cambridge; studied physical science and mathematics before studying philosophy; Fellow (since 1924) and Lecturer, King's College, Cambridge, 1938-53; University Lecturer, 1928-34, and Sidgwick Lecturer in Moral Science, University of Cambridge, 1934-53; Tarner Lecturer, Trinity College, Cambridge, 1945-46; President, Mind Association, 1946; President, Aristotelian Society, 1946–47; Annual Philosophical Lecturer to the British Academy, 1950; since 1953 Knightbridge Professor of Moral Philosophy, University of Cambridge; FBA, since 1953; President British Society of the Philosophy of Science, 1962-63. Deems Lecturer, University of New York, 1962.

Chief publications: *Moral Principles and Inductive Policies* (British Academy Lecture, 1950). *Scientific Explanation*, 1953. *Empiricist Views of the Nature of Religious Belief* (Eddington Lecture), 1955.

R. B. BRAITHWAITE

PROBABILITY AND INDUCTION

THE problem (or pseudo-problem) of the justification of inductive reasoning — the skeleton in the cupboard of Inductive Logic, as C. D. Broad has called it — has been treated by British philosophers in recent years in close connection with the problem of the nature of probability and of probable reasoning. Hume, indeed, whose proof that an empirical generalization (or an unknown instance of it) could not be deduced from knowledge of a limited number of instances first exposed the problem, led up to his analysis of 'necessary connection' by way of a discussion of probability; and subsequent philosophers who have not been satisfied with the two post-Humean ways of trying to justify induction by assimilating it to deduction — Kant's Transcendental Analytic and J. S. Mill's Uniformity of Nature as a supreme major premiss (which, however precisely it is stated, is not strong enough to do what is wanted of it, besides requiring inductive inference for its own establishment) — have turned more and more for assistance to the theory of probability. Induction, if it cannot yield certainty, can yield probability; and Jevons's influential *Principles of Science* (1874) treated the question as an inverse problem in which, instead of passing with certainty from general premisses to particular conclusions, we pass with probability from particular premisses to general conclusions. In our generation J. M. Keynes (Lord Keynes) solved, as he thought, Hume's problem in one part of his *Treatise on Probability* (1921); and his treatment, together with similar treatments which were published about the same time by Sir Harold Jeffreys, D. M. Wrinch and C. D. Broad, has been the principal basis for the discussion of the subject in Great Britain in the period between the two wars. It will therefore be convenient if I talk about probability statements in general before passing on to the inductive problem.

Probability statements are of several different kinds of which the following are typical examples:

(1) The probability of an ideal die falling with five uppermost is $\frac{1}{6}$.

(2) The probability of this particular die (the die I am now holding in my hand) falling with five uppermost is $\frac{1}{6}$.

(3) The probability of a radium atom disintegrating within 1700 years is approximately $\frac{1}{2}$.

(4) It is more probable than not that a new-born child will be a boy.

(5) On the evidence which we have at present Einstein's theory of gravitation is more probable than Newton's.

(6) Influenza is probably a virus disease.

(7) The next swan I shall see will probably be white.

(8) Sonny Boy will probably win the Derby.

The first four of these statements differ in a very important way from the last four. In (1), (2), (3) the statements make explicit reference to a number measuring the probability. In (4), although the statement as given does not include a numeral and so does not explicitly refer to a number, the statement is another way of saying that the probability of a new-born child being a boy is greater than $\frac{1}{2}$, which explicitly refers to a number (just as to say that most of the children born last year in Cambridge were boys is another way of saying that the proportion of children born last year in Cambridge who were boys is greater than $\frac{1}{2}$). Statements (1) to (4) are thus *essentially numerical* probability statements: it would be self-contradictory to hold any of these statements while holding that there was no number which measured the probability in question. The fundamental notion in (1) to (4) is that of probability *qua* numerically measurable.

The situation is quite different in the case of statements (5) to (8). Here, while it is possible to hold (as is held by Jeffreys and was held at one time by C. S. Peirce) that for each probability referred to there is a number which measures it, it is not self-contradictory to deny this while asserting the probability statement. There is no contradiction in saying that Einstein's theory of gravi-

tation is more probable than Newton's and at the same time declining to hold that there are two numbers, the first greater than
the second, of which the first measures the probability of Einstein's theory and the second that of Newton's. Probability as used
in (5) to (8) is not *essentially* a numerical concept: it is essentially a
comparative concept (construing, in (6) to (8) 'probably' as 'more
probably than not'). The fundamental notion concerned is the
relation more probable than. The situation is similar to that of
'attributes of sensation' such as the brightness of a visual sensation.
To say that one visual sensation is brighter than another does not
imply that there are two numbers, the first greater than the second,
measuring the brightnesses of the two sensations respectively. It
may be possible to devise a satisfactory method for measuring
brightnesses numerically, for example Fechner's use of 'just
noticeable difference' as the unit, but to say that one sensation is
brighter than another does not depend upon such a method having
been found. Similarly to say that the sense of probability in (5) to
(8) is essentially a comparative sense does not imply that it may
not be possible to attach numbers to these probabilities. But it is
perfectly possible to interpret the probabilities in (5) to (8) only
comparatively, and this sharply contrasts with the probabilities in
(1) to (4), which have to be interpreted numerically in order to
give sense to the statement.

This distinction between essentially numerical and essentially
comparative probability statements, for the most part unrecognized by writers of the 1920's (e.g. Keynes and R. von Mises), has
been emphasized by more recent writers (e.g. K. R. Popper,
Rudolf Carnap, Bertrand Russell, William Kneale), who have
often given distinctive names to the two types. I will refer to the
first type as concerned with an *essentially measurable probability*
and treat the second type as equivalent to the comparative notion
of *reasonableness of belief.* One of the reasons why the two types
are so frequently confused is that they are often conflated in the
same sentence: to say that it is highly probable that a radium atom
will not disintegrate within one year is to say that it is reasonable
to believe the proposition that the probability of a radium atom
disintegrating within one year is to be measured by a very small

number. Some contemporary philosophers (e.g. P. F. Strawson) would prefer, instead of distinguishing two senses of probability, to distinguish between two 'factors' in the 'strength of the support' which p gives to q in the argument 'p so probably q', one of these factors being the 'degree of completeness' of the generalization underlying the argument (corresponding to my essentially numerical probability), the other being the 'degree of completeness of the support' for this generalization (corresponding to my reasonableness of belief in the generalization). But, whatever be the best way of expressing the distinction, the distinction is now generally recognized; unlike Keynes and von Mises, contemporary logicians, for the most part, do not expect to analyse both ways of using probability by the same method, and do not attempt to reduce essentially numerical probabilities to degrees of reasonableness or vice versa.

Let me say something first about essentially numerical probabilities. Some statements referring to these are theorems, or exemplifications of theorems, in the pure deductive system of probability logic. Just as to say that a Euclidean triangle has the sum of its angles equal to two right angles is to state a necessary consequence of the axioms of Euclidean geometry (together with the definitions of the terms used), so to assert statement (1) — that the probability of an ideal die falling with five uppermost is $\frac{1}{6}$ — is to state a necessary consequence of the axioms of probability logic together with the definition of 'ideal die' as one which is as likely to fall with any one side uppermost as with any other. The proposition is equivalent to a *hypothetical* proposition about an actual die — namely, that if this particular die (which I am now holding in my hand) is an ideal die, then the probability of its falling with five uppermost is $\frac{1}{6}$. There is no peculiar difficulty in the analysis of this logically necessary proposition: it is exactly on a par with the hypothetical propositions of a system of pure geometry.

The problem which has faced logicians of probability in recent years has been the analysis of the essentially measurable probability statements of types (2) to (4), which are all empirical propositions. Statement (2) — that the probability of this particular die falling with five uppermost is $\frac{1}{6}$ — has a *prima facie* resemblance to (1) — the logically necessary statement about an ideal die; but consideration of its relation to experience shows that it is of a different logical category. The logically necessary proposition (1) will not be rejected by any amount of experience with any actual die — all we shall conclude from such experience is that the die is not an ideal die; but the proposition (2) about an actual die will be rejected if, when it is thrown a large number of times, the proportion of times it falls with five uppermost deviates widely from $\frac{1}{6}$. Similarly with propositions (3) and (4) about the disintegration of radium atoms and the male-birth ratio. (3) will not be directly testable by experience, but deductions from it about the diminution in mass of observable pieces of radium will be directly testable, and if these deduced conclusions deviate widely from the values predicted by (3), (3) will have to be rejected. Since under suitable empirical circumstances each of these three propositions will be rejected, they are all empirical propositions. They are all *general* empirical propositions, although the generality is of a special sort which will be called *statistical*. This can be shown by translating them into forms which use instead of probability language some such an expression as 'by-and-large':

By-and-large, one-sixth of the throws of this die yield fives.

By-and-large, half the radium atoms disintegrate within 1700 years.

By-and-large, over half of the children born are boys.

'By-and-large' (or some similar qualification) has to be added because the classes of reference (the class of throws of this die, the class of radium atoms, the class of new-born children) are all 'open' classes, i.e. they cannot be given by specifying their members separately; and none of the propositions is making an assertion about the proportion in any specific 'closed' class (e.g. the first thousand throws of this die, the radium atoms in the Cavendish Laboratory at a particular date, the children born in Cambridge in a particular year).

The problem before the probability logician is thus that of the analysis of an empirical statistical general proposition which may be expressed in either of the forms:

The probability of a throw of this die yielding a five is $\frac{1}{6}$.

By-and-large, one-sixth of the throws of this die yield fives. The clue as to how to treat this problem lies in recognizing that if '1' or '0' is substituted for '$\frac{1}{6}$' in the first of these forms, 'all' or 'none' respectively requires to be substituted for 'one-sixth' in the second and the 'by-and-large' deleted. The propositions then become affirmative or negative universal general propositions. Now the meaning of a sentence expressing a universal proposition, e.g. 'All the throws of this die yield fives' may be regarded as being determined by the fact that this sentence expresses the logically weakest proposition which will be rejected by our finding one throw of the die which does not yield a five. If the meaning of the sentence is given in this way, it will ensure that from the universal proposition thus specified there will logically follow the proposition that, with respect to a particular throw of the die, that particular throw will yield a five, the essential characteristic of a universal proposition. Similarly the meaning of a sentence expressing a statistical general proposition, e.g. 'By-and-large, one-sixth of the throws of this die yield fives', may be regarded as being determined by the fact that the sentence expresses the logically weakest proposition which will be rejected by our finding, in a large set of throws of this die, that the proportion of fives deviates from $\frac{1}{6}$ by more than a certain small amount. Giving the meaning of the sentence in this way will ensure that from the statistical general proposition thus specified there will logically follow, by the theorems of probability logic, the proposition that the great majority of sets of a large number of throws of the die will yield proportions of fives deviating from $\frac{1}{6}$ by less than this small amount.

The difference between a universal proposition (Every A is B) and a statistical general proposition (The probability of an A being a B is p) will then consist in the fact that, whereas from the former there logically follows the proposition that in every set of instances of A all the members of the set have the property B, from the latter there follows the proposition that the great majority of large sets of instances of A will have a proportion of members having the property B which differs by a small amount from p. This is a consequence of the Law of Great Numbers of probability logic.

There is, however, a serious difficulty in explaining statistical general propositions in terms of their method of rejection which does not apply to the explanation of universal propositions by a rejection method. For, since the Law of Great Numbers consequence of the statistical general proposition makes a statement only about the great majority of sets of instances, the rejection method may mistakenly reject the proposition when it is true if the set of instances examined does not fall within this great majority of sets of instances. So the rejection cannot be taken as a definitive rejection (as in the case of universal propositions), but as a rejection which is provisional only, and which is open to revision on further evidence.

Such further evidence can, however, be found to test whether the rejection on the first set of instances was mistaken. This can be provided by examining a very large set of observations and treating this as a large set of large sets of observations, and then seeing whether, within this set of sets, the great majority have a proportion of members with the property B which differs by less than the appropriate small amount from p. If the great majority have such a proportion this second test does not provisionally reject the statistical general proposition and the first provisional rejection must be cancelled: if they have not, the first provisional rejection is confirmed by a second provisional rejection.

Such a second provisional rejection can again be tested by evidence of an even larger set of observations, regarded as a large set of large sets of large sets of observations; and on such evidence it can be cancelled, thereby cancelling also the first provisional rejection, or it can be supported by a third provisional rejection. And so on. Moreover a rejection test at any stage in this endless series of tests may serve provisionally to reject the statistical general proposition even if the previous tests in the series have failed provisionally to reject it. Each rejection test supersedes all previous rejection tests. So the criterion for the definitive rejection of the statistical general proposition would be that at some stage in the series of tests it is provisionally rejected, and that it continues to be provisionally rejected by all the subsequent tests in the endless series.

Does the fact that an endless series of empirical rejection tests would be necessary definitively to reject the statistical general proposition make it impossible to use these rejection tests for giving an empirical meaning to the statement of the statistical general proposition? I do not think so. It would be impossible if it were logically necessary that a statistical general proposition provisionally rejected by one of these tests should have this provisional rejection cancelled by a later test. But this is not the case. It is perfectly possible for the proposition to be rejected by all the tests, or by all the tests from some stage onwards. So the notion of provisional rejection by an empirical rejection test seems to me adequate to give an empirical meaning to the sentence expressing the proposition, although this notion allows for the possibility of the provisional rejection being cancelled. We are perfectly used to the notion of a universal proposition being definitively rejected, but never being definitively accepted, since a further test may always serve definitively to reject it. And the impossibility of 'complete verification' of a universal statement does not prevent its meaning being given by an empirical rejection test, which in the case of universal statements is a definitive one. What I am maintaining is that similarly the meaning of statistical general statements is given by a series of empirical rejection tests, all of which are provisional and subject to revision. That a statistical general statement may nevertheless be true although it has been rejected by the first hundred or thousand in the series of tests is comparable with the fact that an empirical universal statement may be false although it has failed to be rejected by a great number of tests. In each case the empirical tests give empirical meanings to the statements.[1]

This account of the meaning of statistical general statements (i.e. of empirical probability statements) is, I think, no more than the exposition in a form which will satisfy a philosophical logician of the remarks to be found in the standard treatises on statistical mathematics to the effect that, from a statement ascribing the probability p to an A being a B, it logically follows that it is *practically certain* that a random sample of the A's which is *sufficiently large*

---

[1] This account of the meaning of empirical probability statements is elaborated in chapters V and VI of my book *Scientific Explanation* (Cambridge, 1953).

will have a proportion of B's deviating *very little* from p, and that the probability statement is to be rejected if the proportion in an examined sample deviates too widely from p. Statistical mathematicians are usually not concerned explicitly with the meaning of their probability statements: they take the meaning for granted, and give criteria for their use. All I am doing is to take one of their criteria for rejecting a probability statement as giving actually the meaning of the statement. If the meaning is determined in this way, other criteria worked out by the statistical mathematician can be used for practical tests which are more convenient than the series of tests used in my definition.

Since the empirical tests used in my account of empirical probability statements are all in terms of the proportions or 'frequencies' found in samples, the account can properly be classed as a 'frequency theory of probability'. But it does not identify a probability with any actual frequency, nor with the limit (in the mathematical sense) of an infinite sequence of actual frequencies — as in the theories of von Mises, Popper and Hans Reichenbach. The defect of these 'limiting frequency' theories is that the mathematical limit cannot be 'logically constructed' in terms of any finite set of actual frequencies, so it is necessary, one way or another, to 'posit' it; and even so no empirically testable proposition about actual frequencies can be deduced from an infinite sequence of them as having a posited limit. The account given here does not purport to 'construct' probabilities out of observable frequencies: what it does is to take the method in which a probability statement is used as a premiss for deducing propositions about observable frequencies which can be tested against experience, as giving the way to determine the meaning of the numerical probability statement.

This 'frequency' account of the meaning of empirical probability statements is not applicable only to those, like (4) — about the probability of a new-born child being a boy, the evidence for which is that of observed frequencies: it is applicable to all empirical probability statements including those the evidence for which is not that of observed frequencies at all. It is reasonable for me to believe that the probability of this particular die falling with five uppermost lies between 15 per cent and 18 per cent without my having thrown the die at all. My belief is then based upon my observation that the die looks and feels fairly symmetrical and my previous knowledge about a mechanical system (such as a die) in which a small difference in the initial conditions of motion makes 'all the difference' to the final position. Similarly I can reasonably come to believe that a die is biased by doing experiments to find the position of its centre of gravity instead of by throwing it. A Mendelian geneticist may assign a probability on the basis of gene distribution without having observed any instances of the biological species in question. But in all these cases the assignments of probability will be rejected if the observed frequencies turn out to be sufficiently different from those predicted by the probability statement. The meaning of all these empirical probability statements is given by the observable frequencies which would make us reject them: given the meaning of the statements there may well be other, and better, evidence for them than a particular observed frequency.

So much for statements of probabilities which are essentially numerical. Unless they are merely exemplifications of pure mathematical theorems (like statements about a 'true' or 'unbiased' or 'ideal' die), they are all empirical statements whose meaning is given by an empirical test in terms of observable frequencies. The case is quite different for statements asserting probabilities in the sense of reasonableness of belief. Here it is most unplausible to suggest (as was at one time done by Peirce) that reasonableness of belief can be measured in terms of any empirical frequency, e.g. of the proportion of beliefs of the same sort that turn out to be true. Logicians who have wished to treat what I have called reasonableness of belief as analogous to an essentially numerical probability have treated it as being concerned with logical relations between propositions (Keynes, Jeffreys) or with syntactical relations between sentences (Carnap).

The 'logical relation' theories of Jeffreys and Keynes may be described as attempts to give a logical account of the way in which the evidence for a proposition which is not such that the proposition logically follows from it is said to 'support' the proposition.

Supporting is taken to be a logical relation between two propositions analogous to entailment. It is related to reasonable belief in that, if evidence *e* supports proposition *h*, it is reasonable, given knowledge of *e*, to believe *h* with a degree of belief proportional to the degree with which *e* supports *h*. Jeffreys and Keynes both treat their theory of support as accounting for all the uses of probability; but since it makes support a logical notion it cannot account for the cases where, since empirical conditions can be used to reject probability statements, probability must be an empirical notion. But even considered as a theory applicable only to probability in the sense of reasonableness of belief, it has the grave defect that, in order to derive complicated propositions about degrees of support it is necessary to have, besides the theorems of probability logic, initial premisses ascribing degrees of support, equal degrees of support when a Principle of Indifference is used. Since the epistemological status of such initial premisses is highly unsatisfactory, the deductions used are equally unsatisfactory. The probability theory, regarded as a formal system, may be accepted; but will it serve the purposes which its authors intend it to serve?

The difficulty appears in clearest form in Carnap's account where syntactical relations between sentences take the place of logical relations between propositions. Carnap shows precisely how various artificial languages may be constructed in which 'degrees of confirmation' can be defined in relation to the basic sentences of the language. But the question remains as to whether any of these languages bears enough resemblance to the languages of science and of ordinary thinking to throw any light upon the problems of 'support' and 'reasonable belief' as these concepts are here used.

Keynes and Jeffreys developed their doctrines of probability primarily with a view to the justification of inductive inference. They are able, by using theorems of probability logic, to show than an increase in the amount of evidence supporting an inductive hypothesis increases the 'probability' of the hypothesis, always provided that the hypothesis has some *initial* 'probability'. The same difficulty then arises as to the epistemological status of the 'postulate' required to provide such an initial probability. Keynes proposed a Principle of Limited Independent Variety, which would restrict the number of properties in the world which are independent of one another (i.e. not interconnected by universal laws). There is no doubt that, with suitable qualification, this principle can be put into a form in which, if it is taken as an empirical generalization covering particular fields, there are some good reasons for believing it. But the reasons for believing it are inductive reasons, based upon our inductively derived knowledge of various features of the world; so it would be a circular argument to use it to give a justification of induction.

Jeffreys's and Keynes's attempts to justify induction by means of a probability theory may be regarded as the final stage in the attempt to justify induction by assimilating it to deduction — in their case, not as with Mill, to a deduction to a conclusion which would be certainly known, but to one with a conclusion which it would be probable to believe. Without their valiant attempts it would not be as clear as it is today to most empirically minded philosophers that inductive reasoning must be treated on quite different lines from deduction; and that the justification of induction, if indeed it requires one, is to be found from quite different considerations than those relevant to the validity of deductive inference, in which the conclusion follows from the premisses according to principles of inference which are logically necessary.

The justification of induction — if indeed induction ought to be justified. The failure of all attempts to assimilate induction to deduction has led many contemporary philosophers to answer this question in the negative. The doubt as to whether we have any reason to rely upon inductive procedures, it is said, is not a sensible doubt to be allayed by postulating a 'supreme major premiss' or by disclosing a 'presupposition', but is a senseless doubt to be dispelled by recognizing that it is senseless. The way to recognize this is to examine what we mean by applying the epithet 'rational' to a belief arrived at by an inductive inference, or for which inductive reasons would be given if the believer were asked to justify his belief. If we do this, we shall find that we just call an inductively supported belief 'reasonable' if the evidence for it is good inductive evidence. To quote P. F. Strawson, who has recently expressed the no-justification-required view in an admirable manner (largely due to his awareness that 'some attempts to show that the doubt is senseless seem altogether too facile'): 'It is an analytic proposition that it is reasonable to have a degree of belief in a statement which is proportional to the strength of the evidence in its favour ... So to ask whether it is reasonable to place reliance on inductive procedures is like asking whether it is reasonable to proportion the degree of one's convictions to the strength of the evidence. Doing this is what "being reasonable" *means* in such a context.'[1]

Now we may well admit that this is the truth about one way in which we apply the word 'reasonable' without agreeing that this verbal point gives the whole truth about the problem (or pseudo-problem) of the justification of induction. For why do we apply the same epithet 'reasonable' both to beliefs in conclusions of inductive arguments based upon known evidence and to beliefs in conclusions of deductions from known premisses? Although inductions are logically quite distinct from deductions, the general procedure of making inductions must have something in common with that of deducing for the conclusions of both to be called by the same complimentary title.

It is here, I think, that C. S. Peirce's 'justification' of induction in terms of its 'truth-producing virtue' comes in. Deductive procedures have truth-producing virtue in that the truth of the premisses *always* carries with it the truth of the deduced conclusion; inductive procedures have such virtue in that the truth of the premisses 'for the most part' carries with it the truth of the inductive conclusion. Any particular inductively supported belief may be erroneous, but generally speaking the practice of making inferences by inductive procedures can be relied upon to yield true beliefs. It is the truth-producing virtue in general of the use of an inductive procedure, and not a quasi-logical relation in which the premisses stand to the conclusion in a particular use of the inductive procedure, that is at the root of our proper attachment to the

[1] *Introduction to Logical Theory* (London, 1952), chapter IX.

use of such procedures. We are right in believing what scientists tell us because what they tell us is, on the whole, true.

Whether or not this fact should be regarded as a justification for induction, it seems to me clear that our belief in it is our justification for applying the adjective 'reasonable' to belief obtained by inductive procedures. Did we not believe that inductive procedures were, on the whole, reliable, we should not have the use we have at present for the word 'reasonable' in inductive contexts, since inductive inference would lack the truth-producing virtue which is a necessary characteristic of deduction. This is not to say that another use might not be found for the word: lucky guesses might be called reasonable inferences. But if the procedures upon which we rely cease to be reliable, 'reasonable' will cease to be applied to beliefs obtained by means of these procedures.

Peirce specified the non-deductive procedures having 'truth-producing virtue' as being those which *for the most part* carry truth with them.[1] But 'for the most part' is historically unplausible of the usual inductive procedures: it is, however, unnecessarily strong for our purpose. What is required, and what is historically true of the past, is that inductive procedures *frequently* carry truth with them, and that no other procedure does this.

One of the inductive procedures which is frequently truth-producing is induction by simple enumeration — the inference to a generalization from evidence of instances of it (together with no evidence of contrary instances). Although this procedure has been superseded in most parts of science by procedures having greater truth-producing virtue, the reason for using these better procedures is induction by simple enumeration from evidence of their truth-producing virtue in the past. Any new regular procedure for making predictions which is found to be truth producing will be inductively supported by simple-enumerative induction, and Strawson is right in saying that it is an analytic proposition that 'any successful method of finding out about the unobserved is necessarily justified by induction' — namely, by induction by simple enumeration. But there remains the question as to why a pro-

[1] This was the view he expounded in the famous 'Illustrations of the Logic of Science' articles of 1877-8. In the 1900's Peirce preferred to validate induction by its self-corrective character.

cedure which has been found to have truth-producing virtue in the past should continue to have it in the future; and this (as Strawson agrees) is a contingent and not a necessary proposition. It is the 'circularity' involved in justifying this by simple-enumerative induction which is the great philosophical puzzle about induction.

The circularity, however, is not of the *petitio principii* type. It does not consist in the fact that the conclusion that the procedure of simple-enumerative induction has truth-producing virtue is itself a premiss in the inference, but rather in the fact that it is the truth-producing virtue of this procedure which provides the validating principle of the inference. But is it circular to infer a conclusion by the use of a principle of inference whose validity is what is asserted in the conclusion? It is certainly not circular if the procedure of making simple-enumerative inductions is regarded from the outside as the method of working of an inference machine. An inference machine could perfectly well work from a position corresponding to the evidence for a proposition to a position corresponding to the proposition itself according to a method of working whose general reliability this proposition asserted. And it is quite plausible to maintain that such an external, naturalistic, semi-behaviourist way of looking at inductive thinking is the proper one, and that *inductive behaviour* (to use an expression of Jerzy Neyman's) rather than inductive belief is the fundamental concept.

When looked at in this way the onus of proof changes. It is no longer up to the logician to give reasons for inferring inductive conclusions: it is up to the critic to give reasons for abandoning inductive behaviour. A pattern of behaviour as universal and as practically useful as inductive behaviour has been in the past requires positive grounds for condemning it as irrational. Such grounds might be that it was of the nature of obsessional behaviour which had in fact no useful function, or that there was good reason to believe that the world was changing in such a way that to continue to behave inductively would not enable us to make our predictive responses successfully. Reasons can be given for preferring one type of inductive behaviour to another in terms of their relative predictive success: simple-enumerative induction has been largely abandoned in the advanced sciences in favour of the more sophisticated hypothetico-deductive method exactly because the use of this latter has been found to be more predictively successful. But no reasons have been given for abandoning inductive behaviour altogether — except the bad reason that it cannot be 'justified' in a similar way to that in which deductive behaviour can be justified. Belief in the truth-producing virtue of an inductive procedure is essentially a disposition to practise a certain type of inductive behaviour. Though we may have 'opted' (to use Ryle's word) for one type of inductive behaviour rather than for another, we certainly have not opted to behave inductively; we acquired inductive dispositions in infancy when we learned to orient ourselves in the world. And to explain such behaviour by calling it, whether complimentarily or derogatorily, 'primitive credulity' or 'animal faith' conceals the fact that it requires no epistemological justification.

At the beginning of this paper I interpreted the sense of probability in which it was not essentially measurable as the comparative concept of reasonableness of belief. But the reasonableness of belief in an inductively supported hypothesis, such as is expressed in the statement that influenza is probably a virus disease, admits of only two degrees of comparison — reasonableness and unreasonableness. The 'truth-producing virtue' account of induction does not profess to explain what is meant by arranging a series of hypotheses h_1, h_2, h_3, etc., in such an order that it is more reasonable to believe h_1 than h_2, h_2 than h_3, etc.; and a logician who rejects the Jeffreys-Keynes account of the matter will have to try to give some alternative account. All that such logicians have been able to do up to date is to propose criteria that can be considered reasonable ones for preferring one statistical hypothesis to a parallel one based on the same statistical evidence. However, the philosophical critics who have demanded a justification for induction have on the whole not been interested in this difficulty. They have been prepared to admit that acceptance, on inductive grounds, of a well-established hypothesis is usually an 'all-or-none' matter: what they have alleged is that, failing a 'justification', such an acceptance, and the behaviour that goes along with it, is unreasonable.

An accusation of unreasonableness in every context has a moral overtone of blame. We do not, however, blame a man for acting on what he *bona fide* believes to be true factual premisses even if he is mistaken in this belief. Similarly we should not condemn a man as unreasonable for acting as if induction were predictively reliable even if it is not. We may criticize the former for not having taken more trouble to verify his factual premisses, and we may criticize the latter scientist for not having used a better inductive procedure if a better one is to be found. But neither can be properly condemned if he has done everything that it was in his power to do. Since the rise of science mankind has developed inductive procedures so that they have the greatest possible truth-producing virtue. What more can be demanded of us than that we should always be prepared to revise these procedures if they can thereby be made more predictively reliable? To turn the critic's word upon himself — what more can be *reasonably* demanded of us? For what have we failed to do? Our only sin of omission is to have failed to reduce induction to deduction. But, if this is a sin, it derives indeed from the original sin of a Prometheus who dared to engage upon empirical science instead of confining himself to the pure mathematics beloved of the Gods — and the philosophers.

ALICE AMBROSE
and
MORRIS LAZEROWITZ

Ludwig Wittgenstein:
Philosophy, Experiment and Proof

ALICE AMBROSE (Mrs. Morris Lazerowitz) A.B. (Millikin University); M.A., PH.D. (University of Wisconsin); PH.D. (Cantab.); LL.D. (Millikin): born November 25th, 1906; Fellow at the University of Wisconsin, 1930-32; Alice Freeman Palmer post-doctoral Fellow, 1932-33; Marion Kennedy Student, Newnham College, 1933-35; Instructor in Philosophy, University of Michigan, 1935-37. Taught at Smith College since 1937, now Sophia and Austin Smith Professor of Philosophy at Smith College. Editor of the *Journal of Symbolic Logic* since 1953.

Chief publications: *Fundamentals of Symbolic Logic* (with Morris Lazerowitz), 1948 (revised 1962); *Logic: the Theory of Formal Inference* (with Morris Lazerowitz) 1961; Articles in *Mind, Journal of Philosophy, Philosophical Review, Proceedings of the Aristotelian Society* and in various collections of essays.

MORRIS LAZEROWITZ A.B., PH.D. (University of Michigan): born October 22nd, 1907; Fellow at University of Michigan, 1934-36; Alfred H. Lloyd post-doctoral Fellow, Harvard, 1937; taught at Smith College since 1938, now Sophia and Austin Smith Professor of Philosophy at Smith College; Fulbright Lecturer at Bedford College, London, 1951-52.

Chief publications: *Fundamentals of Symbolic Logic* (with Alice Ambrose), 1948 (revised 1962). *Logic: The Theory of Formal Inference* (with Alice Ambrose), 1961. *The Structure of Metaphysics*, 1955. *Studies in Metaphilosophy*, 1964. *Metaphysics: Readings and Reappraisals* (with William E. Kennick), 1966.

ALICE AMBROSE and MORRIS LAZEROWITZ

LUDWIG WITTGENSTEIN: PHILOSOPHY, EXPERIMENT AND PROOF

> I shall light a candle of understanding in your
> heart which shall not be put out. II ESDRAS.

I

LUDWIG Wittgenstein was one of the most original philosophers
of this century and there can be no doubt that the impact of his
perceptions into the nature of philosophical problems will radically and permanently change the course of philosophy in the
future. Unfortunately, the influence of his thought has been
retarded. Apart from a paper in the *Proceedings of the Aristotelian
Society* and his famous *Tractatus Logico-Philosophicus*, he did not
permit any of his work to be published during his lifetime,
although some of his lectures were privately circulated in
mimeographed form among a selected group of his students.
According to all accounts Wittgenstein was a man of compelling
personality and tended to gather a circle of favoured students
around himself. An aura of mystery, not untinged with religion,
was thus created around his work as well as around the special
group of students. Understandably, such an atmosphere might well,
and in fact did, have consequences less than desirable from an
intellectual point of view. Fortunately time has already begun to
disperse the emotional mists and clear up the air; and now that
Wittgenstein's work is being made publicly available, now that it
belongs to the public domain, so to speak, it should make itself
felt widely and objectively in the doing of philosophy. Without
stretching a metaphor unfairly, philosophy up to the present
may be described as an expanding museum of exhibits, a sort of

Madame Tussaud's to which new figures are constantly being added but from which no figures are ever removed. But some things that Wittgenstein said will plant a seed in the minds of philosophers which will in time develop into an improved understanding of the workings of philosophy, enable us to look at it in a new way. And the explanations of theories and arguments flowing from this understanding will not become just further exhibits: they will instead place the exhibits in a light which will enable us to see them for what they are.

Philosophy, over the years, presented itself in a number of different guises to Wittgenstein, some of them the usual ones all of us know, others not. It is, of course, the later ways in which he saw philosophy that are so enlightening and helpful, but to realize how enlightening these are some of the earlier ways need to be looked at. Before considering these, however, it is important to notice a connection between some things G. E. Moore did and insights into philosophy Wittgenstein arrived at later. As is well known, Moore brought philosophical theories (or some of them, at least) down to earth from the Platonic 'heaven above the heavens' where they were protected against our understanding. Placed in the light of the ordinary sun they could be scrutinized under less distorting conditions. Such a general philosophical view as Bradley's, that physical things are not real, or are mere appearance, which casts a spell over the intellect, he would translate into (and perhaps it would not be far off to say, *deflate* into) its concrete implications, for example, that he was not really wearing a waistcoat or that he was mistaken in believing that there was a sheet of paper on which he was writing with a fountain pen. Moore's ostensible purpose in effecting his translations into the concrete was to force on our attention the consequences of an abstract philosophical theory, consequences which we apparently tend to avoid noticing. The point of doing this was, frequently if not always, to refute a theory by subjecting it to 'trial by example'. But what could not fail to emerge, whether grasped consciously or unconsciously, was that construed as having Moore's translations, the theories were altogether too plainly false for anyone to have failed to see *for himself* that they were false. A further puzzling feature attaching to Moore's translations is that many philosophers who became acquainted with them did not give up their views. The idea which inevitably suggests itself is that a philosophical view like 'physical things are unreal' is not what it has been taken to be. The question could not but arise whether the view is actually *incompatible with* a factual proposition such as that Moore is wearing a waistcoat and is writing with a fountain pen. Surprising as it might seem, Moore's translations into the concrete, if they show anything, tend to show that the theories are not open to his translations. The problem then becomes one of understanding rightly how a philosopher is using language when he says, 'Physical things are not real', or 'Physical things exist but are mere appearance'. Wittgenstein's later work shows us the way to a correct understanding of such statements.

In one place Moore observed that it would seem that language, ordinary everyday language, was 'expressly designed to mislead philosophers'.[1] With the same complaint apparently in mind Wittgenstein said that 'Philosophy is a battle against the bewitchment of our intelligence by means of language',[2] and 'A philosophical problem has the form "I don't know my way about"'.[3] Moore resorted to one procedure, that of careful analysis of the meanings of words, to free philosophers from their bewitchment. Wittgenstein also used this procedure to help them find their way through the maze of language. According to him 'A main source of our failure to understand is that we do not *command a clear view* of our use of words — Our grammar is lacking in this sort of perspicuity.'[4] To express the matter with the help of a metaphor of his that has captured the imagination of many philosophers, what will help the fly escape from the fly-bottle is analysis of usage, getting straight about how we ordinarily use words. There is, however, a difference in their procedures which it will be useful to look at. This difference might very well have led Wittgenstein to say that a philosopher of Common Sense ('and that, *n.b.*, is not

[1] *Philosophical Studies*, p. 217.
[2] *Philosophical Investigations*, p. 47.
[3] Ibid, p. 49.
[4] Ibid.

the common-sense man'[1]) is himself captive in the fly-bottle but favours a special corner in it, that in trying to refute positions which go counter to Common Sense he also 'does not know his way about'. For Moore's disagreements with other philosophers result in *philosophical* stalemates, stalemates as old as those between Parmenides and his opponents.

It will be recalled that Moore's defence of Common Sense against the attacks of philosophers, attacks sustained throughout the long history of philosophy, has been rejected as begging the question, and Moore has been criticized as being dogmatic about the 'truisms' he lays down. And in bringing them, unsupported by chains of reasoning, against the counterclaims of philosophers who back their own propositions with analytical arguments, he has, in the opinion of many thinkers, begged the very questions that are in debate. Moore's familiar expletives, 'nonsense', 'absurd', 'obviously false', etc., may momentarily silence a philosopher who goes against Common Sense, but it does not affect the way he continues to think about the 'errors' of Common Sense. Long ago Parmenides said, 'Heed not the blind eye, the echoing ear, nor yet the tongue, but bring to this great debate the test of reason'. We might restate this philosophical recipe to the following effect, without antecedent prejudice to the question as to whether our senses are reliable sources of information or not: Disregard the eye, the ear, and the tongue (for we all pretty much hear the same, taste the same, and see the same), but bring only reasoning to a philosophical investigation. Moore's defence does not do this. Thus, e.g., Moore allows that he neither gives nor attempts to give an argument for *the premises* of what he puts forward as proofs for the existence of external things; and a philosopher who does give arguments against the Common Sense claim that we have knowledge of the existence of things like waistcoats and pens might, with the appearance of justification, charge that Moore is dogmatic and begs the question. And, indeed, Moore does need to explain why calling philosophers' attention

[1] L. Wittgenstein, *Preliminary Studies for the Philosophical Investigations*. Generally known as *The Blue and Brown Books*, p. 48. Subsequent references to this work will be designated *The Blue Book*. Subsequent references to *Philosophical Investigations* will be abbreviated to *Investigations*.

to truths of Common Sense does not bring them back to it nor make them give up their wayward attacks on it. But perhaps an explanation can be found only by looking at philosophy from a vantage point outside it. It may be that only from an external standpoint will it be possible to see the nature of philosophical stalemates.

It can with justice be said that Wittgenstein has been read with too much haste recently and that some of his ideas have been slid over and others have been put into the service of the private needs of philosophers, with consequent gaps and distortions in our understanding of his later work. In the present connection it is important to read with particular care one of his passages on what happens when we philosophize and how we are to be brought back from philosophy to Common Sense without at the same time being brought back to philosophy. The passage also shows how his procedure differs from Moore's. Moore, on the whole, represents the philosopher who departs from Common Sense as having made an error of fact; Wittgenstein frequently represents him as having made an error of language, and identifies the mistake, with the aim of effecting a cure. The following is the passage:

When we think about the relation of the objects surrounding us to our personal experiences of them, we are sometimes tempted to say that these personal experiences are the material of which reality consists. How this temptation arises will become clearer later on.

When we think in this way we seem to lose our firm hold on the objects surrounding us. And instead we are left with a lot of separate personal experiences of different individuals. These personal experiences again seem vague and seem to be in constant flux. Our language seems not to have been made to describe them. We are tempted to think that in order to clear up such matters philosophically our ordinary language is too coarse, that we need a more subtle one.

We seem to have made a discovery — which I could describe by saying that the ground on which we stood and which appeared to be firm and reliable was found to be boggy and unsafe. — That is, this happens when we philosophize; for as soon as we revert to the standpoint of common sense this *general* uncertainty disappears.

This queer situation can be cleared up somewhat by looking at an example; in fact a kind of parable illustrating the difficulty we are in, and also showing the way out of this sort of difficulty: We have been told by popular scientists that the floor on which we stand is not solid, as it appears to common sense, as it has been discovered that the wood consists of particles filling space so thinly that it can almost be called empty. This is liable to perplex us, for in a way of course we know that the floor is solid, or that, if it isn't solid, this may be due to the wood being rotten but not to its being composed of electrons. To say, on this latter ground, that the floor is not solid is to misuse language. For even if the particles were as big as grains of sand, and as close together as these are in a sandheap, the floor would not be solid if it were composed of them in the sense in which a sandheap is composed of grains. Our perplexity was based on a misunderstanding; the picture of the thinly filled space had been wrongly *applied*. For this picture of the structure of matter was meant to explain the very phenomenon of solidity.

As in this example the word 'solidity' was used wrongly and it seemed that we had shown that nothing really was solid, just in this way, in stating our puzzles about the *general vagueness* of sense-experience, and about the flux of all phenomena, we are using the words 'flux' and 'vagueness' wrongly, in a typically metaphysical way, namely, without an antithesis; whereas in their correct and everyday use, vagueness is opposed to clearness, flux to stability.[1]

Looking at a philosophical utterance in this way is enormously helpful, but it is not enough. And Wittgenstein did go beyond this point of view to deeper insights into the way philosophy works, as is shown, for example, by his characterizing a philosophical problem as one which arises 'when language goes on holiday',[2] or 'when language is like an engine idling, not when it is doing work'.[3] The plain implication of these observations and of many other things he has said is that a philosophical problem is not a mere verbal muddle to be cleared up by analysis of usage, but is rather the expression of a special kind of game that can be played with language. On this construction of what doing philosophy consists in, to solve a philosophical problem is just to understand the game that is being played with terminology.

To go back to his earlier work, in the *Tractatus* Wittgenstein states a number of views about the nature of philosophy or of some of its parts. The following statements give the most important of the views he advanced:

(1) Most of the propositions and questions to be found in philosophical works are not false but nonsensical. Consequently we cannot give any answer to questions of this kind, but can only establish that they are nonsensical. . . . And it is not surprising that the deepest problems are in fact *not* problems at all. (4.003)

(2) Philosophy is not a body of doctrine but an activity. A philosophical work consists essentially of elucidations. Philosophy does not result in 'philosophical propositions', but rather in the clarification of propositions. (4.112)

(3) All philosophy is a 'critique of language'. . . . (4.0031)

(4) The totality of true propositions is the whole of natural science (or the whole corpus of the natural sciences). (4.11) Philosophy is not one of the natural sciences. (The word 'philosophy' must mean something whose place is above or below the natural sciences, not beside them.) (4.111)[1]

The inconsistencies among these different things that Wittgenstein said about philosophy are not inconspicuous, and their going unnoticed must have an explanation. But bringing out inconsistencies is not important in the present connection. What is important to see is that philosophy could present such different faces to him. About his own statements in the *Tractatus*, presumably those which concern philosophy, he said: 'My propositions serve as elucidations in the following way: anyone who understands me eventually recognizes them as nonsensical, when he has used them — as steps — to climb up beyond them. (He must, so to speak, throw away the ladder after he has climbed up it.) He must

[1] From the translation by D. F. Pears and B. F. McGuinness.

transcend these propositions, and then he will see the world aright.' (6.54).

This pronouncement, which many people have found exciting, is odd, and the excitement it arouses must derive from some sort of hidden message it conveys. Perhaps, like the Delphic oracle, it 'neither speaks nor conceals, but gives a sign'. On the surface the pronouncement seems to imply that his own statements are nonsensical *elucidations*, and also, according to his own words, that nonsensical elucidations can lead to one's seeing the world aright. The underlying implication would seem to be that philosophers do not see the world aright, and that they can be led by nonsense to see it aright. It must be granted that nonsense seems at times to have remarkable curative powers, but it is hard to think that it could be a 'specific' for philosophers. However that may be, the series of views he advanced, either explicitly or by implication, about philosophy are the following. (a) Most philosophical utterances are devoid of literal intelligibility, in the way in which 'The good is more identical than the beautiful' is without literal intelligibility. (b) No philosophical proposition is true. This follows directly from (4), and parallels something he said at a later time: 'What the philosophers (of whatever opinion) say is all wrong, but what the bedmaker says is all right.'[1] He also seems to have held, (c), that some philosophical propositions are true. Thus, he came out for one of Hume's views about causation: 'Belief in the causal nexus is *superstition*'. (5.1361); and he also came out for the view that a proposition about the future is an hypothesis: 'It is an hypothesis that the sun will rise tomorrow: and this means that we do not *know* whether it will rise.' (6.36311) (d) He held, furthermore, that in philosophy no propositions are advanced. According to one way philosophy presented itself to him, it was just clarification analysis and had no propositions of its own to put forward: there are no 'philosophical propositions' as there are scientific ones.

The claim, (a), that most philosophical utterances are devoid of literal intelligibility is usually linked with the so-called Verifi-

[1] From notes taken by A. Ambrose and M. Masterman in the intervals between dictation of *The Blue Book*. These notes will be referred to subsequently as *The Yellow Book*. (Note. A 'bed maker' is a domestic who services rooms in a Cambridge college: Ed.)

ability Principle, which requires some comment. Moritz Schlick formulated in the following words the principle for determining whether an indicative sentence which does not express an *a priori* proposition has or lacks literal significance. 'Stating the meaning of a sentence amounts to stating the rules according to which the sentence is to be used, and this is the same as stating the way it which it can be verified (or falsified). The meaning of a proposition is the method of its verification.'[1] This version of the principle is usually attributed to Wittgenstein and probably it originated with him. It has commonly been understood, by those who have adopted it as well as by those who have rejected it, to eliminate metaphysical sentences from the class of literally meaningful sentences constructible in a language, and in this way to rid philosophy of its most spectacular if also its most unsatisfactory branch. This understanding of what the job of the criterion is fits in with a number of statements in the *Tractatus*, but a careful reading of the wording of the criterion brings to light the curious fact that it does not eliminate metaphysics and certainly contains within itself the possibility of the return of the rejected. For the criterion, as it is worded, does not preclude the possibility of there being supersensible verification, which would be the kind of verification appropriate to a statement referring to a non-sensible reality. That is, as phrased (and the phrasing cannot be supposed the result of a merely accidental lapse), the criterion is open to the specification, 'The meaning of a metaphysical proposition is the method of its verification'. The criterion does not rule out of court the claims of a philosopher like Husserl, who wrote: 'Under the title of *A Pure or Transcendental Phenomenology* the work here presented seeks to found a new science — though, indeed, the whole course of philosophical development since *Descartes* has been preparing the way for it — a science covering a new field of experience, exclusively its own, that of "Transcendental Subjectivity".'[2]

In the present connection, it is particularly interesting to notice that one idea about philosophy expressed in the *Tractatus* (4.113)

[1] *Gesammelte Aufsätze*, 1926–36 (1938), p. 340.
[2] Edmund Husserl, *Ideas, General Introduction to Pure Phenomenology*, trans. by W. R. Boyce Gibson (1931), p. 11.

is that it 'settles controversies about the limits of natural science'. This would seem to imply the view that at least one task of philosophy is to settle territorial disputes between science and religion. The underlying idea, from which perhaps Wittgenstein never completely freed himself, is that the metaphysician is able to survey reality in all of its parts, supersensible as well as sensible, and, like the guide at the maze in Hampton Court, is able to help those who get lost in the cosmic maze. This idea may have considerable connection with the fact that a number of Wittgenstein's later students have returned to metaphysics. It should be mentioned, however, that some followers of Wittgenstein have taken a different course, also consonant with the criterion. According to him one task of philosophy, perhaps its only task, is to bring to light modes of verification appropriate to different sorts of propositions. Interestingly enough, logic has a similar function, according to Aristotle. Ross describes Aristotle's conception of logic as not being 'a substantive science, but a part of general culture which everyone should undergo before he studies any science, and which alone will enable him to know for what sorts of proposition he should demand proof and what sorts of proof he should demand for them'.[1]

To return to the four different and incompatible views of philosophy to be found in the *Tractatus*: (a) Most philosophical utterances are senseless, (b) Philosophical propositions are not truths, (c) Some philosophical propositions are truths, (d) There are no philosophical propositions. These lie comfortably enough alongside each other, and there is no evidence that Wittgenstein ever attempted to sort them out and select from among them. Nevertheless, it cannot be supposed that in Wittgenstein's active and original mind they could continue indefinitely to live in amity with each other. And their existence shows unmistakably that one of his main preoccupations, perhaps his central one, was to get clear about the nature of philosophy. In his later thinking Wittgenstein did not completely free his mind from his earlier views about philosophy. A few examples will be enough to show this. In *Philosophical Investigations* he writes: 'The results of philosophy

[1] W. D. Ross, *Aristotle* (1930), p. 20.

are the uncovering of one or another piece of plain nonsense and of bumps that the understanding has got by running its head up against the limits of language'[1] and also, 'My aim is: to teach you to pass from a piece of disguised nonsense to something that is patent nonsense.'[2] In *The Blue Book* he sometimes seems to represent philosophers as making false empirical claims, although in this connection he disagrees with Moore as to how they are to be corrected. He wrote:

There is no common sense answer to a philosophical problem. One can defend common sense against the attacks of philosophers only by solving their puzzles, i.e., by curing them of the temptation to attack common sense, not by restating the views of common sense. A philosopher is not a man out of his senses, a man who doesn't see what everybody sees; nor on the other hand is his disagreement with common sense that of the scientist disagreeing with the coarse views of the man in the street.[3]

At times he represents philosophers as making mistaken claims about the uses of terminology, claims which his own investigations are designed to correct. He describes what he does in the following words:

Our investigation is therefore a grammatical one. Such an investigation sheds light on our problem by clearing misunderstandings away. Misunderstandings concerning the use of words, caused, among other things, by certain analogies between the forms of expression in different regions of language. — Some of them can be removed by substituting one form of expression for another; this may be called an 'analysis' of our forms of expression, for the process is sometimes like one of taking a thing apart.[4]

He also wrote:

When philosophers use a word — 'knowledge', 'being', 'object', 'I', 'proposition', 'name' — and try to grasp the *essence* of the thing, one must always ask oneself: is the word ever actually used in this way in the language-game which is its original home? —

---

[1] p. 48.   [2] p. 133.   [3] pp. 58–9.   [4] *Investigations*, p. 43.

What *we* do is to bring words back from their metaphysical to their everyday usage.[1]

At times he seems to represent the philosopher as making two different kinds of mistake simultaneously, one a factual mistake, to be removed by looking or introspection, the other a linguistic mistake, to be removed by noting what an expression is normally applied to. Thus in *The Blue Book* he said: 'Examine expressions like "having an idea in one's mind", "analysing an idea before one's mind". In order not to be misled by them see what really happens when, say, in writing a letter you are looking for the words which correctly express the idea which is "before your mind".'[2] We may gather from this that the Platonist, for example, is led by a common form of words into holding a false factual belief about what is before one's mind; he is misled by a linguistic analogy into forming a wrong notion of the actual application of the expression, 'analysing an idea before one's mind' (compare with 'analysing a substance before one's eyes'). This in turn results in a false belief regarding what *is* before one's mind when one conducts an analysis. The impression gained is that both errors are to be corrected by looking at the facts, both the erroneous idea about usage and the erroneous idea about what takes place when we 'have an idea before our mind'. But plainly the 'linguistic mistake' of the Platonist, who appears to think that there are special refined objects designated by the phrase 'idea before one's mind', is not like that of a person who thinks the word 'horse' is normally used to apply to cows or like that of a person who sees a horse but thinks he sees a cow or thinks he sees what in fact does not exist. Wittgenstein could not have failed to realize this, and, indeed, a new insight into philosophy had begun to develop in his mind.

The direction of his thinking became more and more oriented toward the notion that philosophical problems are muddles, verbal tangles which are to be straightened out by recourse to ordinary usage, with the help of a special device he called 'language games'. A philosopher develops a 'mental cramp', and the therapy for removing it is to bring him back to ordinary usage. The

[1] Ibid, p. 48.   [2] p. 41.

following passage from *The Blue Book* will make this clear. In considering the question whether I can know or believe that someone else has a pain, he wrote:

> But wasn't this a queer question to ask? *Can't* I believe that someone else has pains? Is it not quite easy to believe this? . . . needless to say, we don't feel these difficulties in ordinary life. Nor is it true to say that we feel them when we scrutinize our experiences by introspection. . . . But somehow when we look at them in a certain way, our expression is liable to get into a tangle. It seems as though we had either the wrong pieces, or not enough of them, to put together our jig-saw puzzle. But they are there, only all mixed up; . . . [1]

The thing to do to get straightened out, to cure our verbal malady, is 'to look how the words in question *are actually used in our language*'.[2] When Wittgenstein observed that to call what he did 'philosophy' was perhaps proper but also misleading, and that what he did was one of the 'heirs' of philosophy, he certainly had in mind the technique of examining the actual usage of expressions in the language for the purpose of 'dissolving' philosophical problems. It is worth noticing, in passing, that he conceived his work as beneficially destructive: 'Where does our investigation get its importance from, since it seems only to destroy everything interesting, that is, all that is great and important? (As it were all the buildings, leaving behind only bits of stone and rubble.) What we are destroying is nothing but houses of cards and we are clearing up the ground of language on which they stand.'[3]

To return to the question whether what he did might appropriately be called philosophy, he had in mind not only the procedure of attempting to settle controversies by examining usage — so as to bring philosophers down to the linguistic realities — but also, possibly, the new notion that was beginning to take form. It must be allowed that he did not give very much expression to the insight into the linguistic structure of philosophical theories which gave rise to this notion, nor did he elaborate and develop it; but he did give *some* expression to it and he did make some application

[1] p. 46.   [2] *The Blue Book*, p. 56.   [3] *Investigations*, p. 48.

of it. In *The Blue Book* there occurs this important paragraph:

The man who says 'only my pain is real', doesn't mean to say
that he has found out by the common criteria — the criteria, i.e.,
which give our words their common meanings — that the others
who said they had pains were cheating. But what he rebels
against is the use of *this* expression in connection with *these*
criteria. That is, he objects to using this word in the particular
way in which it is commonly used. On the other hand, he is not
aware that he is objecting to a convention. He sees a way of dividing the country different from the one used on the ordinary map.
He feels tempted, say, to use the name 'Devonshire' not for the
county with its conventional boundary, but for a region differently bounded. He could express this by saying: 'Isn't it absurd
to make *this* a county, to draw the boundaries *here*? But what he
says is: 'The *real* Devonshire is this'. We could answer, 'What
you want is only a new notation, and by a new notation no facts
of geography are changed'. It is true, however, that we may be
irresistibly attracted or repelled by a notation. (We easily forget
how much a notation, a form of expression, may mean to us, and
that changing it isn't always as easy as it often is in mathematics
or in the sciences. A change of clothes or of names may mean very
little and it may mean a great deal.)[1]

The idea that quite unmistakably comes through from this
passage is that a philosophical theory is a misleadingly phrased
introduction of an altered piece of terminology. The form of
sentence in which a philosopher presents his remodelling of
conventional language is the form of sentence ordinarily used to
state a matter of fact; and in presenting his renovated terminology
in this way he makes himself dupe to what he does, as well as
anyone who either sides with him or opposes him. The philosopher imagines himself to be expressing a matter of fact or a theory,
i.e., to be delivering himself on what really is the case or on what
exists or on what cannot exist; and his mistake lies in the construction he places on what he is doing, not in his understanding of the
actual use of terminology. He is mistaken about what he does with

[1] p. 57.

conventions of usage and is not mistaken about what the accepted conventions are:

'The fallacy we want to avoid is this: when we reject some form of symbolism, we're inclined to look at it as though we'd rejected a proposition as false. It is wrong to compare the rejection of a unit of measure as though it were the rejection of the proposition, "The chair is 3' instead of 2' high". This confusion pervades all philosophy. It's the same confusion that considers a philosophical problem as though such a problem concerned a fact of the world instead of a matter of expression.'[1]

This view as to the nature of philosophical statements and of what might be called the 'fallacy of philosophy' quite plainly has great explanatory power. The position that philosophical utterances are about states of affairs, about reality, does not, for one thing, square with the analytical arguments with which philosophers support their theories; neither does it explain, for another thing, how a philosopher can hold his views while not being, to use Wittgenstein's words, 'a man out of his senses, a man who doesn't see what everybody sees'. The position that philosophical utterances use language improperly or are misdescriptions of actual usage does not explain why a philosopher is not corrected by bringing terminology back to its 'original home'. It does not explain why a philosopher who is made to feel embarrassed by being shown the correct use of language nevertheless does not give up his claim, or if he does give it up is able to return to it later. The view which makes philosophical utterances out to be pronouncements embodying covertly revised criteria for the use of expressions explains both these things, and it also explains other eccentricities attaching to philosophical theories. To use Wittgenstein's imaginative metaphor, it explains why the fly cannot be shown the way out of the fly-bottle. The fly cannot be led out because it does not want to be led out. The fly-bottle is only superficially its prison. At a deeper level, the fly-bottle is its home which it has built for itself out of language.

[1] *The Yellow Book.*

A somewhat extended passage from *The Yellow Book* would seem plainly enough to indicate that this was the direction his thinking took about the nature of philosophical theorizing, i.e., about what goes on when we think in a 'philosophic moment', to use Moore's expression. It should be remarked immediately that the passage does not indicate this direction unambiguously and in so many plain words, without indications of other directions. But Wittgenstein's mind does not seem to have worked in straight lines. The following is the passage, and it is well worth a careful reading:

Suppose now I call my body by the name of Wittgenstein. I can now say, 'Wittgenstein has toothache', just as I can say 'Shaw has toothache'. On the other hand I should have to say, 'I feel the pain', and I might feel it at a time when Wittgenstein had not toothache; or when Shaw had. It is only a matter of fact that Wittgenstein has the toothache when I feel the pain.

If I use 'I' and 'Wittgenstein' thus, 'I' is no longer opposed to anything. So we could use a different kind of notation. We could talk of pain in the one case and of behaviour in the other. But does this mean the same as saying that I have real toothache and the other person has not? No, for the word 'I' has now vanished from the language. We can only now say 'There is toothache', give its locality and describe its nature.

In doing this we are keeping the ordinary language and beside it I am putting another. Everything said in the one can, of course, be said in the other. But the two draw different boundaries; arrange the facts differently. What is queer about an ordinary notation is that it draws a boundary round a rather heterogeneous set of experiences. This fact tempts people to make another notation, in which there is no such thing as the proprietor of a toothache. But without the people realizing it, or even realizing that there are two, the two notations clash.

Put it another way. To the person who says, 'Only I can have real toothache', the reply should be, 'If only you can have real toothache there is no sense in saying, "Only I can have real toothache". Either you don't need "I" or you don't need "real". Your notation makes too many specifications. You had much better say, "There is toothache", and then give the locality and the description. This is what you are trying to say and it is much clearer without too many specifications. "Only I have real toothache" either has a common sense meaning, or, if it is a grammatical (philosophical) proposition, it is meant to be a statement of a rule; it wishes to say, "I should like to put", instead of the notations, "I have real toothache", "there is real toothache", or "I have toothache". Thus the rule does not allow 'only I have real toothache' to be said. But the philosopher is apt to say the thing which his own rule has just forbidden him to say, by using the same words as those in which he has just stated the rule.

'I can't know whether another person has toothache' seems to indicate a barrier between me and the other person. I want to point out to you that this is a pseudo-problem. It is our language which makes it seem as though there were a barrier.'

I talked before of the differences which our language stresses, and the differences it hushes up. Here is a wonderful example of a difference hushed up. It is not entirely hushed up; for of course all the notations must have the same multiplicity. Nothing can be said in the one which can't also be said in the others. But a notation can stress, or it can minimize; and in this case it minimizes.[1]

Even a cursory reading of these words exposes a number of different tendencies in Wittgenstein's thinking about philosophy. Thus, he describes the question as to whether it is possible to know that another person has a pain as a 'pseudo-question'. There is also the hint that a philosophical problem is some sort of mix-up, the linguistic symptom of a mental cramp. There is, further, the notion that philosophical theories, or anyway some philosophical theories, introduce alternative forms of expression which translate into expressions in ordinary use, i.e., ' keeping the ordinary language and beside it ... putting another', the difference between the two being that they 'arrange the facts differently'. It may be remarked, to bring into connection what Wittgenstein says here with other things he says about philosophy, that it

[1] *The Yellow Book.*

is hard to see how an alternative notation could in any way be an attack on common sense, to be cured by bringing philosophers back to ordinary language. And it is equally hard to see how a notation which uses 'the words "flux" and "vagueness" wrongly, in a typically metaphysical way, namely, without an antithesis' could translate into ordinary language where 'in their correct and everyday use vagueness is opposed to clearness, flux to stability'. Indeed, it is not hard to see that a notation which translates into the language of common sense cannot be an attack on common sense; and it is not hard to see that a notation in which ordinary words occur without their antitheses cannot translate into, have 'the same multiplicity' as, a language in which they occur with their antitheses. All this only goes to show that on different occasions and in somewhat different connections Wittgenstein tried out different ideas to explain the enigma that is philosophy.

If we do not let ourselves be diverted by the different ideas in the above passage as to what a philosopher does and how he gets himself into difficulties, we are led to the notion, not that the philosopher fails to 'command a clear view of our use of words', but that the perception he has into the uses of words makes him wish to modify or in some way alter those uses. It is evident that the alterations he institutes do not have any of the jobs alternative forms of expression usually have, e.g., to say the same thing with greater economy or with improved efficiency for calculating or with greater vividness or just to avoid monotony of expression. The picture of the philosopher which begins to come into focus is that of someone who scans the intricate map of language, and, unlike the grammarian and the thesaurus compiler, is not satisfied merely to report rules embedded in the language, but in various ways changes the rules. Differences in the uses of expressions which ordinary language does not perspicuously display, differences which it 'hushes up', he is sometimes impelled to try to bring out in sharp relief; and differences in the uses of expressions ordinary language 'stresses' he is sometimes inclined to mute. The reasons, in the form of arguments, that he gives for the changes he introduces quite obviously make negligible or no connection

with the everyday kinds of work language does for us. The conclusion which is at least latent in a good many things he said is
that a philosopher alters ordinary language or 'puts another
language beside it' for the remarkable effects doing this creates.
In the passage above, ordinary language is represented as responsible for the idea that a barrier exists between people which prevents one person from knowing that another has a pain. But it
should be realized at once that the sentence 'I cannot know
whether another person has a toothache', i.e., the sentence which
creates the idea of a barrier, is *not* an ordinary sentence. Wittgenstein was, of course, aware that ordinary language does not put
this idea in the mind of 'the man in the street': in his words, 'we
don't feel these difficulties in ordinary life'. The sentence is a
philosophical production whose job is not at all like that of a
sentence such as 'I cannot know whether Socrates has a toothache;
he endures pain with stoicism.' To describe what is happening in
Wittgenstein's way, a philosopher who says, 'I cannot know
whether another has a pain' is objecting to the conventional use of
'has a pain' but is not aware that he is objecting to a convention.
His sentence announces the academic deletion from the language of
such phrases as 'knows that another person has a pain', 'knows
that another person sees red', and in this way he brings out the
great difference between the use of 'has a pain' and the use of
'has a tooth'. But he introduces his re-editing of language conventions in a way which creates the idea that there is some sort
of barrier between people. It is not everyday language but the
manner in which he announces changes in everyday language
which is responsible for the inappropriate idea.

When Wittgenstein said, 'What we are destroying is nothing
but houses of cards and we are clearing up the ground of language
on which they stand', quite possibly what he intended to convey
was that like the pretence use of cards as building materials a
philosophical theory is constituted by a pretence use of language.
Quite possibly he wanted to convey that to give utterance to a
philosophical theory is not to use language to express a theory but
is only to use language to create the false idea that a theory
is being expressed. And when he observed that 'we may be

irresistibly attracted by a notation', he may have been referring to deeper things in our minds that philosophical utterances link up with. It is not easy to know where one is reading too much and where too little into the mind of an original thinker.

M. L.

II

Certain problems about the nature of mathematics, recurrent in the history of philosophy, were recurrent in Wittgenstein's thinking and were dealt with explicitly and at length in lectures given in Cambridge in 1933-34 and 1939, and throughout his *Remarks on the Foundations of Mathematics*. Of some of these problems he said in the *Investigations* that they are 'something for philosophical *treatment* ... like the treatment of an illness'.[1] We now want to consider certain of these problems in terms of the hypothesis which seems to us one of his most original insights into their nature, and perhaps the one which in later years figured most consistently in his 'treatment' of traditional theories: the hypothesis that these problems arise from the 'confusion which pervades all of philosophy — that considers [them] as though they concerned a fact of the world instead of a matter of expression',[2] whereas 'what [is wanted] is only a new notation'.[3] We shall devote ourselves to a cluster of theories which derive in a general way from the theory about the nature of mathematical propositions that they are *a priori* synthetic. For the moment let us specify this characterization as covering the following pronouncements philosophers put forward as theories: that mathematical propositions state internal connections between objects which are often discoverable in the first instance by observation, that they have some features of both truths of reason and truths of fact.

That mathematical propositions should appear in this light is entirely natural. When one discovers by testing out even numbers that they can be represented as the sum of two primes, one has, as Courant and Robbins put it, 'empirical evidence in favor of the

[1] p. 91.   [2] *The Yellow Book.*   [3] *The Blue Book*, p. 57.

statement that every even number can be so represented'.[1] The proof of the generalization ('Goldbach's conjecture') is still lacking, but if true, it will be true of necessity, and the *a priori* law about even numbers will have been suggested by what has been found by observation. Tables of primes up to 12,000,000 have been computed by means of methods which refine upon Erastosthenes' 'sieve'. These have been said to 'provide us with a tremendous mass of empirical data concerning the distribution and properties of primes. On the basis of these tables we can make many highly plausible conjectures (as though number theory were an experimental science)...'[2] Observation, or experimentation, gives rise to the conjectures, which the mathematician then goes on to prove. Somehow observation manages to be relevant to truths which, on being established, it is entirely irrelevant as support, although the unproved hypothesis seems very like an induction from empirical cases. The situation is the same with the truths of geometry. One discovers by counting that a particular cube has twelve edges, and takes this as warranting an *a priori* generalization about all cubes. Further, a single observation — and even a thought-experiment — is taken to be sufficient warrant. And the proof supposedly proves something about *this* solid as well as about all such solids. Or if not about this solid, then about the ideal geometrical solid to which it approximates.

Analogies between empirical investigation and mathematical investigation, between empirical propositions and mathematical propositions, are many and for the most part obvious. Their existence is I think responsible for the characterization 'synthetic *a priori*'. Kant's application of this description to all propositions of pure mathematics was accompanied by a general account of it that illuminates the considerations which prompt one to claim for these propositions, in various connections, the two diverse features, *synthetic* and *a priori*. The following comment by Wittgenstein is a reminder, by way of an example, of the general features Kant singled out and which we shall find exemplified in various ways in philosophers' descriptions of mathematical propositions.

[1] Richard Courant and Herbert Robbins, *What is Mathematics?*, p. 30.
[2] Ibid, p. 25.

'It might perhaps be said that the synthetic character of the propositions of mathematics appears most obviously in the unpredictable occurrence of the prime numbers. . . . The distribution of primes would be an ideal example of what could be called synthetic *a priori*, for one can say that it is at any rate not discoverable by an analysis of the concept of a prime number.'[1] This assertion calls attention to what Kant called the ampliative character of synthetic propositions, which 'add to the concept of the subject a predicate which has not been in any wise thought in it, and which no analysis could possibly extract from it',[2]. In contrast to these stand analytic propositions, in which 'the connection of the predicate with the subject is thought through identity . . . adding nothing . . . to the concept of the subject, but merely breaking it up into those constituent concepts that have all along been thought in it'.[2] These descriptions make clear that a synthetic proposition, whose predicate term is not a conjunctive part of the subject term, can be expected to provide new information about the subject. Not being of the form *AB is A* (and hence not known to be true 'through the principle of contradiction'), an *a priori* synthetic proposition as surely 'extends our knowledge'[3] as does an empirical proposition. The result of a calculation can be a surprise,[4] proof can establish a previously unpredictable feature. But all writers are anxious to insist that this in no way implies that such propositions are not *a priori*: ' . . . being synthetic . . . does not make them any the less *a priori*.'[5] 'First of all, it has to be noted that mathematical propositions, . . . are always judgments *a priori*, not empirical; because they carry with them necessity, which cannot be derived from experience.'[6] 'Experience tells us . . . what is but not that it must be necessarily so, and not otherwise.'[7]

Some philosophers have held that analytic propositions, equally with those that are *a priori* synthetic, are truths about all possible

---

[1] *Remarks on the Foundations of Mathematics*, pp. 125–6.
[2] *Critique of Pure Reason*, trans. by Norman Kemp Smith, p. 48.
[3] Locke's expression.
[4] Wittgenstein, *Remarks on the Foundations of Mathematics*, p. 161.
[5] Ibid, p. 126.
[6] Kant, op. cit., p. 52.
[7] Ibid., p. 42.

worlds and hence are informative about this one.[1] Locke, as well
as Kant, denied this. Locke characterized the former as 'trifling
propositions' which have 'but verbal certainty' and are not instructive. But about other *a priori* propositions, which Kant later
classified as synthetic, he insisted that they possessed the feature
of 'bringing increase to our knowledge'. The idea that synthetic
a priori propositions state invariant features of all possible universes — and hence of this one — gains support from various
sources. Any given proposition is correctly said to be true or
false, and it is but a short step to conclude that some reality
corresponds to a true one. Given the language of truth and falsity
for both mathematical and empirical propositions, continuing
analogies all conspire to confirm us in viewing both as informative
of a reality corresponding to them. For example, the practical
application of mathematics to real aggregates of things, to real
solids and lines, appears to differ in only negligible ways from the
application of scientific generalizations to fresh cases similar to
those observed.

And yet the assimilation of mathematical propositions to
empirical propositions which illustrates and doubtless prompted
the description '*a priori* synthetic' has paradoxical consequences.
One has but to reflect on the idea of an investigation of real objects in which observation discloses their internal properties to
raise the question, How is this possible? Can one make a physical
discovery which is at the same time a mathematical discovery?
Can one make an experiment and go on to a demonstrative proof
of what was found by experiment? Could a proof, i.e., an *a priori*
demonstration, establish a truth about *this* figure? In his 1939
lectures Wittgenstein commented that there is something true
and yet something absurd in saying that a mathematician makes
an experiment and then proves what he found by experiment. The
absurdity lies in supposing that empirical observation can either
be the same as the observation of an *a priori* fact or support an *a*

---

[1] E.g., H. W. B. Joseph, who held $a = a$ to be a law of things as well as a law of
thought; and C. I. Lewis, who said that the 'genuinely analytic' proposition *All cats are
animals*, which 'can be assured by reference to the meaning of "cat" and "animal" without
recourse to further and empirical evidence . . . also might be established — as well established as most laws of science, for example — by generalization from observed instances
of cats.' *Knowledge and Valuation*, p. 91.

priori truth — or that what is discovered empirically can be the same as what is proved mathematically. And yet it is true that by counting the intersections of a pentagram one finds that they are ten in number, and by looking through the series of integers one finds that primes often come in pairs. The facts cannot be denied, but the description of the facts is paradoxical: that one should use one's bodily eyes — not the eye of the mind, as Plato said, to find a feature whose existence can be known without recourse to the senses, and further, to which the eyes cannot bear witness, since no sense evidence can attest to a necessary connection. Observing that a pentagram has ten intersections or that it fits into a pentagon is like seeing a factual connection which is at the same time necessary. Again, it is paradoxical that a fact arrived at by observation or experimentation should have an *a priori* demonstration. The *a priori* proof, being general, must hold true of the particular case — of this figure, for example; and yet it would seem that it cannot, since a proposition implying the existence of a sensible object cannot be *a priori*. '*This* pentagram has ten intersections' implies 'A pentagram exists'; and if having an *a priori* proof makes the first an *a priori* proposition, then it would follow that an *a priori* true proposition sometimes implies a contingent one — one which could conceivably be false. There is no doubt that one can correctly speak of predicting the result of a calculation and of believing that a mathematical proposition is true, e.g., Fermat's theorem and Goldbach's theorem. But there is a puzzle about *what* is predicted or believed in case it is self-contradictory. How can one predict, or believe, that what is logically impossible is true?

The existence of so much puzzlement suggests a source or sources either in false theories about mathematical investigation and about the propositions which record its results, or in the language we use to describe these. Leaving aside for the present any decision between these alternative explanations, it is important first of all to see whether there is something common and basic to the statement of each puzzle. Philosophy has a long history centering about the distinction between essence and accident, where what is essential and what is accidental are treated as features

of *things*. Finding what is implicit in a concept was taken to dis-
close what is essential to the objects falling under it. By reasoning
one could come to knowledge of real things. 'Is it true of the idea
of a triangle, that its three angles are equal to two right angles?',
asks Locke. 'It is true also of a triangle, wherever it really exists.'[1]
Investigation in mathematics is conceived as a search for essential
features, and its *a priori* truths as assertions about objects. On
Mill's account they state generalizations, of an unusual degree of
certainty, about real things (physical cubes and empirically
observable collections of objects). 'Propositions concerning
numbers have the remarkable peculiarity that they are propositions concerning all things whatever; all objects, all existences of
every kind, known to our experience.'[2] Geometrical truths differ
from those of arithmetic in being 'true of lines only or angles
only'.[3] Mill's claim concerning mathematical propositions was
directed not only against those who denied that they were generalizations about objects of experience but also against those who
asserted them to be about symbols.

What is important about claim and counterclaim is the description of the propositions to which the disputants would all
subscribe: that they are about something. The various statements
put forward by philosophers as theories about the nature of
mathematics can all be understood as differing descriptions of its
subject matter. What is surprising is that between Mill, a conventionalist and Plato there should be so radical a disagreement about
the proper description of such familiar statements as 'Three is two
and one' and 'A circle is a figure bounded by a line which has all
its points equally distant from a point within it'. According to
Plato they are about ideal objects, their certainty deriving from the
possibility of exact description. 'Although [students of geometry,
arithmetic, and the kindred sciences] make use of the visible
forms and reason about them, they are thinking not of these,
but of the ideals which they resemble; not of the figures which they
draw, but of the absolute square and the absolute diameter, and so

---

[1] *An Essay Concerning Human Understanding*, Book IV, ch. 8, p. 289. A. S. Pringle-
Pattison edition.
[2] *A System of Logic*, p. 165.
[3] Ibid, p. 166.

on.'[1] Presumably propositions about the empirical approxima-
tions to these ideals will not be exact descriptions. Of the drawn
equilateral it is not quite true that its sides are equal; but of the
mathematical equilateral it is inconceivable that it not be true.

It is reasonable to suppose that one source of the puzzles detailed earlier is in what is common to all of them, the assumption
that there are objects of which the propositions of mathematics
hold true. And it is fairly obvious that this assumption does figure
in the statement of each puzzle, just as it is obvious that the divergent philosophical theories about the nature of mathematics rest
on divergent descriptions of the field it investigates. What I have
called an assumption is in fact a philosophical theory, which pro-
liferates into three theories according as the objects whose existence it asserts are held to be real or ideal or merely symbols. The
theory itself is outwardly similar to an experiential proposition,
and the theories which presuppose it, about the nature of the objects investigated, also look to be empirical. All are the outcome
of assimilating mathematical to empirical propositions. According
to Wittgenstein this assimilation is the source of the puzzles.

Now what this assimilation comes to and how the philosopher
effects it need to be examined. It might be supposed that its giving
rise to paradox merely shows that to treat mathematical propositions as though they are empirical is a mistake of the sort which
finds expression in a false theory — here the theory that there are
objects, actual or possible, about which mathematical propositions, like empirical ones, make assertions. Wittgenstein has
made it abundantly clear that he does not take the source of puzzlement to be a *false* philosophical theory. If it were, then the philosopher's task would be to replace the false theory by a true one.
Certainly many philosophers would describe their task in this
way. But 'the philosopher does not look at facts more closely
than the ordinary person does. We can neglect philosophic difficulties in a way we can't engineers' because the philosophers'
difficulties, unlike the others, are due to a misunderstanding.'[2]
And the misunderstanding is not due to a misapprehension of fact

---

[1] *Republic*, Book VI, sec. 510 (Jowett translation).
[2] *The Yellow Book*.

but to 'the mystifying use of language'[1] to describe fact. In looking 'for the *source* of [the philosopher's] puzzlement we find that there is puzzlement and mental discomfort, not only when our curiosity about certain facts is not satisfied or when we can't find a law of nature fitting in with all our experience, but also when a notation dissatisfies us.'[2] '[Philosophical problems] are, of course, not empirical problems; they are to be solved rather, by looking into the workings of our language, and this in such a way as to make us recognize those workings: *in despite of* an urge to misunderstand them.'[3]

This latter statement leaves unclear what Wittgenstein supposes the misunderstandings which get reflected in philosophical puzzles to be. When he speaks of 'problems arising through a misinterpretation of our forms of language',[4] and of an 'entanglement in our rules',[5] it is natural to conclude that the existence of a problem betokens a misuse of language on the philosopher's part — not a wilful misuse but one caused by a misapprehension of what the proper usage is. If this conclusion were correct, then a philosopher could be dissuaded from his 'view' by making clear to him how he had misused language and that through his misuse he had failed to express anything true or false, however strong the impression was that he had succeeded. Now there is a feature of philosophical disputation which precludes supposing philosophical problems arise through ignorance of proper usage. And this feature also precludes supposing they arise from false theories. This is that disputation continues despite the presence to the disputants of all facts, both linguistic and non-linguistic. 'A philosopher is not a man out of his senses, a man who doesn't see what everybody sees.' It is unplausible to suppose disagreement would continue if it could be settled by appeal to either linguistic or non-linguistic fact, since a philosopher could be as easily made aware of these facts as anyone else.

For this reason, and despite the fact that what Wittgenstein does in dealing with a specific puzzle could be cited in support of the thesis that a problem is due to an unwitting error in the use of

---

[1] *The Blue Book*, p. 6.   [2] Ibid, p. 59.   [3] *Philosophical Investigations*, p. 47.
[4] Ibid, p. 47.   [5] Ibid, p. 50.

words, we shall proceed on the alternative thesis to which he has given expression: that it is due to a discontent with a notation — with ordinary language. Wittgenstein said in *The Blue Book*, 'Our ordinary language, which of all possible notations is the one which pervades all our life, holds our mind rigidly in one position, as it were, and in this position sometimes it feels cramped, having a desire for other positions as well. Thus we sometimes wish for a notation which stresses a difference more strongly, makes it more obvious, than ordinary language does, or one which in a particular case uses more closely similar forms of expression than our ordinary language.'[1] In many instances this wish expresses itself in an alteration of the present notation: new linguistic boundaries are drawn — in some cases a sharp boundary which 'will never entirely coincide with the actual usage, as this usage has no sharp boundary'.[2] Now we all know that philosophical positions are never explicitly stated as proposals for new usages or as claims (mistaken or otherwise) about actual usage. Wittgenstein remarks that 'it is particularly difficult to discover that an assertion which the metaphysician makes expresses discontentment with our grammar when the words of this assertion can also be used to state a fact of experience.'[3] So admittedly his renovation of current language is concealed — by clothing it in words appropriate to the expression of fact; and the philosopher himself 'is not aware that he is objecting to a convention'.[4] This general hypothesis about what the philosopher is doing, of which his assimilating mathematical to empirical propositions would be an instance, requires support which it is not here the place to give (though it can, we believe, be given). But various remarks by Wittgenstein show that he was aware of a puzzling fact which the usual view of a philosophical assertion as factual leaves unexplained: that philosophical 'discoveries', unlike scientific ones, are in no way felt by the philosopher to augment the facts to which his behaviour must be adjusted. His behaviour is unaltered. The thesis that he is not stating a truth but instead 'recommending his notation'[5] helps explain this phenomenon. For if boundaries

[1] p. 59.   [2] Ibid, p. 19.   [3] Ibid, pp. 56–7.   [4] Ibid, p. 57.
[5] Ibid, p. 60.

are redrawn on the language map 'no facts of geography are changed'.[1] 'We are keeping the ordinary language and beside it [the philosopher] is putting another.'[2] He 'did not tell us a new truth and did not show us that what we said before was false.'[3] If he had, then the new truth should have made a difference.

What method, now, is to be used to remove the puzzlement expressed in such questions as: How can one arrive at a mathematical discovery via an observation? How can one observe a matter of fact about a given figure which is also necessary? How can a proof be given concerning *this* figure? A comment Wittgenstein made about metaphysical propositions serves as a hint: 'What we always do when we meet the word "can" in a metaphysical proposition [is to] show that this proposition hides a grammatical rule. That is to say, we destroy the outward similarity between a metaphysical proposition and an experiential one, and we try to find the form of expression which fulfils a certain craving of the metaphysician which our ordinary language does not fulfil and which, as long as it isn't fulfilled, produces the metaphysical puzzlement.[4] We shall follow this hint in examining philosophical 'theories' about the nature of mathematical propositions. Assuming that the assimilation of mathematical to empirical propositions is responsible for the theories which underlie the various puzzles, our procedure will be to stress the differences between the two, differences which ordinary language, wedded as it is to the category 'true or false', minimizes. 'A notation can stress, or it can minimize',[5] and in this connection some philosophers of mathematics find the differences not minimized enough. The antidote here will be the setting out of these differences. They will be differences of a sort which will be recognized, once they are set out in plain view. Wittgenstein said he would 'draw attention to facts which we know quite as well as he, but which we have forgotten or at least to which we are not immediately attending'.[6] 'I cannot teach you any new facts. But I can help you to recognize certain facts which otherwise you would not recognize.'[7] 'The problems are solved, not by giving new information,

[1] Ibid, p. 57.   [2] *The Yellow Book.*   [3] Ibid.
[4] *The Blue Book*, p. 55.   [5] *The Yellow Book.*   [6] Lecture notes, 1939.
[7] *The Yellow Book.*

but by arranging what we have always known.'[1] This thus spells out what he meant in saying that his work 'consists in assembling reminders for a particular purpose'.[2]

We now proceed to an inventory of features of mathematical investigation and of its resultant propositions for which it may be enlightening to be reminded. Let us begin with the fact that something closely resembling empirical observation can lead to a mathematical hypothesis which one then goes on to prove. The resemblance here is obvious, as is the resemblance to an induction in natural science. On the basis of this resemblance Mill said they *are* inductions, that, e.g., $3 + 7 = 10$ is 'proved by showing to our eyes and our fingers that any given number of objects, ten balls for example, may by separation and rearrangement exhibit to our senses all the different sets of numbers the sum of which is equal to ten'.[3] But people who have no such 'theory' to advance use similar language to describe the discovery of mathematical truths. Discovery of internal properties is often described as empirical. We call attention to examples in geometry cited and discussed by Wittgenstein: discovery by counting what the number of intersections of a pentagram is, seeing what sort of star fits a pentagon, or that a pentagram consists of a pentagon plus five triangles, seeing that two isosceles right triangles make a square, finding that a rectangle divided into squares of which there are twenty-one on one side and thirty-six on the other contains 756 squares in all, or that two rods 2' long placed end to end fit a space of 4', discovery that a square piece of paper can be so folded as to form a boat or hat.

Counting, fitting, dividing, adjoining, folding are all experiential procedures. In the examples cited they *seem* to have yielded a mathematical result. Specifically, that a pentagram has ten intersections, that it fits into a pentagon and itself consists of a pentagon and five triangles, that a square divides into two similar isosceles right triangles, that $21 \times 36 = 756$, that $2' + 2' = 4'$, that a square can be transformed into a three-dimensional hat-figure. How acknowledge the facts about mathematical investigation while avoiding the paradoxical account of it as an empirical

---

[1] *Philosophical Investigations*, p. 47.   [2] Ibid, p. 50.   [3] *A System of Logic*, p. 167.

observation of *a priori* fact or as an empirical support for a necessary truth? or the facts about discovery and proof while avoiding
the paradoxical account of discovery as uncovering factual
connections which proof demonstrates to be necessary? The
answer lies in seeing the *differences* between experiential procedures leading to a hypothesis which though true could be false
and experiential procedures leading to a mathematical proposition.
These differences are muted, 'hushed up', by the form of words
used in describing mathematical investigation, discovery, and
demonstration. Minimizing these differences we construe as a
result of dissatisfaction, for whatever reason, with the differences
our language marks out in the descriptions of *a priori* and empirical propositions.

We shall draw upon Wittgenstein's discussions[1] of these
examples to bring out differences counteracting the impressiveness
of their similarity. Compare the counting of the intersections of a
given pentagram with counting the number of marbles in a row,
and the consequent descriptions: 'This figure has ten intersections',
'the pentagram has ten intersections', 'there are ten marbles
here'. Unless one uses 'this figure' to mean 'the pentagram' one
would call the first statement experiential, and of course also the
last. One records in them the result of the experiment of counting
particular sets of things. But 'the pentagram has ten intersections'
is a geometrical statement. It does not help to distinguish the
two sorts of description to say that in one case one counts the
number in this figure, and in the other the number in the pentagram. What goes on at the time of counting is the same. To claim
one can draw this sort of distinction makes it appear that there are
two different facts described, two different realities to which the
two propositions correspond, as though geometry were 'the
physics of the intellectual realm'.[2] With this description the assimilation of geometrical propositions to empirical ones has already
been effected. But despite its stress on their similarity, does it not
at the same time demarcate their difference? Or is it a *false*
description? The answer might appear to be affirmative except
that differences Wittgenstein points out, instead of showing its

[1] Lecture notes, 1939.   [2] Op. cit.

falsity, tend to remove the temptation to give it. For the differences are not differences between species of the same genera but are differences of an entirely different order. A precise figure and a rough approximation to it are comparable, as are wider and narrower generalizations; but a visual phenomenon (the drawn figure) and a paradigm are not. A report on the drawn figure, recording what is visually experienced at a given time, is a truth, or falsity, about *this* figure, for as long as the visual phenomenon lasts. But when an aspect of the drawn figure is recorded in a mathematical proposition, this aspect becomes a paradigm to which any drawn figure must conform if it is to be called, say, a pentagram. It becomes a standard for future descriptions.

The sentence 'This figure has ten intersections' can be used to express either an empirical or a mathematical proposition, depending on whether the phrase 'this figure' is used to designate a particular visual phenomenon or to mean the same as 'the pentagram'. This fact makes it natural to describe the difference between its two meanings as a difference in the objects its subject term designates, the one apprehended by sight, the other by a conceptual process. One difficulty of this natural description, which assimilates the mathematical and empirical propositions expressed by the sentence, is that the claimed difference between the objects, and between the instruments for apprehending them, is not straightforward, like the difference between drawn squares and rhombuses and between a hammer and a hatchet.

To see the difference between the assertions about this figure and about *the* pentagram requires no comparison of incomparable objects, but only of the uses the particular figure is put to in each case. Is it used as the subject of a particular experiment of counting, or as a model for future descriptions? Between these two uses there is a great difference: the difference between counting the intersections of a figure known to be a pentagram to find their number and counting the intersections of a figure in order to determine whether it is a pentagram. When we say it is impossible to imagine the figure's not having ten intersections, the figure has been taken as a paradigm of what is to be called a pentagram. It is not its certainty which makes this proposition a mathematical one, but its being assigned a particular function.[1] That the sentence 'The pentagram has ten intersections' expresses a mathematical proposition makes it impossible for 'pentagram not having ten intersections' to describe any drawn figure; the phrase is excluded from a use in our language once the drawn figure is used as a paradigm. The function of the mathematical proposition 'is to shew what it makes SENSE to say'.[2] Proof, or a construction, 'determine(s) us to accept this as sense, that not'.[3]

Although this description of the differing uses of mathematical and empirical propositions may serve to displace the description of their difference as resting on the kinds of objects they are about, it nevertheless does little or nothing to mitigate the impression that one often proceeds by an empirical process to an *a priori* generalization. Which is to say that a paradox remains. What now should be examined is the process of counting, a process used, when, e.g., one counts the marbles in a row, to find out what the number is. Is this its use when one counts the intersections of a pentagram? The motions we go through are obviously the same. But there is an important difference, and this is in the result. When one counts the marbles the result could conceivably be otherwise. That there are ten marbles in a row is a mere 'truth of fact', and one could predict, truly or falsely, what the result of counting would be. But counting the intersections of the pentagram is like calculating the result of an arithmetic process: we say that the process 'yields' a certain result; but the result is part of the process.[4] The process fixes the result, so that in repeating the process it includes every step *and the result*. Without *that* result the calculation would contain a mistake. And such a mistake would not be at all like failure to observe the conditions of an experiment, e.g., failing to heat a compound to a certain temperature. A failure of this latter sort has a causal influence on the result; but to characterize it in this way already is to admit that, whatever steps are taken, they might be carried out and the result might, or might not, occur. That is, the description of the experimental steps does not include the result. Or to get at the point in another way, one

[1] *Remarks on the Foundations of Mathematics*, p. 114.   [2] Ibid, p. 77.
[3] Ibid.   [4] Ibid, p. 26.

could repeat an experiment by reproducing the conditions and not obtain the expected result. But in repeating a calculation one must repeat every step and the result.[1] The result of counting the intersections becomes a criterion for the figure's being a pentagram. Similarly, the division of a row of marbles into groups of two, three, and five is taken as a criterion for their being ten in all. Counting off the marbles in such groups in the process of finding out their total number is different from counting them off so as to find a set of numbers whose sum is equal to ten. It is like the difference between using a yard stick and a metre stick to find out the length of something in yards and metres, respectively, and setting one stick against the other to find out how to express metres in terms of inches.[2] If on recounting or remeasuring, different results were obtained, one would say one had counted or measured incorrectly, or that a marble had been added or a length shrunk, but one would not say that $2 + 3 + 5$ sometimes has different results or that sometimes a metre is not 39.37 inches. If counting or measuring is an experimental process then one must accept whatever comes, but if what comes is taken as a criterion for correct counting or measurement, then the process has the result incorporated into it,[3] and is a calculation. 'We use "result" in two different ways. A mathematical process is not such that the process could be what it is and the result a different one. To say a process gives a certain result means giving the result.'[4]

One is tempted, as was Mill, to say that 'by showing to our eyes and our fingers' that ten marbles may be divided into groups of two, three, and five, one proves that $2 + 3 + 5 = 10$, or at any rate that 2 marbles + 3 marbles + 5 marbles = 10 marbles. And of course the similarity of this 'proof' to an experiment is undeniable, inasmuch as the same process of grouping would verify the empirical proposition '*These* marbles fall into the groups two, three, and five'. But whether the process of dividing is an experiment or a calculation shows up in the use it is put to. Wittgenstein

---

[1] *Remarks on the Foundations of Mathematics*, p. 91.
[2] Lecture notes, 1939.
[3] *Remarks on the Foundations of Mathematics*, p. 27.
[4] Lecture notes taken 1934–35 by A. Ambrose.

makes a similar point about pouring two lots of 200 apples together. 'Proof, one might say, must originally be a kind of experiment. . . . This process of adding *did* indeed yield 400, but now we take this result as the criterion for the correct addition — or simply: for the addition — of these numbers. . . . The proof is now our model of correctly counting 200 apples and 200 apples together: that is to say, it defines a new concept: "the counting of 200 and 200 objects together". Or, we could also say: "a new criterion for nothing's having been lost or added".[1]'

Seeing the activity of counting as a calculation with an internal result in contrast to an experimental test with a result which could be otherwise is one step to seeing the lack of analogy between counting intersections and counting marbles. But noticing the difference between calculation and experiment is by itself not enough to rule out the assimilation of mathematical to empirical propositions. For one thing, the difference is matched by an impressive similarity, which Wittgenstein remarks on as follows: '. . . in the calculation I surely wanted from the beginning to know what the result was going to be; *that* was what I was interested in. I am, after all, curious about the result.'[2] Nevertheless, even here there is a difference: I am not curious as to 'what I am *going* to say, but as to what I *ought* to say'.[2] 'To say that something is the right result is quite different from saying that it is the result that I get.'[3] What I ought to say is not determined by the character of my responses to the accepted rules of calculating, but by what is fixed, necessarily, by those rules. 'We mistake the nature of *"experiment"*', says Wittgenstein, if we suppose that "whenever we are keen on knowing the end of a process, it is what we call an "experiment".'[4]

And yet much of our language concerning the results of calculation, proof and investigation is language appropriate to the description of an experiment. A whole class of words carry over from one kind of procedure to the other: such words as 'predict', 'believe', 'convinced by'. It will be useful to canvass the usage of

---

[1] *Remarks on the Foundations of Mathematics*, pp. 75 and 76.
[2] Ibid, p. 95.
[3] Lecture notes, 1939.
[4] *Remarks on the Foundations of Mathematics*, p. 99.

such words in mathematical contexts and then to note the differences which this language tends to cover up. Suppose one says one believes 9 will recur at least once in the expansion of π, or that the result of multiplying 25 by 25 will be 625, or that a group of ten marbles will divide into three sub-groups two of which contain two, or that two isosceles right triangles placed base to base will make a square, or that what holds for a given polygon of $n + 2$ sides, namely, that the sum of its angles is $n \times 180°$, will hold for all polygons. In advance of proof one might even predict that 9 would recur, etc. And then, with proof, one might report that one was convinced of their truth. The use of the future tense in these examples is to be remarked. Is it used in a temporal sense as it is in sentences which express predictions? Compare the following statements: 'You will get 625', 'If you calculate correctly you will get 625'. The first is clearly a prediction of a result someone will get when he carries out the multiplication, say, of 25 by 25. This prediction could be false. But the latter could not but be true. For it is equivalent to saying that the result of the calculation is 625.[1] There is no distinction to be made between what the calculation *does* or *will* lead to and what it *must* lead to. There is no difference between showing that 9 will occur again in the expansion of π and that it must, etc. For all its appearance of being a prediction, '7 will recur' does not state something which is made true by an event occurring at a certain moment in the expansion. This and other considerations indicate that the phrase 'will recur', and the like are non-temporal. 'It does not mean that it will recur with most people or in half an hour.'[2] In fact there is a certain absurdity in construing mathematical propositions temporally. To say it is an eternal truth that 100 apples consist of 50 and 50 or that a rectangle consists of two similar triangles is not to say that this was true yesterday and is true now and will remain true for all times in the future — like the law of free fall. In this context 'consist' is used tenselessly. ' . . . it doesn't mean that *now*, or just for a time, they consist of 50 and 50.'[3]

[1] *Remarks on the Foundations of Mathematics*, pp. 159–62.
[2] Lecture notes, 1939.
[3] *Remarks on the Foundations of Mathematics*, p. 30.

Since it is precluded that they not consist of 50 and 50, the question arises whether one could believe that they do not, and if this is not possible, whether one could *believe* what is true. Although Hardy, for example, said he believed Goldbach's theorem, one is tempted to say one cannot believe a mathematical proposition, even an unproved one. For what is the object of belief (inasmuch as the proposition may be self-contradictory)? Suppose one said one believed, on someone else's assurance, that $13 \times 13 = 196$. What is one believing? 'How deep do you penetrate, one might say, with your belief, into the relation of these numbers? For — one wants to say — you cannot be penetrating all the way, or you could not believe it.'[1] 'The thing is, if one thinks of an arithmetical equation as the expression of an internal relation, then one would like to say: "You can't believe at all that 13×13 yields *this*, because that isn't a multiplication of 13 by 13, or is not a case of something being yielded, if 196 comes at the end." '[1] Such a comment calls attention to the difference between beliefs in mathematical and empirical contexts which the term 'believe' conceals, but it does it in a way which makes the impossibility of belief the same as the impossibility of drawing a round square: to believe what we cannot even conceive is a logical impossibility. In consequence 'believe that $13 \times 13 = 196$' would be a self-contradictory expression, which means 'that one is not willing to use the word "believe" for the case of a calculation and its result — or is willing only in the case in which one has a correct calculation before one.'[1] But suppose one has a *correct* calculation, is it possible even in this case to believe it? Is it possible to believe what could not be otherwise? One is tempted to say, as Wittgenstein notes, ' "One can only *see* that $13 \times 13 = 169$, and even that one can't believe." ... And what am I doing if I say this? I am *drawing a line* between the *calculation* with its result ... and an experiment with its outcome.'[1] ' "But you surely don't believe a mathematical proposition." — That means: "Mathematical proposition" signifies a role for the proposition, a function, in which believing does not occur. '[2]

[1] *Remarks of the Foundations of Mathematics*, p. 32.
[2] Ibid, p. 33.

It should be noted that to draw such a line would be to redraw the boundaries extant in ordinary English. For the expression 'believe that p', where p is a mathematical proposition, has a use. As Wittgenstein points out, 'In certain circumstances I do *say*: "I believe that $a \times b = c$".'[1] His comments on the argument that one cannot believe a mathematical proposition are a quite clear indication of his interpretation of what the philosopher who presents it is doing. Here we have a typically philosophical argument, whose point, Wittgenstein claims, is to make a linguistic change. The argument is ostensibly about what it is possible to believe, not about language. In fact it makes no mention of words at all. But if it were what it appears to be, then the philosopher who advances it commits himself to its linguistic concomitant, that 'I believe that $a \times b = c$', unlike 'I believe it is going to rain', expresses a logical impossibility. At the same time, he could not fail to be aware — in fact he knows perfectly well — that as English is used both forms of words express possible truths. So another construction has to be placed upon his argument: that it shows, not that belief is impossible, but that it should be counted as impossible, the linguistic correlate of which is that limitations should be placed on the use of the word 'believe'. That his argument should lead to the actual alteration of usage in everyday language is of course not to be expected.

Let us consider some differences between being convinced by a mathematical proof and being convinced by empirical evidence. First of all, the word 'convinced' is, as Wittgenstein says, 'taken from the case where there is a direct criterion for something and also indirect ways of being convinced',[2] such as the testimony of others. One is inclined to say that by finding that various even numbers tested are the sum of two primes one has evidence, and may even feel convinced, that all even numbers are so representable, but that only a rigorous proof would conclusively justify one's being convinced. One interesting difference, however, is that in advance of proof one cannot imagine what it would be like to be convinced. To imagine this would be to imagine the proof. And an imagined proof would be as good as any other — for it

---

[1] Ibid, p. 32.   [2] Lecture notes, 1939.

would be a proof. But certainly an imagined experiment would not be an experiment. 'I can *calculate* in the medium of imagination, but not experiment,'[1] Again, in mathematics a *picture* can serve as a proof, whereas 'the picture of an experiment is not itself an experiment'.[2] Suppose one offered as proof that a square consists of two similar right triangles, or that a row of ten marbles consists of two groups of five, a picture of a square cut by its diagonal and a picture of the row of marbles divided. Why should what is done here convince one of anything more than that *this* square consists of two triangles, that *this* row of ten marbles consists of two groups of five? 'But oddly enough if *that* is what you grant, you seem to be granting, not the more modest geometrical proposition [more modest than the generalization concerning all squares], but what is not a proposition of geometry at all.'[3] How is it that the pictured figure, or the pictured row of marbles is a proof — convinces us of a generality (about all squares, all rows of ten)? Have we 'won through to a piece of knowledge in the proof? . . . Why should I not say: in the proof I have won through to a *decision*?'[4] (the decision to count a figure a square if its diagonal divides it into isosceles right triangles, to count a group as ten if it divides into two groups of five). 'Proof, one might say, must originally be a kind of experiment.[5] But to accept a proof is to take it as a *model* which 'shews us the result of a procedure (the construction)'.[6] '. . . It is part of proof to have an accepted criterion for the correct reproduction of a proof'.[7] To accept a proof is to be 'convinced that a procedure regulated in *this* way always leads to this configuration'.[8] It comes to taking the square cut by its diagonal and the row of ten divided into two groups of five as pictures of what any future processes of division must lead to — to taking each as 'our model for a particular *result's being yielded*'.[9] And this comes to accepting the result as part of the process.[10]

Other things Wittgenstein says, and of which there is already an indication here, throw a further light on what he supposes

[1] *Remarks on the Foundations of Mathematics*, p. 29.   [2] Ibid, p. 13.
[3] Ibid, p. 19.   [4] Ibid, p. 77.   [5] Ibid, p. 75.
[6] Ibid.   [7] Ibid.   [8] Ibid.
[9] Ibid, p. 76.   [10] Ibid, p. 26.

accepting a proof comes to. Not only does accepting the construction as proof that a square is divisible into triangles serve as a criterion for correctly reproducing the proof. 'When we say that the construction must convince us of the proposition, that means ... that it must determine us to accept this as sense, that not.'[1] 'Let us remember that in mathematics we are convinced of *grammatical* propositions; so the expression, the result, of our being convinced is that we *accept a rule*.'[2] And what sort of rule? 'I go through the proof and say: "Yes, this is how it *has* to be; I must fix the use of my language in *this* way." I want to say that the *must* corresponds to a track which I lay down in language.'[3] 'The proof puts a new paradigm among the paradigms of the language.'[4] We shall not *call* a figure a pentagram if its vertices cannot be fitted to those of a pentagon, nor a row of marbles ten if it cannot be divided into two groups of five. Were Goldbach's conjecture proved, we should not call a number even which was not the sum of two primes.

That a proof should induce one to accept a rule about the use of language, as no 'empirical' proof would do, is a very different account of proof than the one many philosophers find quite natural: that it establishes that certain properties necessarily belong to pentagrams, or groups of ten, i.e., that it arrives at truths about them guaranteed by the fact that those properties *are* essential. As a counter to this standard view stands Wittgenstein's assertion that in a most important sense Euclidean geometry 'isn't *about* length. It gives rules for the application of the words "equal length" and so on. In the same way arithmetic doesn't talk of numbers ... but gives us rules for the use of number words.'[5] In mathematical and empirical contexts ' "being about" means two entirely different things.'[5] The reality corresponding to a sentence in mathematics, like the reality corresponding to the word 'two', is that it has a use.[6]

Suppose that in opposition to Wittgenstein's account it is held that the mathematician's investigation is in no sense linguistic, that it is the farthest from his aim to delineate the criteria for the

[1] Ibid, p. 77.   [2] Ibid.
[3] Ibid, p. 78.   [4] Ibid.
[5] Lecture notes, 1939.   [6] Ibid.

use of words. Wittgenstein admits the inaptness of his description in admitting that when our attention is drawn to a new aspect we feel as if we were 'penetrating into the essence of the thing',[1] and as if this aspect were something which is there whether attention is drawn to it or not. Suppose we see a pentagram as consisting of a pentagon and five triangles. A pentagram seen under this aspect, says Wittgenstein, 'consists of them so long as we look at it'.[2] That is, it is a visual, therefore temporal, phenomenon. 'On the other hand we could adopt the geometrical expression "pentagram = pentagon + five triangles". This can't be seen — it's a rule. Of course the rule may have been suggested by seeing it thus.'[3] What is being said here is that seeing a figure under a certain aspect and seeing that the aspect is 'essential' are processes different in kind. 'It is not the property of an object that is ever "essential", but rather the mark of a concept.'[4] 'Suppose we visually divide ' ' ' ' into two and two. As long as we look at it in a "two and two way" our picture consists in a division into two and two. This is a temporal phenomenon. Visual division is one of the many processes we call division. It is a phenomenon like any other. To say the picture *consists* in division into two parts provokes the reply that it does so long as the phenomenon of division lasts. Some say the division is timeless. What phenomenon is this? If we use "consists" to mean that 4 consists of 2 and 2 in the sense of $2 + 2 = 4$, then we can't *see* this. There is no phenomenon of seeing that a proposition of grammar holds.'[5] Seeing the strokes ' ' ' ' in pairs *suggests* the rule, but is not the same as seeing the rule.

Wittgenstein admits there is a temptation to say that if ' ' ' ' weren't as it is it *couldn't* be divided into two and two, as though any other division would present an insuperable difficulty. However, 'the man who tells me I can't divide ' ' ' ' into three and three doesn't admit of a description of what it is like to divide into three and three except in the case where one starts with six'.[6] That is, he has accepted the rule: 'I will say that a group is of the form A [' ' ' '] if and only if it can be split into two groups like

[1] Lecture notes, 1934-35.   [2] Ibid.   [3] Ibid.
[4] *Remarks on the Foundations of Mathematics*, p. 23.   [5] Lecture notes, 1934-35.
[6] Ibid.

B and C [′ ′] and [′ ′].'[1] The experience of seeing may have suggested the rule, but that experience and seeing that the rule holds are very different.

What Wittgenstein has said in various places, some of them already quoted, justly warrants attributing to him a conventionalist position concerning necessary propositions. 'If you talk about *essence*,' he says, 'you are merely noting a convention.'[2] On the other hand he also says, 'we do not look at the mathematical proposition as a proposition dealing with signs . . . '[3] With good will, the difference he wishes to remark between mathematical and empirical propositions can be put in an unobjectionable way: To see that a *sentence* expresses a necessary proposition is to recognize a criterion for the use of certain words in it. E.g., to know that 'a row of ten marbles divides into two groups of five' expresses a necessary proposition is to know that the words 'ten marbles not divisible into two groups of five' has no application, does not, as English is used, describe any set of things. And when a proof in a newly invented branch of mathematics convinces us, as we say, of a new truth, e.g., the early proof that $x^2 = -2$ has two roots, we are in fact persuaded to accept an extension of our notation, here, that '$x^2 = -2$ has two roots' expresses a necessity.

Having canvassed differences which Wittgenstein has brought to the fore between mathematical and empirical propositions and between the investigations leading to them, we shall try now to indicate their bearing on philosophical theories about mathematics and the paradoxes they give rise to. What is the point, or the importance, of citing differences which Wittgenstein would say 'we know quite as well as he'? Quite evidently he brings them forward as a counter to something he considers to underlie the philosophical theories. We have construed this to be the assimilation of mathematical to empirical propositions, and of mathematical investigation to empirical procedures. We want now to give the anatomy of this assimilation, and to do this by proceeding on one hypothesis about the nature of philosophical theories to which Wittgenstein has given expression: This is the hypothesis that they arise from a discontent with a notation, and that this discontent manifests itself in emphasizing or minimizing, in the guise of a theory, what the present notation emphasizes too little or too much. The radical difference between mathematics and natural science is of course abundantly apparent. The philosopher of mathematics who finds their similarity being overshadowed by this difference counters with a description which makes them appear similar: mathematical investigation discloses essential properties of what it investigates, and the truths it arrives at, sometimes on the prompting of empirical observation, are truths about its special subject matter. Necessary facts about mathematical objects are the realities which make them truths.

Presumably this description covers all that differentiates mathematical from empirical investigation. But what makes the description impressive is its analogy to a description which could be given of natural science. Compare, e.g., a Platonist's description of an invariant relation amongst mathematical objects with Galileo's words: 'Nature is governed by immutable laws which she never transgresses.' The analogy is reinforced by language we quite properly use: that such-and-such is *true*, that we *believed* it and later, through proof, were *convinced* of it, that it is *about* prime numbers, say. To see how this stress on their analogy has been effected it is useful to revert to the Kantian characterization, *a priori* synthetic, which sums up diverse features of mathematical propositions. When Poincaré objected to viewing mathematics as a set of tautologies he was expressing awareness of the non-trivial character of its propositions. They are not mere formal identities. As Kant put it, the predicate adds something to the subject 'which no analysis could possibly extract from it . . . by mere dissection'. In this respect mathematical propositions are like empirical ones, and this fact is signalized by the philosopher of mathematics in the classification 'synthetic'. Of course the fact that they are not of the form *AB is A* does not gainsay their *a priori* character. But it is a first step in their assimilation to empirical propositions to see that they are not, to use Leibniz' term, 'identical truths'. For example, a syllogism is not an identical truth, the conclusion of which is a conjunct in the set of its premises. The premises of the syllogism, 'All London philosophers speak Hindustani and all who speak Hindustani speak English; hence all London philosophers speak English', are false, and do not break down into a conjunction of propositions at least one of which is true; whereas the conclusion is true. Hence the conclusion is not a proposition which can be extracted from the premises by a process of dissection.

Now a fact can be stressed or minimized, and a philosopher who claims that mathematics is informative has, without being aware of it, stressed the difference between mathematical propositions and those of the form *AB is A*, and minimized their difference from empirical propositions. Not to stress their *a priori* character is to minimize their difference of role, to gloss over the function of a necessary proposition in proscribing the descriptive use of certain expressions. In fact it turns attention away from their bearing on our use of language. Having gone this far it is natural to carry the assimilation a further step, by claiming them to be *about* something. If, as Locke said, mathematical propositions 'bring increase to our knowledge' in a way that what he called 'trifling propositions' do not, then the information they provide must be about what their form of assertion indicates: Just as 'Mature elephants weigh at least four tons' is about elephants, so 'A square is divisible into two right triangles' is about squares. Being *a priori*, the latter informs us of an essential property they have. The fact that its truth-value is intrinsic to it, so that no observation of squares in any measure supports it is ignored, or else covered over by holding it to be true in all possible worlds and hence in this one. To justify the fact that what real squares are like neither confirms nor upsets it, it is held that the proposition is not about these but about ideal squares — to quote Wittgenstein, 'as if, in fact, the "mathematical [square]" were a [square]'.[1] On this he comments: ' "The symbol '*a*' stands for an ideal object" is evidently supposed to assert something about the meaning, and so about the use, of "*a*". And it means of course that this use is in a certain respect similar to that of a sign that has an object, and that it does not stand for any object. But it is interest-

---

[1] *Remarks of the Foundations of Mathematics*, p. 135.

ing what the expression "ideal object" makes of this fact.'[1] By means of it the philosopher of mathematics is able to retain his emphasis on the similarity between empirical propositions and mathematical ones. 'Ideal object', like 'imaginary object', still seems to stand for an object.

The interesting thing about this assimilation, which expresses itself in the form of words appropriate to the expression of a true-or-false theory about a domain of objects, is that it is a nominal assimilation only. The mathematician who is at the same time a philosopher does not treat mathematical propositions like empirical ones when he does mathematics. For whatever reasons, he has stretched the word 'about' and the word 'informative' so as to make the analogy between the two more evident, and he thus alleviates his discontent with the prominence our ordinary way of describing mathematical and empirical propositions gives to their contrast. But mathematical proof is the same whether described as being about ideal objects or about marks on paper or about nothing at all. 'If someone believes in mathematical *objects* and their queer properties — can't he nevertheless do mathematics?'[2] The truth or falsity of the philosopher's claim that there are objects which he investigates, unlike a similar claim by a physicist, in no way alters what is called a truth *in* his field. Which suggests that his assimilation of mathematical propositions to empirical ones does not find expression in a true or false theory. Quite regardless of it, mathematical investigation remains what it is, and physical investigation remains what it is, each distinct from the other. Nothing has been changed but a way of talking, the point of which is to bring out a similarity between the two. But the way of talking can be of great importance to some people, for it can create the delusive idea that the mathematician is a physicist of the supersensible. It can bring to them the comfort of an illusion. This is perhaps what 'the *deep* need for the convention'[3] reflects. To imitate Hilbert's remark about Cantor's transfinite number theory, the metaphysician of mathematics has created a paradise from which no one can drive him out.

A. A.

---

[1] Ibid, p. 136.   [2] Ibid.   [3] Ibid, p. 23.

BIOGRAPHICAL · BIBLIOGRAPHICAL NOTES

LUDWIG WITTGENSTEIN was born in Vienna on April 26th, 1889. He was educated at home until the age of 14 and for three years thereafter at a school in Linz in Upper Austria, then at the Technische Hochschule, in Berlin-Charlottenburg (1906-8). He was at the University of Manchester from 1908 to 1911, and at Trinity College, Cambridge in 1912-1913. He was a Fellow of Trinity (1930-36; 1939-47); Lecturer in Moral Sciences in the University of Cambridge (1930-39), and Professor of Philosophy at that University from 1939 to 1947. He died on April 29th, 1951. A biographical sketch by G. H. Von Wright is contained in Norman Malcolm's *Ludwig Wittgenstein. A Memoir* (London, Oxford University Press) 1958.

Published writings: *Tractatus Logico-Philosophicus*. The only work published by Wittgenstein during his life. 1st edition 1921, London, Routledge & Kegan Paul. 2nd edition (retranslated) 1961.

The following writings were published after his death: *Philosophical Investigations*, Oxford (Blackwell), 1953. *Remarks on the Foundations of Mathematics*, Oxford, 1956. *The Blue and Brown Books*, Oxford, 1958. *Notebooks 1914-16*, a selection from the few surviving notes made by Wittgenstein during the period in which he was writing the *Tractatus*. Dictated by Wittgenstein, and in his own words. (All writings posthumously published and edited by G. E. M. Anscombe, R. Rhees and G. H. Von Wright).

Unpublished records: There are in addition unpublished notes taken by students. Among the most important are:

1. Notes taken by Alice Ambrose and Margaret Masterman in 1933-34 of informal talks by Wittgenstein between intervals in the dictation of *The Blue Book*. This was called by then the *Yellow Book* and is so referred to in the foregoing paper.

2. Lecture notes taken by Alice Ambrose in 1932-35.

3. Lecture notes taken by members of his class.

Commentaries: Anscombe, G. E. M., *An Introduction to Wittgenstein's Tractatus*, New York: Hillary House Publishers, Ltd., 1959. Black, Max, 'Some Problems Connected with Language', reprinted as Wittgenstein's *Tractatus* in *Language and Philosophy*, Ithaca: Cornell University Press, 1949. Appeared originally in *Proceedings of the Aristotelian Society*, XXXIX (1938-39). Black, Max, *A Companion to Wittgenstein's Tractatus*, Cambridge University Press, 1964. Plochmann, C. K. and Lawson, J. B., *Terms in their Propositional*

Contexts in Wittgenstein's Tractatus: An Index, Carbondale: Southern Illinois University Press, 1962. Griffin, J., *Wittgenstein's Logical Atomism*, Oxford University Press, 1964. Maslow, A., *A Study in Wittgenstein's Tractatus*. Berkeley: University of California Press, 1961. Malcolm, Norman, 'Wittgenstein's Philosophical Investigations', reprinted in *Knowledge and Certainty: Essays and Lectures*, Englewood Cliffs, N.J.: Prentice-Hall, Inc., 1963. Appeared originally in the *Philosophical Review*, LXIII (1954). Moore, G. E. 'Wittgenstein's Lectures in 1930-33', reprinted in *Philosophical Papers*, London: George Allen and Unwin; New York: The Macmillan Co., 1959. Appeared originally in *Mind*, LXIII, 1954, LXIV, 1955. Pitcher, George, *The Philosophy of Wittgenstein*, Englewood Cliffs, N.J.: Prentice-Hall, Inc., 1964. Pole, David, *The Later Philosophy of Wittgenstein*, London: The Athlone Press, University of London, 1958. Shwayder, D. S., *Wittgenstein's Tractatus, A Historical and Critical Commentary*, D.Phil. thesis at Oxford, 1954. Stenius, Erik, *Wittgenstein's Tractatus*, Oxford: Basil Blackwell & Mott, Ltd., 1960.

G. E. MOORE

Visual Sense-Data

GEORGE EDWARD MOORE, O.M., LITT.D. (Cantab.): born November 4th, 1873, and died on October 24th, 1958. Educated at Dulwich College, 1882-92, and Trinity College, Cambridge; Fellow of Trinity, 1898-1904; Lecturer in Moral Science at Cambridge, 1911-25, and Professor of Philosophy, 1925-39; Visiting Professor at several colleges and universities in the U.S.A., 1940-44; Fellow of Trinity (since 1925) and Emeritus Professor after retirement; Hon. LL.D. (St. Andrews), 1918; married 1916, D. M. Ely; two sons.

Chief publications: *Principia Ethica*, 1903. *Ethics* (Home University Library), 1911. *Philosophical Studies*, 1922. 'Reply to Critics and Autobiography', *Philosophy of G. E. Moore*, Library of Living Philosophers, (Ed. Schillp), first edition 1942, second edition 1952 with addendum to *A Reply to my Critics*. This books contains a bibliography of Moore's writing up to 1952. *Some Main Problems of Philosophy* (Lectures given in 1910-11) 1953. 'Wittgenstein's Lectures in 1930-33', *Mind*, Vols. LXIII and LXIV, reprinted in *Philosophical Papers*, 1959.

Posthumous publications: *Philosophical Papers* (including two papers not previously published), 1959. *Commonplace Book 1919-53* (Edited by C. Lewy), 1962.

Among important obituary notices and other similar publications are: R. B. Braithwaite: 'George Edward Moore 1873-1958', *Proceedings of the British Academy*, Vol. XLVIII, 1961. C. D. Broad: 'G.E. Moore', published in the *Manchester Guardian*, October 25th, 1958, republished in *Philosophical Papers*, 1959. Leonard Woolf: *Sowing: An Autobiography of the Years 1880-1904*; 1960 contains recollections concerning Moore's life.

Commentaries on Moore's philosophical writings published since the second edition of *The Philosophy of G. E. Moore* (1952), include: A. R. White, *G. E. Moore: A Critical Exposition*, Oxford, Blackwell, 1958. A. C. Ewing: 'The Work of G. E. Moore', *The Indian Journal of Philosophy*, Vol. I, 1959. C. D. Broad: 'G. E. Moore's latest published Views on Ethics', *Mind*, LXX, 1961. C. Lewy: *G. E. Moore on the Naturalistic Fallacy*, British Academy Lecture, 1964.

G. E. MOORE

VISUAL SENSE-DATA

IT seems to me quite plain that one of the commonest senses in which the word 'see' can be correctly used in English, perhaps the commonest of all, is that in which a particular person can be said, at a particular time, to be 'seeing' such objects as, e.g. a particular penny, a particular chair, a particular tree, a particular flower, or a particular horse, his own right hand, the moon, the planet Venus, etc. etc. — objects which I will call 'physical objects'. I have, indeed, once met a philosopher who told me I was making a great mistake in thinking that such objects are ever seen. But I think this philosopher was certainly wrong, and was thinking that the various correct uses of 'see' are limited in a way in which they are not in fact limited. I think there is no doubt whatever that the word 'see' can be correctly used in such a sense that, e.g. the words 'I have often seen pennies' or 'I have often seen the moon', when used by me and by many other people, are correct ways of expressing propositions which are true. I, personally, have in fact often seen pennies and often seen the moon, and so have many other people. But, nevertheless, I think there is a puzzle as to how the word 'see' is being used in this common usage.

There are two kinds of physical objects which we may at a particular moment be said to be 'seeing' in this common sense, viz. (1) objects which are transparent, like a drop of clear water or any ordinary glass tumbler or wine-glass, and (2) objects which are opaque, like a penny or the moon. In the former case it seems possible that you may, in certain cases, see the whole object at once, both every part of its surface and its inside: it is, at all events, not clear that, in certain cases, you don't do this. But, in the case of opaque objects, it seems perfectly clear that you can be correctly said to be 'seeing' the object, in cases where (in another sense of 'see') you are *only seeing* one or several 'sides' of the opaque object, i.e. *some* part of its surface, but emphatically *not* all parts of its surface nor its inside. It seems, indeed, doubtful whether you can be correctly said to be seeing *it* unless you are seeing a *sufficiently* large part of its surface; and I am inclined to think that *how large* a part of its surface is 'sufficient' to entitle you to say you are seeing *it* is different in the case of different objects: e.g. it is quite plain that you can be correctly said to be seeing the moon when you *only see* the very thinnest crescent, whereas if you only saw such a small part of the surface of a penny, it would be doubtful if it could be correctly said that you were seeing that penny: you would be inclined to say that you did not see *it*, but only a small part of its rim. But where, for instance, you see the whole of the 'tail' side of a penny, but *don't* see the 'head' side, there is no doubt whatever that you can be correctly said to be seeing the penny. What is meant by 'seeing' the penny in such a case? There seems to me no doubt that, if you said to yourself, as you might, 'That is a penny', the demonstrative 'that' would be short for a phrase of the kind which Russell has called a 'definite description'; and, if you only said this to *yourself*, there would, of course, be no need for you to point at or touch anything, in order to show which object you were referring to, since you would be able to identify the object without any such gesture. The 'definite description' for which your 'that' would be short would be 'the object of which *this* is part of the surface'; and if 'know by description' were used in the way in which Russell uses it in *The Problems of Philosophy* (ch. v) you could be said to 'know' the penny 'only by description', although you can also correctly be said to be seeing the penny. I think, however, that this is an incorrect use of the word 'know'. We do not use the words 'See' or 'Perceive' in such a way that what you see or perceive is necessarily 'known' to you at all. Perhaps we might say that the penny in such a case is only 'seen by description'. But the important point is that, if in your 'That is a penny', the demonstrative 'that' is short for a definite description, then your proposition 'that is a penny' is a proposition which is 'about' or 'refers to' two objects at once, *not* only to one. This can be easily seen by looking at an example similar to what Russell gives as an example of a sentence which contains a definite description. Consider the sentence, 'The author of Waverley was a Scot.' It is undeniable that the proposition expressed by these English words says *something* about two objects, and not only about one. It says something *both* about the novel 'Waverley' *and* about its author. About the novel *Waverley* it says that it had one and only one author, and does *not* say that this novel was a Scot. But it does also say something not about the novel, but about its author; for it is of its author that it says he was a Scot.

But now, it is quite clear that, in the sentence, 'The author of *Waverley* was a Scot', the word 'Waverley' is also short for a description. It may be short, on different occasions, for a number of different descriptions. What do I mean by saying, as is true, that I possess a copy of *Waverley?* I might mean, and this is one of the simplest possible descriptions, 'I possess a copy of *the* book which was called *Waverley* by its author.' But, quite certainly, the novel *Waverley* is not being directly perceived by me now, though I am making a proposition about it. May it not be the case that, in our sentence 'the object of which *this* is part of the surface', the word 'this' is also short for a description? This seems to me to bring out the really puzzling question about the meaning of 'see' where the physical object which is seen is opaque; and there is a similar question where the physical object is perfectly transparent. I will only try to explain what the question seems to me to be in what is the simplest, but, also, I think, far the commonest case. The case in question is the case in which *both* (1) We are not seeing the physical object 'double', i.e. are not having what is often called a 'double image' of it, *and* (2) are not seeing two or more parts of the object's surface which are separated from one another by parts of its surface which we are not seeing, because they are hidden by intervening opaque objects. It is, I think, quite clear that you can correctly be said to 'see' a particular physical object in the common sense, even in cases where one or both of these conditions is (or are) not fulfilled; but I think far the commonest case is that in which both are fulfilled, and I propose to confine myself to that case.

What *is* the puzzle in the case of opaque objects seen under these conditions? It arises from the fact, which everybody knows, that, even where there is only one single part of an opaque object's surface which a man is seeing, and that part is large enough to entitle him to say correctly that he is seeing the object, yet the part of its surface in question may 'look' different to two different people who are both seeing that surface at the same time. For it seems to me quite plain that what is meant by saying that the same surface 'looks' different to two different people is that each is 'seeing', in a sense which I have called 'directly see', an entity which really *is* different from what the other is seeing. I have tried to explain what I mean by 'directly see' by saying that I use that expression to mean that sense of 'see' in which, if you look at, e.g. an electric light, then close your eyes and 'get', while your eyes are still closed, what is often called an 'after-image' of the light, you can be said to 'see' this after-image. It seems to me quite plain that 'see' can be correctly used in such a way that, in such a case, you do see the so-called 'after-image', although, in that case, you are certainly not seeing in the common sense any physical object whatever. And it also seems to me plain that, to say that, e.g. if I am wearing blue spectacles, a wall which is white but *not* bluish-white 'looks' bluish-white to me, is merely another way of saying that I am directly seeing an expanse which really is of a bluish-white colour, and which at the same time has to the surface which is not bluish-white a specific relation which, for the moment, I will call 'R' — a relation which entitles me to assert that, in directly seeing that bluish-white expanse, I am seeing the surface of the wall which is *not* bluish-white.

If I am *not* directly seeing a bluish-white expanse which *has* some such relation to a wall which is *not* bluish-white, how can I possibly know that that wall *is* looking bluish-white to me? It seems to me quite plain that I cannot 'see' in the common sense any physical object whatever without its 'looking' *somehow* to me, and, therefore, without my directly seeing some entity which has R to the object I am said to see, if the object is transparent and I am seeing the whole of it; and, if the object is opaque, under the conditions we are assuming, has R to the part of its surface which is the *only* part of its surface which I am seeing. And I think it is true that I so use the phrase 'visual sense-datum' that, from the fact that any entity is 'directly seen', in the sense explained, that entity *is* a visual sense-datum.

It is, I think, important to notice that it is only if 'looks' is used in one particular sense, that to say that a wall which is not bluish-white looks bluish-white to me involves the proposition that I am directly seeing a bluish-white expanse which has R to a surface that is not bluish-white. For there is another sense in which the word 'looks' is, I think, often used such that this consequence is *not* involved. What the two senses of 'looks' are can, I think, be very easily seen by considering the fact that if you see (in the common sense) two boats on the sea, one of which is quite near and the other at a considerable distance, you may be able to say with truth both (1) that the distant boat looks much smaller than the near one and (2) that the distant boot 'looks as if it were' much larger than the near one. Now, if 'looks' is used, as I think it some-times is, to mean the same as what I have just expressed by 'looks as if it were', then proposition (2) could be expressed by 'The distant boat looks much larger than the near one', which would be inconsistent with proposition (1), unless 'looks' were being used in a different sense in expressing (2) from that in which it is used in expressing (1). But the two propositions are obviously *not* incon-sistent with one another, hence 'looks', if it is used to express 'looks as if it were', must be used in a different sense from that in which it is used in (1). It is *only* if it is used as in (1) that it seems to me quite plain that the proposition that a physical surface looks bluish-white to me, entails that I am directly seeing an entity that *is* bluish-white.

Professor Ayer seems to have entirely misunderstood my view as to the relation of what I call a 'visual sense-datum' to such a proposition as is expressed by 'This is a penny'; for he asserts, twice over, that I take a visual sense-datum to be the *only* object about which we are making an assertion when we say 'This is a penny'.[1] I never, of course, held any view so silly. If I had, I should have been asserting that a visual sense-datum is what is

---

[1] *Philosophical Essays*, p. 78, note 3.

being asserted to be a penny! He seems to have failed to understand that my view was that the demonstrative 'this', in such an expression, is short for a definite description, and that, therefore, in saying 'This is a penny' we are making a proposition about *two* objects, and *not* about one only, just as, when we say 'The author of *Waverley* was a Scot', we are making an assertion (but a different one) *both* about the novel *Waverley* and about its author. I do hold that, in making the assertion 'This is a penny', I am asserting *something* about a sense-datum, just as in 'The author of *Waverley* was a Scot', I am asserting *something* about the novel *Waverley*. But in both cases I am 'referring to' and 'denoting' (but in different senses) two different objects and not one only. It does not seem to have occurred to him that 'this', even when it 'refers to' an object which we are, in the common sense, 'seeing', may be short for a definite description; and that I was holding that in, 'This is a penny', it *is* short for a definite description, and, therefore, 'refers to' at least two objects, though in different senses. It is true I have said that, in such a case, a visual sense-datum is 'the real or ultimate subject' of our judgment,[1] which, of course, implies that it is *not* the *only* subject: but this expression is perhaps, nevertheless, misleading, and ought not to have been used. I used it because I was so impressed, as I still am, by the extreme difference between a 'this' which is short for a definite description and a 'this' which 'refers to' a visual sense-datum which is being directly perceived at the moment.

But I have to own that I now think I was mistaken in supposing that, in the case of 'seeing' an opaque object, where in seeing it you are seeing only one visual sense-datum, the sense-datum can possibly be identical with that part of the opaque object's surface which you are seeing. I now think that it cannot possibly be identical with that part of the object's surface, i.e. that the relation which I have called 'R' above cannot possibly be the relation of identity. Until very recently I had thought that, though some of the arguments that purported to show that it cannot were strong, yet they were not conclusive, because I thought that, e.g. in the case where you directly see an 'after-image' with closed eyes, it

1 *Philosophical Studies*, p. 236.

was just possible that the after-image only looked to have certain colours and shape and size, and did not really have them. I made this suggestion in *Some Judgments of Perception*, but said there, several times, that it was perhaps nonsensical.[1] I well remember that, at the Aristotelian meeting at which I read that paper, Russell said that the suggestion certainly *was* nonsensical. I now feel sure that he was right; but, if so, then, when the same surface looks different at the same time to different people, the sense-datum which the one directly sees is certainly not identical with that which the other directly sees, and, therefore, they cannot both be identical with the surface which both are seeing. I was, therefore, certainly mistaken in supposing that, where an opaque object is seen, in the common sense, and only one sense-datum is directly seen in seeing it, the sense-datum in question is *always* identical with the part of the object's surface which is being seen. I was misled by the fact that it seems to me that you can always rightly say, in such a case, of a sense-datum which you are directly seeing, '*This* sense-datum *is* a part of the surface of a physical object.' I took it that the *is* always expresses identity, but it now seems to me that it certainly does not. But I still think that no philosopher, so far as I know, has explained clearly what the relation R is, where it is not identity.

[1] Ibid., pp. 245, 247, 252.

A. J. AYER

Perception

ALFRED JULES AYER, M.A. (Oxon), F.B.A.: Wykeham Professor of Logic in the University of Oxford. Fellow of New College, Oxford; Hon. Fellow of Wadham College, Oxford. Born October 29th, 1910; educated at Eton and Christ Church, Oxford; Lecturer in Philosophy at Christ Church, 1933, and Student, 1935; served in Welsh Guards and in Military Intelligence, 1940-45; Fellow and Dean of Wadham College, 1945-46; Grote Professor of the Philosophy of Mind and Logic in the University of London 1946-59; Visiting Professor at N.Y. University 1948-49, City College, N.Y. 1961-62.

Chief publications: *Language, Truth and Logic*, 1936 (revised edition, 1946). *The Foundations of Empirical Knowledge*, 1940. *Thinking and Meaning* (Inaugural Lecture), 1947. *British Empirical Philosophers* (edited), 1952. *Philosophical Essays*, 1954. *Problems of Knowledge*, 1956. *Logical Positivism* (Ed.), 1959. *Privacy* (British Academy Lecture), 1960. *Philosophy and Language* (Inaugural Lecture), 1960. *The Concept of a Person and Other Essays*, 1963 together with articles in philosophical and literary journals.

A. J. AYER

PERCEPTION

AMONG the many things that a later generation of philosophers has
learned from G. E. Moore is that it is not for them to query the
truth of such everyday judgments of fact as 'this is a human hand'.
To be able to decide whether such a judgment is true, we have to
know its context. This now seems to us so clear that we are tempted
to conclude that philosophers who have put forward theories from
which it would follow that such judgments never were true could
not have been serious. Rather than allow that these philosophers
denied obvious facts, we prefer to think that they did not literally
mean what they said. What, in that case, they really did mean,
remains obscure. It appears to us hardly less strange that philosophers should have treated the validity of these judgments as being even open to doubt. Thus there is a tendency to hold that
Berkeley and Locke and even Hume were not really in this position. What they were doing, whether or not they were fully aware
of it, was not to evaluate the truth of these ordinary perceptual
judgments, but to analyse their content.

I still think that a good case can be made out for this view. It is
an interpretation of the work of these philosophers that does not
do any great violence to their texts. My objection to it is that it
misrepresents their manner of approach. If the modern analytical
philosopher is like a librarian, reviewing his stock of books and
trying to sort them into their proper shelves, these earlier empiri-
cists were more like detectives who assembled their clues and then
went on to see what, if anything, they could legitimately infer from
them. Their first problem was to decide what were the clues. They
wished to set out from what Bertrand Russell, who stands in the
same tradition, has called 'hard-data'. To the extent that they were
able to build anything on this foundation, their achievement can

be represented as a work of analysis; its effect, for those who deny philosophy the power to put any matter of fact in question, is simply to show how different levels in the construction are related to one another. But the investigation was actually carried out as a work of discovery. The hard-data were thought to be secure: but it was treated as an open question whether anything further could be made to rest upon them.

Now it is a matter of general agreement among those, from Descartes onwards, who have adopted a method of this kind that the hard-data do not include physical objects. This has not always prevented them from taking words which are commonly used to stand for physical objects as referring to hard-data. Berkeley, for example, claimed to follow common sense in holding that trees and books and tables were directly perceived. But if we consider what is ordinarily meant by a physical object, I think that we must allow that nothing can properly be called a physical object unless it is accessible, at least in theory, to more than one sense, and to more than one observer. Various other properties are requisite, including the property of occupying space and of having more than a momentary duration, but for our present purposes these are the most important. The point is that it must always be significant to say of one and the same physical object that it is perceived by different people and that it is, for example, touched as well as seen. But these conditions are not satisfied by the objects which Berkeley, and most other philosophers, have regarded as hard-data. What, according to them, is immediately given in perception is an evanescent object, called an idea, or an impression, or a presentation, or a sense-datum, which is not only private to a single observer but private to a single sense.

This contention that we directly perceive sense-data rather than physical objects is not easy to interpret. What sort of a statement is it? In the first place it is not an empirical statement of fact. A philosopher who thinks that he directly perceives physical objects does not for that reason expect anything different to happen from what is expected by one who believes that he directly perceives sense-data. Each is claiming to give an account of all perceptual experience, whatever form it may take, so that no experiment can settle the issue between them. Neither can the statement that we can see and hear and touch sense-data be construed as a comment on the ordinary usage of words like 'hear' and 'touch' and 'see'. It is true that there is a familiar use of words like 'hear' and 'taste' and 'smell' according to which the objects heard, or tasted, or smelled, are private to a single sense. We commonly talk of hearing sounds, as well as of hearing the things which make the sounds, and whereas the things which make the sounds can usually be perceived in other ways as well, the sounds themselves can only be heard. But neither sounds nor tastes nor smells are ordinarily regarded as being private to a single observer: it makes perfectly good sense to speak of two different persons hearing the same sound or smelling the same smell. The only sounds that are private to a single observer are those that he hears in his mind's ear, those, in fact, that make no sound at all. And when we come to the most important senses, those of sight and touch, we find that ordinary usage does not provide them with accusatives on the analogy of sound and hearing. One may speak indifferently of hearing a clock or hearing its tick, but one does not speak of touching the feel of a clock or of seeing its look. What one is ordinarily said to touch and feel is the clock itself. And the clock which is seen is the very same object as the clock which is touched. There are objects such as mirror-images which are private to the sense of sight, but they again are not private to a single observer. It is only the things that one sees in one's mind's eye that are exclusively one's own.

Thus it appears that those who would have it said that the only immediate objects of perception are sense-data are making a fairly considerable departure from ordinary usage. They are assimilating all forms of perception to the perception of mental images, achieving the paradoxical result of taking as the standard case of sense-perception something that is ordinarily contrasted with it. To put it fashionably, their thesis is a linguistic recommendation. The interesting question is why it should be made.

The answer I believe is this. The main reason for bringing in this new notation is that our ordinary way of describing what we perceive appears to make a stronger claim upon the facts than the perception itself can cover. There may be no doubt, for example, that I am now looking at an ash-tray, but in saying that I see an ash-tray, which implies that there really is an ash-tray there, I am making an assertion which does more than merely report the content of my experience. It is consistent with my having this experience that I should not in fact be seeing an ash-tray, since it is at any rate logically possible that the perception should be partly or totally hallucinatory: it is consistent with my having the experience which I am having that there should not be an ash-tray there at all.

The difficulty with this argument lies in the interpretation of such expressions as 'the content of my experience'. If I am asked to say what experiences I am having at this moment, and if I interpret this somewhat unusual question as requiring me to say, among other things, what it is that I am seeing, then it is natural and proper for me to reply that I am, among other things, looking at an ash-tray. And if the experience which I am having is that of looking at an ash-tray, then it is not true that in saying that I see an ash-tray I am making an assertion which goes beyond the content of my experience. But then, it will be argued, though natural and legitimate, this is not a strict description of what is visually given to me. In saying that this object really is an ash-tray, I am implying that it can be touched as well as seen: I am implying that in suitable conditions other people could see it too. But this is not something that I now can 'see'. If I found that what I now take to be an ash-tray eluded my attempts to touch it, if I had reason to believe that other people could not touch it either, or even see it, then I should at least become hesitant about the truth of my statement that I saw an ash-tray. But whether or not these further claims are justified, the perception on which they are based, the purely visual experience, remains the same. Accordingly, if I am to be really circumspect, to give the fewest possible hostages to fortune, I must not say anything so bold as that I am seeing an ash-tray: I must say only that it now seems to me that I am seeing an ash-tray. The next step is to convert sentences like 'it now seems to me that I am seeing an ash-tray', which allows for the possibility that I am really seeing something else which I mistake for an ash-tray, or not really seeing anything at all, into 'I really am now seeing a seeming-ash-tray'. And this seeming-ash-tray, which lives only in my present experience, is an example of a sense-datum. Applying the same procedure to all other cases of perception, we thus arrive at the conclusion that only sense-data are given, or in other words, that it is always a seeming-object, of whatever sense it may be, that is directly perceived.

I think that there is a justification for the withdrawal from 'I am seeing x', where 'x' stands for a physical object or at least for something that is publicly observable, to 'it seems to me that I am seeing x'. Admittedly this use of 'it seems to me that' is somewhat unconventional. In the ordinary way, one does not say 'it seems to me that' unless one is in some way hesitant about the fact in question. It would be odd for me to say 'it seems to me that I am now looking at an ash-tray' when I have no doubt whatsoever, nor any reason to doubt, that there really is an ash-tray there. But the oddity is not so great that there need here be any difficulty in understanding what is meant. We are to use 'it seems that' in all cases where we wish to describe the character of what we see or hear or touch or otherwise perceive, in such a way as not to imply that the perception either is, or is not, veridical, but simply to leave the question open. Thus whenever it is true that I am perceiving a physical object it will also be true that it seems to me that I am perceiving it, but the converse will not necessarily hold.

What appears more dubious is the step by which we pass from saying 'it seems to me that I am seeing x' to 'I am seeing a seeming-x'. For here by a stroke of the pen we create a whole new realm of private objects and, what is more, imprison ourselves inside it. We are then faced with the problem how, if all that we are ever directly aware of in perception is our own sense-data, we can ever know anything about the external world. It is not surprising therefore that philosophers who are disposed to regard such problems as artificial should prefer to dispense with sense-data. But philosophical problems are not settled simply by our taking care that they should not arise. If the introduction of sense-data is legitimate, then there exists a problem about the way in which they are related to physical objects. The mere fact that this question can be raised entitles it philosophically to an answer.

There are, however, philosophers who maintain not merely that sense-data are a nuisance, or that their introduction serves no useful purpose, but that it is not legitimate. Thus, Professor Ryle has argued in his *Concept of Mind* that 'this whole theory [of sense-data] rests upon a logical howler, the howler, namely, of assimilating the concept of sensation to the concept of observation'.[1] His reason for thinking that this is a howler is that if observing something entails having a sensation, then having a sensation cannot itself be a form of observation: for if it were we should be involved in an infinite regress. Moreover the sort of things that can be said about observation, or perception, cannot significantly be said about sensation. 'When a person has been watching a horse race, it is proper to ask whether he had a good or a bad view of it, whether he watched it carefully or carelessly, and whether he tried to see as much of it as he could.'[2] But no one asks questions of this sort about sensations, 'any more than anyone asks how the first letter in "London" is spelled'. Sensations, although they can be noticed and attended to, are not 'objects of observation', and 'having a sensation cannot itself be a species of perceiving, finding or espying'.[3] This last statement is based on the assumption that it is impossible to perceive anything without having at least one sensation, that to speak of someone's seeing something without having any visual sensations, or of someone's hearing something without having any auditory sensations, would be self-contradictory. But Ryle himself subsequently concludes that this assumption is false. Reversing what he said before, he in the end maintains that 'this primary concept of sensation is not a component of the generic concept of perception, since it is just a species of that genus'.[4] To have a sensation is to feel something, and since one can see and hear without feeling anything, seeing and hearing do not entail having sensations. Even in the cases where they are accompanied by sensations, such as a sense of strain in the eyes, or a tingling in the ears, these sensations are not representations of what is seen and heard. They are not visual, or auditory impressions, in the sense in which philosophers have used this term. Such impressions do not, indeed, exist at all. They are invented by philosophers who

[1] P. 213.   [2] P. 207.   [3] P. 214.   [4] P. 242.

think that something is required to mediate between external objects and the mind. 'Impressions are ghostly impulses, postulated for the ends of a para-mechanical theory.'[1]

However much truth there may be in these remarks, I do not think that they are in any way fatal to the sense-datum view. In the first place even if it were correct to say that the advocates of sense-data treat sensation as a form of observation, what must here be meant by observation is not something which itself entails sensation. Consequently, it does not follow that they are committed to an infinite regress. There are special reasons, as I have tried to show, for analysing the perception of physical objects into the sensing of seeming-objects: but these reasons do not apply in turn to the sensing of seeming-objects. We are not obliged to analyse that into the awareness of seeming-seeming objects: there is no question of our having to adopt the general rule that no object is approachable except through an intermediary. Professor Ryle has indeed considered the possibility of some such defence: and his rejoinder is that it 'in effect explains the having of sensations as the *not* having any sensations':[2] if having a sensation is construed as an awareness of a sensible object then one may have sensations without being sensitively affected. But this rejoinder seems to me very weak. To talk of someone's sensing a sense-datum is, on this interpretation, just another way of saying that he is sensitively affected: the manner in which he is affected reappears as a property of the sense-datum: there is no need to say it all twice over.

But let us suppose that Professor Ryle is right, and that sensing a sense-datum cannot be made to do duty for having a sensation. This is still not a decisive objection to the sense-datum theory. For the theory does not in fact require that the two should be identified: it does not have to be interpreted as referring to sensations at all. To talk of sense-data is to talk of the ways things seem, in the somewhat peculiar sense of seeming that I have tried to explain. The question whether someone's seeming to perceive something, in this sense, coincides with what is ordinarily meant by his having a sensation may be regarded as irrelevant. Neither is there any call for the sense-datum theorists to hold that the sensing of sense-data is a form of observation, if calling it a form of observation is to imply that everything that can significantly be said about seeing, hearing and the rest, in the more familiar senses of these terms, can equally be said about it. Accordingly Ryle's comments on the every-day vocabulary of sensation and perception need not trouble them; it is certainly a fact that we do not ordinarily talk in the way that for philosophical purposes only they propose that we should, but this in itself is no objection to them. Historically, it may well be that some of the philosophers who have introduced impressions, or their equivalents, into the analysis of perception, have been guilty of the confusions which Ryle imputes to them. But the introduction of sense-data is not necessarily linked with any such confusions. No doubt there are ways in which it may prove misleading, but it may also serve a useful purpose.

Finally, it is to be remarked that the problem of justifying statements about physical objects on the basis of statements about sense-data, which I take to be the main traditional problem of perception, can still be raised even if we refuse to admit sense-data, or their equivalents, into our philosophical vocabulary. For this problem to arise we need not take the final step of translating 'seeming to see an object' into 'seeing a seeming-object', though it is convenient to do so for the purpose of discussing it. It can take the form of asking how we are justified in saying what things really are on the basis of what they seem to be. However we choose to formulate it, all that is required to constitute the problem is the admission that our ordinary judgments of perception claim more than is contained in the experiences which give rise to them. It is only if this admission is mistaken that the problem is illusory.

II

Assuming the problem not to be illusory, it takes its place among a set of philosophical problems which, though superficially dissimilar, exhibit a common pattern. In every case the data which are available to us appear to fall short in some uncompromising way of the conclusion which we hope to reach; the problem is to remove or bridge the gap. Thus, the apparent difficulty of passing to physical objects from sense-data is paralleled by the difficulty of passing from present experiences to past events, by the difficulty of inferring what goes on in other people's minds from their observable behaviour, and by the problem of induction, the passage from statements of fact to statements of law. These problems are interconnected in the sense that the solution of one of them may be taken for granted in the formulation of another. In raising the problem of other people's minds, we take for granted that we can observe their bodies: in dealing with the problem of induction we credit ourselves with knowledge of past events. Thus the level of what we count as data varies, but the difficulty of advancing beyond the data presents very much the same aspect in each case.

The answers which philosophers give to these problems fall into five main divisions:

(1) *Scepticism*. There is a gap and it cannot be bridged. We have no good reason to believe in the existence of physical objects. For all that we can prove there have never been any past events. It is an unjustifiable assumption that the course of nature continues uniformly the same. We can not know anything about the experiences of others. We can not really know anything at all, except perhaps what we are ourselves immediately experiencing.

(2) *Intuitionism*. Abolishing the gap by bringing the evidence up to the conclusion. Memory is a form of direct knowledge. We are directly acquainted with other people's minds. Our justification for believing scientific laws is that we apprehend necessary connections. In the case of perception, this kind of answer takes the form of naive realism: physical objects are directly perceived.

(3) *Reductionism*. Abolishing the gap by bringing the conclusion down to the evidence. Statements about the past are equivalent to statements about the present and future. Statements about other people's thoughts and feelings are equivalent to statements about their observable behaviour. Universal propositions are truth-functions of elementary propositions. In the case of perception, this method of approach gives us phenomenalism: physical objects are logical consructions out of sense-data.

(4) *The Scientific Approach*. There is a gap but we can work to build a bridge. Physical objects are inferable as the causes of sense-

data. Belief in the existence of other minds can be justified by an argument from analogy. Statements about the past are to be regarded as probable hypotheses. Induction can be justified as the basis of the theory of probability.

(5) *Analysis as a Form of Reassurance.* There is a gap but it does not matter. The relation between statements about sense-data and statements about physical objects, and the corresponding relations in the other cases, are not deductive, nor can they be made so by any multiplication of the data. They are what they are, and each of them justifies the relevant conclusion in its own particular way. This type of answer is often allied to a linguistic treatment of philosophical questions. There being no problem, or at any rate no general problem of justification, we are left only with the task of describing the conditions in which these various types of statement can properly be asserted. What we have to consider is how the sentences which express them are actually used.

Neither the sceptical nor the intuitionist answers need detain us long. The merit of the sceptic is that he focuses the problem. He sees that there is a gap to be bridged and the reasons which he gives for saying that it cannot be bridged are very often such as to give us a clearer understanding of its nature. But his conclusion is empty. Rejecting all the ordinary canons of proof, except the deductive canon which does not here apply, it puts nothing in their place. The peculiarity of the sceptic's position is that he will be satisfied with nothing less than what, on his showing, is logically unattainable. Granting that his premises are correct, his sceptical conclusion is without interest, just because he makes it a necessary truth.

As for intuitionism, it is not so much a move in the game as a refusal to play. It is true that we perceive physical objects. Anyone who says that we do not is either denying plain empirical facts or else giving an unusual meaning to the word 'perceive'. In saying that we perceive them 'directly', the naive realist, on the most favourable interpretation of his position, is declining to be moved by the considerations which lead some philosophers to say that we directly perceive sense-data. He is in fact, rejecting the antithesis between 'direct' and 'indirect' perception altogether, except per-

haps in the unphilosophical sense in which one might talk of seeing an object indirectly if it appeared as a reflection in a looking glass
or a projection on a screen. So long as he remains aloof in this way,
the naive realist's position is secure. It is only if he can be lured
into the game that it becomes vulnerable. Thus Professor Price, in
his book on *Perception* makes his naive realist admit that it is
sense-data that are given; and he then attributes to him the view
that visual and tactual sense-data are parts of the surfaces of physical objects. But this view is very easily refutable. It can be saved
from contradiction only if the expression 'part of the surface of a
physical object' is understood in a Pickwickian sense, which is
contrary to the spirit of naive realism. Price takes this course because he thinks it undeniable that there are sense-data. And he is
right in as much as he uses the word 'sense-datum' to describe what
are undoubtedly facts. But since these facts can also be described
in more familiar ways, it remains open to the naive realist to refuse
to recognize the need for introducing any such word at all. The
worst that can then be said of him is that he is philosophically un-
enterprising. If the sceptic has too little common sense, the intuitionist has, for a philosopher, too much.

The causal theory of perception owes the attraction that it has
for many people to the prestige of science. We learn about light
and sound waves, about cerebral cortices and the workings of the
nervous system, and as the result of this we are led to think that
the objects which we should ordinarily say that we perceived, the
objects which constitute the coloured, noisy, redolent world of
common sense, are very much our own creation. We never perceive the contemporary state of an object, for light and sound and
nerve impulses take time to travel: and even assuming that the object has not changed, or gone out of existence, in the interval, we
still do not see its natural face; it never appears in public unmade-
up. We cannot remove this make-up, just because it is we who put
it on, but we can theoretically discount it. We can allow for the
influence of the medium of observation, and of the character and
situation of the observer. And we can then work out what the object must in itself be like in order to have, in such conditions, the
effects on us that it does. It is in fact what science tells us that it is.

The famous distinction between primary and secondary qualities is not a distinction between those perceived qualities that are not affected by the conditions of observation and those that are: there is no such distinction, as Berkeley saw. The primary qualities of the object are just those properties with which science credits it.

This causal theory has fallen somewhat out of favour with philosophers, partly perhaps because its exponents have not been sufficiently circumspect in their use of the word 'cause'. But if all that is being claimed is that we are entitled to postulate a world of 'external' objects as a means of explaining our perceptual experiences, it seems innocent enough. It may be asked how we can be justified in holding that two classes of things are causally connected when the members of one of them, being unobservable, never have been, or could be, found in conjunction with the members of the other. But the answer to this is that 'finding' an object need not here be construed as directly observing it. There must indeed be some empirical tests by which the truth of what is said about the object is to be determined; but they need not be such as to make the object more than indirectly observable. There are serious problems about the interpretation of statements which refer to such scientific entities. It has to be decided whether they are reducible to statements which describe what is, or what comes nearer to being, directly observable. And if, as will probably be the case, it turns out that they are not so reducible, it then becomes a question whether the objects which they mention must be taken to be real, or whether it is still open to us to treat them as convenient fictions. It also has to be considered how far we are justified, on the basis of the observations which we are able to make, in putting these statements forward. The proof that we have some justification is that the way in which words like 'atom' or 'electron' are actually used is such that our having the relevant experiences does count as evidence for the statements which they serve to make. At the same time, this evidence is in general weaker than that which we have for believing in the existence of such material objects as stones and trees and chairs and tables. We could give up current physical theory without being logically committed to denying the existence of things of these familiar sorts. Consequently, if the causal theory of perception is regarded as offering an analysis of what is ordinarily meant by saying that such things are perceived, it has to be rejected. But it is at least permissible not to take it in this sense.

If the causal theory is not interpreted as a theory about the analysis of ordinary perceptual judgments, there need be no conflict between it and naive realism. It is open to anyone to hold both that such things as chairs and tables are directly perceived and that our sense experiences are dependent upon physical processes which are not directly perceptible. This is indeed a position which is very widely held, and it is perfectly consistent. All the same, there is a way in which acceptance of the causal theory does undermine naive realism. It does so by casting doubts upon the adequacy of the picture which the naive realist forms of the external world. The naive realist is not alone in thinking that things like chairs and tables may continue to exist when no one is perceiving them. His peculiarity is that he pictures them as existing unperceived in exactly the same form as that in which we normally do perceive them. This picture is not a logical ingredient in his theory, but it is its natural accompaniment. The causal theorist spoils it by pointing out that the ways in which these things appear to us are causally dependent upon the conditions which attend our perception of them. The suggestion is that when an object ceases to be perceived, it cannot reasonably be thought of as retaining properties which it owes to its being perceived. This argument does not demolish the naive realist's picture; he can reply that the object retains the properties in the sense that it could be perceived to have them: but it does at least mar its purity. If he replies in this way, he is taking a step in the direction of phenomenalism.

The causal theory also has its accompanying picture. Following the suggestion that the physical objects, which we should commonly say that we perceived, are somehow disguised by our perception of them, it represents their unperceived existence as a matter simply of their dropping their disguise. But this picture is muddled in a way that the naive realist's picture, for all its naivety, is not. It divests the object of its colour and its other secondary qualities, leaving a skeleton to occupy its spatial position. But if the perceptible colour of the object is to be taken from it, just because it is perceptible, so must its perceptible figure and extension. And if all its perceptible qualities are taken from it, as well as from all the other objects which surround it, its perceptible location vanishes too. There can be no half measures in this case. If a curtain is to be drawn between things as they really are and things as they appear to us to be, if we are never to be allowed to make perceptual contact with the things themselves but only with their effects on us, then the objects which we perceive fall in their entirety on our side of the curtain and so does the space in which they are located. What remains on the other side is the world of scientific objects with its appropriate space. These worlds do not interpenetrate, though one may be regarded as accounting for the other. There is no reason why a model of the 'external' world should not include features which are drawn from the world which we perceive; indeed, to the extent that the model is pictorial, this cannot be avoided. But confusion results when a composite picture is made out of the two. It is thoroughly misleading to suggest that the external objects come before us disguised as their own effects. In fact, the metaphor of disguise is inappropriate in this case. Again, the acceptance of this metaphor is not an integral part of the causal theory, but it is very intimately associated with it. Without it, the causal theory is hardly a theory of perception at all, in the philosophical sense. It simply gives us the assurance that phenomena can be scientifically explained. The problems which it raises belong to the philosophy of science.

Just as the causal theory is, in this anodyne form, compatible with naive realism, so is it compatible with phenomenalism. The phenomenalist need not deny that the occurrence and character of sense-data are to be explained in terms of entities which are not themselves observable. He must, however, maintain that to talk about such unobservable entities is, in the end, to talk about sense-data. His position is that every empirical statement about a physical object, whether it seems to refer to a scientific entity, or to an object of the more familiar kind which a naive realist would claim directly to perceive, is reducible to a statement, or set of statements, about sense-data. And what he is ordinarily taken to mean by saying that a statement S is reducible to a set of statements K is first that the members of K are on a lower epistemological level than S, that is that they refer to 'harder' data, and secondly that S and K are logically equivalent. The notion of logical equivalence is, in this context, not so clear as one could wish, but it requires at least that it should not be possible for us to find, or even to describe, a set of circumstances in which one statement would be true and its supposed equivalent false.

The first difficulty which the phenomenalist has to meet is that physical objects, unlike sense-data, can exist without being perceived. To say this is not to beg the question against Berkeley. It is simply that we so define our terms that it is a necessary condition for anything to be a physical object that it makes sense to say of it that it exists unperceived. This is not, in itself, to say that there are physical objects, and one might understand Berkeley as maintaining that there are not, or, more precisely, that there could not be. I doubt, however, if this would be an altogether just interpretation of Berkeley. He did allow that things, which commonly passed for physical objects, could continue to exist when only God perceived them; and to say of something that it is perceived only by God is to say that it is not, in any ordinary sense, perceived at all. In any case the phenomenalist does not deny that there are physical objects; his contention is that they are constituted by sense-data. But the fact that they can exist unperceived obliges him to hold that the statements about sense-data, into which statements about physical objects are to be translated, are predominantly hypothetical. They will for the most part have to state not that any sense-data are actually occurring, but only that certain sense-data would occur if the appropriate conditions were fulfilled. Furthermore, these hypotheticals cannot be construed as statements of material implication; for in that case they would all be true provided that their antecedents were false, which would put the phenomenalist in the position of holding that anything whatsoever existed so long as it was unperceived. The hypotheticals which he mainly needs are subjunctive conditionals: but their correct analysis presents a problem.

Some critics base an objection to phenomenalism not so much on the difficulty of interpreting these unfulfilled conditionals as on the fact that they are brought in at all. They maintain that when statements about physical objects are categorical, as they very frequently are, no rendering of them, however complicated and ingenious, into merely hypothetical statements about sense-data can possibly be adequate. 'Such a categorical existential material object sentence', says Mr. Berlin, 'as, "the table is next door" or "there is a table next door", is used at the very least to describe something which is occurring or being characterized at the time of speaking . . . ; and being characterized or occurring, unless the contrary is specifically stated or implied, not intermittently but continuously, and in any case not "hypothetically". For to say that something is occurring hypothetically is a very artificial and misleading way of saying that it is not, in the ordinary sense, occurring at all . . .'[1] I cannot myself see that there is any logical force in this objection. It is quite true that sentences which express hypothetical statements about sense-data are not used to assert that any sense-data are occurring, but it does not follow that they are not used to assert that any physical events are occurring, or that any physical objects exist. On the contrary this is exactly what they do state if phenomenalism is correct. There is no more difficulty of principle in replacing categorical statements about chairs and tables by hypothetical statements about sense-data, than there is in replacing categorical statements about electrons by hypothetical statements about Geiger counters, or whatever it may be, or in replacing categorical statements about people's unconscious feelings by hypothetical statements about their overt behaviour. Whether the translation can even theoretically be carried out in any of these cases is another question. As we shall see, there are strong reasons for concluding that the phenomenalist's 'reduction' is not feasible: but its possibility cannot be excluded merely on the ground that it substitutes hypothetical statements at one level for categorical statements at another.

What is puzzling about Mr. Berlin's position is that he is prepared to allow, at least for the sake of argument, that categorical statements about physical objects and hypothetical statements

---

[1] I. Berlin. 'Empirical Propositions and Hypothetical Statements', Mind, vol. LIX, no. 235, pp. 300-1.

about sense-data may 'strictly entail' each other, which is surely all
that any phenomenalist requires. He objects only that even if they
do entail each other they are not identical in meaning, and in some
legitimate sense of 'identical in meaning' he is no doubt right. His
main point is, I think, that these different types of statement have,
as it were, a different 'feel'. As he truly says, 'common sense and
the philosophers who are in sympathy with it, have always felt dissatisfied (with phenomenalism). The reduction of material object
sentences into what we may, for short, call sense-datum sentences,
seemed to leave something out, to substitute something intermit-
tent and attenuated for something solid and continuous'.[1] In fact,
if the phenomenalists are right, nothing is left out: any statement
which implies that there are solid and continuous objects in the
world will re-appear in the form of the appropriate statements
about sense-data. But even if nothing is left out, it is natural that
something should seem to be. For there is no picture associated
with phenomenalism in the way that the picture of things continuing to exist in much the same form as we perceive them is associated with a naive realist theory of perception, or the picture of
things existing stripped of their disguise is associated with the
causal theory. A permanent possibility of sensation is not something that can very well be pictured. In Plato's myth, the shadows
in the cave are contrasted with substantial objects outside. Phenomenalism seems to leave us with nothing but the shadows.

This may account for the psychological resistance with which
phenomenalists so very often meet, but it does not prove that their
thesis is false. However hard they may make it for us to construct
an imaginative picture of the physical world, they may still be
right in claiming that statements about physical objects are reducible to statements about sense-data. To do them justice this
claim must be submitted to a purely logical examination. But even
so I do not think that it succeeds. It requires, among other things,
the elimination from sense-datum statements of any explicit reference to an observer or to public space and time: and this raises
serious difficulties, as I have remarked elsewhere.[2] But even if we

[1] Op. cit., p. 291.
[2] 'Phenomenalism', *Proceedings of the Aristotelian Society*, 1947-48.

suppose these difficulties to be overcome, there remains a more general objection which the phenomenalist is not, so far as I can see, in a position to meet. If phenomenalism is true, the existence of a physical object of a certain sort must be a sufficient condition for the occurrence, in the appropriate circumstances, of certain sense-data; there must be a deductive step from physical reality to possible, if not to actual, appearances. And conversely, the occurrence of the sense-data must be a sufficient condition for the existence of the physical object; there must be a deductive step from actual, or at any rate possible, appearances to physical reality. The objection is that neither of these requirements can be satisfied.

The denial that statements which imply the existence of physical objects can be logically deduced from any finite set of statements about sense-data is often expressed in the form that no statement about a physical object can be conclusively verified. The probability of illusion can be diminished to a point where it becomes negligible, but its possibility is never formally excluded. However far they may be extended, our sense-experiences can never put the truth of any statement about a physical object beyond question; it remains consistent with them that the statement be false. But is this really so? Is it not very paradoxical to suggest that there can be any doubt of the existence of the table at which I am seated, the pen with which I am writing, the hand which is holding the pen? Surely I know for certain that these physical objects exist. And if I do know this, I know it on the basis of my sense experiences. Admittedly my present experiences, taken by themselves, are not sufficient for the purpose: the mere fact that I now seem to see and feel a table does not conclusively prove that there is a table there: it does not prove it even in the case of my own right hand. But when they are taken in conjunction with all my past experiences, then, it may plausibly be argued, these experiences are sufficient. They put it beyond question that these physical objects exist. The run of favourable evidence may indeed come to an end; it is at any rate logically possible that from this moment onwards there ceases to be any indication in experience that these objects exist, or ever have existed. But even if this were to happen it would not follow that they do not exist now or even that their present existence has not been conclusively established. It would, according to this argument, be a contradiction to deny that these physical objects exist while allowing that I have had the sense-experiences that I have.

But what must these experiences have been for this result to obtain? The difficulty is that any description of the way things seem, whatever the number of its details and however much they may corroborate each other, would still appear to admit of their really being otherwise. No doubt there soon comes a point at which the suggestion that things are not what they seem ceases to be serious; but this is not to say that it is formally excluded. It would, indeed, be absurd for me to query the truth of such statements as that this is a piece of paper or that this is my right hand. I can at this moment quite properly claim to know that these statements are true. But from the fact that I know these statements to be true, and even that I know them to be true on the basis of my sense-experience, it does not follow that they are logically entailed by any set of statements which describe my sense-experience. But surely, it may be objected, if this is so it is only because your sense-experience is too limited; if it were suitably increased the entailment would hold. We speak of illusions only in the cases in which there is a conflict among our sense-experiences; that is, when the expectations to which some of them give rise are not fulfilled by the others. But when they are all mutually corroborative, not even the logical possibility of illusion remains; to speak of all human experience as illusory would be meaningless. It is a necessary truth that you cannot fool all the people all of the time. But the answer to this is that while it may be meaningless to assert in a general way that all experience is illusory, it is not meaningless to say this of any particular description of experience, however far it is extended. The statement that the experiences so described are as a whole illusory may be false and even certainly false, but it will not be self-contradictory. For the phenomenalist to succeed, it is not enough that he can establish the general thesis that if all experience is as if there are physical objects, then there are physical objects. He must be able to find at least one specimen set of statements about sense-data from which a statement which implies the existence of a given physical object logically follows. And this, it seems to me, he cannot do.

Neither, I now think, can he make good the converse claim that the existence of a given physical object is a sufficient condition for the occurrence of certain sense-data. It is sometimes asserted, as by Berkeley, that to say, for example, that the earth moves is to say that 'if we were placed in such and such circumstances, and such or such a position and distance, both from the earth and sun, we should perceive the former to move — .'[1] But it might happen that when we were placed in these circumstances we did not perceive this at all, not because the earth was not moving, but because we were inattentive, or looking in the wrong direction, or our view was in some way obscured, or because we suffered from some physiological or psychological disorder. It may be suggested that these difficulties can be provided for. We might, for instance, attempt to rule out the possibility of the observer's suffering from some physiological disorder by adding a further hypothetical to the effect that if a physiologist were to examine him, or rather were to seem to be examining him, it would seem to the physiologist that his vision was unimpaired. But then we should require a further hypothetical to guard against the possibility that the physiologist was undergoing an illusion; and so *ad infinitum*. This is not to say that the fact that some physical object fails to be observed is never to be counted as a proof that it does not exist; it is on the contrary the very best proof obtainable. But it is not a demonstrative proof. From the fact that in the specified conditions the requisite sense-data do not occur it does not follow logically that the physical object which is in question does not exist, or that it does not have the properties with which it has been credited. In many cases, this is the obvious, indeed the only reasonable, explanat on of the apparent facts; but the possibility of an alternative explanation must always remain open.

It might seem that this difficulty could be met by stipulating that the test for the presence or absence of the physical object was to be carried out in normal conditions by a normal observer: and indeed this is an assumption that is generally made by those who

[1] *Principles of Human Knowledge*, LVIII.

maintain that to speak of such an object as existing unperceived is to imply that if one were in the appropriate situation one would be perceiving it. But this is merely a way of concealing the difficulty, not of resolving it. If we are to understand by 'normal' conditions those that permit an observer to perceive things as they really are, and by a 'normal' observer one who in such conditions does perceive things as they really are, then indeed it will follow from the fact that there is a physical object in such and such a place that if a normal observer were there he would under normal conditions be perceiving it. But it will follow only because it is made to follow by our definition of normality. And the difficulty which we are trying to avoid reappears immediately as the difficulty of mak-sure that the conditions and the observer really are, in this sense, normal. Again, we may attempt to make sure by stipulating that if tests were made for every known source of abnormality, their results would all appear to be negative. But once more we shall need an infinite series of further hypotheticals to guarantee the tests themselves. Nor is it logically necessary that the sources of abnormality that are known to us are all the sources that there are. It follows that the step from physical reality to possible appearances cannot by this method be made formally deductive. Neither, so far as I can see, can it be made so by any other.

It appears then, if my reasoning is correct, that the phenomenalist's programme cannot be carried through. Statements about physical objects are not, in general, translatable into statements about sense-data. In itself, indeed, this conclusion is not startling. It is rather what we should expect if we reflected merely on the way in which sentences which refer to physical objects are actually used. That phenomenalism has commanded so strong an allegiance has been due not to its intrinsic plausibility but rather to the fact that the introduction of sense-data appears to leave no other alternative open. It has been assumed that since statements about physical objects can be verified or falsified only through the occurrence of sense-data, they must somehow be reducible to statements about sense-data. This is a natural assumption to make, but I now think that it is false. There is a parallel here with the case of scientific theories which ostensibly refer to such things as atomic particles or unconscious mental states. The cash value of such theories is to be sought in the lower-level statements on the truth or falsehood of which their validity depends: at the same time, the statements of the theory are not simply reformulations of these lower-level statements. In this sense, I suggest that statements about physical objects are theoretical with respect to statements about sense-data. The relation between them is not strictly deductive; and to say that it is inductive leaves its exact nature still to be explained. In the end, therefore, we are brought by elimination to the fifth of the methods which I listed for dealing with the problem of perception; that which I entitled analysis as a form of reassurance. In its way our examination of the problem has itself been an exercise in this method: I hope that we have taken the preliminary step of making the issues reasonably clear.

GILBERT RYLE

The Theory of Meaning

GILBERT RYLE: born August 19th, 1900; educated at Brighton College and Queen's College, Oxford; Classical Scholar, Queen's College, Oxford; Waynflete Professor of Metaphysical Philosophy in the University of Oxford.

Chief publications: *The Concept of Mind*, 1949. *Dilemmas*, 1954. Various papers in *The Proceedings of the Aristotelian Society* and in philosophical journals. Editor of *Mind* since 1947.

GILBERT RYLE

THE THEORY OF MEANING

WE can all use the notion of *meaning*. From the moment we begin to learn to translate English into French and French into English, we realize that one expression does or does not mean the same as another. But we use the notion of meaning even earlier than that. When we read or hear something in our own language which we do not understand, we wonder what it means and ask to have its meaning explained to us. The ideas of understanding, misunderstanding and failing to understand what is said already contain the notion of expressions having and lacking specifiable meanings.

It is, however, one thing to ask, as a child might ask, What, if anything, is meant by 'vitamin', or 'abracadabra' or '$(a+b)^2 = a^2 + b^2 + 2ab$'? It is quite another sort of thing to ask What are meanings? It is, in the same way, one thing to ask, as a child might ask, What can I buy for this shilling?, and quite another sort of thing to ask What is purchasing-power? or What are exchange-values?

Now answers to this highly abstract question, What are meanings? have, in recent decades, bulked large in philosophical and logical discussions. Preoccupation with the theory of meaning could be described as the occupational disease of twentieth-century Anglo-Saxon and Austrian philosophy. We need not worry whether or not it is a disease. But it might be useful to survey the motives and the major results of this preoccupation.

Incidentally it is worth noticing that many of these issues were explicitly canvassed — and some of them conclusively settled — in certain of Plato's later Dialogues, and in the logical and other works of Aristotle. Some of them, again, were dominant issues in the late Middle Ages and later still with Hobbes; and some of them, thickly or thinly veiled in the psychological terminology of 'ideas', stirred uneasily inside British epistemology between Locke and John Stuart Mill. But I shall not, save for one or two back-references, discuss the early history of these issues.

The shopkeeper, the customer, the banker and the merchant are ordinarily under no intellectual pressure to answer or even ask the abstract questions What is purchasing-power? and What are exchange-values? They are interested in the prices of things, but not yet in the abstract question What is the real nature of that which is common to two articles of the same price? Similarly, the child who tries to follow a conversation on an unfamiliar topic, and the translator who tries to render Thucydides into English are interested in what certain expressions mean. But they are not necessarily interested in the abstract questions What is it for an expression to have a meaning? or What is the nature and status of that which an expression and its translation or paraphrase are both the vehicles? From what sort of interests, then, do we come to ask this sort of question? Doubtless there are many answers. I shall concentrate on two of them which I shall call 'the Theory of Logic' and 'the Theory of Philosophy'. I shall spend a good long time on the first; not so long on the second.

(1) *The Theory of Logic.* The logician, in studying the rules of inference has to talk of the components of arguments, namely their premisses and conclusions and to talk of them in perfectly general terms. Even when he adduces concrete premisses and conclusions, he does so only to illustrate the generalities which are his proper concern. In the same way, he has to discuss the types of separable components or the types of distinguishable features of these premiss-types and conclusion-types, since it is sometimes on such components or features of premisses and conclusions that the inferences from and to them pivot.

Now the same argument may be expressed in English or in French or in any other language; and if it is expressed in English, there may still be hosts of different ways of wording it. What the logician is exploring is intended to be indifferent to these differences of wording. He is concerned with what is said by a premiss-sentence or a conclusion-sentence, not with how it is worded.

So, if not in the prosecution of his inquiry, at least in his explanations of what he is doing, he has to declare that his subject-matter consist not of the sentences and their ingredient words in which arguments are expressed, but of the propositions or judgments and their constituent terms, ideas or concepts of which the sentences and words are the vehicles. Sometimes he may say hat his subject matter consists of sentence-meanings and their constituent word-meanings or phrase-meanings, though this idiom is interestingly repellent. Why it is repellent we shall, I hope, see later on. So in giving this sort of explanation of his business, he is talking *about* meanings, where in the prosecution of that business he is just operating *upon* them.

For our purposes it is near enough true to say that the first influential discussion of the notion of meaning given by a modern logician was that with which John Stuart Mill opens his *System of Logic* (1843). He acknowledges debts both to Hobbes and to the Schoolmen, but we need not trace these borrowings in detail.

Mill's contributions to Formal or Symbolic Logic were negligible. It was not he but his exact contemporaries, Boole and de Morgan, and his immediate successors, Jevons, Venn, Carroll, McColl and Peirce who, in the English-speaking world, paved the way for Russell. On the other hand, it is difficult to exaggerate the influence which he exercised, for good and for ill, upon British and Continental philosophers; and we must include among these philosophers the Symbolic Logicians as well, in so far as they have philosophized about their technical business. In particular, Mill's theory of meaning set the questions, and in large measure, determined their answers for thinkers as different as Brentano, in Austria; Meinong and Husserl, who were pupils of Brentano; Bradley, Jevons, Venn, Frege, James, Peirce, Moore and Russell. This extraordinary achievement was due chiefly to the fact that Mill was original in producing a doctrine of meaning at all. The doctrine that he produced was immediately influential, partly because a doctrine was needed and partly because its inconsistencies were transparent. Nearly all of the thinkers whom I have listed were in vehement opposition to certain parts of Mill's doctrine, and it was the other parts of it from which they often drew their most effective weapons.

Q

Mill, following Hobbes's lead, starts off his account of the notion of meaning by considering single words. As we have to learn the alphabet before we can begin to spell, so it seemed natural to suppose that the meanings of sentences are compounds of the components, which are the meanings of their ingredient words. Word-meanings are atoms, sentence-meanings are molecules. I say that it seemed natural, but I hope soon to satisfy you that it was a tragically false start. Next Mill, again following Hobbes's lead, takes it for granted that all words, or nearly all words, are names, and this, at first, sounds very tempting. We know what it is for 'Fido' to be the name of a particular dog, and for 'London' to be the name of a particular town. There, in front of us, is the dog or the town which has the name, so here, one feels, there is no mystery. We have just the familiar relation between a thing and its name. The assimilation of all or most other single words to names gives us, accordingly, a cosy feeling. We fancy that we know where we are. The dog in front of us is what the word 'Fido' stands for, the town we visited yesterday is what the word 'London' stands for. So the classification of all or most single words as names makes us feel that what a word means is in all cases some manageable thing that that word is the name of. Meanings, at least word-meanings, are nothing abstruse or remote, they are, *prima facie*, ordinary things and happenings like dogs and towns and battles.

Mill goes further. Sometimes the grammatical subject of a sentence is not a single word but a many-worded phrase, like 'the present Prime Minister' or 'the first man to stand on the summit of Mt. Everest'. Mill has no qualms in classifying complex expressions like these also as names, what he calls 'many-worded names'. There do not exist proper names for everything we want to talk about; and sometimes we want to talk about something or somebody whose proper name, though it exists, is unknown to us. So descriptive phrases are coined by us to do duty for proper names. But they are still, according to Mill, names, though the tempting and in fact prevailing interpretation of this assertion differs importantly from what Mill usually wanted to convey. For, when Mill calls a word or phrase a 'name', he is using 'name' not, or not always, quite in the ordinary way. Sometimes he says that for an expression to be a name it must be able to be used as the subject or the predicate of a subject-predicate sentence — which lets in, e.g. adjectives as names. Sometimes his requirements are more stringent. A name is an expression which can be the subject of a subject-predicate sentence — which leaves only nouns, pronouns and substantival phrases. 'Name', for him, does not mean merely 'proper name'. He often resisted temptations to which he subjected his successors.

Before going any further, I want to make you at least suspect that this initially congenial equation of words and descriptive phrases with names is from the outset a monstrous howler — if, like some of Mill's successors, though unlike Mill himself, we do systematically construe 'name' on the model of 'proper name'. The assumption of the truth of this equation has been responsible for a large number of radical absurdities in philosophy in general and the philosophy of logic in particular. It was a fetter round the ankles of Meinong, from which he never freed himself. It was a fetter round the ankles of Frege, Moore and Russell, who all, sooner or later, saw that without some big emendations, the assumption led inevitably to fatal impasses. It was, as he himself says in his new book, a fetter round the ankles of Wittgenstein in the *Tractatus*, though in that same book he had found not only the need but the way to cut himself partially loose from it.

I am still not quite sure why it seems so natural to assume that all words are names, and even that every possible grammatical subject of a sentence, one-worded or many-worded, stands to something as the proper name 'Fido' stands to the dog Fido, and, what is a further point, that the thing it stands for is what the expression means. Even Plato had had to fight his way out of the same assumption. But he at least had a special excuse. The Greek language had only the one word ὄνομα where we have the three words 'word', 'name' and 'noun'. It was hard in Greek even to say that the Greek counterpart to our verb 'is' was a word but not a noun. Greek provided Plato with no label for verbs, or for adverbs, conjunctions etc. That 'is' is a word, but is not a name or even a noun was a tricky thing to say in Greek where ὄνομα did duty both for our word 'word', for our word 'name' and, eventually, for our word 'noun'. But even without this excuse people still find it natural to assimilate all words to names, and the meanings of words to the bearers of those alleged names. Yet the assumption is easy to demolish.

First, if every single word were a name, then a sentence composed of five words, say 'three is a prime number' would be a list of the five objects named by those five words. But a list, like 'Plato, Aristotle, Aquinas, Locke, Berkeley' is not a sentence. It says nothing, true or false. A sentence, on the contrary, may say something — some one thing — which is true or false. So the words combined into a sentence at least do something jointly which is different from their severally naming the several things that they name if they do name any things. What a sentence means is not decomposable into the set of things which the words in it stand for, if they do stand for things. So the notion of *having meaning* is at least partly different from the notion of *standing for*.

More than this. I can use the two descriptive phrases 'the Morning Star' and 'the Evening Star', as different ways of referring to Venus. But it is quite clear that the two phrases are different in meaning. It would be incorrect to translate into French the phrase 'the Morning Star' by 'l'Étoile du Soir'. But if the two phrases have different meanings, then Venus, the planet which we describe by these two different descriptions, cannot be what these descriptive phrases mean. For she, Venus, is one and the same, but what the two phrases signify are different. As we shall see in a moment Mill candidly acknowledges this point and makes an important allowance for it.

Moreover it is easy to coin descriptive phrases to which nothing at all answers. The phrase 'the third man to stand on the top of Mt. Everest' cannot, at present, be used to refer to anybody. There exists as yet no one whom it fits and perhaps there never will. Yet it is certainly a significant phrase, and could be translated into French or German. We know, we have to know, what it means when we say that it fits no living mountaineer. It means *something*, but it does not designate *somebody*. What it means cannot, therefore, be equated with a particular mountaineer. Nor can the meaning conveyed by the phrase 'the first person to stand on the top of

Mt. Everest' be equated with Hillary, though, we gather, it fits him and does not fit anyone else. We can understand the question, and even entertain Nepalese doubts about the answer to the question 'Is Hillary the first person to conquer Mt. Everest?' where we could not understand the question 'Is Hillary Hillary?'

We could reach the same conclusion even more directly. If Hillary was, *per impossibile*, identified with what is meant by the phrase 'the first man to stand on the top of Mt. Everest', it would follow that the meaning of at least one phrase was born in New Zealand, has breathed through an oxygen-mask and has been decorated by Her Majesty. But this is patent nonsense. Meanings of phrases are not New Zealand citizens; what is expressed by a particular English phrase, as well as by any paraphrase or translation of it, is not something with lungs, a surname, long legs and a sunburnt face. People are born and die and sometimes wear boots; meanings are not born and do not die and they never wear boots — or go barefoot either. The Queen does not decorate meanings. The phrase 'the first man to stand on the top of Mt. Everest' will not lose its meaning when Hillary dies. Nor was it meaningless before he reached the summit.

Finally, we should notice that most words are not nouns; they are, e.g. adverbs, or verbs, or adjectives or prepositions or conjunctions or pronouns. But to classify as a name a word which is not even a noun strikes one as intolerable the moment one considers the point. How could 'ran' or 'often' or 'and' or 'pretty' be the name of anything? It could not even be the grammatical subject of a sentence. I may ask what a certain economic condition, moral quality or day of the week is called and get the answer 'inflation', 'punctiliousness' or 'Saturday'. We do use the word 'name' for what something is called, whether it be what a person or river is called, or what a species, a quality, an action or a condition is called. But the answer to the question 'What is it called?' must be a noun or have the grammar of a noun. No such question could be answered by giving the tense of a verb, an adverb, a conjunction or an adjective.

Mill himself allowed that some words like 'is', 'often', 'not', 'of', and 'the' are not names, even in his hospitable use of 'name'. They cannot by themselves function as the grammatical subjects of sentences. Their function, as he erroneously described it, is to subserve, in one way or another, the construction of many-worded names. They do not name extra things but are ancillaries to the multi-verbal naming of things. Yet they certainly have meanings. 'And' and 'or' have different meanings, and 'or' and the Latin 'aut' have the same meaning. Mill realized that it is not always the case that for a word to mean something, it must denote somebody or some thing. But most of his successors did not notice how important this point was.

Even more to Mill's credit was the fact that he noticed and did partial justice to the point, which I made a little while back, that two different descriptive phrases may both fit the same thing or person, so that the thing or person which they both fit or which, in his unhappy parlance, they both name is not to be equated with either (or of course both) of the significations of the two descriptions. The two phrases 'the previous Prime Minister' and 'the father of Randolph Churchill' both fit Sir Winston Churchill, and fit only him; but they do not have the same meaning. A French translation of the one would not be a translation of the other. One might know or believe that the one description fitted Sir Winston Churchill while still questioning whether the other did so too. From just knowing that Sir Winston was Prime Minister one could not infer that Randolph Churchill is his son, or *vice versa.* Either might have been true without the other being true. The two phrases cannot, therefore, carry the same information.

Mill, in effect, met this point with his famous theory of denotation and connotation. Most words and descriptive phrases, according to him, do two things at once. They *denote* the things or persons that they are, as he unhappily puts it, all the names of. But they also *connote* or signify the simple or complex attributes by possessing which the thing or person denoted is fitted by the description. Mill's word 'connote' was a very unhappily chosen word and has misled not only Mill's successors but Mill himself. His word 'denote' was used by him in a far from uniform way, which left him uncommitted to consequences from which some of his successors, who used it less equivocally, could not extricate themselves. For Mill, proper names denote their bearers, but predicate-expressions also denote what they are truly predicable of. Fido is denoted by 'Fido' and by 'dog' and by 'four-legged'.

So to ask for the function of an expression is, on Mill's showing, to ask a double question. It is to ask Which person or persons, thing or things the expression denotes? in one or other of Mill's uses of this verb — Sir Winston Churchill, perhaps — ; but it is also to ask What are the properties or characteristics by which the thing or person is described? — say that of having begotten Randolph Churchill. As a thing or person can be described in various ways, the various descriptions given will differ in connotation, while still being identical in denotation. They characterize in different ways, even though their denotation is identical. They carry different bits of information or misinformation about the same thing, person or event.

Mill himself virtually says that according to our ordinary natural notion of meaning, it would not be proper to say that, e.g. Sir Winston Churchill is the meaning of a word or phrase. We ordinarily understand by 'meaning' not the thing denoted but only what is connoted. That is, Mill virtually reaches the correct conclusions that the meaning of an expression is never the thing or person referred to by means of it; and that descriptive phrases and, with one exception, single words are never names, in the sense of 'proper names'. The exception is just those relatively few words which really are proper names, i.e. words like 'Fido', and 'London', the words which do not appear in dictionaries.

Mill got a further important point right about these genuine proper names. He said that while most words and descriptive phrases both denote or name and connote, proper names only denote and do not connote. A dog may be called 'Fido', but the word 'Fido' conveys no information or misinformation about the dog's qualities, career or whereabouts, etc. There is, to enlarge this point, no question of the word 'Fido' being paraphrased, or correctly or incorrectly translated into French. Dictionaries do not tell us what proper names mean — for the simple reason that they do not mean anything. The word 'Fido' names or denotes a particular dog, since it is what he is called. But there is no room for anyone who hears the word 'Fido' to understand it or misunderstand it or fail to understand it. There is nothing for which he can require an elucidation or a definition. From the information that Sir Winston Churchill was Prime Minister, a number of consequences follow, such as that he was the leader of the majority party in Parliament. But from the fact that yonder dog is Fido, no other truth about him follows at all. No information is provided for anything to follow from. Using a proper name is not committing oneself to any further assertions whatsoever. Proper names are appellations and not descriptions; and descriptions are descriptions and not appellations. Sir Winston Churchill *is* the father of Randolph Churchill. He is not *called* and was not christened 'the father of Randolph Churchill'. He is called 'Winston Churchill'. The Lady Mayoress of Liverpool can give the name *Mauretania* to a ship which thenceforward has that name. But if she called Sir Winston Churchill 'the father of Sir Herbert Morrison' this would be a funny sort of christening, but it would not make it true that Morrison is the son of Sir Winston Churchill. Descriptions carry truths or falsehoods and are not just arbitrary bestowals. Proper names are arbitrary bestowals, and convey nothing true and nothing false, for they convey nothing at all.

Chinese astronomers give the planets, stars and constellations names quite different from those we give. But it does not follow that a single proposition of Western astronomy is rejected by them, or that a single astronomical proposition rejected by us is accepted by them. Stellar nomenclature carries with it no astronomical truths or falsehoods. Calling a star by a certain name is not saying anything about it, and saying something true or false about a star is not naming it. Saying is not naming and naming is not saying.

This brings out a most important fact. Considering the meaning (or Mill's 'connotation') of an expression is considering what can be said with it, i.e. said truly or said falsely, as well as asked, commanded, advised or any other sort of saying. In this, which is the normal sense of 'meaning', the meaning of a sub-expression like a word or phrase, is a functional factor of a range of possible assertions, questions, commands and the rest. It is tributary to sayings. It is a distinguishable common locus of a range of possible tellings, askings, advisings, etc. This precisely inverts the natural assumption with which, as I said earlier, Mill and most of us start, the assumption namely that the meanings of words and phrases can be learned, discussed and classified before consideration begins of entire sayings, such as sentences. Word-meanings do not stand to sentence-meanings as atoms to molecules or as letters of the alphabet to the spellings of words, but more nearly as the tennis-racket stands to the strokes which are or may be made with it. This point, which Mill's successors and predecessors half-recognized to hold for such little words as 'if', 'or', 'all', 'the' and 'not', holds good for all significant words alike. Their significances are their rôles inside actual and possible sayings. Mill's two-way doctrine, that nearly all words and phrases both denote, or are names, and connote, i.e. have significance, was therefore, in effect, though unwittingly, a coalition between an atomistic and a functionalist view of words. By the irony of fate, it was his atomistic view which was, in most quarters, accepted as gospel truth for the next fifty or seventy years. Indeed, it was more than accepted, it was accepted without the important safeguard which Mill himself provided when he said that the thing or person denoted by a name was not to be identified with what that name meant. Mill said that to mean is to connote. His successors said that to mean is to denote, or, more rarely, both to denote and to connote. Frege was for a long time alone in seeing the crucial importance of Mill's argument that two or more descriptive phrases with different senses may apply to the same planet or person. This person or planet is not, therefore, what those phrases mean. Their different senses are not their common denotation. Russell early realized the point which Mill did not very explicitly make, though Plato had made it, that a sentence is not a list. It says one thing; it is not just an inventory of a lot of things. But only much later, if at all, did Russell see the full implications of this.

I surmise that the reason why Mill's doctrine of denotation, without its safeguards, caught on, while his truths about connotation failed to do so, were two. First, the word 'connote' naturally suggests what we express by 'imply', which is not what is wanted.

What the phrase 'the previous Prime Minister of the United Kingdom' signifies is not to be equated with any or all of the consequences which can be inferred from the statement that Churchill is the previous Prime Minister. Deducing is not translating. But more important was the fact that Mill himself rapidly diluted his doctrine of connotation with such a mass of irrelevant and false sensationalist and associationist psychology, that his successors felt forced to ignore the doctrine in order to keep clear of its accretions.

Let me briefly mention some of the consequences which successors of Mill actually drew from the view, which was not Mill's, that to mean is to denote, in the toughest sense, namely that all significant expressions are proper names, and what they are the names of are what the expressions signify.

First, it is obvious that the vast majority of words are unlike the words 'Fido' and 'London' in this respect, namely, that they are general. 'Fido' stands for a particular dog, but the noun 'dog' covers this dog Fido, and all other dogs past, present and future, dogs in novels, dogs in dog breeders' plans for the future, and so on indefinitely. So the word 'dog', if assumed to denote in the way in which 'Fido' denotes Fido, must denote something which we do not hear barking, namely either the set or class of all actual and imaginable dogs, or the set of canine properties which they all share. Either would be a very out-of-the-way sort of entity. Next, most words are not even nouns, but adjectives, verbs, prepositions, conjunctions and so on. If these are assumed to denote in the way in which 'Fido' denotes Fido, we shall have a still larger and queerer set of nominees or *denotata* on our hands, namely nominees whose names could not even function as the grammatical subjects of sentences. (Incidentally it is not true even that all ordinary general nouns can function by themselves as subjects of sentences. I can talk about *this* dog, or *a* dog, or *the* dog which . . .; or about *dogs*, *all* dogs, or *most* dogs, and so on. But I cannot make the singular noun 'dog' by itself the grammatical subject of a sentence, save inside quotes, though I can do this with nouns like 'grass', 'hydrogen' and 'Man'.) Finally, since complexes of words, like descriptive and other phrases, and entire clauses and sentences have unitary meanings, then these too will have to be construed as denoting complex entities of very surprising sorts. Now Meinong in Austria and Frege in Germany, as well as Moore and Russell in this country, in their early days, accepted some or most of these consequences. Consistently with the assumed equation of signifying with naming, they maintained the objective existence or being of all sorts of abstract and fictional *entia rationis*.

Whenever we construct a sentence, in which we can distinguish a grammatical subject and a verb, the grammatical subject, be it a single word or a more or less complex phrase, must be significant if the sentence is to say something true or false. But if this nominative word or phrase is significant, it must, according to the assumption, denote something which is there to be named. So not only Fido and London, but also centaurs, round squares, the present King of France, the class of albino Cypriots, the first moment of time, and the non-existence of a first moment of time must all be credited with some sort of reality. They must *be*, else we could not say true or false things of them. We could not truly say that round squares do not exist, unless in some sense of 'exist' there exist round squares for us, in another sense, to deny existence of. Sentences can begin with abstract nouns like 'equality' or 'justice' or 'murder' so all Plato's Forms or Universals must be accepted as entities. Sentences can contain mentions of creatures of fiction, like centaurs and Mr. Pickwick, so all conceivable creatures of fiction must be genuine entities too. Next, we can say that propositions are true or false, or that they entail or are incompatible with other propositions, so any significant 'that'-clause, like 'that three is a prime number' or 'that four is a prime number', must also denote existent or subsistent objects. It was accordingly, for a time, supposed that if I know or believe that three is a prime number, my knowing or believing this is a special relation holding between me on the one hand and the truth or fact, on the other, denoted by the sentence 'three is a prime number'. If I weave or follow a romance, my imagining centaurs or Mr. Pickwick is a special relation holding between me and these centaurs or that portly old gentleman. I could not imagine him unless he had enough being to stand as the correlate-term in this postulated relation of being imagined by me.

Lastly, to consider briefly what turned out, unexpectedly, to be a crucial case, there must exist or subsist classes, namely appropriate *denotata* for such collectively employed plural descriptive phrases as 'the elephants in Burma' or 'the men in the moon'. It is just of such classes or sets that we say that they number 3000, say, in the one case, and 0 in the other. For the results of counting to be true or false, there must be entities submitting to numerical predicates; and for the propositions of arithmetic to be true or false there must exist or subsist an infinite range of such classes.

At the very beginning of this century Russell was detecting some local unplausibilities in the full-fledged doctrine that to every significant grammatical subject there must correspond an appropriate *denotatum* in the way in which Fido answers to the name 'Fido'. The true proposition 'round squares do not exist' surely cannot require us to assert that there really do subsist round squares. The proposition that it is false that four is a prime number is a true one, but its truth surely cannot force us to fill the Universe up with an endless population of objectively existing falsehoods.

But it was classes that first engendered not mere unplausibilities but seemingly disastrous logical contradictions — not merely peripheral logical contradictions but contradictions at the heart of the very principles on which Russell and Frege had taken mathematics to depend. We can collect into classes not only ordinary objects like playing-cards and bachelors, but also such things as classes themselves. I can ask how many shoes there are in a room and also how many pairs of shoes, and a pair of shoes is already a class. So now suppose I construct a class of all the classes that are not, as anyhow most classes are not, members of themselves. Will this class be one of its own members or not? If it embraces itself, this disqualifies it from being one of the things it is characterized as embracing; if it is not one of the things it embraces, this is just what qualifies it to be one among its own members.

So simple logic itself forbids certain ostensibly denoting expressions to denote. It is at least unplausible to say that there exist objects denoted by the phrase 'round squares'; there is self-contra-diction in saying that there exists a class which is a member of itself on condition that it is not, and *vice versa*.

Russell had already found himself forced to say of some expres-sions which had previously been supposed to name or denote, that they had to be given exceptional treatment. They were not names but what he called 'incomplete symbols', expressions, that is, which have no meaning, in the sense of denotation, by themselves; their business was to be auxiliary to expressions which do, as a whole, denote. (This was what Mill had said of the syncategorematic words.) The very treatment which had since the Middle Ages been given to such little words as 'and', 'not', 'the', 'some' and 'is' was now given to some other kinds of expressions as well. In effect, though not explicitly, Russell was saying that, e.g. descriptive phrases were as syncategorematic as 'not', 'and' and 'is' had always been allowed to be. Here Russell was on the brink of allowing that the meanings or significations of many kinds of expressions are matters not of *naming* things, but of *saying* things. But he was, I think, still held up by the idea that saying is itself just another variety of naming, i.e. naming a complex or an 'objective' or a proposition or a fact — some sort of postulated *Fido rationis*.

He took a new and most important further step to cope with the paradoxes, like that of the class of classes that are not members of themselves. For he now wielded a distinction, which Mill had seen but left inert, the distinction between sentences which are either true or false on the one hand, and on the other hand sentences which, though proper in vocabulary and syntax, are none the less nonsensical, meaningless or absurd; and therefore neither true nor false. To assert them and to deny them are to assert and deny nothing. For reasons of a sort which are the proper concern of logic, certain sorts of concatenations of words and phrases into sentences produce things which cannot be significantly said. For example, the very question Is the class of all classes which are not members of themselves a member of itself or not? has no answer. Russell's famous 'Theory of Types' was an attempt to formulate the reasons of logic which make it an improper question. We need not consider whether he was successful. What matters for us, and what made the big difference to subsequent philosophy, is the fact that at long last the notion of meaning was realized to be, at least in certain crucial contexts, the obverse of the notion of the nonsensical — what can be said, truly or falsely, is at last contrasted with what cannot be significantly said. The notion of meaning had been, at long last, partly detached from the notion of naming and re-attached to the notion of saying. It was recognized to belong to, or even to constitute the domain which had always been the province of logic; and as it is at least part of the official business of logic to establish and codify rules, the notion of meaning came now to be seen as somehow compact of rules. To know what an expression means involves knowing what can (logically) be said with it and what cannot (logically) be said with it. It involves knowing a set of bans, fiats and obligations, or, in a word, it is to know the rules of the employment of that expression.

It was, however, not Russell but Wittgenstein who first generalized or half-generalized this crucial point. In the *Tractatus Logico-Philosophicus*, which could be described as the first book to be written on the philosophy of logic, Wittgenstein still had one foot in the denotationist camp, but his other foot was already free. He saw and said, not only what had been said before, that the little words, the so-called logical constants, 'not', 'is', 'and' and the rest do not stand for objects, but also, what Plato had also said before, that sentences are not names. Saying is not naming. He realized, as Frege had done, that logicians' questions are not questions about the properties or relations of the *denotata*, if any, of the expressions which enter into the sentences whose logic is under examination. He saw, too, that all the words and phrases that can enter into sentences are governed by the rules of what he called, slightly metaphorically, 'logical syntax' or 'logical grammar'. These rules are what are broken by such concatenations of words and phrases as result in nonsense. Logic is or includes the study of these rules. Husserl had at the beginning of the century employed much the same notion of 'logical grammar.'

It was only later still that Wittgenstein consciously and de-liberately withdrew his remaining foot from the denotationist camp. When he said 'Don't ask for the meaning, ask for the use', he was imparting a lesson which he had had to teach to himself after he had finished with the *Tractatus*. The use of an expression, or the concept it expresses, is the rôle it is employed to perform, not any thing or person or event for which it might be supposed to stand. Nor is the purchasing power of a coin to be equated with this book or that car-ride which might be bought with it. The purchasing power of a coin has not got pages or a terminus. Even more instructive is the analogy which Wittgenstein now came to draw between significant expressions and the pieces with which are played games like chess. The significance of an expression and the powers or functions in chess of a pawn, a knight or the queen have much in common. To know what the knight can and cannot do, one must know the rules of chess, as well as be familiar with various kinds of chess-situations which may arise. What the knight may do cannot be read out of the material or shape of the piece of ivory or boxwood or tin of which this knight may be made. Similarly to know what an expression means is to know how it may and may not be employed, and the rules governing its employment can be the same for expressions of very different physical compositions. The word 'horse' is not a bit like the word 'cheval'; but the way of wielding them is the same. They have the same rôle, the same sense. Each is a translation of the other. Certainly the rules of the uses of expressions are unlike the rules of games in some important respects. We can be taught the rules of chess up to a point before we begin to play. There are manuals of chess, where there are not manuals of significance. The rules of chess, again, are completely definite and inelastic. Questions of whether a rule has been broken or not are decidable without debate. Moreover we opt to play chess and can stop when we like, where we do not opt to talk and think and cannot opt to break off. Chess is a diversion. Speech and thought are not only diversions. But still the partial assimilation of the meanings of expressions to the powers or the values of the pieces with which a game is played is enormously revealing. There is no temptation to suppose that a knight is proxy for anything, or that learning what a knight may or may not do is learning that it is a deputy for some ulterior entity. We could not learn to play the knight correctly without having learned to play the other pieces, nor can we learn to play a word by itself, but only in combination with other words and phrases.

Besides this, there is a further point which the assimilation brings out. There are six different kinds of chess-pieces, with their six different kinds of rôles in the game. We can imagine more complex games involving twenty or two hundred kinds of pieces. So it is with languages. In contrast with the denotationist assumption that almost all words, all phrases and even all sentences are alike in having the one rôle of naming, the assimilation of language to chess reminds us of what we knew *ambulando* all along, the fact that there are indefinitely many kinds of words, kinds of phrases, and kinds of sentences — that there is an indefinitely large variety of kinds of rôles performed by the expressions we use in saying things. Adjectives do not do what adverbs do, nor do all adjectives do the same sort of thing as one another. Some nouns are proper names, but most are not. The sorts of things that we do with sentences are different from the sorts of things that we do with most single words — and some sorts of things that we can significantly do with some sorts of sentences, we cannot significantly do with others. And so on.

There is not one basic mould, such as the 'Fido'-Fido mould, into which all significant expressions are to be forced. On the contrary, there is an endless variety of categories of sense or meaning. Even the *prima facie* simple notion of naming or denoting itself turns out on examination to be full of internal variegations. Pronouns are used to denote people and things, but not in the way in which proper names do so. No one is *called* 'he' or 'she'. 'Saturday' is a proper name, but not in the same way as 'Fido' is a proper name — and neither is used in the way in which the fictional proper name 'Mr. Pickwick' is used. The notion of denotation, so far from providing the final explanation of the notion of meaning, turns out itself to be just one special branch or twig on the tree of signification. Expressions do not mean because they denote things; some expressions denote things, in one or another of several different manners, because they are significant. Meanings are not things, not even very queer things. Learning the meaning of an expression is more like learning a piece of drill than like coming across a previously unencountered object. It is learning to operate correctly with an expression and with any other expression equivalent to it.

(2) *The Theory of Philosophy*. I now want to trace, rather more cursorily, the other main motive from which thinkers have posed the abstract question What are meanings? or What is it for an expression to have a certain sense?

Until fairly recently philosophers have not often stepped back from their easels to consider what philosophy is, or how doing philosophy differs from doing science, or doing theology, or doing mathematics. Kant was the first modern thinker to see or try to answer this question — and a very good beginning of an answer he gave; but I shall not expound his answer here.

This question did not begin seriously to worry the general run of philosophers until maybe sixty years ago. It began to become obsessive only after the publication of the *Tractatus*. Why did the philosophy of philosophy start so late, and how did it come to start when and as it did?

It is often not realized that the words 'philosophy' and 'philosopher' and their equivalents in French and German had for a long time much less specific meanings than they now possess. During the seventeenth, the eighteenth and most of the nineteenth centuries a 'philosopher' was almost any sort of a *savant*. Astronomers, chemists and botanists were called 'philosophers' just as much as were Locke, Berkeley or Hume. Descartes's philosophy covered his contributions to optics just as much as his contributions to epistemology. In English there existed for a long time no special word for the people we now call 'scientists'. This noun was deliberately coined only in 1840, and even then it took some time to catch on. His contemporaries could not call Newton a 'scientist', since there was no such word. When a distinction had to be made, it was made by distinguishing 'natural philosophy' from 'moral' and 'metaphysical philosophy'. As late as 1887, Conan Doyle, within two or three pages of one story, describes Sherlock Holmes as being totally ignorant of philosophy, as we use the word now, and yet as having his room full of philosophical, i.e. scientific, instruments, like test-tubes, retorts and balances. A not very

R

ancient Oxford Chair of Physics still retains its old label, the Chair of Experimental Philosophy.

Different from this quite important piece of etymological history is the fact that both in Scotland and in England there existed from perhaps the time of Hartley to that of Sidgwick and Bradley a strong tendency to suppose that the distinction between natural philosophy, i.e. physical and biological science on the one hand and metaphysical and moral philosophy, perhaps including logic, on the other, was that the latter were concerned with internal, mental phenomena, where the former were concerned with external, physical phenomena. Much of what we now label 'philosophy', *sans phrase*, was for a long time and by many thinkers confidently, but quite wrongly equated with what we now call 'psychology'. John Stuart Mill sometimes, but not always, uses even the grand word 'metaphysics' for the empirical study of the workings of men's minds. Protests were made against this equation particularly on behalf of philosophical theology, but for a long time the anti-theologians had it their own way. A philosopher, *sans phrase*, was a Mental and Moral Scientist — a scientist who was exempted from working in the laboratory or the observatory only because his specimens were collected at home by introspection. Even Mansel, himself a philosophical theologian with a good Kantian equipment, maintained that the science of mental phenomena, what we call 'psychology', was the real basis of even ontological or theological speculations.

So not only did the wide coverage of the word 'philosophy' encourage people not to look for any important differences between what scientists, as we now call them, do and what philosophers, as we now call them, do; but even when such differences were looked for, they were apt to be found in the differences between the investigation of physical phenomena by the laboratory scientist and the investigation of psychological phenomena by the introspecting psychologist.

As I see it, three influences were chiefly responsible for the collapse of the assumption that doing philosophy, in our sense, is of a piece with doing natural science or at least of a piece with doing mental science or psychology.

First, champions of mathematics like Frege, Husserl and Russell had to save mathematics from the combined empiricism and psychologism of the school of John Stuart Mill. Mathematical truths are not mere psychological generalizations; equations are not mere records of deeply rutted associations of ideas; the objects of geometry are not of the stuff of which mental images are made. Pure mathematics is a non-inductive and a non-introspective science. Its proofs are rigorous, its terms are exact, and its theorems are universal and not merely highly general truths. The proofs and the theorems of Formal or Symbolic Logic share these dignities with the proofs and theorems of mathematics. So, as logic was certainly a part of philosophy, not all of philosophy could be ranked as 'mental science'. There must, then, be a field or realm besides those of the material and the mental; and at least part of philosophy is concerned with this third realm, the realm of non-material and also non-mental 'logical objects' — such objects as concepts, truths, falsehoods, classes, numbers and implications.

Next, armchair mental science or introspective psychology itself began to yield ground to experimental, laboratory psychology. Psychologists like James began to put themselves to school under the physiologists and the statisticians. Scientific psychology began first to rival and then to oust both *à priori* and introspective psychology, and the tacit claim of epistemologists, moral philosophers and logicians to be mental scientists had to be surrendered to those who used the methods and the tools of the reputable sciences. So the question raised its head What then were the objects of the inquiries of epistemologists, moral philosophers and logicians, if they were not, as had been supposed, psychological states and processes? It is only in our own days that, anyhow in most British Universities, psychologists have established a Faculty of their own separate from the Faculty of Philosophy.

Thirdly, Brentano, reinforcing from medieval sources a point made and swiftly forgotten by Mill, maintained as an *a priori* principle of psychology itself, that it is of the essence of mental states and processes that they are *of* objects or contents. Somewhat as in grammar a transitive verb requires an accusative, so in the field of ideas, thoughts and feelings, acts of consciousness are directed upon their own metaphorical accusatives. To see is to see something, to regret is to regret something, to conclude or suppose is to conclude or suppose that something is the case. Imagining is one thing, the thing imagined, a centaur, say, is another. The centaur has the body of a horse and does not exist. An act of imagining a centaur does exist and does not have the body of a horse. Your act of supposing that Napoleon defeated Wellington is different from my act of supposing it; but what we suppose is the same and is what is expressed by our common expression 'that Napoleon defeated Wellington'. What is true of mental acts is, in general, false of their accusatives or 'intentional objects', and *vice versa.*

Brentano's two pupils, Meinong and Husserl, happened, for different reasons, to be especially, though not exclusively, interested in applying this principle of intentionality or transitivity to the intellectual, as distinct from the sensitive, volitional or affective acts of consciousness. They set out, that is, to rectify the Locke-Hume-Mill accounts of abstraction, conception, memory, judgment, supposal, inference and the rest, by distinguishing in each case, the various private, momentary and repeatable acts of conceiving, remembering, judging, supposing and inferring from their public, non-momentary accusatives, namely, the concepts, the propositions and the implications which constituted their objective correlates. Where Frege attacked psychologistic accounts of thinking from the outside, they attacked them from the inside. Where Frege argued, for instance, that numbers have nothing psychological or, of course, physical about them, Husserl and Meinong argued that for the mental processes of counting and calculating to be what they are, they must have accusatives or objects numerically and qualitatively other than those processes themselves. Frege said that Mill's account of mathematical entities was false because psychological; Husserl and Meinong, in effect, said that the psychology itself was false because non-'intentional' psychology. The upshot, however, was much the same. With different axes to grind, all three came to what I may crudely dub 'Platonistic' conclusions. All three maintained the doctrine of a third realm of non-physical, non-psychological entities, in which realm

dwelled such things as concepts, numbers, classes and propositions.

Husserl and Meinong were both ready to lump together all
these accusatives of thinking alike under the comprehensive title
of Meanings (*Bedeutungen*), since what I think is what is conveyed by the words, phrases or sentences in which I express what
I think. The 'accusatives' of my ideas and my judgings are the
meanings of my words and my sentences. It easily followed from
this that both Husserl and Meinong, proud of their newly segre-
gated third realm, found that it was this realm which provided a
desiderated subject-matter peculiar to logic and philosophy and
necessarily ignored by the natural sciences, physical and psychological. Mental acts and states are the subject-matter of psychology.
Physical objects and events are the subject-matter of the physical
and biological sciences. It is left to philosophy to be the science of
this third domain which consists largely, though not entirely, of
thought-objects or Meanings — the novel and impressive entities
which had been newly isolated for separate investigation by the
application of Brentano's principle of intentionality to the specifically intellectual or cognitive acts of consciousness.

Thus, by the first decade of this century it was dawning upon
philosophers and logicians that their business was not that of one
science among others, e.g. that of psychology; and even that it was
not an inductive, experimental or observational business of any
sort. It was intimately concerned with, among other things, the
fundamental concepts and principles of mathematics; and it
seemed to have to do with a special domain which was not be-
spoken by any other discipline, namely the so-called third realm of
logical objects or Meanings. At the same time, and in some degree
affected by these influences, Moore consistently and Russell spas-
modically were prosecuting their obviously philosophical and
logical inquiries with a special *modus operandi*. They, and not they
alone, were deliberately and explicitly trying to give analyses of
concepts and propositions — asking What does it really mean to
say, for example, that this is good? or that that is true? or that centaurs do not exist? or that I see an inkpot? or What are the differences between the distinguishable senses of the verb 'to know' and

the verb 'to be'? Moore's regular practice and Russell's frequent practice seemed to exemplify beautifully what, for example, Husserl and Meinong had declared in general terms to be the peculiar business of philosophy and logic, namely to explore the third realm of Meanings. Thus philosophy had acquired a right to live its own life, neither as a discredited pretender to the status of the science of mind, nor yet as a superannuated handmaiden of *démodé* theology. It was responsible for a special field of facts, facts of impressively Platonized kinds.

Before the first world war discussions of the status and rôle of philosophy *vis-à-vis* the mathematical and empirical sciences were generally cursory and incidental to discussions of other matters. Wittgenstein's *Tractatus* was a complete treatise dedicated to fixing the position mainly of Formal Logic but also, as a necessary corollary, the position of general philosophy. It was this book which made dominant issues of the theory of logic and the theory of philosophy. In Vienna some of its teachings were applied polemically, namely to demolishing the pretensions of philosophy to be the science of transcendent realities. In England, on the whole, others of its teachings were applied more constructively, namely to stating the positive functions which philosophical propositions perform, and scientific propositions do not perform. In England, on the whole, interest was concentrated on Wittgenstein's description of philosophy as an activity of clarifying or elucidating the meanings of the expressions used, e.g. by scientists; that is, on the medicinal virtues of his account of the nonsensical. In Vienna, on the whole, interest was concentrated on the lethal potentialities of Wittgenstein's account of nonsense. In both places, it was realized that the criteria between the significant and the nonsensical needed to be systematically surveyed, and that it was for the philosopher and not the scientist to survey them.

At this point, the collapse of the denotationist theory of meaning began to influence the theory of philosophy as the science of Platonized Meanings. If the meaning of an expression is not an entity denoted by it, but a style of operation performed with it, not a nominee but a rôle, then it is not only repellent but positively misleading to speak as if there existed a Third Realm whose denizens are Meanings. We can distinguish this knight, as a piece of ivory, from the part it or any proxy for it may play in a game of chess; but the part it may play is not an extra entity, made of some mysterious non-ivory. There is not one box housing the ivory chessmen and another queerer box housing their functions in chess games. Similarly we can distinguish an expression as a set of syllables from its employment. A quite different set of syllables may have the same employment. But its use or sense is not an additional substance or subject of predication. It is not a non-physical, non-mental object — but not because it is either a physical or a mental object, but because it is not an object. As it is not an object, it is not a denizen of a Platonic realm of objects. To say, therefore, that philosophy is the science of Meanings, though not altogether wrong, is liable to mislead in the same way as it might mislead to say that economics is the science of exchange-values. This, too, is true enough, but to word this truth in this way is liable to make people suppose that the Universe houses, under different roofs, commodities and coins here and exchange-values over there.

Hence, following Wittgenstein's lead, it has become customary to say, instead, that philosophical problems are linguistic problems — only linguistic problems quite unlike any of the problems of philology, grammar, phonetics, rhetoric, prosody, etc., since they are problems about the logic of the functionings of expressions. Such problems are so widely different from, e.g. philological problems, that speaking of them as linguistic problems is, at the moment, as Wittgenstein foresaw, misleading people as far in one direction, as speaking of them as problems about Meanings or Concepts or Propositions had been misleading in the other direction. The difficulty is to steer between the Scylla of a Platonistic and the Charybdis of a lexicographical account of the business of philosophy and logic.

There has been and perhaps still is something of a vogue for saying that doing philosophy consists in analysing meanings, or analysing the employments of expressions. Indeed, from Transatlantic journals I gather that at this very moment British philosophy is dominated by some people called 'linguistic analysts'. The word 'analysis' has, indeed, a good laboratory or Scotland

Yard ring about it; it contrasts well with such expressions as 'speculation', 'hypothesis', 'system-building' and even 'preaching' and 'writing poetry'. On the other hand it is a hopelessly misleading word in some important respects. It falsely suggests, for one thing, that any sort of careful elucidation of any sorts of complex or subtle ideas will be a piece of philosophizing; as if the judge, in explaining to the members of the jury the differences between manslaughter and murder, was helping them out of a philosophical quandary. But, even worse, it suggests that philosophical problems are like the chemist's or the detective's problems in this respect, namely that they can and should be tackled piecemeal. Finish problem A this morning, file the answer, and go on to problem B this afternoon. This suggestion does violence to the vital fact that philosophical problems inevitably interlock in all sorts of ways. It would be patently absurd to tell someone to finish the problem of the nature of truth this morning, file the answer and go on this afternoon to solve the problem of the relations between naming and saying, holding over until tomorrow problems about the concepts of existence and non-existence. This is, I think, why at the present moment philosophers are far more inclined to liken their task to that of the cartographer than to that of the chemist or the detective. It is the foreign relations, not the domestic constitutions of sayables that engender logical troubles and demand logical arbitration.

STUART HAMPSHIRE

The Interpretation of Language:
Words and Concepts

Stuart Hampshire, m.a. (Oxon.), f.b.a. Professor of Philosophy, Princeton University: born October 1st, 1914; educated at Repton and Balliol College; elected Fellow of All Souls College, 1936; Lecturer in Philosophy, Oxford, 1936-39; served in the Army during the war, and in the Foreign Office immediately after the war; Lecturer in Philosophy, University College, London, 1948-51; Fellow of New College, Oxford, 1951-55; Research Fellow and Domestic Bursar of All Souls College, Oxford, 1955-59; Grote Professor of Philosophy of Mind and Logic in the University of London, 1960-63.

Chief publications: *Spinoza*, 1950; *Thought and Action*, 1959; *Feeling and Expression* (Inaugural Lecture), 1960. Various articles in *Mind*, *Proceedings of the Aristotelian Society*, and other philosophical journals.

STUART HAMPSHIRE

THE INTERPRETATION OF LANGUAGE: WORDS AND CONCEPTS

THERE are many languages, constantly changing and widely different from each other, not only in vocabulary, but also in structure. It would be a mistake to think of Language, with a capital L, as some Platonic ideal language to which actual languages in different degrees approximate. Different languages have enough in common, as signalling systems, and serve sufficiently similar purposes in social behaviour, to make us call them languages. But we do not in philosophy need to state precisely what are the necessary and sufficient conditions for calling a signalling system a language; for we are not particularly concerned with defining the word 'language'. Nor are we concerned with a systematic classification of the different grammatical forms of language; the interest of contemporary philosophers in forms of speech neither is, nor should be, scientific or systematic. They describe the use of particular idioms in particular languages, and the adaptation of the idioms to particular purposes, only as instances of different functions in speech; and the instances are not selected as evidence in support of some generalization about Language; there is no serious attempt to arrive by induction at a list of ultimate categories or ultimate functions of language. (Philosophy is not an inductive inquiry; its statements of fact are the citation of examples, not the production of evidence.) This painstaking description of actual, contemporary English or German idiom has so far had a largely negative and destructive purpose: to upset philosophical preconceptions about the necessary forms and functions of language, particularly the preconceptions of Hume and Mill and Russell. No positive conclusions about the necessary forms of language could properly be based on such narrow and haphazard investigations. Perhaps it may sometimes seem that the linguistic analysts are themselves deceived, and that they have some preconceptions of their own about the necessary and universal forms of language. They sometimes write as if there were just so many statable functions which language must fulfil, or (worse) they sometimes write as if all languages must be intertranslatable dialects of the Platonic ideal language. With unacknowledged provincialism, they seem sometimes to be generalizing about a whole range of discourse on the basis of a few contemporary idioms. They sometimes ignore the history of the concepts which they examine, where a 'concept' is a whole family of related idioms taken together. Every concept has a history, and the clearest way of introducing the concept is to trace its history, the changes through which it has passed, as old idioms drop out and new idioms come in. If philosophers were positively and primarily interested in describing and distinguishing the different uses of language, as they sometimes now claim that they are, they would be historians before all else; but they are conspicuously not historians. They are in fact content with a haphazard selection of instances from any one field of discourse, because, whether they acknowledge it or not, they are generally making a negative point — that the discourse of the kind examined does not serve the purposes which previous philosophers had implied that it must serve.

Ambiguity of purpose in linguistic analysis might mislead philosophers seriously; they might step outside the purely negative conclusions, and try to deduce philosophical conclusions from the description of a few English idioms. I will give two examples of how this mistake may be made:

(a) In the characterization of moral judgments;

(b) In the characterization of mental concepts, and in recent discussions of the concept of mind.

In learning a language, which is part of a civilization largely different from one's own, one would expect to be able to pick out a class of utterances which play a part in social behaviour analogous to the part played in our own behaviour by what we call moral judgments; and one would also expect, with rather less confidence, that there would be sentence-forms which occupy, within this unfamiliar language, some place analogous to the place occupied by ought-sentences, or by quasi-imperative or (perhaps) gerundive forms, in English or Latin. If both these expectations were correct and there was this identifiable class of utterances having some distinguishing grammar of its own, it still would not follow that our moral judgments would be translatable, in any ordinary sense of 'translation', into the strangers' language, or that theirs would be translatable into ours. We might have to say that they had a central concept (e.g. of 'virtue') which we had not got, and that they did not have our corresponding concept of 'virtue', i.e. the concept which would seem to have the nearest corresponding place in our terminology. We might learn to understand their language, in the sense of being able to use it in full communication with them, producing the appropriate expressions in the appropriate situations; we should so far have entered into their manner of thought and into their way of classifying and assessing human behaviour. Partly because we understood their idioms so well, in this ordinary sense of 'understand', we might see that it was impossible to find any equivalents in our own store of moral terms for those expressions which we have singled out as their moral terms; when we lay one language over the other, as a piece of tracing paper, we find that the lines and divisions do not sufficiently coincide at any point. To take a comparatively trivial and easy example: we find this non-correspondence even in Greek discussions of 'virtue', and we find it wherever no distinction of any kind is marked between the moral and natural qualities of persons. A choice is then presented: we may say, if we choose, that the users of this language have a radically different morality from ours, that their moral views and attitudes are altogether different: or we may say that, strictly speaking, they do not make what can properly be called moral judgments at all. It is not incorrect to take the first alternative, provided this kind of difference of moral view is distinguished from the difference of view which is adopted, as a matter of choice and reflection, within a common terminology providing for the expression of other views. And it is not incorrect to take the second, or Kantian alternative, provided that it is made plain that 'moral judgment' is not now being used to single out a speech-function, and is no longer on the same level as 'factual statement', 'command', 'recommendation', etc. It is of little importance for philosophers to decide what makes a moral judgment a moral judgment, that is, to settle the necessary and sufficient conditions for the use of the *expression* 'moral judgment'. But it has been useful, again negatively, to insist that we would in any language single out a class of utterances as moral judgments at least partly on the ground that they are used to prescribe or recommend conduct, where the conduct is not directed towards some given end. This characterization of moral judgments as essentially prescriptive or quasi-imperative is not (or should not be) intended to be precise — indeed the explicatory terms are themselves vague in their application. It is intended solely to counter certain accounts which previous philosophers had given or implied of the use and function of moral judgments. It was a denial of the assumption that they must function in those ways, and in accordance with that logic, which current philosophies recognized; it was negative only, a warning against a false assimilation.

But we are seriously misled if we begin to generalize about the nature of moral judgment on the basis of some examination of the form of our own arguments on moral questions; for then it will seem that there cannot be very different terminologies in which recognizably moral questions (questions of 'What is it, or was it, right to do?'), can be discussed. Here again some study of history is needed in order to engender a decent scepticism. Examination of idioms, and forms of argument, used in current moral discussion, cannot by itself lead to any positive answer to any question posed in moral philosophy; at the most it can lead to an historically interesting description of one conventional morality. It is possible for someone fully to understand, and to be able to use correctly, the idioms of conventional morality, while rejecting this whole terminology as superstitious or as in some other way inadequate. For instance, he may fully understand, in the ordinary sense of 'understand', the familiar Protestant-Christian notion of personal responsibility, and the distinction now conventionally accepted between the moral and the natural qualities of persons. He may be able always to apply this distinction correctly in particular cases, and he may be able to state in general terms how the line of distinction is ordinarily drawn, that is, to give an analysis of the notion of moral responsibility as it now occurs in ordinary language. But he may at the same time consider that the distinction itself is untenable, when all its implications are traced to the end; he may even intelligibly deny that there is such a thing as personal responsibility, while admitting that he understands the ordinary rules of application of the term. He is then in a position similar to (but not the same as) that of the anthropologist, or the student of comparative religion, who learns to use and to understand a language, or part of a language, while denying that many of the distinctions and classifications involved in the language correspond to any reality.

It is not possible consistently to maintain both of the following two propositions: (1) that to understand an expression is to be able to use the expression correctly, and to recognize the standard occasions of its use: and (2) that existential statements have no place among philosophical conclusions, philosophy being solely concerned to analyse the actual meanings of terms in use. One may deny proposition (1), and give reasons for saying that many expressions which have, or have had, an easily recognizable and statable use in this or that language, are strictly meaningless. This was the paradoxical way of the earlier positivists. Alternatively, one may allow that arguments on philosophical questions, arguments which are in no ordinary sense empirical, may properly terminate in existential statements of the form — 'there are no so-and-so's'. This seems to me the more honest and less misleading way out of the dilemma, and certainly it involves no departure from ordinary usage; for this is the form of statement which has generally been used in repudiating a concept. Entirely unrestricted and unqualified existential statements of the form 'There are no so-and-so's' are perhaps uncommon, but their characteristic use is in expressing quasi-philosophical conclusions: 'There is no God' or 'There are no entirely disinterested actions' or 'There is no such thing as sin'. Many examples could be cited, in which the unrestricted existential form is commonly used to repudiate the use of a concept, or of a distinction, on grounds which are not in any simple sense empirical. The step from these quasi-philosophical existential statements to strictly philosophical conclusions is much smaller than the step from 'meaningless' (ordinary use) to 'meaningless' (philosophical use). A man who understands and can explain what is ordinarily meant by 'sin' cannot properly say that the word is meaningless. But he can properly say that there is no such thing as sin. He is not objecting to the *word*, as having no established place in the vocabulary, and no recognized conditions of use; he is objecting to the concept, that is, to the customary application of the whole set of distinctions which are involved in the use of the word. To reject a concept is to reject a whole system of classification as in one way or another inadequate; and the sufficient grounds for the rejection cannot be given without some comparison between different terminologies and systems of classification, a comparison which involves stepping outside any one terminology, and contrasting its method of application with that of some other. A description of the actual use of any one terminology cannot by itself yield an answer to any problem of moral philosophy, since the problem always lies in the choice, and in the grounds of choice, between different terminologies. Methods of classifying, assessing and prescribing human conduct, with the patterns of argument which support the assessments and prescriptions, come into being and disappear in history one after the other, and they are often mutually exclusive. The lines drawn cannot always be made to coincide and translations are not always possible; we have to find grounds for thinking and talking in one set of idioms rather than another. A moral philosopher must to this extent moralize himself, or he will be confined to the purely negative work of indicating the difference between moral judgments and judgments of other kinds.

The concept of mind has a long and various history, extending through many languages; it is a history which it would be difficult to write, even if one were confined to Greek, Latin, French, German and English. The outlines of the concept of mind have largely changed in the last fifty years, even more largely since Descartes wrote on the passions of the soul, or since Hume wrote on the sentiments and passions. Mind, motive, passion, sentiment, character, mood, heart, soul, temperament, spirit — these are words for which there have at many times been no translations in other languages, or which have radically changed their meanings in complicated ways. The conception of human beings as having master passions, and constant dispositions, has come into being and passed away more than once. The concept of will, or a concept closely related to it, has existed at some time in some languages, and at other times and in other languages it has not existed at all in any easily recognizable form. There have been times and phases in the history of some languages, when states of mind were conceived as entities easily and definitely identified and labelled, very much as physical things are identified and labelled. Our whole conception of personality, and of the limits of self-knowledge and of knowledge of the minds of others, has changed often, and will certainly change again. Regarded as linguistic analysis, Descartes's and Hume's discussions of the concept of mind are largely out of date; and, regarded as linguistic analysis, Professor Ryle's discussion will soon seem out of date also. But through all the phases of its history, the concept of mind preserves some rough continuity; there is something common to the various different vocabularies which have been used to talk about human personality and experience. Just as there are largely different moral terminologies, which yet form a single type of discourse, to be called 'moral', so one can speak of different conceptions of human personality as conveyed in different vocabularies. A philosopher may be concerned, not to clarify the conventions of use of any one vocabulary, but rather to take instances to show the conditions of use of any such vocabulary; if so, the proper title of this work is 'The Concept of Mind', and not the word 'mind'. Professor Ryle, like Descartes and Hume before him, takes examples from the contemporary English vocabulary to illustrate the requirements which any such vocabulary must satisfy in its application. His philosophical thesis consists of the statement of these requirements, in direct opposition to the conditions of application which Descartes and Hume insist upon. This is where their philosophical difference lies — that

s

they each have a pattern, a different one, of the conditions under which statements can be confirmed, and expressions applied, with the greatest possible confidence and clarity; and they compare and criticize the actual use of psychological expressions by reference to this standard. From this comparison emerges a general thesis about the proper outlines of the concept of mind. But I must first explain what I mean by the conditions of application of an expression.

To understand an expression in common use involves being able to recognize the standard occasions of its use, and the normal way to explain its meaning is to give specimens of these standard occasions. For every element of the vocabulary of a language which we understand, we could describe some conditions which would be the ideal conditions for the application of the expression in question; we could also describe some contrasting conditions in which its application would have to be qualified as dubious and uncertain. When we have described the conditions of certainty and uncertainty, we have given the conventions of application for the expression in question. One can draw the outlines of the concept of mind, as it is embodied at any one time in any one language, by giving the conventions of application (the method of verification in this sense) of a whole cluster of expressions in the vocabulary; this would so far be a purely descriptive and historical work (e.g. The Greek concept of the soul — The concept of the passions in the eighteenth century). But a more fundamental inquiry may suggest itself: among all the different types of expression in the present vocabulary — descriptions of states of mind, of sensations, dispositions, processes of thought and many others — there are some that seem, in the conventions of their application, entirely clear and unproblematical; for the conditions of certainty in the application of them are not peculiar and have evident parallels in other familiar and unquestioned kinds of discourse; for this reason they do not provoke doubt or philosophical scepticism. There are other types of expression which seem to have altogether peculiar conditions of certainty, without parallel outside this one kind of discourse; and it is at this point that philosophical scepticism and inquiry begins. 'Can we ever be really certain that anything is a so-and-so? When we claim to know, do we really know?' In any period there is a tendency to take one method of confirmation, appropriate to some one type of expression, as the self-explanatory model to which all other types of expression are to be assimilated. To Hume a direct description of a feeling or sensation seemed the type of expression which, in the standard conditions of its use, provided the model of certain knowledge; the different conditions of certainty appropriate to expressions of other types seemed to him open to challenge; it seemed to him that there could not be any certainty comparable with the certainty attached to the description of a sensation. In some contemporary philosophy the model of certainty has become almost exactly the reverse of Hume's. The conditions of certainty appropriate to descriptions of sensations seem problematical and peculiar, the model being descriptions of the behaviour of bodies; therefore a contrary thesis is developed, which tries to assimilate the conditions of certainty for descriptions of sensations to the conditions of certainty appropriate to descriptions of bodily behaviour. The philosophical thesis in each case consists in the assimilation of the different methods of confirmation in actual use to some single self-explanatory pattern. In the ordinary use of language, and until philosophical doubts arise, every type of description in any language is accepted as having its own appropriate conditions of certainty and its own appropriate method of confirmation. The philosophical doubt takes the form of a more general comparison of the degrees of certainty obtainable in the use of different expressions, a comparison which deliberately cuts across the divisions of type. A philosopher in effect says: 'I know of course that these are the conditions which are ordinarily taken as the standard conditions for the use of expressions of this type: but can we ever be certain about the application of any expression of this type, in the sense in which we can have certainty in the application of expressions of this other type?' In asking this question, he is in effect challenging the accepted rules of application for the family of expressions considered; he is suggesting that the concept is otiose, since, when we reflect, we realize that there is no satisfactory way of determining whether something falls under the concept or not. It is a mistake, in exaggerated respect for established usage, to represent this form of scepticism as a pointless eccentricity of philosophers. Even outside philosophy we do make these comparisons between the certainty which can be obtained in the application of expressions of different types, and we do sometimes become dissatisfied with the vagueness of the conventions of application of a whole range of expressions. The family of expressions then tends to drop out of the language and to be replaced by others, which have clearer and more definite (as it seems) conventions of application; this is the process by which concepts are modified, and which makes their history. One example: I may have learnt to use a vocabulary which permits me to explain human behaviour in terms of a small range of passions, each taken to be definitely identifiable. I might be able to use this vocabulary correctly myself, and be able to distinguish, among statements expressed in these terms, those which are certainly true, given the conventions of the vocabulary, from those which are certainly false. But I might at the same time wish to reject the whole vocabulary, perhaps on the ground that its classifications are 'inadequate to the complexity of the facts'. I know how the passions are conventionally identified, but the identification seems to me too uncertain, when judged by some external standard of certainty which I have taken as a model. I might argue that the conditions under which certainty is conventionally claimed in the application of such expressions do not sufficiently resemble the standard conditions of certainty for expressions of similar type. Even in the more favourable conditions for distinguishing one passion from another, there too often remains a greater possibility of doubt than would be allowed in (for instance) the identification of natural kinds. The proportion of borderline cases to unchallengeable cases is too high, and higher than the form of the statements themselves would suggest. If I am persuaded that, judged by these external standards, no ideally certain case of the identification of a passion exists, or could exist, then I am persuaded that the use of this vocabulary is radically misleading; the concept of simple passions will be discredited. I could correctly express my conviction that the whole terminology is inapplicable by saying that in reality there are no simple passions to be found, and that the facts cannot in general be represented within this framework. Many modern writers, not

mainly philosophers, have in fact wished to make exactly this negative existential statement ('There are no simple passions'), and
their influence, together with the influence of Freudian psychology, has been enough to make the old classifications of motives
almost obsolete over a large range of human conduct: or if not
obsolete, at least suspect, so that in conditions in which the identi-
fications would formerly have been made confidently and without
qualification, they are now made tentatively and with qualifications
and this, if pressed far enough, will amount to a change in the
conditions of use of the expressions, and so will amount to a change
in their meaning. The concept of the passions will no longer be
what it was. Ordinarily sections of the vocabulary become obsolete, and concepts (e.g. the concept of motive) change their outlines, very gradually and without conscious planning or decision;
the conventions of application of expressions of different types are
not explicitly compared, and the scepticism about a particular
range of expressions is felt in practice, rather than worked out in
theory. As soon as scepticism is based on a weighted comparison
between the conditions of certainty attached to expressions of
different types, one has entered the domain of philosophy; this is
the form of argument to be found in Professor Ryle's *Concept of
Mind*, no less than in all his predecessors. And the argument
naturally leads him, for the reasons which I have suggested, to
make unqualified existential statements, e.g. in denying the existence of acts of will or of impalpable mental processes, and in
asserting the existence of hankerings, cravings and itchings. He
has been criticized for expressing any conclusions in an existential
form, on the grounds that no existential conclusions can follow
from a second-order inquiry into the common uses of words. But
the criticism is misplaced, since he is not merely describing the
actual uses of words. He quotes instances of the conventions of
application of different expressions, and then tries to represent
these conventions of application as fitting into a common pattern.
In respect of any expression taken as an example, his first questions always are — 'How do we know when to apply it? What are
the standard and most favourable conditions for its use?' He cir-
cumscribes the permissible uses of psychological expressions by

reference to his own standard of verification. And so he can maintain that there could not be a 'neat sensation' vocabulary, since nothing which he would count as verification, or as certainty in application, would be attached to expressions so used. The conventions of application suggested for a vocabulary of this type diverge too widely from what he takes to be the standard; for he finds this standard of certainty in the conventions governing the use of physical descriptions. He argues his thesis against Hume and Russell by trying to show that, even in apparently recalcitrant cases, the actual conventions of application attached to expressions of different types conform more nearly to his standard than to theirs; and this is the relevance of the instances from ordinary language to the general philosophical thesis. But it remains true that it is a positive thesis, setting up one standard of clear discourse as against another.

In order to define somebody's philosophy, it is enough to discover what existential statements he takes to be unproblematical and in need of no further explanation. And in order to discover what existential statements he takes as unproblematical, it must be enough to discover what kind of discourse provides him with his model of absolute certainty in the use of language — 'this is as certain as anything can be' (e.g. 'as that $2+2=4$', or 'as that I am sitting in this room'). There has always been this connection between the so-called theory of knowledge — i.e. the critical comparison of the conditions of certainty in application attached to expressions of different types — and metaphysics; in fact the two cannot be separated, or even in the end distinguished. Someone who, in exaggerated respect for the common sense of the moment, refuses to make such weighted and critical comparisons, refuses to enter the domain of philosophy. Any vocabulary that we use carries with it its own existential implications; if, applying the actual conventions in use, one distinguishes between true and false statements about acts of will, or about motives, or character, or the soul, it is inevitable that one should sometimes pause to ask whether these conventions provide that kind of certainty in identification which, unreflectingly, we had assumed that they do provide. If, after the comparison, we have lost confidence in our ordinary method of identifying the passions (it was more unlike the standard cases of identification than it seemed), we shall properly say that there are no simple emotions to be identified. This will not imply that there is no difference between what we have counted, by applying the ordinary conventions, as true and as false statements about the passions; it will imply only that the difference between a particular passion existing or not existing was not as sharply marked as we had assumed, before we noticed the enormous possibilities of uncertain and borderline cases and the few possibilities of certain cases. And when we draw attention to this misleadingness, we go beyond the mere plotting of the ordinary uses of words. This plotting is a necessary check upon philosophy, but it is not philosophy itself.

POSTSCRIPT

THIS thesis has been a continuing concern of mine (also '*Are All Philosophical Questions Questions of Language?*' Proc. Arist. Soc. *Supplementary Volume*, 1948, 'Words and Concepts' in *Contemporary British Philosophy*, Allen and Unwin, 1956, and in *Thought and Action*, Chatto and Windus, 1959). I still believe that the main thesis is correct: namely that there are existential (or, as some prefer, ontological) conclusions of typical philosophical arguments. These typical philosophical arguments make comparisons between the conditions of application attached to concepts of widely different types: and by 'conditions of application' I understand the conditions in which certainty can properly be claimed in applying the concepts in question. When the conditions of application, in this sense, attached to a whole set of concepts fall short of a standard of definiteness, the sense of the concepts in question is indeterminate, in comparison with those fully determinate concepts which are taken as a standard. This comparative indeterminacy of sense is a feature of the disputed concepts as they are ordinarily applied; I am assuming that the doubt is not merely a doubt about the correct, established use of an expression, as, for example, when an expression is used in two or more different senses. Rather the correct use is known, but it provokes further doubts about the conditions of and confirmation implied by it. The consequence of indeterminacy is that to propositions asserting the existence of something falling under these concepts we cannot consistently apply the law of excluded middle: we are not in a position to insist — 'Either there is a so-and-so here or there is not'. We are not in a position to say that any proposition involving such concepts must be either true or false. In determining whether so-and-so's are present, we have no method that can yield determinate results, which must be either positive or negative. That this is so may come as a discovery, and typically a philosophical discovery. Common habits of speech, and linguistic analogies, had concealed this indeterminacy from us. Reality is not, as our habits of speech had suggested to us, divided into cases of so-and-so and cases that are not cases of so-and-so.

I would modify, at one important point, the argument, as originally stated. The examples of indeterminate, and therefore disputable, concepts that I chose are mental concepts. But I confused the issue by including moral concepts among them. For these are essentially disputed concepts, and to reject a moral concept is not necessarily to deny the existence of something. The important contrast at this time is between the concepts of the physical sciences, and some, at least, of the mental concepts that we employ in the ordinary transactions of private and public life; this is a fundamental contrast in the present state of our knowledge. The conditions of application of many mental concepts are systematically subject to philosophical dispute. ('In what sense, if any, are there acts of will?' 'In what sense, if any, is there an unconscious mind?') These are philosophical disputes, just because the conditions of application of a whole range of concepts are being assessed on a standard of certainty derived from other disciplines. There is a range of questions of this kind in the philosophy of mind, which are still more speculative than the similar questions in the philosophy of the advanced sciences. Every man's morality and practical policies incorporate assumptions about the existence or non-existence of the will and of the unconscious mind and of dispositions and powers of different types. The truth or falsity of these assumptions, like the truth or falsity of a man's religious opinions, cannot in general be finally established: but they do call for argument. Any clarity and conviction in moral and political philosophy must depend upon arguments of this type.

S. H.

September, 1962.

MARGARET MASTERMAN

Metaphysical and
Ideographic Language

MARGARET MASTERMAN (Mrs. R. B. Braithwaite), M.A. (Cantab.): born 1910, married 1932, son born 1937, daughter 1940; daughter of the Rt. Hon. C. F. G. Masterman, member of Liberal Government of 1906-1914; educated at Hamilton House, Tunbridge Wells, and subsequently at the Sorbonne, Paris; obtained major scholarship in Modern Languages at Newnham College, Cambridge; graduated in Modern Languages and Modern Sciences and was the first woman to hold the Burney Studentship for Philosophy of Religion; became first a professional theatre manager and later organizer of relief work for refugees from Nazi Germany; in 1948 lectured for Cambridge Modern Sciences Faculty, and later became Director of Studies at Fitzwilliam House and St. Catharine's Colleges; Director of Research of Cambridge Language Research Unit.

Chief publications: papers in *The Proceedings of the Aristotelian Society, Semantic Message Detection for a Machine using an Interlingua* (contribution to First International Conference on Machine Translation, 1961), H.M.S.O.; Papers (with W. Haas), on 'Translation' in *Proceedings of the Aristotelian Society,* Joint Session 1961; on 'The Intellect's New Eye' in *The Times Literary Supplement,* 1962; on the 'Guberina Hypothesis' in the *Estratto Rivista Methodos,* 1963; and on 'The Writer and Semantics', *Arena,* 1964. Has also contributed to many non-philosophical journals and has published three novels.

MARGARET MASTERMAN

METAPHYSICAL AND
IDEOGRAPHIC LANGUAGE

IN these two lectures, working within a general conceptual framework of what, in the United States, is called Logical Empiricism,
and in this country, 'the philosophy of language', I propose to
revive the question 'What is metaphysics?'

The purpose of the first lecture is to say that, in that sense of
'discovery' in which alone we can speak of 'a philosophic discovery', the time is now ripe for us to *discover* what metaphysics
is; not *to advance the opinion* as to what metaphysics is. It is the
purpose of this lecture, further, to give reasons for this statement;
and to say, though only in the tersest terms, what kind of thing
metaphysics, so discovered, would have to be.

The purpose of the second lecture, which carries on in more
detail the argument of the first, is to explore, just a little, the metaphysical countryside: to take fugitive, preliminary glimpses of
some metaphysical orderings in language. The argument of the
second lecture is by no means complete, both because the glimpses
of metaphysical orderings given are extremely fragmentary, and
because no formal system is constructed within which, in any
sense, they can be contained. Not only would it be quite out of
place, however, here to provide a complete *basis fundamentaque
linguae metaphysicae*, but also, to do so would take away all suggestive value from the argument itself. For the value of this kind of
suggestive, piecemeal approach to the analysis of any general notion
lies less in what it says than in what it implies. And 'in this case
what is implied is only: 'this *sort of* method of combining symbols, instances of which — once we notice them — surround us

everywhere, is the *sort of* thing metaphysical system-making has nearly always, in the past, turned out to be'.

So the second lecture's argument is not even meant to be complete. Provided always that it is judged to be sufficiently definite for those who do not agree with it to see how to reject it, it will be sufficiently definite also to achieve its end. For this end — at this stage — is merely to enable the essential logical structure of the metaphysical towers dimly to be seen. We look from the suburban viewpoint of the logical empiricist foothills — and we obtain our view mainly by progressively filtering and thus dissipating the stifling, all-pervasive, extrapolated clouds of 'Logical-Positivist' smog.

I. TOWARDS A LOGICAL DEFINITION OF METAPHYSICS

§1: *The Stages of a Philosophic Discovery*

What is it to make a philosophical discovery? Why do some people say, for instance, that certain modern theologians *advance the opinion* that theological facts take place in a supra-polar sphere, while other people say, for instance, that Wittgenstein, following Russell, and independently of Post, *discovered* that all logical and mathematical propositions were tautologies?

Do such people mean merely that, as between two contentions given, they approve the second, and disapprove of the first? I do not think that this is all they do mean, though I think, undoubtedly, that this is part of what they mean. But a man might say, 'Spinoza advanced the opinion that, in the last analysis, there is only one Substance; and personally I agree with him'. In this last case, we should not dispute the speaker's right to agree with Spinoza in this matter; but neither should we wish to say that Spinoza discovered that there was only one Substance. We might, however, very easily wish to say that Spinoza advanced the opinion that there was only one Substance, and that this is an opinion with which many people have agreed.

It seems, then, that making a philosophical discovery may be something different in kind from advancing a philosophical opinion, and not simply something of the same kind, though rather stronger. We feel inclined to say, for instance, in a rough and ready manner, that a man makes an *intellectual* discovery when there is some antecedent scientific or logical problem which (probably by inventing some new logical or mathematical or experimental technique) he *solves*. Why, however, if this is so, do we talk of a *philosophical* discovery? How, on this view, is a philosophical discovery different from, say, a logical or scientific discovery? And if it is not different, why do we behave as though it were by calling it 'philosophical'?

It would take a long time to work out all possible senses in which philosophical 'discoveries' and the uses which are made of them, could be said to be like or unlike logical or scientific ones. Among British philosophers, John Wisdom has made a notable attempt to do something like this in a long paper on G. E. Moore, entitled *Moore's Technique*.[1] Winston Barnes has made a very much less successful attempt in his survey of philosophy entitled *The Philosophical Predicament*.[2] (Other writers have provided a large literature disagreeing with one another on the nature of philosophic propositions, or statements: but they do not stress, in these, the element of discovery.)

I am going to advance here what seems at first sight to be a cynical view that, in fact, a philosophic discovery is usually said to be made when, and only when, the following five intellectual stages occur in the public discussion of any philosophical difficulty. (These five stages need not all occur within the span of the intellectual development of one single philosopher. It is far more likely that they will occur more slowly than that; that is, within the collective span of thinking of a series of philosophers.)

First stage: progressive limitation of the problem. By a general, intuitive, unspoken agreement, a progressively limited problem is substituted for a general philosophical query.

Second stage: Focus upon the problem. The nature of the problem is clarified still further, so that it becomes apparent what kind of technical step would be necessary to solve it.

[1] John Wisdom, *Moore's Technique*. (*The Philosophy of G. E. Moore*, The Library of Living Philosophers, 1944); also reprinted in John Wisdom, *Philosophy and Psycho-Analysis* (Blackwell, 1953).
[2] Winston H. F. Barnes, *The Philosophical Predicament* (Adam and Charles Black, 1950).

Third stage: Solution of the problem. A philosopher takes the technical step which solves the problem.

Fourth stage: The solution is generalized. Having solved the limited problem in a technical manner, the philosopher (or his successors) now proceed to generalize the solution in such a way that it bears on the original philosophical query; even though, once the solution is thus generalized, there is no longer any compelling technical reason, as there was at stage three, for holding that the new generalization is true.

Fifth stage: philosophic public opinion signifies its approval. Although perfectly well aware that the generalization undertaken at stage four removes the cogency from the step undertaken at stage three, yet public opinion still holds that 'somehow or other so-and-so was quite right'; 'by taking the x technical step he solved the problem'; and by doing so 'he made a philosophical discovery'.

Thus Russell — and other philosophers, such as Broad, who have followed Russell — was partly right, but also partly wrong when he said that all philosophical questions, if sufficiently exactly stated, would resolve themselves into separable and technical problems the technical answers to which would finally be found. What Russell should have said (that is, if the general description of philosophical discovery given above is a right one) is that there are certain philosophic situations in which public opinion judges that the solution of a limited, technical problem bears sufficient analogy to the answer to a cognate general philosophical query for the solution of the first to count as the answer to the second. This was the sense in which Wittgenstein discovered that all logical and mathematical propositions are tautologies. And this is the sense in which I hold that recent work done by various English-speaking philosophers should enable us, progressing little by little, to *discover* (taking as already achieved stages one and two of the procedure given above) that metaphysical statements must be taken as statements with a special type of logical structure; and to say — embarking on stage three of this same 'discovery-procedure' — what that special type of logical structure is. Since the assertion that philosophical discovery-procedure is of this nature is thus evidently central to my argument I have documented the stages of Wittgenstein's discovery.[1]

§2: *The progressive limitation of the problem*

Now, given that Wittgenstein, following Russell, has 'discovered' what mathematics is, where are we, in the case of metaphysics? I suggest that we are already well past the stage of making the first limitation of the problem. The first stage in limiting the problem was, actually, to remove it, by saying, as Carnap said and Ayer also said (that Hume and Wittgenstein had already said) that whereas all logical and mathematical propositions gave rules for language-making — that is, though in a widened, generalized

---

[1] In his *Introduction to Mathematical Philosophy*, which was published in May 1919, Russell wrote:

'All the propositions of logic have a characteristic which used to be expressed by saying that they were analytic, or that their contradictories were self-contradictory. This mode of statement, however, is not satisfactory. The law of contradiction is merely one among logical propositions; it has no special pre-eminence; and the proof that the contradictory of some proposition is self-contradictory is likely to require some other principles of deduction besides the law of contradiction. Nevertheless, the characteristic of logical propositions that we are in search of is the one which was felt, and intended to be defined, by those who said that it consisted in deducibility from the law of contradiction. This characteristic ... for the moment we may call tautology....'

The naming of the missing characteristic of logical propositions, made by Russell in the above passage, was the essential step which first turned the general query, as to what logical and mathematical propositions were, into a specific problem which could be solved. This general query had already received its first limitation by the work done by Russell and Whitehead in *Principia Mathematica*. For this work suggested (reversing and elaborating the earlier suggestion made by Boole), that the nature of the propositions of mathematics could be found by looking at the propositions of logic; that, as Russell himself put it, 'logic is the youth of mathematics'.

Once this new limitation had been put on it, the *query* became, and firmly remained, a *problem*. Max Black, for instance, giving the history of the matter in his *Introduction to Carnap's article on The Unity of Science* (published in English in the series of Psyche Miniatures, in 1943) said:

'... The most effective influences on ... [the Logical Positivist] trend of thought were the researches, in Logic and the Foundations of Mathematics, of Russell and others of the "logistic" school (especially through *Principia Mathematica*, 1910). Russell's influence has since been reinforced by Wittgenstein's *Tractatus Logico-Philosophicus* (published in book form in 1922) *which solved one of the major problems of an empiricist outlook by providing a more satisfactory solution of the nature of Logic and Mathematics....*' (Italics mine.)

That it was Wittgenstein, and not himself, who incorporated mathematics into the general empiricist outlook — that is, who took the third step, the technical step, and solved the now doubly limited query which had become a problem — Russell acknowledges again and again. See, particularly, the chapter on 'Mathematics and Logic' in his *Introduction to Mathematical Philosophy* (pp. 204-5) where he says:

'It is clear that the definition of "logic" or "mathematics" must be sought by trying to give a new definition of the old notion of "analytic" propositions. Although we can no longer be satisfied to define logical propositions as those that follow from the law of contradiction, we can and must still admit that they are a wholly different class of propositions from those that we come to know empirically. They all have the characteristic which,

288 BRITISH PHILOSOPHY IN MID-CENTURY

sense, they were tautologies — all metaphysical propositions were gibberish, nonsense; that (taking up the mathematical analogy again) they were just not well-formed formulae in language.

This attempt to remove the problem altogether progressively broke down. To start with, to say this was to make a distortion of the argument of the *Tractatus Logico-philosophicus*; a distortion to be obtained only, as Max Black pointed out, by taking over the second part of the *Tractatus* while rejecting the first.[1] Then an in-

[1] Max Black, *Introduction to Carnap's article on the Unity of Science* (Psyche Miniatures, 1934).

---

a moment ago, we agreed to call "tautology". This, combined with the fact that they can be expressed wholly in terms of variables and logical constants (a logical constant being something which remains constant in a proposition even when all its constituents are changed) will give the definition of logic or pure mathematics. For the moment, I do not know how to define "tautology". . . .

'*Note*. The importance of "tautology" for a definition of mathematics was pointed out to me by my former pupil Ludwig Wittgenstein, who was working on the problem. I do not know whether he has solved it, or even whether he is alive or dead. . . .'

Wittgenstein, however, was not dead, and the technical solution to the now purely technical problem was given by him (as also, independently, by Post), in the *Tractatus Logico-Philosophicus*, first published in 1921. There Wittgenstein defined 'tautology' as follows:

'5.43 . . . Among the possible groups of truth conditions [of elementary and molecular propositions in the propositional calculus] there are two extreme cases.

In the one case the proposition is true for all the truth-possibilities of the elementary propositions. We say that the truth-conditions are *tautological*.

In the second case the proposition is false for all the truth-possibilities. The truth conditions are *self-contradictory*.

In the first case we call the proposition a tautology, in the second case a contradiction. . . .'

'6.1 The propositions of logic are tautologies.'

'6.11 *The propositions of logic therefore say nothing. (They are the analytic propositions.)*. . .' (final italics mine.)

Finally, the solution was generalized. In the last chapter of his *History of Western Philosophy* (1946), Russell made, with widespread public approval, a series of statements of which the final statement (in my italics, below) derives its authority from Wittgenstein's definition of a tautology as a sub-class of propositions within the propositional calculus, but which, in the widened form that all logical knowledge is verbal knowledge, there is no reason whatever to believe. Nevertheless, we feel that Russell is somehow right, in that (somehow or other) a discovery has been made:

'In philosophy ever since the time of Pythagoras there has been an opposition between the men whose thought was mainly inspired by mathematics and those who were more influenced by the empirical sciences . . . In our day [however] a school of philosophy has arisen which sets to work to eliminate Pythagoreanism from the principles of mathematics, and to combine empiricism with an interest in the deductive parts of human knowledge . . . [It has] dethrone[d] mathematics from the lofty place it has occupied since Pythagoras and Plato, and . . . destroy[ed] the presumption against empiricism which has been derived from it. Mathematical knowledge, it is true, is not obtained by induction from experience . . . But it is also not *a priori* knowledge about the world. *It is, in fact, merely verbal knowledge* . . . [Thus] modern analytic empiricism . . . differs from that of Locke, Berkeley and Hume by its incorporation of mathematics and its development of a powerful logical technique. . . .'

numerable cloud of 'metaphysically-minded' philosophers, headed by Urban[1] began pointing out that if, according to the arguments of Ayer's *Language, Truth and Logic*, all metaphysical propositions were gibberish, nonsense, then the arguments of *Language, Truth and Logic* were also gibberish, since, on Ayer's own criteria, these were metaphysical. A not very articulate attempt to answer these attacks led to a distinction being made between important and unimportant nonsense; a distinction which Wittgenstein himself made verbally in his middle period, but against which F. P. Ramsey rightly protested[2]. If, Ramsey said in effect, the analogy between a language and a calculus, which has served so well in enabling us to explain logical and mathematical propositions, is to be maintained at all, it has got to be maintained seriously. In terms of that analogy, metaphysical propositions are just not well-formed formulae; they are just gibberish. Now gibberish cannot be either important or unimportant; it is just a mathematical mistake; you throw it away.

This was a poser; and there was not any answer to it. And so, gradually, the empiricist world faced the unpalatable truth that Mill and Russell had underestimated the difficulties of the empiricist position. If the general empiricist position were to be maintained (and the spectacular advances continually made within science increased every day the general case for maintaining it) then not only had the nature of logical and mathematical propositions to be explained (as indeed they had been, in our sense, by saying that they were tautologies); but also the nature of metaphysical propositions had to be explained; *and in such a way that the analogy between a language and a game or calculus did not altogether break down.* For if the analogy between a language and a calculus did altogether break down, then the explanation of the nature of logical and mathematical propositions, which had been given in terms of this analogy, broke down also. And if this happened, we should be back in Mill's extremely unsatisfactory position of wondering whether mathematical propositions were very

[1] Wilbur Marshall Urban, *Language and Reality, The Philosophy of Language and the Principles of Symbolism* (New York, 1939).
[2] Frank Plumpton Ramsey, *The Foundations of Mathematics and other Logical Essays* (Kegan Paul, 1931), section entitled 'Philosophy', p. 263.

T

general empirical propositions or not, and of having no way of deciding what they were. And (so the whole empiricist philosophical world intuitively felt) this was a return upon our tracks which must positively be prevented at all costs.

Gradually, then, philosophers who were perfectly aware of the gains to be had by developing the analogy between a calculus and a language began to give explanations of what metaphysics was which did not consist in saying that metaphysical propositions were nonsense. These explanations were at first very cloudy and vague. Among English-speaking philosophers D. M. Emmet, in *The Nature of Metaphysical Thinking*,[1] said that typical metaphysical statements drew key analogies; but she never explored the logical nature of analogy sufficiently for her general line of approach to be followed up by logicians. W. M. Urban said that metaphysical systems were somehow subject-predicate pictures,[2] and that metaphysics-making was as inescapable a human activity as breathing; but he said nothing more about the logical structure of the 'pictures'; nor did he sufficiently indicate what their use really was. Philipp Frank, one of the philosophers of the original Vienna Circle, studied metaphysical propositions occurring within a science. These were, he said, picturesque simplifications, designed to connect the modern technical languages with what we miscall 'the language of common sense'.[3] The one thing upon which these neo-apologists of metaphysics agreed was that metaphysical statements could not be straightforwardly either true or false, being unsubjectable to an 'operational' test. There was another thing, too, upon which they all agreed, though they themselves mostly did not realize it; and that was, that the missing definition of metaphysics, when it came, would have to be a logical one, not one in terms of facts. For metaphysical statements could no longer be defined primarily by their subject-matter, once it was agreed that they were not such as to have truth-values; and (it was realized) it was a consequence of this that no one now knew what their subject-matter was. They would have, then, to be defined by their

[1] Dorothy M. Emmet, *The Nature of Metaphysical Thinking* (Macmillan, 1945).
[2] W. M. Urban, op. cit., pp. 631 et seq. (Section on 'The Language of Metaphysics'.)
[3] Philipp Frank, *Modern Science and its Philosophy* (Harvard, 1941): chapter 16, 'The place of Logic and Metaphysics in the advancement of Modern Science.'

logical form. 'Metaphysical systems and statements are about Being; they give the most general characteristics of Reality'; this was the sort of definition everyone was now slow to give, and reluctant to take seriously. Thus the general query received its first limitation. What was wanted was a logical definition of what metaphysics was.

The problem received its second limitation at the hands of a quite different school of philosophers; at first sight, of a far more esoteric school. Among the philosophers who were conscious of the possibilities of logical exploration opened up by comparing a language with a calculus were some who, following, as they thought, the teaching of the later Wittgenstein, made their whole philosophic argument depend on analysis of concrete statements, and who shunned generalization of every kind. These confined their overt philosophical writing and lecturing to setting out (comparatively) concrete examples of actual and possible uses of a concept or a phrase; 'testing concepts to destruction', as Ryle, using an engineering metaphor, once said.[1] These philosophers assumed (while denying) the analogy between a language and a calculus or a game, as was shown both by the fact that they developed a whole jargon based on it, and also by the fact that their aim, as they said, was to make a language-map.[2] But they would not use any scale-maker or map-signs; like Lewis Carroll's German Professor,[3] they preferred to use ordinary language as its own map; with the result that, also as in Carroll, the scale of this map was of a mile to a mile. This device — of using ordinary language as its own exemplification — also had its remote origin in Wittgenstein's *Tractatus Logi-*

[1] Gilbert Ryle, *Philosophical Arguments, An Inaugural Lecture* (Oxford, 1945), p. 6.
[2] They also talked about 'playing language-games', and described any step in a philosophic argument as 'a move'.
[3] 'What a useful thing a pocket-map is!' I remarked.
'That's another thing we've learned from *your* nation,' said Mein Herr, 'map-making. But we've carried it much further than *you*. What do you consider the *largest* map that would be really useful?'
'About six inches to the mile.'
'Only *six inches!*' exclaimed Mein Herr. 'We very soon got to six *yards* to the mile. Then we tried a *hundred* yards to the mile. And then came the grandest idea of all! We actually made a map of the country, on the scale of *a mile to the mile!*'
'Have you used it much?' I inquired.
'It has never been spread out, yet,' said Mein Herr: 'the farmers objected: they said it would cover the whole country, and shut out the sunlight! So now we use the countryside itself, as its own map, and I assure you it does nearly as well.'
Lewis Carroll, *Sylvie and Bruno Concluded, The Man in the Moon.*

co-Philosophicus, in his contention that the simplest thing to do about the enormously complicated orderings of ordinary language was to give them all; owing to their variety no simpler thing could be done.[1] This 'take-nothing-but-the-concrete-case' technique gave the University seminars and lectures in which it was employed a concrete-yet-symbolic, a poetic, almost a Far Eastern flavour. And in fact there was an analogy (as other philosophers were not slow to point out) between this device and the devices used in Zen Buddhism which are designed to break the confidence of the disciple of Zen in the validity of the achievement of the generalizing mind.

Actually, of course, the 'ordinary-language philosophers' have not thrown over the language-calculus analogy; what they are doing is drastically refining it. The realization that the rules of no one calculus can reproduce the richness of any natural language, this belief, if strongly enough held, can pass over easily to a complete refusal to use any formal procedures to indicate logical form, and to an insistence on contenting one's self with giving a concrete instance of the logical form in question, leaving the reader or hearer to generalize as he may see fit. Nor do these philosophers, *de facto*, always abhor the habit of generalization which they renounce *de jure*. For general remarks, such as that 'there exists a special class of performatory statements', or (as we shall see) that 'metaphysical statements are paradoxes', are among the generalizations which they do not hesitate to make, anti-generalizers though they are. What these philosophers fear, like the Buddhist sages before them, is that philosophic generalization shall turn to dogma and thus stifle thought and cramp imagination. They make their philosophic generalizations, therefore — when they do make them — in the most provisional and fugitive forms which they can find. Those of them, however, who have been in close contact with scientists, fear the dangers of dogmatization less, and therefore generalize in writing far more freely, than those who have been educated entirely in the literary and religious traditions. The fugitive, provisional nature of good philosophic generalization seems for these former to be like the fugitive provisional nature of in-

[1] L. Wittgenstein, *Tractatus Logico-Philosophicus*, 5.55, 5.555, 5.5561, 5.5562, 5.5563.

formal theoretic guesses in science. A good scientific guess, freely made, and cast in the form of a didactic and unqualified generalization, inspires a scientist's experimental work for a time; then it breaks down; something is seen to go wrong with it; it is forgotten; finally it is gone.

So there are two kinds of 'ordinary-language' philosopher; those who generalize freely and fancifully (like the present writer), treating their own strongest generalizations, however, like guesses made in an extremely inexact science; and those who, in theory, eschew generalizations altogether, except as a new kind of Tibetan Ear-Whispered Teaching — that is, as a teaching which will be vulgarized and ossified if written down. Both schools of thought, in fact, regard the use of the device of generalization as inevitable; both schools of thought are concerned that generalizations shall not harden into dogmata; and both, when possible, throw the weight of argument on to analysis of actual concepts set in statements — that is, caught as they are when actually being used. So the two kinds of 'ordinary-language' philosopher are not as different from one another as they look.

In spite of all precautions, however, certain generalizations tend to be quasi-permanently passed around, even in the inner circles of anti-generalizers. And among those generalizations which members even of the stricter sect allow themselves to formulate is one (made by Wisdom in a Presidential Address to the Aristotelian Society) to the general effect that metaphysical statements are not nonsense because they are gibberish; they are nonsense because, speaking logically but not mathematically, they are paradoxes; attempts, that is, to say something which, in terms of ordinary logic, can't be said.[1] This point of view, like the vaguer view that metaphysical thinkers drew key analogies, has had its immediate English-speaking *précurseurs*. Collingwood[2] earlier stressed that metaphysical propositions could be understood more easily as meaningful when the framework of their historical context was

[1] John Wisdom, 'Metaphysics' (Presidential Address to the meeting of the Aristotelian Society, 1950), pp. 236-259, *Other Minds* (Blackwell, 1952).

See also 'Philosophy, Anxiety and Novelty', 'Philosophy and Psycho-Analysis' and 'Philosophy, Metaphysics and Psycho-Analysis' from *Philosophy and Psycho-Analysis* (Blackwell, 1953) by the same author.

[2] R. G. Collingwood, *An Essay on Metaphysics* (Oxford, 1940).

present to diminish their apparent paradoxicality. Price (in the Presidential Address which he gave at the first Joint Session of the Aristotelian Society and Mind Association to take place after the second world war) stressed that 'sensible, clear propositions' were not enough; a new truth often broke linguistic rules by exhibiting itself as oxymoron, as paradox.[1] Thus the general idea was already in the air that metaphysical propositions, looked at logically, were paradoxes; but no one has carried this general idea any further. Only William Empson, originally a Cambridge mathematician, poet and literary critic, has made any attempt to examine, in greater detail, the kinds of logical form which poetical or metaphysical paradoxes might turn out to have.[2] Even he, however, only asked this question incidentally, in the course of carrying out another inquiry. Thus, again, it has gradually become more and more clear that the 'ordinary-language philosophers' have not solved the problem of what metaphysics is: what they have done is to bring a new limitation to it. For not only do they assume that the problem is a logical one, not one of content; that is, that any statement, if analysed and used metaphysically, can become, or rather, be envisaged as, metaphysical. They have asumed further — and this is a new assumption — that the philosophical problem of what metaphysics is will be solved when the logical form can be defined not of the interconnections between the parts of a whole metaphysical system, but of the interconnections between the terms of a single metaphysical statement. And to say this is both to impose on the problem a second limitation, and also, speaking logically, to make it a more fundamental one.

Now, if, for the time being, you will allow that we may all of us be in the throes of a 'discovery-procedure' (in the sense of 'discovery' defined above) and also that, in the process of corporately hatching this discovery-procedure, we have got through the essentials of stages one and two, the question arises, what steps can we take to enter upon stage three? Where can we find a technique to solve this now technical problem?

[1] H. H. Price, 'Clarity is Not Enough' (Presidential Address). (*Proceedings of the Aristotelian Society*, Supplementary Volume XIX, 1945.)
[2] William Empson, *The Structure of Complex Words* (Chatto & Windus, 1951).

§3: *Focusing and refocusing on the limited problem*

The first trail (which seems at first glance to be a *cul-de-sac*) lies, obviously, in a closer examination of the general nature of paradox. There is an immense English literary critical literature on paradox[1] which at first sight seems to lead one philosophically nowhere. Closer inspection, however, shows that the study of this is not as philosophically sterile as it appears. For this study leads one to stress with increasing earnestness, in the order given, the following literary-cum-linguistic 'truths' about paradox which, if a metaphysical statement is going to be a paradox, are truths which have got to be accounted for. The following, that is to say, are the provisional generalizations which come out of the literary-critical literature on paradox, 'paradox' being here taken in the Oxford Dictionary sense.

(i) *Speaking logically (though not formally) about a linguistic and poetic phenomenon, paradox is the most extreme kind of metaphor, just as metaphor is the most extreme kind of simile.*

If I say, 'That hat — well it's rather like a piece of architecture', then I'm drawing a simile. If I say, 'That hat — it's the Taj Mahal',[2] then, because I'm saying that it *is* the Taj Mahal, not that it is merely *like* the Taj Mahal, the critics' thesis is that I'm alleging a greater and more clear-cut similarity between a piece of architecture and the hat than if I said merely that the hat was like any particular piece of architecture. Of course, in fact, it is even more blatantly far-fetched and untrue (in the scientific and common-sense senses of 'truth') to say that the hat *is* the Taj Mahal than it was to say that the hat was *like* a piece of architecture (nature of resemblance between the two unspecified). But now, suppose I carry the whole thing a stage further. Suppose I say, 'Yes, this hat, it's like the Taj Mahal, and then again, it's not like the Taj Mahal. It's like the Taj Mahal; and it's also like a shaded blue whirlwind rising out of a deeper blue pool, with rhythmic waves flowing

---

[1] For example, I. A. Richards, *The Philosophy of Rhetoric* (Oxford, 1936). William Empson, *The Structure of Complex Words.* Owen Barfield, *Poetic Diction, A Study in Meaning* (Faber & Faber, 1922), etc. etc. (There is an extensive if carelessly compiled further bibliography on this subject in Empson's book.)

The reader should be warned that this extensive literary critical literature is tangled and ambiguous. The interpretation of it given here is therefore open to controversy.

[2] John Wisdom, *Philosophy, Metaphysics and Psycho-Analysis* (see note 14).

round it, and with crenelated edges. It's one of those hats of which you could say "It's One, and it's Many". It's one of those hats of which you could say, "It's vegetable, and it's mineral". It's one of those hats of which you could say, "It's One and it's Five".' If I take to saying this sort of thing, it could be said that I land myself in asserting a series of paradoxes, in the assertion of one at least of which I have broken, by implication, Aristotle's Law of the Excluded Middle. Thus, logically speaking, I have done something even more preposterous and extreme in asserting a paradox such as 'this hat — it's One and it's Many', than I did when I asserted that the hat was the Taj Mahal—that is, if it be held that there is a formal contradiction involved in asserting of an object x that it is both one and many, whereas there is no formal contradiction in asserting of it that it is the Taj Mahal. Actually, of course, in so far as I have further clarified the mental image which I have of the hat, I have said something less preposterously untrue (in the common-sense and scientific senses of 'true') by asserting the whole string of paradoxes with regard to the hat, than I did when I metaphori-cally asserted that it was the Taj Mahal; because each paradox 'waters down' the others, so that, when all are asserted concur-rently, the contradiction is destroyed. Logically, however, the situation is different from what common sense says it is, in that the breach of what we always assume to be normal logical convention is more flagrant in the case of an assertion which formally breaks the Law of the Excluded Middle than in the case of an assertion which merely untruly says that x is y; just as the breach of normal logical convention is more flagrant in the case where the persistent assertion is untruly made that x is y, than in the case where the merely surprising assertion is made that x is like y. This — speak-ing logically, though about a linguistic phenomenon — paradox (x is not x) is the limiting case of metaphor (x is y, asserted when x is patently not y), and metaphor (x is y, asserted when x is patently not y), is the limiting case of simile (x is like y, asserted when x is patently not very like y).

As unthinking, rough-and-ready logicians, as I say, we assume all this. But of course, speaking strictly, the logical difficulties of assuming all this are immense.

(ii) *Linguistically and poetically speaking, but not logically speaking, 'All language is metaphoric';*[1] *(and therefore, by implication, also potentially paradoxical).*

As it stands, this general assertion, which is widely made by contemporary poets and literary critics, is singularly unhelpful, since it is too obscure even to discuss. For if metaphor-making, and metaphor-extending, are to be taken as the two most fundamental linguistic operations (as this assertion, taken logically, suggests that they will have to be) then it is clear that 'metaphor' and 'metaphoric', as used in the assertion and in current explanations of it, must refer to the result of the operation of some basic linguistic transformation-rule — to some operation, that is, which is carried on *whenever* statements are constructed out of concepts — *whenever* bits of language — of *any* language — are manipulated. And if this is so, then the terms 'metaphor' and 'metaphoric' must refer to something so much more fundamental than that figure of speech known as metaphor, which is analysed in so many English eighteenth-century rhetoric books, that it seems absurd and merely misleading to give the same name to both.

Thus this assertion is not self-explanatory, as it stands. It is useful, mainly, in stimulating the further question, 'Where, then, do we look for the most fundamental kinds of metaphor and of paradox?'

The third assertion attempts to answer this.

(iii) *From the rhetorician's point of view, though not from that of the linguist, the kinds of metaphor which most cry out for logical analysis are to be found, not in poetry, but in ancient metaphysical and doctrinal statements, nearly all of which push metaphor to the point of paradox.*[2]

If this assertion is true, then it is supported by assertion (i), namely that paradoxes exemplify a stranger and more fundamental logical form than those statements which are usually analysed as

[1] I. A. Richards, op. cit.
Cf. also Suzanne K. Langer, *Philosophy in a New Key* (Harvard, 1942).
[2] William Empson, op. cit.
Cf. also Margaret Masterman, *Analysis of a Religious Paradox* (*Epiphany Philosophers' Conference Report*, 1954).

normal examples of metaphor and simile. This new assertion states
that examples of these extreme cases of metaphor are to be found
both in statements taken from original documents, and also in
statements which are parodies of these. 'God is Three and God is
One.' 'Thou art This and That.' 'The right Faith is that we believe
and confess: that our Lord Jesus Christ, the son of God, is God
and Man . . .' And in parody; 'War is Peace.' 'For the Snark was a
Boojum, you see.' 'All animals are equal; but some are more equal
than others.' . . .

This assertion leads directly to assertion (iv), which is a more
general one, and, therefore, a more philosophic one, and, therefore, to a philosopher, much more baffling and perplexing even
than the linguistic and poetic assertions which have been made so
far.

(iv) *Even when a paradox, occurring in ordinary language, looks
at first sight as though it were a flagrant breach of terminological or
logical rule, it is only a paradox with regard to the particular terminology within which that particular terminological or logical rule holds.*

That this fourth assertion should be made at all shows how
great has been the persuasive power, during the last fifty years, of
the development of the analogy between a language and a calculus. The difficulty of drawing it in this context, however, lies in
determining what is really meant — as soon as we move to speaking in terms of *language* from speaking in terms of *calculus* — by
the concepts of 'terminological' and of 'terminology'. Nevertheless a truth is being asserted (we feel); a genuine point is somehow
being made. The vital question at issue, however, which is never
discussed, can be reached only by questioning the assumption
underlying the philosopher of language's whole point of view.
For when you are starting to think in this kind of way, the precise
question at issue always turns out to be: 'Just how far and in which
directions, in discussing paradox, can the language-calculus comparison be made to go?'

What the poet wants to say is comparatively simple; and it is
simple because he is talking simply and inexactly about a very
simple and inexact sort of paradox. He wants to say, with regard

to any paradox (in the Oxford Dictionary sense of 'paradox') that it is impossible to see whether or not it is a paradox until you have first seen how it is embedded in the particular units of discourse within which it occurs. Thus (for instance) the assertion that the Snark was a Boojum does not sound at first sight as though it were at all paradoxical, until one discovers that it is opposed, all through the text, to the assertion that the Snark was a Snark, and that it thus invalidates, with regard to that particular unit of discourse, the logical principle 'not both p and not-p'. Similar considerations could be applied, *mutatis mutandis*, to all the other paradoxes given above. For the poet, then, a paradox is just a statement consisting of two comparable parts which do not fit, the non-fitting of the two parts being due to the fact that each is meaningful only within its special kind of context. For the mathematical logician, however, a paradox (say that of the Liar) is something different, namely, a statement which can be deduced from an apparently consistent set of premisses, but which contradicts one of them. The question here is: is there an analogy between the simpler and vaguer Oxford Dictionary sense of 'paradox' and the more complex and exact mathematical sense 'of paradox'? The answer is that there is such an analogy, but that it has itself to be described in such very vague terms that no direct intellectual use can be made of it. In the simple kind of paradox two mutually inconsistent regions of an over-variegated total context 'throw up' two descriptive statements which, when placed together, do not logically fit; as happens, for instance, in the case of the two parts of the paradox, 'Jesus Christ is God, and he is man', or 'God is Three, and God is One'. In the complex case, two or more of an actually over-variegated, because ambiguous, set of premisses deductively 'produce' two statements which, when confronted with one another, do not 'fit'. The Cretan said, 'All Cretans are liars', and his witness was true. But if it was true then he himself was a liar, and so it wasn't true. His witness, therefore, has to be both true (or there is no premiss) and false (or there is no consequence), thus making a first-type paradox to the effect that 'The Cretan's witness was both true and false'. Clearly, therefore, for this paradox to be resolved, the Cretan's witness has to be true as a premiss, in Context I, and the deduction 'true', in

Context II; and the underlying analogy between the two kinds of paradox is shown by the fact that 'context' can be interpreted here both in a vague linguistic sense, in which the relationship between the contexts is not fully determined, and also in an exact mathematical sense, in which the relationship between the two 'contexts' can be made explicit and exact, the meaning of 'context' being changed in the course of doing this.

Since it is only by being vague about the exact case as well as about the vague case that the analogy between the two can be shown, there is no way of carrying the train of thought which shows it any further. But it is clear, from the whole general line of the argument, that the idea that there can be different kinds of system within the general body of mathematics is encouraging the poet and critic to think that there may be, analogously, different terminologies, or units of discourse, within a language. Moreover, (the poet thinks) if it be the case, in mathematics, that an axiom such as Boole's $xx=x$, which it is perfectly right to have within a Boolean system, can look highly paradoxical (in the Oxford Dictionary sense of 'paradox') when considered in relation to, say, the calculus of natural numbers, may not it analogously be the case that a statement, such as 'God is Three and God is One', may be a right and well-informed statement within one kind of universe of discourse, although it looks highly paradoxical with regard to another?

This last thought leads straight to assertion (v).

(v) *Considered as a prose statement in ordinary English, a paradox is an ellipsis; that is, for any paradoxical statement* x, *there is a longer ordinary English statement* y, *which, somehow or other, gives the full meaning of* x, *and yet which is not itself a paradox.*

Considered, however, as it really ought to be considered, i.e. 'in terms of its own logic', a paradox is a perfectly normal statement, which could have its own kind of paradox-logical relations with other ['*equally paradoxical*'] *statements occurring within a total paradox-logical unit of discourse, such that no breach of paradox-logic occurred.*[1]

[1] William Empson, op. cit.
Margaret Masterman, op. cit. Cf. also 'The Pictorial Principle in Language' (*Proceedings of the XIth International Congress of Philosophy*, 1953, Vol. XIV).

'In the logic of prose a paradox may sound queer; but in the logic of poetry it takes its proper place — and poetry really has its own logic, you know.' This is the kind of thing a poet might say in trying to express his final feeling about paradox; and he, like the mathematician but unlike the philosopher, does not find it difficult to believe that there may be 'another logic', a logic of poetry, of paradox, in terms of which everything that is said in prose (that is, in a linguistic form governed by ordinary logic), seems queer and everything that, when placed in the context of prose and of forms of argument governed by ordinary logic, seems queer, now looks perfectly normal. For the logic of poetry — or what the poet, speaking to himself, calls 'the logic of poetry' — is impressed, at every level of consciousness, upon the poet's mind and upon his heart. He feels, rightly or wrongly, that he intuitively knows it; he feels, too, that he knows — and in the most definite and clear-cut way — when he is writing in poetry and when in prose.

For the philosopher, however, this poet's estimate of the logical situation with regard to paradox is really very difficult indeed. What kind of thing, for instance, is the statement y which, from the prose-writer's point of view, logically legitimizes the thought contained in the paradox x? What is paradox-logic? What kind of thing are paradox-logical relations? What are the similarities and differences (if any) between paradox-logic and poetic logic? And, above all, in what sense or senses, through all this argument, is the word 'logic' being used?

I think that the only thing which we can do (that is, if we are to take seriously the suggestion given in this last and fifth assertion, which forms the climax of the literary critics' thought) is to give ourselves practice in the activity of making and unmaking paradox. Firstly, we must try and find a complex situation, a description of which we can sum up paradoxically (i.e. given y, find x); then also we must try to find a paradox which we can extend into a description of a complex situation (i.e. given x, find y). More than that we cannot possibly do; because that is as far as the philosopher, without further technical devices, can follow the poet. For he cannot be presumed, *qua philosopher*, to have the poet's intuitive 'inner eye' to guide him in his philosophic search for the logic of metaphor and of paradox. Unlike the poet, he can only write in prose. His first reaction, therefore, to the poet's assertions will be one of intense philosophic exasperation, and it will be difficult for him to realize that the thought, 'I shall never be able, speaking logically, to think like a poet unless I have some special logical device to enable me to do so' is one which, in the long run, is likely to be productive not of truistic indolence but of creative enterprise. Only experience can show that the continued pressure on him of this poet's attitude can so serve to exasperate and further focus his thought, that he gets finally to that fully ripened state of tense despair, out of which alone some unforeseen intellectual leap can come. For notice how strongly the poet-cum-literary-critic, thinking turgidly perhaps but also persistently and progressively, has been stimulating the philosopher and also goading him on. 'This paradox-logic that you say you can't even imagine gives the form, according to us, of the most fundamental operations which can take place in any language' (assertion ii). 'Paradox is only an extreme case of metaphor, and metaphor an extreme case of simile (assertion i). Granted always that you won't even try to understand paradox, are you also going to say, and that indefinitely, that you won't try to understand metaphor or simile?' 'Critics and linguists talk about there being different logical universes of discourse, or terminologies, or sub-schemata, occurring within the same total language (assertion iii). You say that you cannot understand what we mean. But the philosopher Wittgenstein talked similarly about there being different notations which could occur within the same, natural language. You won't listen to us; will you also not listen to him?' 'You spend a great deal of your time looking for subtle differences of usage and use of concepts which occur in natural language. These differences which you look for must be logical differences; and yet when we say that there is a logic of poetry, and of paradox (assertion v) you won't believe us. You look for subtle and evanescent differences of logical form; are you blind to permanent and gross ones?'

Goaded thus, over and over, beyond endurance, one attempts to take, in the end, the missing, apparently impossible, technical step, the object of which is to enable one, logically, to follow what the poet intuitively does. Either that; or one abandons the whole train of thought altogether, and returns to the older, G. E. Moore form of analysis as being the only clear intellectual activity left in an impossible and repellent logical world. It is important to see, however — if one decides on this final retreat — that in that case all the books of contemporary descriptive linguists, as well as those of poets and literary critics, must all be thrown mentally right out of the window, where they will no longer cause trouble; and, what's worse, their poetry books — and those of Elizabethan poetry too — must be thrown away after their critical works. Now we were prepared enough (that is, when we first read *Erkenntnis* and *Language, Truth and Logic*) to throw religious philosophy and metaphysics bravely on to Hume's bonfire. But are we prepared, here and now, to jettison all poetry as well?

Of course not. And therefore there is only one alternative left open to us.

Before, however, desperately and blindly, we take our technical step, let us finish our encounter with the vaguer world of the critics and poets by trying to make and unmake paradox in prose. Suppose now that we are trying to make a brief even if paradoxical picture of the present state of organizer-theory in biochemistry, as this is described in a recent paper by Holftreter.[1] In the first section of his paper Holftreter contrasts the present state of the theory with the very recent past of the state of the theory. Put briefly (I simplify drastically and philosophically) the situation used to be that there were thought to be two morphologically different kinds of cell. There were firstly, organizer-cells, which, when grafted on to undifferentiated tissue would induce specialization leading to the development of full morphological organization; and secondly, there were ordinary cells, which could be subjected to this process but could not initiate it. Now, however, further experiment has shown firstly, that when maltreated to a certain point in various ways, ordinary cells can acquire the morphological properties of organizer-cells; secondly, that other substances and other objects can, under certain circumstances, act as organizer-cells; and

[1] Johannes Holftreter, *Concepts on the Mechanism of Embryonic Induction and its relation to Parthenogenesis and Malignancy.* (*Growth*, Symposia of the Society for Experimental Biology II (Cambridge, 1948).)

thirdly, that if, under certain other, only slightly differing, circumstances cells are maltreated, they can become, not organizers, but cancerous and pathogenic; that is, both (in this context) degenerate in themselves and also capable of transmitting, by mitosis, their own degenerate form of organization to other cells. Now this is a situation which would certainly invite a poet to paradox, were there to arise a poet sufficiently interested for it to inspire him to become paradoxical. Taking, therefore, as our *y* the whole of the first section of Holftreter's exposition (which is written mainly in biological Greek and which we will call *Hy*) one could well summarize his argument in what one might call a series of cell-paradoxes, which, speaking very roughly, would go as follows (and which, taken together, we will call *Hx*).

Hx: 'Cells, the fundamental form of life, are at once organizers, reproducers and receptors; reproducers, as touching their method of propagation; receptors, as touching their hierarchical position; organizers, as touching their biochemical potentialities. As for the biochemical potentialities of cells, these are both developmental and pathogenic; sufficiently constant to be chemically analysable, and yet morphologically ambiguous in action. One could sum the whole matter up, in fact, by saying that, speaking biochemically, cells both operate causally, and also in such a way as to render meaningless the whole causal conception upon which biochemical theory is based. Thus, in any generalized context within which we examine them, they both are and are not *a*, or *b* or *c*; that is, they have the whole combination of properties which the mutually inconsistent biochemical experiments give them. This conclusion, which so destroys our sense of fact, is what is imposed upon us by the facts. It is, therefore, what every true scientist must believe if biochemical science is to continue to be the truly scientific study which it now is.'

If it be provisionally granted that *Hx* sums up the situation which Holftreter exposes in his paper (the situation, indeed, which it is his purpose in writing it to disentangle); and if it also be provisionally granted that *Hx* be considered, broad and large, as one long paradox, then it becomes possible for us to ask ourselves what we can find out, speaking logically, by comparing *Hy* (the extended statement) with Hx (the paradox). Let us, however, defer this question until we have first tried the reverse process, i.e. that of getting from paradox to extended statement, from x to y.

Let us take as x, this time, a short paradox, namely, the theological paradox which we have just quoted, 'God is Three and God is One'. This, in its context, is poetic, since it is the second line of Newman's hymn which forms the credal confession of the dying Gerontius.[1] We will call this paradox Tx; and the question which we have now immediately to consider is how, starting with this, we are to construct Ty.

It is at once clear that, if we are to construct Ty in anything like a natural and unselfconscious manner, Ty will neither be a logically homogeneous statement nor a logically simple one. For the first thing which we want to say about Tx is something like this:

$Ty(i)$ [first attempt at Ty]:

'Tx is a compound statement which is of the logical form p *and* q and which also has this exceptional logical characteristic, that the two halves of it make sense in different contexts.[2] For in certain contexts "divinity", or "God" is a finite and empirical causal concept. It impels certain men to certain actions, and does not impel certain other men to certain other actions. It causes the occurrence of certain events, and prevents the occurrence of certain others. It sometimes is in action, and sometimes not. In these contexts ascetic theologians have found it helpful to subdivide this causal agency into three aspects (*personae*, strands) each of which exercises a stronger force, as it were, than the last. The "Holy Ghost", according to them, is the gentlest of the three. Thus "He" acts until the power of action of the second *persona*, "Christ", manifests itself within the personality, of which manifestation there are certain empirical signs. This second *persona* then takes over, and from then on the impact of the Christic force gets stronger and stronger, until, in the hypostatic union, which, from the point of view of the person concerned, is (theoretically) cognizable by the onset of the "Beatific Vision", the direct power of action of the last

[1] J. H. Newman, *The Dream of Gerontius*, Part I.
[2] Cf. on this: F. Waismann, 'Language Strata', from *Essays on Logic and Language*, ed. Flew, second series (Blackwell, 1953), p. 22.

U

persona or strand, that of "the Father" comes into full effect from then on.

Thus, in this highly esoteric kind of context, "God is Three" makes perfectly good sense; and it could be provisionally granted that this kind of context is an empirical one. But there are certain other, metaphysical, contexts in which, to a metaphysician, it makes sense to say that "God is One" (as for instance in the deductive "proofs" of the existence of God), and in such contexts dogmatic theologians, if they possibly can, always avoid any mention of the fact that "God is Three". In such contexts, moreover, the meaning of the concept "God" tends to become more and more general, until we reach the limiting case of Spinoza's *Deus sive Natura*, in which "God" means the same as "all that is".'

So much for our first approximation to Ty, which we will call $Ty(i)$. Now the length of $Ty(i)$, especially when compared with that of Tx, is all but intolerable; and yet, long as it is, $Ty(i)$ is far from being complete or self-explanatory. Let us, however, shorten Ty drastically, so as to produce a statement comparable in length to Tx:

$Ty(ii)$, [shortened version of $Ty(i)$]:
'The meaning of the compound statement "God is Three and God is One", when this statement is taken as a whole, is that there are some contexts (call them A) in which the simple statement "God is Three" makes sense, and there are other contexts (call them B) in which the simple statement "God is One" makes sense but that A need not coincide with B.'

Now suppose we further provisionally assume that $Ty(ii)$ is what we have been looking for, i.e. the extended form of the paradox Tx such that

(i) $Ty(ii)$ gives the full meaning of Tx, and
(ii) $Ty(ii)$ is not itself a paradox,

even then what more that is helpful can we say about the logical relationship of $Ty(ii)$ to Tx?

We can say, firstly, that $Ty(ii)$ is a meta-statement, that is (speaking vaguely), that it is a statement about Tx and not about the world. And we can say, secondly, that Tx, if it is a paradox, will be such as to make 'paradox', in the sense in which Hx and Tx are paradoxes, to be very roughly definable in the following terms:

A paradox, in the Oxford Dictionary sense, is an apparently nonsensical compound statement consisting of a conjunction (stated or implied) of two simpler substatements. These simpler substatements

(i) are so closely connected with one another in content as to be, in some sense 'parallel' the one to the other, and

(ii) are of the same logical form, but

(iii) are such that each, taken separately, can be placed in contexts within which it can be made to make sense, and

(iv) are such also that the two groups of contexts will significantly differ from one another. Moreover, these substatements

(v) are such that in order to make each of them make sense it may be necessary to rewrite it in some kind of 'standard form', to bring out clearly its meaning when it is taken as an isolated statement, and this means rewriting it in such a way that, in its rewritten version, the logical parallelism between it and the other part of the total paradox will be destroyed.

If the above definition gives a first approximation to a general description of the logical form of a paradox, then it becomes evident why $Ty(ii)$ is a meta-statement. This is indeed the third of the things which we can significantly say about the logical relations which hold between Tx and Ty, and, more generally, about the logical relations of x and y. For if y is to give the 'fields of significance' of the two parts of x, then either y must include, as Holftreter's paper does, exemplifications of all the contexts involved, in which case y will be of enormous length, or it must give a defining characteristic, in each case, of the two types of context involved, in which case it is bound to be a meta-statement, i.e. a statement not about the world but about the contexts of Tx.

Now all this, vague as it is, undoubtedly gives a certain general intellectual satisfaction, in so far as it makes us feel (if we agree with the argument) that we know more than we did before about the logical nature and function of paradox. But this kind of thinking gives us no exact or clear satisfaction. It gives us no logical satisfaction as soon as we use logic in the strict sense. What's worse, it has explained paradox in such a way that no light at all is thrown upon the problem of the nature of metaphysics which is the one which we originally started out to solve. For paradox, envisaged like this, is not really a very interesting logical form; and it is hard to see how this method of analysing it throws any light at all upon the logical analysis of metaphysics. Come to think of it, is metaphysics really paradox, even in the weaker Oxford Dictionary sense of paradox? Take some of the definitions of the first book of the *Ethics* of Spinoza:

'*I. Per causam sui intelligo id, cuius essentia involvit existentiam: sive id, cuius natura non potest concipi nisi existens* . . .'
('In so far as the essence of a thing involves its existence, I shall understand it as being the cause of itself. I shall use the same expression to describe a thing the nature of which can only be conceived as existent') . . .
'*III. Per substantiam intelligo id, quod in se est, et per se concipitur* . . .'
('By substance I understand that which both is, in itself, and also which is created through itself . . .')
'*IV. Per attributum intelligo id quod intellectus de substantia percipit, tanquam eiusdem essentiam constituens.*'
('By attribute I understand what the intellect perceives of substance and therefore takes as constituting its essence.')
'*V. Per modum intelligo* . . .' *etc.*
('By mode I understand . . .')
'*VI. Per Deum intelligo eus absolute infinitum* . . .'
('By "God", I understand completely unlimited being . . .')

You may say that these Spinozan definitions are obscure, or that they are, empirically speaking, ridiculous, or that they are perverse; but (with the possible exception of I or III), here is no paradox; at least none in the sense in which we have been using the term. Nothing would be gained, either in the case of the total statement formed by conjoining all the individual definitions or in the case of any individual definitions (e.g. Definition III) which can be analysed so as to consist of a conjunction, by considering separately the 'fields of significance' of the parts of the conjunction so that each, taken on its own, made sense; in fact much, every way, would be lost by doing this. And if we once grant Spinoza his definitions, then his propositions also won't be paradoxes.

So where do we get? Has our whole long train of thought come to an end, having produced the not very interesting considerations which we have just made?

The alternative is that we pursue the far more difficult suggestion contained in the second part of the poets' fifth assertion, since not much result has been achieved by following the thoughts contained in the first. It will be remembered that this second part of the poets' thought was that, if we are to understand the logical form of paradox, it can only be by coming to create or understand some form of what was there called 'paradox-logic'. It was agreed, too, that in order to achieve this we should have to make use of some new and hitherto untried technical device; that we should have, as it were, to take a technical step.

The technical step which I suggest that we take is to create a new universe of discourse: to imagine a new language. We will call this (for philosophers) 'ideographic language', though we shall, in fact, imagine it from the start as having the pauses and stresses of a spoken language; we shall think of it as a spoken language with an ideographic script. For mathematical logicians we shall call it 'elemental language' — meaning by this that it is founded upon combinations of homogeneous elements, not upon combinations of symbols recalling subjects and predicates. For linguists we will call this same language not 'isolating language', which is misleading both to philosophers and to mathematicians, but 'grouping language' (from Meriggi's suggestion in 'La Structure des Langues Groupantes').[1] By this we shall intend to stress the fact that the distinguishing characteristic of this language is to build its elements — which we shall envisage as significant syllables, or *semes* — into groups smaller than, and more logically fundamental than, clauses or statements, but larger than words.

[1] H. Meriggi, 'La Structure des Langues Groupantes' (*Journal de Psychologie*, 1933).

Thus, we shall speak (for philosophers), of '*clusters* of ideographs'; we could also speak, for mathematicians, of '*sequences*, or strings, of *elements*'; and, for descriptive linguists, of '*prosodies* of semes'. And the total act of imagining such a language we shall speak of, in general, as 'doing ideography' — and we shall speak of the philosopher who engages in such an activity without further qualification as 'an ideographer'.

It might be said that, in the next lecture, we make no real suggestion because we create no language. All that we do — it might very well be said — is to create a cumbrous analytic notation, which can be used to analyse some statements in metaphysics. This notation, doubtless, has an algebraic feel about it; but it is far too complicated for any algebraist ever to be able to use it, and thus it is of no real mathematical or logical interest. We apply it, possibly capriciously, to various bits of English and Chinese, which are then so analysed as to make them sound metaphysical; but the whole procedure is intuitive and crude; all we are really saying is, 'English is like Chinese: and both are like metaphysics'.

All this is true, but it is not a sufficient criticism; for it presupposes ignorance on the part of the critic as to the right way of developing a logical analogy. Either, in doing this, you must start with language as it is — in which case you will never achieve a logic, but only a notation — or you must start with some logic or some algebra, axioms and all, just as it is, and interpret it ideographically; in which case you will never achieve anything which looks like language. Of these two, the first course, which demands the greater imaginative effort, is almost certainly the one with which to start. For in going from empirical material to theory, in any field, you have got to have analogies before you can have predictions; you have got to have principles before you can have axioms; you have got to have notations before you can have systems. And if these first notations go so far as actually to display an algebraic analogy, even without doing anything to develop it, then the forerunning leap of the logical imagination has been good. For experience shows that sooner, or later, out of notation, there does emerge system; and that theory, in the end, and by successive stages, is projected from analogy.

In the next lecture I do not do nearly as well as this, for I do not thoroughly take either the first or the second course. As was said at the beginning, I create no calculus and my claim is to imagine, rather than to analyse, a new kind of language. But not much time will be spent in debating the question of whether, in fact, such a language could or does exist — though since the nature of it will be presented by examples, in old and new Chinese, and also in English, the sense in which it is 'purely imagined' is clearly fanciful. It cannot be too much stressed that my present purpose, in drawing the attention of philosophers towards the possibility of doing ideography, is to draw attention also to the analogy between it and forms of language used in actual metaphysics. What I want to say, in fact, in answer to our original query, is that metaphysics is a form of thinking which builds up comparable or contrasting clusters of ideographs, rather than, as it has been thought to be in the past, a form of thinking which builds up series of independent statements. Thus I shall speak, in a Whiteheadian manner, of ideographs, (or λόγοι, or Words) firstly, as metaphysical elements or units; i.e. as discrete philosophic symbols each of which stands for a general idea: 'Substance', 'Mode', 'Accident', 'Space', 'Time', 'Deity'. Secondly, I shall speak of them as discrete and homogeneous semantic units embedded, I shall say, at the very heart of natural language: 'flow', 'go', 'flower', 'san^1', '$wang^2$', '$ching^3$'. Thirdly, as I have already said, I shall speak of them as potential logical units, or elements out of which might be constructed an ideographic calculus. (It is not contended, however, that if such a calculus were constructed it would, when interpreted, 'give' the fundamentals of all natural language. It is merely suggested that it might serve to throw light on one very fundamental form in natural language.)

These ideographs (taking 'ideograph' here in all three senses, philosophic, logical and linguistic), must be envisaged as having a special kind of logical build-up, a logical build-up characteristic of sequences of ideographs, but uncharacteristic of sequences of other kinds of logical unit. These sequences of ideographs, as imagined by me, can be of two kinds. The simpler kind of sequence, the formation and transformation-rules of which include

312 BRITISH PHILOSOPHY IN MID-CENTURY

many rules which a child playing with marbles might find out and use, I shall call, as I have said, *ideographic clusters*. The more complex kind of sequence, in which certain ideographs are set aside to be used as operators, I shall call *ideographic statements*. Both from ideographic clusters, and from ideographic statements, I shall imagine that there can be constructed *ideographic expansions*, recurrent or quasi-recurrent ideographic patterns which recall, without being quite the same as, the parallelisms and clumsy extended statements which we have encountered in discussing paradox.

The immediate philosophic result of suggesting that we create ideography is that it now becomes possible also to suggest that we create also two new, logical, senses of 'metaphysics'. Thus the concept 'metaphysical', as used in the rest of this argument, will mean (i) any sequence of ideographs; and/or (ii) any ideographic expansion, or unit of discourse, in which ideographic clusters predominate rather than ideographic statements; and/or (iii) any such expanded sequence of ideographic clusters which treats of a particular religious-cum-abstract subject-matter, i.e. that of traditional Metaphysics: the narrowest sense of all, sense iii.

Before we proceed, however, to analyse actual examples, there is one concluding query which must be allowed. In what sense is a translation into ideography, in the sense in which we have just now defined it, a technical step in the sense in which we have defined 'technical step'; and what is the technical problem which it 'solves'?

The answer to this, I think, could be put thus. This technical problem requires for its solution a new logical form — a new way, that is, of stringing language-symbols together — and the technical step which I suggest provides a new logical form. But since this whole discussion of the nature of metaphysics (i.e. of 'metaphysics' in senses ii and iii, above, not in sense i,) has only been narrowed into becoming thus technical (i.e. we have only been pushed into the fundamental enterprise of looking for the principles of metaphysics, sense i by a process of progressive limitation and of focusing on the more superficial senses of 'metaphysics', senses ii and iii,) this new logical form, if it is to 'solve' the 'problem', must be such as to be consistent with all the assertions and provisos which have been made in the course of limiting the general query. For it is only by accepting all of these assertions and provisos that we have succeeded in getting the original query finally focused into the narrow but fundamental query which it has now become. Thus, the logical form in question must be 'fundamental to all language'; it must provide, that is, a logical analytic tool in terms of which units of discourse in all languages can be analysed. It must preserve, moreover, some form of the language-calculus analogy; it must lead, somehow, to new formal logical calculation. It must throw light on metaphor; it must 'explain' paradox. And yet it must do all this in such a way as to make sense, not nonsense, of the subtleties of logical distinction produced by the 'philosophers of ordinary language', since it is they who, by their fundamental digging-down below recognized linguistic and logical forms, have done more than any other living philosophers to limit the problem and thus to present it as it now is.

To justify ideography as providing the technique which is required to give satisfaction in all these many contexts would take us far beyond the confines of our main argument. Moreover, it is by no means certain that it can be shown that, in the crude first form in which it is presented here, ideography can give adequate satisfaction in any of them. The present situation, in terms of racing metaphor, is rather that, in this new logical field-event, ideography is unfortunately the only starter. Surely, therefore, it would be better to pursue the more detailed trains of thought to which consideration of the principles of ideography leads[1] than to try to form an inevitably premature judgment as to how exactly and how completely the suggestion to use ideography 'solves' all aspects of the technical problem outlined above.

Two trains of thought, however, one philosophic and one philological, are so closely connected with the nature of the suggestion as here put forward that they deserve, and indeed must have, special mention. Philosopher after philosopher has suggested

[1] And, notably, to deploy the logical forms which are permissible in a very simple ideographic language by first constructing, and then interpreting as sequences of ideographs, the formulae of an algebraic calculus.

hat if we wish to 'see deeper into language' we should base our philosophy of it not upon the grammatical and logical forms of an Indo-European language but upon those of an ideographic language such as Chinese.[1] Sinologue after sinologue has stressed that the ancient Chinese language does embody genuine logical forms of thought, and that these are both different and more fundamental than those superficially suggested by Indo-European languages.[2]

Our next business, however, is logical exploration; to establish principles and, in accordance with them, analyse examples. We must make an excursion into paradox-logic; and thus find ourselves in a new — and yet at the same time old and hauntingly familiar — logical countryside.

II. METAPHYSICAL SEQUENCES IN LANGUAGE

§1: *The Five Basic Characteristics of Ideography.*

(1) *An ideographic language is a system of discrete sound-symbols (i.e. of semantic units or ideographs) in which each symbol represents a general idea.*

On this criterion, and applied to this context, the age-long philosophic controversy about universals makes clear what linguistic and logical controversy does not always make clear, namely that in this wide sense of 'ideograph', all linguistic symbols in all languages are ideographs. It is often thought that this is not really so; that, for instance, only generic nouns are ideographs. But even such a symbol as the '-er' in 'work*er*' in fact stands for a general idea, namely the idea of 'the one who does' something; and in ideographic language this '-er', which is the same sort of symbol as the Chinese *jê*, has its own separate ideograph.

Thus all ideographs are alike universals, some of these being used as operators, and some as arguments. What then, the philosopher immediately asks, is the status in this language of index-

[1] The suggestion that the study of esoteric languages, and especially Chinese, might prove philosophically fruitful, has already been made many times by philosophers, and explicitly, in this century, by Whitehead, H. D. Oakeley, B:oad and Waismann.

[2] See especially, on this, the work of Maspéro and of Demiéville; and, in all probability, the forthcoming work of Dobson.

ical symbols — of words, that is, which have such meanings as 'this', 'here' and 'now', and which, according to Russell, stand for the only true particulars? The answer is that the ideographic symbols for 'picking out', for 'presentness', for 'simultaneity' differ from the rest only that they stand for the most general ideas; so that these also, in ideographic language, count as universals.

No ontological status, however, need be assigned to the ideas. There is no philosophical difficulty in the conception that when we speak we compare various kinds of situation, not with any archetypes, but directly with one another. Speaking philosophically, one might say that the realists have described the basic principles of ideographic language-structure, while the nominalists have given the essential hint as to its interpretation.

(2) *An ideographic language is a system of semantic units in which not more than one form of one symbol represents any one general idea.*

Such a language, speaking philosophically, would be perfectly Platonic, in that in it every ideograph would stand for just one Platonic Form. Seen philologically, it would consist entirely of root-words, of Words each of which was a symbol for a whole family of words. Thus 'work', 'works', 'worked', 'working', 'work-', '-work', 'worker', and any other forms which might be taken in some other language by the basic root idea of doing work in this language would be presented by a single unchanging ideograph.

On this criterion, no natural language is fully ideographic, but natural languages can be ordered with respect to ideography. If they are so ordered, languages such as old Chinese would head the list, and a *lingua franca* such as Basic English would be high up on on it, with languages such as French and Latin low down. If, however, in the highly inflected languages, all forms of prefix, infix and suffix are represented by operator-ideographs (in other words, if the highly inflected languages are first split up into significant syllables and then rescripted on an ideographic principle) such languages may be moved much higher up the ideographic list.

That this rescripting process can be done has been long known to all students of language from Bishop Wilkins onwards. No technical use, however, has as yet been made of this fact.

(3) *An ideographic language is a system of semantic units in which the basic principle of symbol-combination consists in limiting, by making more determinate and specific, concepts which before limitation were indeterminate, unconditioned, universal.*

In other words, an ideographic language, as it *extends* its statements, *reduces* their scope until a sufficiently specific meaning is attained. Thus an ideographic language 'goes from the abstract to the concrete'[1] not, as it is often wrongly said that all language goes, 'from the completely concrete conception to the ever-unstatable abstract'. (The more correct thing to say, speaking logically, is that ideographic language goes from the more indeterminate to the more specific; but for some reason literary men and linguists dislike these terms.)

What has hindered philosophers from having a correct view of the logical deployment of such language is that they have been guided not by the use of the significant sound but by the shape of the graph. The fact that concrete visual forms have to be employed to stand for indeterminate ideographs has led such thinkers to make quite unbased assertions about the ancient method of usage of the word (that is, speaking linguistically, about the spoken element, or *seme*) which was, in fact, a great deal more sophisticated than they ever allow for. The sinologue Bernhard Karlgren has protested against this, but, as far as philosophers are concerned, his protest is ignored.[2]

(4) *An ideographic language is logically a fundamental language, as can be seen from observing the logically fundamental and 'primitive' nature of the logical principles which it employs.*

It is because ideographic language, as thus imagined, is meant to be, in some sense, basic to all language, that only a logic founded upon ideographic forms can be, for translation purposes, a true interlingua — an *interlingua*, that is, as opposed to a *lingua*

---

[1] Cf. Gustave Haloun, *Provisional Analysis of Classical Chinese* (checked by the lecturer: unpublished).

[2] Cf. Bernard Karlgren, *Grammata Serica* ,p. 13.

franca. For what makes translation between languages impossible,
logically speaking, is the impact of expressions built of fundamental logical forms, in use in language *A*, upon expressions built
of logical forms which are, in fact, derived forms when considered in language *A*, but which are taken as logically primary in
language *B*. *B*-primary units can't split, so to speak, to make
themselves into *A*-primary ones. There is no comparable difference the other way round, that is, in the process of translating
from *B* to *A*; since sufficiently close analogues of the derived
forms can nearly always be built up out of combinations of the
fundamental ones.

The sense in which ideographic operations must be envisaged
as logically fundamental is hard to make precise without manipulation of calculi. Roughly speaking, all that can be done is: first,
to select those features of thinking, of system-making and of
language which logicians, mathematicians and linguists have each
tended to look on as fundamental to their own special disciplines,
and then to envisage or find all these in ideographic language.
Thus, ideographs in ideographic language, as we are here conceiving of it, tend to function either, in extreme cases, as arguments or as operators, or, in intermediate cases, as blends of the
two; i.e. as operators with a limited scope:[1] and this graded
difference between argument and operator (speaking logically,
between the descriptive sign and the logical sign) is usually considered, by philosophical logicians, to be one of the deepest
logical 'gradings' which there is. Then again, ideographically-
portrayed *semes*, in the actual language of Chinese, are usually
considered, by Far Eastern linguists, less as being fixed in particular parts of speech than as being always in one of the mathematically fundamental states of being *bound* or *free*, and these terms are
used, by Far Eastern linguists, in an only slight extension of the
mathematical sense. And lastly, the primary methods of combination of the ideographs can be seen as extensions of the combinations produced in such a calculus as H. B. Curry's combinatory

[1] The existence of a large class of words which are 'grammatico-lexical' in character,
as well as of words which are 'purely lexical' in character, and of words which are 'purely
grammatical' in character, is thought by some linguists to be the distinguishing mark of
East Asian languages.

logic — which was specially designed to be more logically fundamental, in certain ways, than any other.

For information on the further development of this conception,
see note at the end of this lecture.

(5) *A sequence in an ideographic language is asymmetric, building
up, to right or left, to a centre of emphasis.*

This type of asymmetric concatenation occurs in fact in all
languages, since it is the principle according to which progressive
stress is built up within a long unit of discourse. In ideographic
language, however, this principle is also used to build up the
separate symbols into a sequence.

As will be seen, it is this asymmetry, more than any other characteristic of ideography, which makes possible the reassessment of
paradox. For under this rule — that is, unless any conflicting rule
operates — if the same ideographic concept is used in two positions in the same sequence, its meaning in the first position will
always be more indeterminate than its meaning in the second
position, so that there will be neither identity of meaning, as between the two meanings, if the concept is repeated, nor, if one of
the two concepts is negated, will there be contradiction.

In a similar sort of way this principle also 'solves' (for ideography) Moore's famous 'paradox of analysis'. For in an asymmetric analysis-statement, the *analysandum* will always be more
indeterminate than the *analysans*; so that correctness in the
analytic procedure will no longer imply triviality.[1]

In a recent paper entitled 'How to Talk: some Simple Ways',
J. L. Austin analyses a closely analogous asymmetry; one more
fundamental than any produced by the subject-predicate principle.[2] The kind of ideographic language which is here envisaged
shows this principle pervasive throughout a language.

In order, informally, to illustrate these characteristics and the

---

[1] 'Moore's paradox' is that an analysis of a concept or statement must be either incorrect
or trivial. If the *analysans* means something different from the *analysandum* the analysis is
incorrect; if they mean the same it is trivial.
[2] J. L. Austin. 'How to Talk: some Simple Ways'. (*Proceedings of the Aristotelian Society*, 1952-53).

principles which flow from them, we will now proceed, without further explanation, to analyse various ideographic sequences in languages. We will start, in two forms of Chinese, three forms of Latin and one form of English, with an incantatory sequence from an English nursery-rhyme; 'Three Blind Mice'. We will continue with a sentence which, in English, is usually thought to need a quantifier, but which, in Chinese, is formed with a form of double negative characteristic of the language. The only reasonable translation of this sentence is: 'Absolutely all men must eat and drink.' Finally, we will track down paradox in its native country-side by analysing an untranslatable-and-yet-translatable Chinese paradox which says that a man is truly human only in so far as he performs acts of kindness; the paradox, 'humanity is humānity'.

In all this, though not always appearing to do so, we shall in fact be pressing the analogy with metaphysics (senses i, ii, iii). For in our first example — in characterizing, that is, an ideographic concept — we shall be trying also to characterize the conception of a metaphysical Word. In the second example, we shall in effect be reassessing the similarities and differences between metaphysical statements made by using only very indeterminate notions — statements like 'cats eat fish', and 'Mankind is, in his origin, wholly good' — with more specific, but also more clearly universal statements like '*All* cats eat fish', '*All* men, in origin, are wholly good'. Thus here, inevitably, we shall contrast and compare the forms of language which, *par excellence*, have been traditionally thought of as metaphysical (senses ii and iii) with the only form of language which modern formal logicians, such as Quine, will allow as being legitimately 'metaphysical'. Finally, we shall reassess paradox, not because we now want to say that all Metaphysical argument (sense iii) is paradoxical, but because, much more fundamentally, we now want to say that the adoption of forms of language which permit the reassessment of paradox will also give the clue to the essential logical nature of forms of language used in metaphysical argument (using 'metaphysical' now in senses i, ii and iii.)

Thus we shall hope to put ourselves in a position, by finishing our series of examples with a poetic example (in Chinese), a philosophic example (in Chinese), and actual Metaphysical examples (in Latin and in German) from Spinoza and from Wittgenstein, to show how, when all these forms of language are regarded ideographically (in our sense) they become extremely like to one another.

Exactly how like they become to one another, and exactly what are the implications of that likeness, are questions, however, into which we shall not enter here.

As will appear, the predominance of examples in the Chinese language is irrelevant to the main argument of this lecture, which is philosophical, except in so far as the logically favourable nature for this purpose both of the Chinese language's build-up and of its script forces us, philosophically, to 're-see' logical problems. To that extent, Chinese examples are irreplaceable.

§2: *Analysis of ideographic examples:*

(i) *'Three Blind Mice'*
(*to illustrate the notion of a metaphysical concept, or Word*)

This phrase, according to ordinary ideas of logic, is an elliptical form of the statement, 'There are three blind mice'. Thus, a Latin equivalent might be found for it in some such way as the following:

Vidistin? curriculo edepol currunt tres musculi caeci

and the normal logical analysis of the 'proposition' thought to underly it would be:

There are distinct individuals, x, y, z, such that:
x is a mouse and is blind
y is a mouse and is blind
z is a mouse and is blind

The ideographic analysis of this phrase, however, makes of it not a statement, but a cluster of Words or concepts, which can be taken as being quite complete in itself. For the process of making an ideographic analysis consists in first defining the root ideas behind the words 'three', 'blind' and 'mice' in order to bring out their indeterminacy as concepts, or as Words, and then of finding a method of combining them according to ideographic principles, so that the 'flavour' of an ideographic cluster, or simple sequence, comes out.

In a way we need not redefine the words, if we can once change our attitude to them. We need to re-see these words; to re-see them, in a sense analogous to that used by Wittgenstein in Part II of *Philosophical Investigations*, as 'concepts' which themselves do not change their forms, but which are re-seeable under different 'aspects'. Perhaps it will suffice, in order to re-see them, to re-write them larger, or to spell them with capital letters: 'Three', for 'three', 'Blind' for 'blind', 'Mice' for mice'. Or perhaps shutting the eyes and chanting the words will help: singing them drowsily, slowly, in time with the respiratory rhythm, each word one note lower than the last, *mi, ré, doh*:

> 'Three | Blind | Mice
> Three | Blind | Mice
> Three | Blind | Mice'

But if neither of these two devices opens our inner eyes: if neither of these two devices helps us, when saying 'blind', to 'see' the striped blind nestling behind the adjective 'blind', or what staring at the sun does, or the generic name of the people who have to feel their way, or that pattern of action, in war and in conjuring, which consists in pretending to do something or other, and in fact only doing it 'for a blind', then there are still two more fundamental devices which remain. The first, which is grammatically unsatisfactory, lies in redefining the words as Words, as I have said: 'the Triple Principle', for 'three', 'Blindness' for 'blind' and 'Mousery' for 'mice'. The second, which is that adopted and, so far, retained by the Chinese people, consists of 'logicizing' the concepts by scripting them in an ideographic script. This device, which bears a considerable analogy to the geometrical devices actually used by Wittgenstein when he was endeavouring to explain his idea of the totality of relations between a concept and its aspects, is logically and mathematically the deepest device of all, since it is itself a kind of logical reformalization. If this device won't restore freshness of logical vision, then nothing will.

There are, however, various ways of making ideographs, and

x

by no means all of them have the effect desired. In Text Fig. 1, for instance, the 'clusters' *A*, *B*, *E*, *H* and *I* are all ideographic representations of this Triple Principle-Blindness-Mousery sequence; but by no means all of them represent 'concepts' with 'aspects'. For Text Fig. 1, *A* represents a *cartoon* of three comic-strip mice who have blindfolded themselves; not unless they were made to resemble eminent politicians would even a glimpse of the concepts lurking behind them begin to come out. Text Fig. 1, *B* is, if anything, more misleading. For it consists of three illustrated counters from an old-fashioned children's game, the object of which was to teach small children English words. Thus, in these counters the pictorial indeterminacy is nullified by being tied down to the actual words. *I, C i, ii, iii* and *I, D, i, ii*, on the other hand, represent transitions to a more truly ideographic (in our sense) state of affairs. For *I, C, i, ii, iii* all represent pictures not of a mouse, but of a square Universe limited by Mousery. *C, i* represents this universe as limited by a general surrealist feeling of Mouse; *C, ii* is a copy of a Japanese artist's drawing of Mouse; *C, iii* is the ideograph for *shu*[3], the general ancient Chinese rodent-like idea. And *D, i* and *D, ii* give an actual example of the highly Metaphysical way in which ancient Chinese philologists and grammarians represented to themselves the meanings of their own generic Words. The graph on the right, *D, ii*, is the graph for *wang*[1], the Chinese Word for 'Royalty' or 'Kingship'. The graph on the left, *D, i*, is the graph for *san*[1], the general triple principle. The words in brackets stress one aspect of this concept, namely, that aspect in which 'Three' stands not for any number, but for the totality of primal things, 'Heaven, Earth and Man'. Thus the upright stroke in the *wang*[1] graph, if superimposed on that of *san*[1], can be naturally interpreted in its turn as the religious principle behind royalty; as that redemptive, self-sacrificial characteristic of the Chinese legendary king, by virtue of which he embodied the principle of harmonious joining, of mediation, between the totality of primal things, heaven, earth and man. Now of course, if one looks only at the shape of the graph, it is possible, without any very great penetration, to guess that the graph of *san*[1] represents, not any three primal things, but — in all probability — three notches made on a stick; and similarly, the shape of the graph for *wang*[1] can be seen either as the royal jade ear-ring, or the royal ceremonial axe, according to one's taste in sinologues. But except as a first, very rough, guide to the generic meaning, the shape of the graph is logically trivial; it is irrelevant. It is logically far more important to see, as the Chinese themselves saw, that *wang*[1] and *san*[1] were both generic Words, that is, concepts with aspects. And Western commentators, in concentrating on the provenance of the graphs, have shown themselves not more logically sophisticated than the ancient Chinese themselves, but, logically speaking, incomparably more naive; and that even when, as comparatively rarely happens, they succeed in agreeing as to what, in any particular case, the provenance of the graph actually was. This failure to recognize general, if unusual, logical remarks about language, and to distinguish these from particular and detailed linguistic descriptive devices, still bedevils current Far Eastern linguistic controversy.

To return to our ideographs: I, *E* represents an artificially constructed *Triple principle-Blindness-Mousery* asymmetric sequence constructed according to the pure principles of ideography. The graphs for *san*[1] and for *shu*[2] have already been explained; the middle one, that for *mong*[4] represents a sightless eye-socket. The whole has to be interpreted 'The total universe in its aspect of Mousery (limited by) Blindness — (the whole consisting of these two being in its turn limited by) the Triple Principle.' Thus the brackets merely impose an ordering on the limitations; and the whole thing *could* be made to mean 'Three Blind Mice'. But as a matter of fact, this sequence, as it stands, is too indeterminate for actual communication; it would not communicate; further specificity — the conveyance of more information, if you like — is required. And so I, *H*, *yu*[2] *mong*[4] *shu*[2] *san*[1] and I, *J*, represent the sequence in two forms of actual language. In I, *H* the *san*[1] is moved back, to show that it is here to be interpreted as a number, and a pointing-out symbol (the graph is sometimes said to represent a right hand pointing at the moon) is put in front of the sequence, to show that actual entities are here involved. This symbol, in this position, is usually, and often misleadingly, translated 'there are . . .'; a better translation, logically, which is also more like the French and German *il y a* and *es gibt*, would be 'Establishing entities as follows': An alternative translation of this Ancient Chinese sequence might therefore run: 'Item: blinde mouse iii'. I, *I* represents the sequence in Modern Pekinese. It has now been made specific by the insertion of two operators (that is [see later], by ideographs formalized by Arabic letters with bars). Its literal 'translation' would thus be: '*Three*-entities: *Blind*-like; Old-*Ratty*'; but since it is close to the English, both in grammar and in feeling, it can be translated, without further qualm or comment, as 'Three Blind Mice'. It is worth remarking, however, that though I, *H* and I, *I* are both more specific than the skeleton-form I, *E*, they still, like I, *E*, both embody the five principles of ideography. For I, *H*, if ordered by its brackets only, reads $(d(a(b(c))))$; and I, *I*, if read by its biggest brackets only, gives the form $(a(b(c)))$. Thus one instance, at least, of our imagined Ideographic Language, can be shown to exist in two typical phrases taken from two stages of an actual grouping language.

It becomes clear, too, from this, why, once you are dealing with indeterminate concepts, you lose the temptation to say, ' "Three blind mice", in correct English, really means "There are three blind mice" '. There may be three blind mice, or there may not be three blind mice: there may be many esoteric ways of interpreting 'Three Blind Mice' and there may be also many straight ways — who cares? For this form of analysis, in halting the progress from indeterminacy to specificness by isolating the still highly indeterminate cluster as it stands, prevents all the thorny logical questions which have to do with the existence of actual entities — together with the even thornier questions which have to do with the existence of fictional entities — from ever being able to arise. We can, of course, raise up logical difficulties for ourselves by insisting on the continuation of the rhyme. But we needn't. If we choose to sing 'Three Blind Mice' three times, and then stop, and say that we have no particular urge to continue, then we have not done something incomplete. We have stopped at the end of the most fundamental ideographic unit, the cluster; we have undoubtedly communicated something highly indeterminate; but nothing illogical has been done: that is quite all right.

Moreover, a very strong case could be made out for saying that it is not only the Chinese language which consists of concepts, and not only colloquial English which has clusters. The translation of 'Three Blind Mice' in Latin, for instance, which was given at the beginning of this section, is by no means the only form of translation which one could make. What about

Mures caeci tres edepol!

just like that without further explanation; or, again as in English,

Caecati musculi tres
Ecce celeriter currunt

The point which we are making here is a logical point; it does not depend upon the structure of any language.

Nevertheless, that it may be seen how far a language can go in providing an empirical basis for the notion of indeterminate concept, actual definitions of two Chinese words are given, together with an example of their use in an $((a(b))(c))$ combination, another variant in actual use of the basic cluster-combination, $(a(b(c)))$. The actual definitions are:

Text Fig. II, A, i), *Tsê*⁴ 'Character'

> to nourish, breed, bring up, treat with fatherly love, cherish; (a 'brought-up' person) name or 'style' taken at 20 years; name, appellation; word, written character, letter.
> The graph shows a child under a roof.

Text Fig. II, A, ii) *Ching*¹ 'Warpery' — the Warping Principle; warp in a loom; (geographical warping principle) meridians of longitude; (the moral 'warp'): rules of conduct, rule, law, classical book, canon, sûtra; prayer; regulate; follow a rule, pass along; pass, past, already.

> The graph shows, on the left, silk; on the right, an underground stream.[1]

[1] These definitions are based on those in Karlgren's *Analytic Dictionary*. See also his discussion in *Sound and Symbol in Chinese*, p. 85.

Clearly, these two are concepts which have many aspects. On the other hand, the meaning of Text Fig. II, *A, iii* is, in the actual language, quite unambiguous. It is the name of a twelfth-century Chinese school-book, the characters of which are arranged in groups of three.

Analysis of ideographic examples:

(ii) *the 'metaphysical' statement: 'Absolutely all men must eat and drink.'*

This next example brings up so many of the fundamental problems of ideography that it is impossible to analyse it properly here. For it exemplifies four secondary ideographic principles: the Double Reference Principle (a restricted form of which we know in ordinary philosophical logic as the Subject-Predicate Principle): the Principle of Progressive Definition by Performance Displacement (that principle which accounts for the emergence of heterogeneity of function among homogeneous ideographs): the Principle of Cluster-forming by Juxtaposition of Comparables (which produces an *a-and-b* form, but not the *p and q* form of ordinary propositional logic): and, finally, the Principle of the Reversal of the Nullification of Totality (which turns the ideographic equivalent of 'cats eat fish' into the ideographic equivalent of 'Absolutely all cats must eat fish'). In short, the whole difficulty of analysing this sequence can be tersely put by saying that this is the point at which an ideographic sequence comes nearest to being capable of analysis in terms of ordinary logic without, however, ever quite coming within the purview of ordinary logic. And it is obvious that an investigation of why exactly it is that such a sentence never comes within the purview of ordinary logic will be crucial to our estimate, as general philosophers, of the value of logic itself; since such an investigation may be calculated to throw a lot of light also on why it is that Metaphysical, poetic and colloquial sentences also never come within the purview of modern logic: to modern logic's all but irreparable loss.

For the exponents of modern logic — pledged to investigate the very foundations of symbolism itself—always flinch from the problem of trying to discover the true nature of symbol manipulation in language. Logicians have now been deflected so definitively from the deeper operation — that of discovering the principles of combination of concepts — to the more shallow operation of trying to find the principles of combination of mathematical concepts, that the greater number of them are now tempted to pretend that to discover the basic principles of the combination of concepts was never their desire. Not so have the very greatest logicians, Aristotle, Boole, Russell, Whitehead, envisaged their task. When Boole said that all reasoning can be reduced to the discussion of attributes, which could be identified with the classes of objects possessing them, and that such attributes could be designated either by adjectives or generic nouns, — he was not side-stepping the question of discovering the principles of combination of all concepts.[1] When the mathematician Birkhoff, writing on logic and commenting on Boole, further states that the notion of an attribute (also called 'property' or 'quality' or 'generic noun') is so fundamental that no definition of it in more fundamental terms is possible, — he also is not side-stepping the fundamental problem of trying to discover what are the basic units which have to be combined in order for it to be possible for thought to occur. Why men of the mathematical calibre of Boole and Birkhoff[2] having started with such a deep initial insight, fail to make progress with this most fundamental problem, is that they then proceed to adopt uncritically two further assumptions. The first of these is that the primary methods of combination of attributes (which we will now call Attributes, in order to equate them not, Aristotelianwise, with determinate qualities and properties, but Platonically, with basic Words, or ideographs, or concepts, or Fundamental Ideas, or generic nouns) are by means of the propositional connectives 'and' and 'or', together with the operations of inclusion and negation. The second is that Attributes, like attributes, are determinate. That the propositional and inclusion con-

[1] G. Birkhoff, in *Lattice Theory* (1940), chapter on 'Applications of Lattice-Theory to Logic' (pp. 122 et seq.) gives and comments on all the relevant quotations from Boole.
[2] Contemporary professional logicians are tending to become more and more chary of saying what the fundamental units of symbolic thought are. Not so 'polymaths', such as Birkhoff (loc. cit.) and Weil, *The Philosophy of Mathematics and Natural Science* (1949), chapter 1, 'Mathematical Logic, Axiomatics'.

BRITISH PHILOSOPHY IN MID-CENTURY

nectives are not either the only ways or the primary ways of combining concepts, however, could have been seen, and seen *a priori*, from the start. For if all reasoning consists in manipulating Attributes, what about the propositional connectives, the inclusion-sign and the negator? Are these Attributes? And if they are not, what are they? This question always remains unanswered. And so the acknowledged fundamental unit of the generic noun, or Attribute, always tends to fall into the logical background, while the connectives, which, as a second sort of fundamental conceptual unit, should never, in the context of this problem, have been allowed to come to the fore at all, tend to become the very stuff of thought itself. Then, for traditional reasons, and also in order to provide something for the now high and dry connectives to join, there has to be invented that eternally elusive entity, the discrete, atomistic, logical building-block of the 'sentence' or 'proposition'. And so logic, by losing its Attributes, loses its hold also on actual language, and through language, on the problem of determining the foundations of thought itself. Then the fictional replacement of generic Attributes by determinate propositions sets in motion an equally delusional competitive race towards greater and greater mathematical rigour and exactness; and it requires shocks such as Gödel's Theorem, and actual experience of wrestling with the paradoxes which this straining after exactness, if it goes too far, itself produces, to cause logicians to go back to the reconsideration of what their basic field of study really is.

Once such reconsideration is embarked on, however, the power and depth of meta-mathematics and of logic — as opposed to the intellectual triviality of much of current philosophy of language and linguistic analysis — immediately shines out like a seascape catching the sun. For the fact that the propositional connectives do not apply to ideographs does not mean that mathematical and logical ideas are irrelevant to ideography. Far from it. Wittgenstein has now reimagined Attributes, even more fundamentally than Boole, as interacting (and therefore indeterminate) concepts.[1] Moreover he (from the side of logic) and Brouwer (from the side of mathematics) have equally dreamed of a process of progressive

[1] Ludwig Wittgenstein, *Philosophical Investigations* (1953), Part II.

general redefinition of mathematical concepts in which these are conceived of as occurring and then re-occurring in freely developing sequences. Thus, if this train of thought is applied also to generic concepts as well as to mathematical ones, and thus made as fundamental as it will go, the static, brick-like proposition becomes dynamic, a segment — acted upon and within itself interacting — of an infinite continuously developing free sequence; something much more like what an unpunctuated piece of language, seen logically, actually is.

To return now from these general considerations to the particular sequence which we have set out to examine, which exemplifies how some ideographic concepts primarily combine. It is evident that if we are to form a logic entirely of generic nouns, of concepts, of Attributes, that we are up against two great difficulties, right from the start. The first of these is to show, from actual examples in language, what concepts which are normally conceived of as being unalterably in other logical categories can possibly look like when they are re-envisaged as generic nouns. The second is to show what forms of language which we have been accustomed to think of as different forms of statement can possibly look like when they are re-envisaged as indeterminate asymmetric sequences. Both of these difficulties are starkly brought to the fore by the example given here. And the secondary ideographic principles referred to earlier are precisely those designed to meet one or other of these two difficulties, and that is why they are relevant to this particular analysis.

To return then to the old Chinese sequence translatable as: 'absolutely all men must eat and drink', given in Text Fig. I, G. In disentangling this sequence's analysis, we come first to those black lines, above and below some of the elements, which separate its central core from its periphreral parts. This black-line-drawing device applies the basic ideographic principle governing sequences with Double Reference. Such sequences break into two conceptual parts: the first part, which displays some aspect of the situation which has been already given: and the second part, which displays some aspect of it which is new. It is difficult to put oneself into the frame of mind in which one could conceive it possible that there may be nothing more to the so-called Subject-Predicate principle than this. Two thoughts help. The first is that obviously, in ideographic language, the Subject-Predicate principle cannot be conceived of as the application to a subject of a predicate, since here we have a language all of generic nouns. The second is that the Subject-Predicate principle can be conceived immediately as far more generalized as soon as the units which are supposed to exemplify it can be envisaged as indeterminate. Let us take an example to illustrate this fact. Imagine a bare valley, full of stones. One stone differs from the rest: it is a red stone. A man using ideographic language points to this conspicuous stone and says, 'Red *Stone*'; i.e. he uses the language-form $(a(b))$. Now, if we conceive of the elements of this sequence as determinate, all sorts of horrible logical questions immediately arise; e.g. Does a man who says 'Red Stone' and points, assert that there actually are red stones, and thus make a statement? or, Does 'red' in the so-called phrase 'red stone' mean the same as 'red' in the so-called 'sentence' 'this is red'? and so on. But now, loosen the logical bands: make the concepts indeterminate: and therefore don't let us decide anything about this sequence except what we absolutely have to decide. Changing our question, let us therefore now ask ourselves, 'What is the indeterminate concept "Red" used to do when, in this sequence, it is applied to the conspicuous stone?' Since it is used here, in the dry bare valley, mainly to distinguish one stone from the rest, it is evidently being used here, not so much in its aspect as a colour symbol as in its aspect as an indexical symbol, or logical proper name, so that the whole phrase means, more or less, '*That* stone'. But now consider another situation. We have picked up the stone; we have then taken it home; and we now intend to examine it closely under a good light. We talk to one another about it (we know already, all too well, that it's a stone): do we say again, speaking ideographically, 'Red *Stone*'? No, we do not; we reverse the concepts and say 'Stone: *Red*'. And this time, not only has the sequence a double reference, back to the valley situation and forward to the present one, but also a reversed process of aspect-choosing takes place. For this time it is the 'Stone' concept which appears in an aspect which is indexical, to mean, '*this* old thing, which I have taken all the trouble to lug home'. But 'Red' here is in an aspect which is anything but indexical, since it is used either to convey, or to re-stress, a piece of information which, in this changed context, is new and strange. The stone isn't sapphire-blue, agate, jet, topaze or turquoise, it's *red*. Now then (we shall then ask) what exact kind of shade of redness is it? And what, in this new context, does this exact kind or shade of redness signify?

And so we have it: the ideographic rule of Predicative Displacement, used to produce a Sequence with Double Reference out of a sequence with only single reference: $(a(b))$ is convertible into $(b:(a))$; and in the Text Figs., in order to preserve more simply the principle of asymmetric concatenation, the displacement, instead of being indicated by a colon, is indicated by hat-shaped black lines above the displaced concepts and below. Moreover, if $(a(b))$ is to be convertible into $(b:(a))$, whenever the $(b:(a))$ form first occurs in an ideographic unit of discourse, a previous occurrence of b (say, in the title) must be presumed to have previously occurred, in order that, when it occurs in the form $(b:(a))$ it may stand for the Given — 'that old thing' — not for any element of surprise, that is, the New. Stories must have titles, in ideography; sentences must have prefixes; and before there can be a 'statement' there must have been a cluster first.

Now, displacement being in our minds, let us turn to the next principle. This is the Principle of Progressive Definition by Performance in Displacement, which accounts for the gradual appearance, in use, of progressive heterogeneity of function, in a language conceived as made up of homogeneous indeterminate units. This principle is a pure and bold invention, which is reached by a theoretic creative act. It owes nothing to historical linguistics, a good deal to Brouwerian logic, and something, but not very much, to the current philosophy of language. It will be evident, however, that the real development of language-concepts in actual languages and over millennia must be so complicated that nothing theoretic can be done about it; it will always be more complicated than anything which we can imagine. What is wanted here, as in other such sophisticated empirical situations, is a principle which is both simple enough to be itself capable of further sophistication, and also powerful enough to account for at least some of the categorical profusion and variety which there is. Here is postulated no ancient proto-language to which we look back: only a logical device for interrelating and handling what occurs.

Imagine an ordinary ideographic asymmetric sequence, $(a(b(c)))$. Imagine now that this is indefinitely prolonged:

1. $(a(b(c(d(e(f(g(n)))))))))$

Imagine finally, that this sequence has to be interpreted as we have been interpreting such sequences: 'n limited, or qualified, by g, the whole, *n-qualified-by-g*, being then qualified by f, the whole, '*n-qualified-by-g*',*-the-whole-being-then-qualified-by-f*, being then qualified by e ... up to ... 'being qualified by a'. It is difficult, of course, to imagine an actual speech-situation in which any such string of Attribute-concepts could ever occur; nevertheless, since we are doing not linguistics but logic, let us imagine that such a speech situation has been found. It is now evident that, in such a situation, owing to the effect on the indeterminacy of the asymmetry, heterogeneity of function will develop as between the concepts. For the concept on the right in 1, n, will tend to become, as it becomes more qualified, more and more particular, until, in the limiting case in which it can refer only to a single occurrence at time t of a fleeting event, it comes to mean something like the South London phrase, 'This 'ere, quick'. And the concept on the left, in 1, will tend to become so extremely general that it serves, in the end, as an almost purely abstract determinator, that is, as a piece of punctuation placed at the beginning of the sequence to indicate the kind of talk which the sequence is going to contain: '*item*, blinde mouse iii'; '*Goings-on* as follows': 'Proceeding now to a *royal communication*' ('The king said:') '*Message starts* here': punctuational indicators like these.

Let us concentrate here on the first of these two extreme cases, since there is a sense in which they both yield pointers rather than arguments, the first a pointer to the occurrence of a particular kind of event in the world, the second a pointer to the occurrence of a particular kind of sequence in language. We will take as an example the concept of 'Play', or 'Playing', and we will imagine this, arbitrarily, as meaning primarily a kind of physical action which is taken part in by one or two parties. 'Children *Play* Ball', 'White *Play* Black' — these would exemplify the kind of way in which this concept is to be used. And this use tends to put the concept 'Play' into the middle rather than at the beginning or end of a sequence; though we can imagine this sequence as having itself evolved by Predicative Displacement from another, shorter, kind of primary sequence: 'Child Play', 'Ball Play', 'White-Black Play'. So we get the imagined first stage in the positional evolution of 'Play':

2.   (a(Play))
3.   (a:((Play (c))))

Now, however, let us imagine the aspect of 'Play' which is used in a more complicated notion, though of the same kind; for instance in the sequence, 'The playing of the impromptu cadenza of the last movement of the first performance of so-and-so's Horn Concerto at the 1955 Edinburgh Festival'. Ideographically, this phrase would become something like: '1955-Edinburgh-Music Festival-So-and-So-Horn-Concerto-First-Performance-Last-Movement-Impromptu-Cadenza-Play'. In such a long specifying phrase, as we have said, the 'Play' concept will tend to become indexical: it will stress, in the concept 'Play', first the aspect of 'actual play' and then the concept of '*that* actual play'.

Now imagine that, for historical reasons, in the case of the concept 'Play' this kind of stressing is the kind which always occurs. To imagine this, we should have to think ourselves into a musical universe of discourse where every event was fleeting and was called a Play (an analogy to this use of 'play' for 'event' sometimes occurs when we say 'Play' after there has been an interval of 'no-play' in playing a game). In such a universe, 'Play', when asserted, would mean almost entirely '*that* play', so that, in the end, in spite of its basic indeterminacy, it might well come to mean entirely something like 'That (pl'y)', with only the ideographic sign of the graph (say, two hands playing a pipe), to mislead scholars into thinking that there once existed a separate but homologous word meaning 'Play'.

Now, in the course of all this, what has happened to the concept 'Play'? It has been subjected to a process of Progressive Definition, in which it is imagined that its past performance contributes to its present meaning. In order to get rid of the element of time, which is indigestible in logic, we will represent each progressive stage of definition as a re-occurrence of 'play' in a linear sequence. In this sequence, the recurrent musical subsequence $(a(b(c(d(e(f(\ldots)))))))$, which must be imagined as essentially stable, if it is to force the progressive redefinition of 'Play', we will call M, and its recurrences M_1, M_2, M_3 . . . M_n. Thus, omitting everything except the bare bones of the process, we get a quasi-recurrent pattern, thus:

4. $\{ \; M_1 \; (Play)) \; \{ \; (M_2 \; (Actual \; Play)) \; \{ \; (M_3 \; (That \; Actual \; Play)) \; \{ \; (M_4 \; (\textit{That} \; (pl'y) \;))\}\}\}\}$

So far, however, we have only progressive redefinition; we have no displacement. The whole M-performance of 'Play' has occurred so far in the position B in the recurrent pattern $(A(B))$.

But now imagine that the concept '*That* (pl'y)', retaining its contextual history, comes to mean also '*Those* (pl'y)'. It will now, in all probability, sharply change its position. For it will now become extremely useful, in an Attribute language referring to a musical universe of discourse, to indicate that the whole sequence which follows refers to chains of non-persistent events which are heard, not seen; and this means putting it over from the extreme right in a sequence to the extreme left. Thus, in this use of 'Play' we will tend to get forms like:

5. $(\textit{Those} \; (pl'y) \; (a\!: \; (b(c))))$

Moreover, if this musical universe of discourse becomes sufficiently developed for individual instances of '*Those* (pl'y)' to have names, instead of being individually referred to, with the aid of pointing, as 'That (pl'y)', the part of speech which we so misleadingly refer to as a 'pronoun' will immediately be required. And what symbol could be more appropriate to us for this than the now largely unemployed 'That (pl'y)'? So you get the final positional displacement of 'Play', to the 'subject' or 'object' position in complex sentences with Double Reference. In the sequence-form which follows, the name of the individual 'That (pl'y)' will be replaced by the symbol I, and the rest of the sequence with Double Reference by the symbols X and Y:

6. $\{ I \{ pl'y: (X(Y)) \} \}$ 'with regard to I, $\begin{cases} pl'y \, Xs \, Y \\ 'it' \end{cases}$

7. $\{ I \{ X: (Y(pl'y)) \} \}$ 'with regard to I, $X \, Ys$ $\begin{cases} pl'y \\ 'it' \end{cases}$

Thus, the Principle of Progressive Definition, in this case, has so acted upon an originally verb-like concept, 'Play', that, firstly, it has become a final positional verbal noun, 'Playing'; then it has become an indexical symbol, 'That (pl'y)': then it has become a generalized form of this, 'Those (pl'y)': then, finally, it has become the unstressed substitute-symbol, '(pl'y)'. And through all this, though it may change its stress, its form will not change; and it will retain, together with its original graph of two hands playing a pipe, just enough of the restriction placed upon it by its original meaning to make it refer throughout only to patterns of non-recurrent sound-events, apprehended by the ear.

Now it is evident that no logical notation can hope to convey the progressive vagaries of all the positional displacements through which ideographic concepts, as we have imagined them, may pass. It is, however, possible to have a steady opinion about the logical order in which such positional displacements may be imagined to occur. In Text Figs. I and II, only this indication is given of performance-displacement, that concepts which are thought of as having been displaced once are marked with one bar; concepts which are thought of as having been displaced twice with two bars. When whole sequences, as opposed to single concepts, are imagined to have been displaced, as in Predicative Displacement, straight lines drawn above and below the displaced sequences are used to replace the bar.

So much, in its turn, for the principle of Progressive Definition by Positional Displacement, of which, if desired, the Principle of Predicative Displacement can be regarded as a special case. Once the full logical flavour of these two principles becomes absorbed, it becomes easier to see why it is impossible, by combining the indeterminate, interacting, progressively definable concepts of ideographic logic, for any logical entity really analogous to the brick-like 'proposition' to be obtained. It becomes easier, too, to appreciate the difficulty which the ideographer will come up against, once he wants, for translation-purposes or otherwise, to make an ideographic sequence stop. For, within the universe of discourse of ideographic language (as also within that of Meta-physical language (sense iii), the trouble is not to make the flow of speech go on, but to get it, logically speaking, ever to cease. For how can we know — on the principles which I have given — that a speaker who stops hasn't just been cut off short? We can't know; there is a sense in which he always has been cut off short; clearly a logical stop-rule is what is required.

This device is called the Principle of Cluster-forming by Juxta-position of Comparables; and it is, as we shall see, the principle which enables one to say 'cut here'. The effect of it is not to say that the cut must be made in one place; but to make immaterial to the amount and kinds of specificness established so far in a sequence any further limiting information which may come in. Like all ideographic principles, it applies equally to single concepts and to sequences. What the principle says is that when a pair, or sequence, of concepts are so highly comparable, both in form and meaning, that the comparison is evident when they are juxtaposed with the most important first; then, the concepts or sequences are to be interpreted according to parallel aspects, which has the effect of bracketing them so closely all together, that both before and after the sequence one can say 'cut here'. Because, in such sequences, the most important of the comparable set is always put first, the sequence consisting of them is bracketed, in the Text Figs., with square brackets which work asymmetrically to the left, instead of working to the right, thus: [[a]b]. 'A-and-B' would be the interpretation of such a sequence; 'Ten-and-Two', 'To be-and-not to be', 'Boy-and-Girl'. Within such clusters also can operate a special rule of conjunctive displacement; for when, within such a cluster, the positional order is reversed — so that [[a]b] becomes converted into [[b]a], then the hyphenating link between the two comparables is imagined to have been made even closer than before, so that the two fuse into a single concept: i.e. 'Twenty', 'Non-Existence', 'Girl-Child'. When it is sequences, not concepts, which are in question, it is in most cases not practical for the permutation to be made. But it is consonant with the genius of this kind of language that, in its modern form, the logically basic form of asking a question is to fuse a sequence and its opposite, making $[[A]non\text{-}A]$. Since, in this form, there occurs no permutation, the fusion of comparables is shown in the Text Figs. by a hyphen on the middle bracket, not by a bar on the second concept.

A moment's reflection will establish the fact that if, in ideographic language, this principle of cluster-forming be conceived as the only true stop-rule, it follows that the cluster-form is more important than that of the 'statement'; the logical unit, in this language, is $[[A_1]A_2]$. We can substitute for this $[[p]q]$, if we like; we shall then lean heavily, as other logicians have before us, on the graphic resemblance between the letter-form 'p' and the letter-form 'q'. For this 'and', which we here interpret by means of square brackets, and which needs, itself, no special ideograph, is not the dot of the Propositional Calculus; it is a hyphen; it is also the main English 'and' of everyday life. And this brings up the further very awkward question as to whether, in colloquial English as in ideographic language, the fundamental logical unit isn't really the sub-paragraph, or cluster; whether we don't, in fact, rely, in understanding one another, upon a phenomenon of logical parallelism which, in logical theory, we ignore.

As soon as we think this, however, the awkward case occurs to us; the case of the supposedly isolatable, factual statement which speakers in any language will have to use. If this is to be conceived of as the A_1 half of an $[[A_1]A_2]$ sequence-form, where on earth is the other half, A_2? Well, there is only one thing, in ideography, which the missing second half of the parallelism can possibly be; namely, that indexical sign which stands, in such a statement, in a final position, and which means: 'To find the other half of the parallelism, look directly at the world itself.' Frege's assertion-sign, |-, will do to represent this, so long as this isn't then inter-preted, in the customary manner, as a full stop. The Text Figs. have a very beautiful ideograph, meaning 'Fact' (and with a graph which is supposed by some to represent a striking cobra) which, when displaced to a completely final position, means just this. And, of course, though logical difficulties still remain if you think hard enough about them, sequences built in this fundamental, elemental kind of way can be taken more easily than propositional sequences can as 'pictures', which can then be imagined to parallel (somehow or other) sequences of elemental fact.

In any case, we can take it that we now get our cluster, the alternative form to $[[A_1]\,A_2]$ being $[[A]|-]$. And now we can turn, at long last, back to our original example, and exhibit our last ideographic principle by analysing 'Absolutely all men must eat and drink'.

The ideographic analysis of this remark is given in Text Fig. I, G, underneath an ideographic sequence which has the symbol for 'Man' (or, 'Humanity') on the left, and the cobra-symbol for 'Fact' on the extreme right. The ideographs for 'Eating' and 'Drinking' are thought so closely to resemble one another that the actual graph of the first is included in the graph of the second.

To construct the sequence we first imagine a universe of dis-course $([[d]e]\,(a))$: 'Humanity qualified by the idea of Eating-and-Drinking': a human eating-and-drinking universe. We now trans-pose the two halves of this, by Predicative Displacement, to give $(a:([[d]e]$; 'Men eat and drink'. As, by the Principle of Conjunction of Comparables, this is not complete, we now add 'Fact', to give the $[[A]|-]$ form, which gives $[[(a([[d]e]))]|-]$: 'Men eat and drink: Fact.' (N.B. As the notation in the Text Figs. is designed for graphs, and is therefore so constructed that the 'Fact' ideograph, which in the actual language is highly mobile, can be both identi-fied by meaning and also barred, the squared brackets are not also used to mark its occurrence, but any brackets which are con-venient, so long as they build up to the left, not the right.)

But now we have to do something to turn 'A man eats and

drinks, and that's a fact', into 'Absolutely all men must eat and drink'. And to do that we have to call on a new (and last) Principle: The Principle of the Reversal of the Nullification of Totality. Another way of putting this difficulty logically is by saying that just as on our principles the difficulty earlier was to stop an ideographic sequence, not to make it go on, so the difficulty now is not to introduce totality — since every indeterminate ideograph will have a total aspect — but to specify the kind of totality which we want to get out of our sequence, and then make sure that no further limitation is subsequently allowed to act upon it.

We do this by constructing a characteristic kind of double negative. First, with the aid of c, a cancelling ideograph (the graph has once been compared to a wheeling bird, which it is helpful for logical purposes to think of as a kind of weathercock, or action of going back upon one's tracks) we cancel our eating and drinking universe; thereby leaving nothing. Now, this aspect of this cancelling, negating symbol can be conceived of logically as a nullifier, that is, as a symbol adding all possible further limitations to an already partially limited total universe of discourse, so as to cancel the whole thing; to make it replaceable by the symbol O. But to see this, one must be explicit about the totality which was once in it. One must make sure, in other words, that the indeterminate symbol for 'Humanity' really does get interpreted Metaphysically, i.e. interpreted as 'Humanity' or as 'Mankind'; not as 'a man', or 'men', or, 'other men', which it can also mean. To secure this, I am here going to replace a by $(a(I))$, using 'I' here to mean the total universe of discourse. In the Text Fig., to indicate this same thing, a is barred; and it is barred because it is pushed into the most general possible position in the sequence, i.e. right over on the extreme left, thus becoming an extremely neat instance of the operation of the principle of Progressive Definition by Positional Displacement. Here, however, to shorten the present analysis, we will leave it as it now is, making:

$$[[(c (((a(\mathrm{I})): ([[d]e])))]|\text{-}]$$

'It is not the case that there is a human eating and drinking universe'; 'The fact of human eating and drinking is a non-fact'.

And now, of course, we negate the nullifier. We use a symbol, of which the logical meaning would be $\sim (\exists x)$, i.e. 'it is not the case that there is an x' — but for the awkward fact that, in this logic, there is no way of asserting $(\exists x)$, (since $(\exists x)$ would always mean, 'There is a total universe of discourse'), — and we use it to limit, or reverse, or qualify, the nullifier. The basic idea of this second negating notion is 'Disappearance', and part of the graph means, comparatively reliably, the sun disappearing behind a tree as it goes down. We then get $(b(c))$, instead of c, in the formula given above. We finally move a over to the extreme lefthand position, both to make sure that it is interpreted in its general aspect, i.e. as $(a(I))$, and also so that it can limit the double negation, thus turning b, the indeterminate idea of 'None', into 'Nobody'. Thus we finally get:

$$[[\ (\ (a(\text{1}))\ (\ (b(c))\ (\ [[d]e]))] \ [\text{-}\ ]$$

'In all cases — that is, in the case of absolutely everybody — nobody does not eat and drink: and that's a fact'; i.e.

'Absolutely everybody must eat and drink.'

No wonder that Mo-Tzu, the Chinese Aristotle, established as the first principle of reasoning the general truth which is given in Text Fig. I, F:

'[The First Principle of Reasoning is that] that which is not limited is universal.'[1]

Analysis of ideographic examples, (iii): the paradox, 'Humanity is Humanity'. Last lecture we spent a very long time misanalysing paradox. Now, with paradox established in its native countryside, the analysis of it can be given in a few lines.

Only one *caveat* is here necessary. The analysis of this paradox, 'Humanity is humanity', which is scripted here according to a suggestion made by the Chinese grammarian Chao[2] spreads

[1] 'What is not limited is universal'. Mo-Tzu, *The Minor Illustrations*, chapter 45.
[2] Yuan Ren Chao, 'The Logical Structure of Chinese Words' (*Language*, XXII (1946), p. 4: presidential address read at the regional meeting of the Linguistic Society of America, 1945.

over Text Fig. I, *J*, *K*, *L*, and includes forms, i.e. Text Fig. *I*, *K*, *L*, which, like Text Fig. I, *E*, are too indeterminate to occur, as they stand, in any language. They are inserted here in order to show the stages in which — speaking now logically but not linguistically — the heterogeneity of 'Humänity is Humănity' is built up.

We can say depressing things, in English, like 'War is War', and 'Business is business', but we cannot say hopeful things, like, 'Humanity is humanity' — 'to be fully human *is* to be humane'. Let us see how we can say this, ideographically, in Chinese.

We start with the primary sequence $(a_1(a_2))$, which, if it existed, would mean, vacuously, 'Human Humanity'. We reverse this by Predicative Displacement; to give the statement, *'Humanity is Humanity'*, $(a_2:(a_1))$, which would probably be misread as $[[a_1]a_2]$ and interpreted 'Man-and-man', i.e. men. We then add the 'Fact' notion to each half of our sequence, giving, 'Humanity, indeed, is human: fact,' $([[a_2]]-]: [[a_1]]-])$). But now, since this is not only too trivial, but still too indeterminate, we add a concretizing symbol, *g* (for the meaning of the graph of which no suggestion whatever is available, but which is analysable as having one general use, namely that of making concrete and/or specific whatever cluster precedes it). The sequence now has to mean, 'The specific aspect of the concept of humanity indeed is human in fact', and the only aspect of the 'Humanity' concept which answers this description is the one which means 'benevolence', 'actual humane deeds'. So we get 'as for what is indeed humane, it is what is in fact human' — which is by no means vacuous or trivial; but the better translation is probably Chao's, 'Humanity is humanity', which leaves the indeterminacy while also leaving the hearer free, if he wish, to structure ideographically what has been said.

§3: *Metaphysical expansions in language*

We have now exemplified metaphysical Words, or concepts, a metaphysical statement, and a metaphysico-poetic statement, or paradox. The final question, which now presses, is: what about actual Metaphysics? What about forms as used in Metaphysical argument (sense iii)?

In the last lecture, it will be remembered, we established three interconnected senses of 'metaphysical' statement. A metaphysical statement, in sense i, meant any sequence of ideographs; a metaphysical statement, in sense ii, meant any sequence of ideographs in which clusters predominated, rather than statements; and a metaphysical, or Metaphysical, statement, in sense iii, meant a sequence of ideographs in which both it was the case that clusters predominated, rather than statements, and also which was concerned with traditional very general, very fundamental subject-matter.

We can now proceed a little further with this triple definition. We have dealt with sense i, in the sense that we have endeavoured to exhibit sequences of ideographs. It is now time to become a little clearer about sense ii. For to say, ideographically, that a metaphysical statement, in sense ii, is one in which clusters predominate, rather than statements, is ambiguous in this context. It can mean that such sequences do not include the notion of 'Fact', placed in a final position; that the metaphysical form, *par excellence*, is $[[A_1]A_2]$, not $[[A]]$-]. That this indeed tends to be the case will appear; but there is more involved in this definition of metaphysical, sense ii, than that. For this definition is meant to postulate a more general requirement that the constructions readily identifiable as Metaphysical (sense iii) should be as ideographically simple as possible; and in particular, that they should be, when possible, such as to make the minimum use of the Principle of Progressive Definition by Positional Displacement. In other words, Metaphysical examples, in senses ii and iii should not, as actual colloquial examples do, tend to represent ideography at its subtlest; but that they should represent it at its starkest, at its least differentiated, at its most indeterminate, in those forms in which the sequences are as it were exploding with totality.

Thus the definition of metaphysics in sense ii requires that in order to think of ideographic language-forms as Metaphysical (sense iii), we must first think of the concepts in them as being at their most basic, and then of the sequence-forms as being ideographically the simplest possible, the most compact, the simplest, the most stark. But it must not be thought, because of this, that

Metaphysical thought, seen thus, will be logically monotonous; for it already foreseeable, from the examples which we have given, that this will be very far from being the case.

Let us try to imagine some basic patterns, usable in such metaphysics; usable, that is, in metaphysics, (sense ii). To do this, let us imagine that we have marbles of different colours, and that we are going to pretend that these marbles are ideographs. Different marbles of the same colour will represent, in this game, different occurrences of the same ideograph. Let us put them on a track, so that they have to be in a line. Now let us fiddle with them, and let our fiddling instincts have full play; and then let us see what kind of thing we get.

We can already foresee the kind of thing which will come out:

pattern I: a marble of colour *a* is put next to a marble of colour *b*, producing *ab*. Try out the effect of contrasting different colours.

(compare Text Fig. II, A, iv, v, vi, vii, viii.)

pattern II: starting with a string of marbles of different colours, *a b c d*, double each, producing *aa, bb, cc, dd*.

(compare Text Fig. II, B, i to iv.)

pattern III: having made a pattern, say of two marbles, *ab*, reverse it, producing *ba*.

(compare Text Fig. II, C, i to iii.)

pattern IV: make a repetitive pattern, *aabb baab ccdd dccd*, etc.

(compare Text Fig. II, D, i and ii)

pattern V: make a recurrent pattern, according to a scheme; e.g. *a c e b d   a c f b d   a c g b d*, etc.

(compare Text Fig. II, F, which shows a more complicated form of this)

pattern VI: make a pattern which is almost recurrent, but which 'works up'; e.g. *a c e b d   a c e e b d   a c e e e b d*, etc.

(compare Text Fig. II, E, which shows, rather untidily, a reversed form of this)

Thus it becomes clear that, even taking marbles of not more than five colours, there are a good many patterns which can be made. The number increases immediately, of course, as soon as one puts back the ideographic brackets, as can be seen from the examples given in Text Fig. II.

for instance,

pattern I can have variants: (a(b)), ((a)b), [[a]b], [[a]b], a:b, (*a*(*b*))

Not all of these forms are exemplified in the examples given; in particular, ((a)b) is left out, as in this form the *b* is always in fact barred, and we want to consider metaphysical sequences (sense ii); that is, sequences in which as few symbols are barred as possible. In the examples given, Text Fig. II, A, iv usually means, in context, 'king of the state', or 'state-king'; Text Fig. II, A, v means, 'to rule the state', or 'to king the state'. Text Fig. II, A, vi is a man's proper name; an analogous feeling is given by the words 'Bridge-it Head'. Text Fig. II, A, vii means, in its context, 'His name (style) was Wings', and is a complete sequence occurring in the *Annals*. Text Fig. II, A, viii means 'If your sister-in-law is drowning . . .' a moral dilemma which is referred to by Confucius.

Many other examples of such forms could be found.

pattern II can have variants: (a(a)), [[a]a], (a 'a'). In Text Fig. II, B, i means in its context 'to govern the state', or 'to make statelike the state'; ii means, in its context, 'He sent an envoy'; iii means, 'generation and generation', which, in a temporal context, means, 'from generation to generation'. Text Fig. II, B, iv is a piece from a sequence from Confucius. It means 'to call, or treat, fathers as fathers and sons as sons'.

pattern III can have variants including (a(b)) *cv* b:a; and [[a]b] *cv* [[b]a]. '*cv*' here means 'is convertible into'.

In the examples given, only examples of the second variation are provided, since that of Predicative Displacement has already been extensively discussed. In Text Fig. II, C, i the two halves of the pattern give in context 'boys and girls', or 'children', and 'girl-child', i.e. 'girl'; in ii 'twelve', i.e. '10+2', and 'twenty', i.e. '2 × 10'; in iii 'to be and not to be' and 'non-existence', used in context to mean 'it is not thus'.

These examples suffice to make clear the vast variety of pattern which ideography allows. The patterning of Text Fig. II, D, incidentally, only makes sense within a larger context. There it means 'to call the right "The Right" ' ... and, by contrast with this, 'to call the wrong "The Wrong" ' ... and it is from Mo-Tzu. We are now, however, in a position to give an ostensive definition of a *cluster*, as this term is used in the definition of metaphysics (sense ii). For we can now say that we will call any sequence a cluster in which these operations, and only these operations, occur.

This definition may seem, at first, wrong-headed and disingenuous, and for two reasons. The first of these is that by including Predicative Displacement we have included in our cluster the form most analogous to the traditional logical 'statement'; and that by this inclusion metaphysical language becomes just language. But this is not so; our Predicative Displacement is *not* the ordinary 'Subject-Predicate' form; it is merely the simplest form of progression from Given to New. To get an analogue of the ordinary logical 'statement', you must not have the form $(a:(b))$, but the form $[[(a:(b))]]-]$; and this form, under the definition of metaphysics (sense ii) cannot occur. The second criticism is that we have included in ideography at its starkest a procedure for producing a person's proper name. But this also is not — at least, not at all straightforwardly — analogous to the normal idea of doing the same thing. For proper-name making can be envisaged as a form of abstraction, since it leads to such a great deal of positional displacement, though it does not lead to progressive redefinition of the kind we have discussed. Consider the concept 'Plum', when used in its aspect in which it means the name of the man 'Plum'. At first we say: 'this is the most concrete possible aspect of 'Plum'; after all, Plum is an actual man; we can shake hands with, and have dinner with 'Plum' '. Consider, however, not the definition of this aspect, but its use; the fictional Plum; the immortal soul, or the literary style of Plum; the Plum family; the Plum-faction, or political party; the district in the new territory of Plum. Would any other aspect of the concept 'Plum' and especially the aspect meaning the plum tree, have produced a positional performance so varied and mobile as that meaning the man Plum? If this is so, and if mobility of positional performance be thought to be, as it here is, a form of abstraction rather than the reverse, then it is evident that in metaphysical thinking (senses ii and iii), this kind of abstraction is likely to be frequently used.

And, as a matter of fact, it is frequently used. From now on to the end, in the short space that is left to us, we shall tend to lose interest in ideographic examples, and to concentrate, in so far as we have time, on examples from Metaphysics (sense iii). And when we begin to ask ourselves just what kind of thing, speaking logically, it is which gives its particular 'feel' to Metaphysical thinking (sense iii), we shall have to answer that one of its outstanding characteristics consists of applying, to a concept which is already very general and indeterminate, a so-called proper name which is more general and abstract yet. Look for instance, at the following quotation from the Athanasian Creed, *Symbolum Athianasium*:

Alia est enim persona Patris, alia Filii, alia Spiritus Sancti:
Sed Patris, et Filii, et Spiritus Sancti una est divinitas, aequalis
  gloria, coaeterna majestas.
Qualis Pater, talis Filius, talis Spiritus Sanctus,

'For there is one person of the Father, another of the Son: and
  another of the Holy Ghost.
'But the Godhead of the Father, of the Son, and of the Holy
  Ghost is all one: the Glory (is) equal, the Majesty (is) co-
  eternal.
'Such as the Father is, such is the Son: and such is the Holy
  Ghost',
    and so on.

Here 'God the Father', 'God the Son' and 'God the Holy Ghost' are used as proper names; but nobody would say that we were here using a concrete sequence. Moreover, every sequence here is in a sense predicative; and yet we have a feeling of absorbing parallel clusters, rather than of making statements, from first to last. One thing remains, though; progression from Given to New.

This progression is fundamental to all thinking done in language. Otherwise, I think that few people would deny that in such a passage as this we have Metaphysical thinking (sense iii) in a form which, in sense ii shows ideography at its simplest, most compact and most stark.

Yes but, you will now ask, if we take now a passage of Metaphysics in sense iii, where is the argument? In our next example we shall try to give the barest indication of the kind of form which Metaphysical argument (sense iii) typically takes.

The enterprise of approaching Metaphysical argument in this sort of way was first suggested by a very talented young Cambridge philosopher, R. G. Bosanquet, who was killed in action in the second world war. It is from his 'Remarks on Spinoza's Ethics', published posthumously,[1] that all which follows here about Spinoza's 'proofs' has been derived. (It is, of course, possible for a critic to argue that not all Metaphysical argument has the same form as the form of a 'proof' in the Latin of Spinoza. This is true, but at this stage need not affect our argument. For the right line to take at this stage is to bring forward for consideration striking and poetic examples of Metaphysics, not 'normal' and discursive ones. After taking an argument in Latin from Spinoza, we shall take one from Mencius and one, in German, from Wittgenstein; thus saying, by implication, if this isn't Metaphysical argument, what is?' For the logical definitions which we have given of metaphysics (senses i and ii), judged from the point of view of theory of language, are so fundamental, that if the striking examples of Metaphysical argument (sense iii) which we shall give, can be examined without strain in terms of them, then the more discursive and less striking examples should be able, by taking trouble, to be fitted in.)

In the *Remarks on Spinoza's Ethics*, then, Bosanquet says, after remarking that all Spinoza's 'proofs' are formally invalid, though not necessarily wrong:

'The proof of [any] proposition, [even a proposition in Euclid], may be looked upon as a way of persuading people to accept a

[1] R. G. Bosanquet, 'Remarks on Spinoza's *Ethics*' (*Mind*, Vol. LIV, N.S. No. 215, July 1945).

certain criterion of whether something falls under a certain concept; in other words, the proof of a proposition may be looked upon as an amplification of the definitions. Much the same can be said of metaphysical proofs. When Spinoza proves that a good act is one which is active and not passive, he is introducing a new criterion of goodness. He is trying to make us use 'Good' in such a way that an act is not good unless it is in this sense 'active' . . . Thus his proof that p consists in building up a connection between p and some definition d. This connection consists in showing that p can be included in d in the sense that p can be used as a criterion for d. In the case of mathematical calculi, there is a fairly clear-cut distinction between the propositions which can and the propositions which cannot be connected in this way with a certain definition. But in a metaphysical calculus there is considerable latitude allowed to the author of the calculus; that is to say, it is to a considerable extent a matter of choice whether a proposition can or cannot be proved.

'We can now see more clearly the machinery of proof which uses sentences with abnormal meanings. Spinoza starts with a word which is normally used in a certain unprecise sense w; and he defines it in a certain sense w'. He then "proves", in the way indicated above, a certain proposition p'; and this leads one to suppose that the normal sense p of that proposition is true. But in fact the proof does not show in the direct way that p is true; what it does is to attempt to persuade us to use words in the Spinozistic rather than in the normal sense. And in the Spinozistic language w' does entail p'. All this, of course, depends upon w and p being nearly the same as w' and p'; and Spinoza's proof can be considered as a proof that w almost entails p.'

Now it is clear, from the above, that Bosanquet is feeling after the idea that there may be a special metaphysical kind of logic, in terms of which one can construct metaphysical proofs. He envisages this logic as being operated with unprecise concepts, moreover, and with concepts the Spinozistic meaning of which is established by a process of Progressive Definition by Position Displacement.[1] The result of this progressive redefinition, however,

[1] R. G. Bosanquet, loc. cit., beginning passage.

in this case, is not to force a concept into new types of grammatical use; but to force it into new types of abstract meaning by a sort of focusing process produced by putting it into carefully chosen contexts, 'context' here being interpreted as 'linguistic sequence'. Moreover, these contexts, these sequences, form recurrent parallel patterns; like the $[[A_1]A_2]$ recurrent patterns which we have been discussing, but much stricter, and much longer. Then these expansions, these patterns, are themselves graded, or ordered, to form the connections between given and new of which Bosanquet speaks; and the final result is a relationship of 'almost entailment', between the first sequence and the last in this long chain, which is not quite like any form of ordinary entailment, but yet not quite like anything else either.

Now in order to find out more about this relationship of 'almost entailment', I suggest that we turn back for a moment to ideography. In Text Fig. II, F and G are two contrasting examples, the one of two lines taken from a Chinese poem, the other of two lines taken from a Chinese argument. The two lines from the Chinese poem read something like this:

'Flower Tree Know Spring to be not long-lasting;
In a hundred ways Red Mauve are Clashing Smell, Scent'

'Flower and Tree
Knowing that May soon fades
In Red and Mauve
Clash hundred Fragrance-shades.'

All through there is an ambiguity, consciously maintained, between flower and tree-blossom clashing and women, feeling youth rushing from them, frenziedly competing with one another in display; and an intense feeling is also conveyed of the almost painful over-exciting impact of the wild uprush of colour of the final stage of spring. In short, it is a highly accomplished poem. But the logical point about it here is that though the parallelism of sound and form required by Chinese poetry is maintained, both between these two lines and between the other, further two lines, not given, with which they are matched, it would be impossible to give a strict logical definition of this match; this poem is, in the sense just given, a metaphysical *expansion*, i.e. it is of the $[[A_1]A_2]$ form, but it is not an expansion with an ascertainable expansion-rule.

Contrast this now with Text Fig. II, *G*, the Chinese argument. This, which is in the first book of Mencius, says something like this:

'In a state of ten thousand chariots, if the king is assassinated, the man who did it is sure to be the lord of a clan of 1000 chariots;
In a state (clan) of 1000 chariots, if the king (clan lord) is assassinated, it is sure to be by the lord of a clan (sub-clan) of 100 chariots'
And so on.

'At the 10,000-chariot-state-level, a 1000 clan-lord regicide is a sure bet;
At the 1,000 chariot-state-level, a 100 clan-lord-regicide is a sure bet':

'Though serfs and slaves receive the harder stings,
It is Prime Ministers who kill their kings.'

Now, owing to the ideographic principles of build-up of the old Chinese language, Mencius here, in order to produce his argument, only has to alter the numerical ideographs in his expanded sequence, *and nothing else*; and these, of course, he can alter according to a rule. This rule says that the number four places from the end of S_1, in the expansion, is the number at the extreme left-hand place in S_1 divided by ten; and the number right at the beginning of S_2, which is to be constructed in all other points like S_1, is the same number as that four places from the end in S_1. Thus, by this rule, not only can the number four places from the end in S_2 be ascertained; but also, if necessary, S_3 could be constructed on the same pattern as S_1 and S_2, and following the same rule. Further than S_3, however, we could not sensibly go; it makes no sense to say that in a state of ten chariots, the king-killer will be the owner of one chariot; this is a political generalization, not a family one. But the logical point here is that this expansion has a rule; and the construction of such expansions according to, usually, interrelated rules, and the subsequent grading of them, forms the core and backbone of Chinese philosophical argument.

Let us consider, for a moment, the characteristics of such argument. Because of the intolerance of most language-speakers to the logical device of expansion, which they consider as merely a sing-song sort of chanting, even the most logically minded sinologues have failed to see its logical advantages. These are (1) that if the reasoner so wishes, every expansion he makes can be constructed according to a different expansion-rule from every other, and (2) that however many such forms of expansion he creates, and however indeterminate the concepts he needs to use in them, the forms both of the expansion-rules, and of the interrelations which hold between them, will in every case be explicitly ascertainable; since it is quite explicit and clear — once it is an ideographic language which is being used for purposes of reasoning, and not a so-called exact, Indo-European language — which concepts in the pattern the reasoner wishes to change for purposes of inference, and which he does not.

Now it can be held that all this is also the case in syllogistic inference. But it is not the case in our much more frequently used analogical inferences ('*a* is like *b*; *therefore* . . .') in the finished formulation of which a state of the very greatest vagueness and indeterminacy usually obtains. 'My love is like a red, red rose.' One can almost hear the ideographic reasoner say, 'Yes, but how like? And in just what way? If you can give me the formulation of the expansion-rule of likeness between your love and the rose, then, and only then, shall I be able, satisfactorily and accurately, to state the logical bounds of your analogy in a valid ideographic expansion; that is, an expansion which, taken as a whole, shall correspond with the facts.'

Now, with this form of ideographic inference in our minds, let us come back to consider an example of an argument in Spinoza. The beginning of Prop. 5, Part I, of the *Ethics*, states:

Si daruntur plures distinctae [substantiae], deberent inter se distingui vel ex diversitate attributorum, vel ex diversitate affectionum (per Prop. praeced.)

'If several distinct substances be given, they must be distinguished one from the other either by the difference of their attributes or by the difference of their modifications (prev. Prop.)'

Let us now replace the abbreviation *per Prop. praeced.* by the proposition itself.

We then get:

S_1: Si darentur plures distinctae [*substantiae*], deberent inter se distingue vel ex diversitate attributorum, vel ex diversitate affectionum.

S_2: Duae aut plures *res* distinctae, vel inter se distinguuntur ex diversitate attributorum substantiarum, vel ex diversitate earundum affectionum.

'Two or more distinct *things* are distinguished one from the other either by the difference of their attributes or the difference of their modifications'

Now suppose we try, which Spinoza does not do, to construct S_3. Can we say, for instance:

S_3: Duae aut plures *ideae* distinctae, vel inter se distinguuntur ex diversitate attributorum earum, vel ex diversitate earundem affectionum.

'Two or more distinct *ideas* are distinguished one from the other either by the difference of their attributes or by the difference of their modifications.'

The answer is, no, of course, we cannot say this, although the temptation to say it is often very strong: cf., for instance, Part I, Props. 1 and 2, to the effect that God, the only Substance, is a thinking and an extended thing: Prop. XX, Part I, coroll: to the effect that particular things are nothing else than modifications

or attributes of God; Prop. VII, Part II, to the effect that the order
and connection of ideas is the same as the order and connections of
things, etc. We conclude, therefore, that the simple expansion-
rule, 'As substance is to thing, thing is to idea', is one which, in
this universe of discourse, does not hold. But this sets us thinking.
Might there not be a more complex expansion-rule, one which, to
be made explicit, would require the development of not one but
several expansions, each with its own rule, and connected to the
others by a connecting rule, by means of which we could finally
connect *substance, thing* and *idea?* And so we find ourselves first
constructing Spinozan 'proofs' — that is, expansions which are not
in the *Ethica* — and then deciding which to reject among them by
reference to the propositions of the *Ethics* itself. No, this one
definitely won't do (we say); once expand that way and you make
it totally impossible for any subsequent expansion, however complex, however gradual, to start from, or end with, the assertion
that there is only one Substance. On the other hand this expansion
is much better . . . it will almost do . . . with a little more change
in the rule it might do . . . And so it goes on. . . .

If Spinoza's proofs can be conceived as ideographic expansions,
much more can the 'reiterations' of Wittgenstein's *Tractatus
Logico-Philosophicus*:

S_1 2.203   *Das Bild enthält die Möglichkeit der Sachlage, die es
darstellt.*
'The picture contains the possibility of the state of
affairs which it represents.'

S_2 3.02   *Der Gedanke enthält die Möglichkeit der Sachlage die
er denkt.*
'The thought contains the possibility of the state of
affairs which it thinks.'

S_3 *Der Satz enthält die Möglichkeit der Sachlage die er
bezeichnet.*
'The proposition contains the possibility of the state
of affairs which it signifies.'

S_1 [transposed] *Die Gesamtheit der Tatsachen ist die Welt.*
1.1   'the totality of facts is the world'

S₂ 3.01   *Die Gesamtheit der wahren Gedanken sind ein Bild der*
           Welt.

           'the totality of true thoughts is a picture of the world'

S₂ 4.11   *Die Gesamtheit der wahren Sätze ist die gesamte*
           Naturwissenschaft.

           'the totality of true propositions is the total natural
           science'

These are only two examples, and not very good ones, out of
the many and complex expansions which could be found in the
text of the *Tractatus Logico-Philosophicus.* The interesting one is
the one which comprises the whole book.

And, of course, next we could approach forms of thought in
Hegel. . . .

The underlying argument of this lecture, like that of the last,
rests on the possibility of the analogy between forms of ideographic thinking and forms of Metaphysical thinking being sufficiently real and close for the elucidation and exploration of the
first to count as pointing the way to the 'discovery' of the logical
nature of the second. If the existence of this analogy be granted,
even if only to a limited extent, then it becomes clear that Metaphysical expansions and sequences, though they can well be
criticized for being indeterminate, cannot, without qualification,
be called 'non-sensical'. For within the ideographic universe of
discourse some sequences will not be well-formed according to the
principles, and will thus be non-sensical, and most will be well-
formed; that is, according to the principles of ideography, they
will 'make sense'. Moreover, our whole argument has tended to
stress that the fact that Metaphysics (sense iii) is built of indeterminate concepts does not prevent these concepts being combin-
able in specific combinations; nor indeed, prevent specific metaphysical rules (sense i) emerging which specify the interrelations of these concepts in a rigorous and exact way. And even
though it is paradox, Chinese poetry, and Metaphysics (sense iii)
which show, portrayed, as it were, in sharp relief, logical forms of
language which are metaphysical (in sense ii), yet it is also true, in

a sense, that all language, and not merely poetry, paradox and Metaphysics, can be construed as metaphysical (in sense i). And thus (perhaps only for the sake of continuing to work out the present argument), if the existence of the metaphysical and ideographic analogy be granted, it will be the case that in the attempt to 'discover' what metaphysics is, the technical step of devising a new metaphysical logical form will have been embarked on, and this means that, in our sophisticated sense of 'discovery', the vital 'discovery' will have started to be made.[1]

---

[1] Since the above was written, further work towards an attempt to construct a metaphysical calculus, which will yield a restricted language called Platonic Pidgin, has been done by Margaret Masterman and A. F. Parker-Rhodes, of the Cambridge Language Research Unit.

FIGURE I

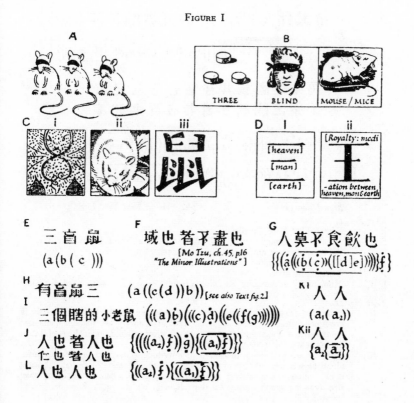

FIGURE II

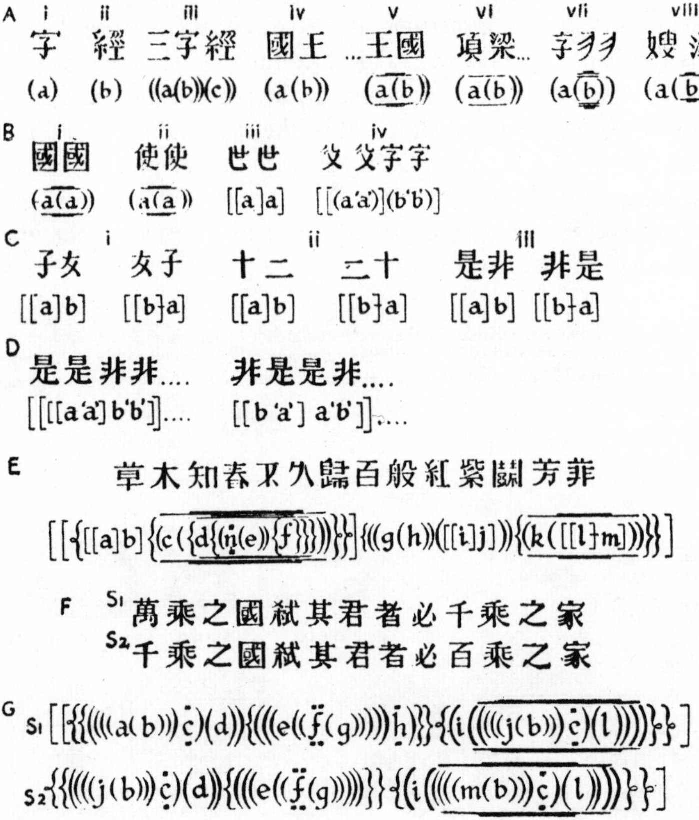

A   i   ii   iii   iv   v   vi   vii   viii

字　經　三字經　國王 …王國　頃梁…　孛羽　嫂溺…

(a) (b) ((a)b))c)) (a(b)) (a(b̄)) (a(b̄)) (a(b̄)) (a(b̄))

B   i   ii   iii   iv

國國　使使　世世　夊夊字字

(a(a)) (a(a)) [[a]a] [[(a'a')(b'b')]

C   i   ii   iii

子夊　夊子　十二　二十　是非　非是

[[a]b] [[b]a] [[a]b] [[b]a] [[a]b] [[b]a]

D 是是非非….　非是是非….

[[[[a'a'] b'b']]…. [[b 'a'] a'b']]….

E 草木知春又入歸百般紅紫鬮芳菲

[[{ [[a]b] { c ({ d ({ h (i(e)) { f } })) } } { ((g(h))((i]j))) { k([[l]m]) } }]]

F S₁ 萬乘之國弒其君者必千乘之家
    S₂ 千乘之國弒其君者必百乘之家

G S₁ [[{ { (((a(b))) ċ)(d) } { (((e((f̣ (g)))) ḥ) } } { (i ((((j(b)) ċ)(l))) } }]]

S₂ { { ((((j (b))) ċ)(d) } { (((e((f̣ (g)))) } } { (i ((((m(b)) ċ)(l))) } }]

Translations, in context, of the examples given in Text Figs. I and II

Text Fig. I
E   'Three Blind Mice' (artificial).
F   'What is not limited is universal' (that which is universal is not limited).
G   'All men must eat and drink' (see also text).
H   'There are three blind mice.'
I   'Three blind mice.'
J, K, L   'Humane-ity is humanity' (he who is truly human is humane). (See also text.)

Text Fig. II.
A (i)   'character' (to breed, nourish, bring up, treat with fatherly love, cherish; (a brought-up person:) name or 'style' taken at twenty years; name, appellation; word; written character, letter — the graph shows a child under the roof, i.e. in the house).

(ii)   'warp' (warp in a loom; meridians of longitude; ('warp' in the body:) larger blood vessels, nerves; (the moral 'warp':) rules of conduct, rule, law, classical book, canon, sûtra; prayer; regulate; follow a rule, pass along, pass, past, already — the graph shows, on the left, silk; on the right, an underground stream).

(iii)   'Three Character Classic' (name of a twelfth-century Chinese school-book).
(iv)   'King of the State.'
(v)   'To rule the State.'
(vi)   (Man's proper name: analogue; Bridge-it Head).
(vii)   'His name (style) was Wing.'
(viii)   'If your sister-in-law is drowning . . .' (a moral dilemma referred to by Confucius).

B (i)   'to govern the State . . .'
(ii)   'He sent an envoy . . .'
(iii)   'From generation to generation . . .'
(iv)   'To treat fathers as fathers and sons as sons . . .'

C (i)   'Boys and girls' (i.e. children): girl-child (i.e. girl).
(ii)   'twelve' (i.e. 10+2): 'twenty' (i.e. 2 × 10).
(iii)   'to be, or not to be' (i.e. being and/or not-being); 'it is not thus' (i.e. not-being — being).

D.   ' . . . to call the Right "right" and the Wrong "wrong" . . .
to call the Wrong "right" and the Right "wrong" . . .'
                                                     (from Mo-Tzu)

E.   'Flower, tree, knowing Spring soon flees,
In a hundred ways red, mauve, clashing smell, scent.'
'(Miss) Flower, (Miss) Tree, knowing that May soon fades,
In a hundred reds, mauves, clash their fragrance-shades.'

F.   'In a State of ten thousand chariots, the regicide, if there is one, will be sure to be the chief of a thousand-chariot clan,
In a State of a thousand chariots, the regicide, if there is one, will be sure to be the chief of a hundred-chariot clan.'
                                                     (from Mencius)

POSTSCRIPT

In Part II of this paper a notion was suggested of 'doing ideography'; that is, of analysing language in a new and fundamental, but at the same time, empirical, way. No actual 'ideographic' system of language was given. Actual sentences, however, in Chinese, Latin and English, were analysed 'ideographically' ('ideographically' being taken as synonymous with 'metaphysically'). Since then, an actual ideographic logical system, or operating device, has been constructed. This, though largely ignored by philosophers, has been used technologically; in research on Mechanical Translation and for mechanically generating four-point analogies. (See M. Masterman, 'Translation' (*Aristotelian Society Supplementary* Vol. XXV, 1961), and M. B. Hesse, 'On Analogy' (*Proc. Arist. Soc.*, 1959–60).)

This device consists in taking, as the units of the system, the 'heads' (or paragraph headings) of a synonym-dictionary, such as *Roget's Thesaurus* — each of which could be represented by an ideograph. These are then envisaged as points on a finite lattice (so as to enable joins and intersections to be made both of them and of the word-uses occurring within them. (See Masterman, 'Translation', as above, and Masterman, Needham and Sparck-Jones, 'The Analogy between Information Retrieval and Mechanical Translation', (*Proceedings of International Conference of Scientific Information*, Washington, 1959, and Masterman, 'Semantic Message Detection, Using an Interlingua', *Proceedings of First International Conference on Mechanical Translation and*

Applied Language Analysis, National Physical Laboratory, 1961).) Thus there now exists a primitive 'ideography' or 'head language', within which every expression in head language is by definition metaphysical.

That this trick, which enables an 'ideographic' system, in the sense of 'ideographic' given in the paper, to be actually constructed, did not occur to me while I was writing it is due to the fact that the paper contains a mistake (on p. 311). There, 'ideographs', or 'λόγοι', or 'Words', are identified (1) with metaphysical elements or units; i.e. with discrete philosophic symbols each of which stands for a general idea: 'Substance', 'Mode', 'Accident', 'Space', 'Time', 'Deity'; and (2) with 'semantic units embedded at the very heart of natural language: "flow", "go", "flower". This double identification is wrong. These two types of unit are not the same, but are of different logical categories. In the ideological synonym-system, the metaphysical units, the headings or 'heads' are interlingual and form a finite set, and it is this set which form the points of the lattice. The sets of word-uses which occur under the headings are unilingual, i.e. they differ with each natural language; and there are indefinitely many of them. The system can be so formed they they always map on to the heads; but there is considerable complication about the mapping. The technical name for the set of uses of a word in the system is a *fan*; so that the total system consists of fans mapped on to structured heads. The fan of uses of the English word 'blind', which is discussed in the text, is given, mapped on to Roget heads, in the appendix attached.

By using the system, primitive metaphysical formulae of exactly the type which are given in the text (on p. 343), can be built up. These are now called *semantic squares*. There is reason to think that we can correlate the square-points in these squares with the phoneticians' main 'choice-points' of heard speech; that is, by the *heads* and *nuclei* of the phoneticians' overall intonational *tunes*, or forms, as these occur in languages.

Thus this investigation, which began by being philosophical, has ended, as so often happens, by becoming technical. It is possible to hold, of course, that as soon as any investigation becomes technical it ceases to be philosophical. In that case, however, it will be necessary to hold also that the construction of a model metaphysical system is irrelevant to metaphysics.

M. M.

THEODORE REDPATH

Some Problems
of
Modern Aesthetics

ROBERT THEODORE HOLMES REDPATH, M.A., PH.D. (Cantab.): born August 17th, 1913; educated at Oatlands School, Harrogate, 1922-26, Leys School, Cambridge, 1927-31, St. Catharine's College, Cambridge (Scholar in English), 1931-36, and St. John's College, Cambridge (Strathcona Research Student for Philosophy), 1937-39; Ph.D., Cambridge, 1939, Army Service, 1940-46, ending as Major, General Staff; called to the Bar at the Middle Temple, 1948; Fellow and Director of English Studies, Trinity College, Cambridge, 1950 to date; Assistant Lecturer in English, University of Cambridge, 1951; Lecturer in English, University of Cambridge since 1954; Tutor at Trinity College, Cambridge, since 1960.

Chief publications: 'Essay on Bacon' in Vol. II of the *Penguin Guide to English Literature*, 1955. *Donne's Songs and Sonnets, an edition for University Students and the General Reader*, 1956. *Tolstoy*, 1960, (with P. Hodgart). *Romantic Perspectives*, 1964, ed. (with W. G. Ingram). *Shakespeare's Sonnets*, London, 1964, New York, 1965. *John Locke and the Rhetoric of the Second Treatise*, 1964. Also articles in the *Atti del XII Congresso Internazionale de Filosofia*, Venezia, 1958, in *Atti del Simposio de Estetica*, Venezia, 1958, in *Proceedings of the Fourth International Congress of Aesthetics*, Athens, 1960, and in *Etudes sur le Contrat Social de Jean-Jaques Rousseau*, Paris, 1964.

THEODORE REDPATH

SOME PROBLEMS
OF
MODERN AESTHETICS

(1) THE MEANING OF A POEM

LIKE some of the other lecturers on this course, I intend in my
lectures not to render an account of recent British philosophy on
my subject, but to try to exemplify a way of thinking characteristic of at least one trend in recent British thought. The way of
thinking is one which I believe I have learned by studying philosophy at Cambridge: but I do not wish to attribute either my
method or my conclusions to any one of the Cambridge philosophers under whom I have studied, i.e. Moore, Broad, Wittgenstein, Wisdom or Russell. None of these philosophers have, in any
case, discussed questions of aesthetics very much: and so even
someone trained in philosophy at Cambridge, if he tries to philosophize about problems in aesthetics, is under the disadvantage of
moving in a field uncharted by them. The only Cambridge philosophers who have recently discussed aesthetics at all largely are
C. K. Ogden and I. A. Richards, and while I have certainly
learned much from them, as so many others have, I have neither
followed their methods nor come to their conclusions.

The problems I have chosen for discussion are problems that
have interested British aestheticians recently, though I would not
pretend that this interest in them is peculiar to this country. The
problems I shall discuss in this first lecture concern aesthetic interpretation: those I shall discuss in the second lecture concern
aesthetic evaluation. That has seemed to me a fair division.

Let me make a start on the first problem, then, which is this: 'Is
the meaning of a poem the meaning the poet intended it to have?'

Some high modern authorities would certainly reply to this question in the negative. Roger Fry, for instance, speaking of works of art in general, once said: 'I'm certain that the only meanings that are worth anything in a work of art, are those that the artist himself knows nothing about.'[1] Let us look into the question.

It is perhaps first worth asking what evidence there could be as to the meaning that the poet intended his poem to have. Some theorists would maintain that there can be no evidence, external or internal, as to what the poet intended his poem to mean, where that meaning would differ from the meaning of the poem as it stands. The American literary theorists, Professors Monroe C. Beardsley and W. K. Wimsatt, Jr., for instance, who have given this problem careful attention,[2] maintain (1) that 'to pretend that the author's aim can be detected internally in the work even where it is not realized . . . is merely a self-contradictory proposition', and (2) that 'there can be no evidence, internal or external, that the author has conceived something which he did not execute'.

Both these statements seem to me to be false.

I think that it is sometimes possible to detect from inspection of a poem, particularly in the case of an inferior poem, that the poet has not said exactly what he meant to say; that is, that the poem, as it stands, does not mean exactly what the poet intended it to mean. Thus the claim 'that the author's aim can be detected internally in the work even where it is not realized', so far from being self-contradictory, is, in my view, not even false, but, on the contrary, absolutely valid, in some cases.

Again, I believe, contrary to (2), that there can be both internal *and* external evidence 'that the author had conceived something which he did not execute'. I have spoken in the last paragraph of the internal evidence; but there could easily be external evidence as well. We have, for example, a poet's own word about the process of poetic creation. Shelley, in his *Defence of Poetry*, writes in terms of great generality: 'when composition begins, inspiration is already on the decline, and the most glorious poetry that has ever

---

[1] Quoted by Virginia Woolf, *Roger Fry*, Hogarth Press (1940), pp. 240-1.

[2] See their article 'Intention' in *A Dictionary of World Literature* (ed. J. T. Shipley), New York, 1944, pp. 326-9 and the fuller treatment of intention in their article, 'The Intentional Fallacy' (*Sewanee Review*, Summer 1946, pp. 468-88).

been communicated to the world is probably a feeble shadow of the original conceptions of the poet'. This seems to me itself evidence of great weight. A poet is telling us that the words of poets do not mean what they were intended to mean. He is even taking precisely the opposite view to that of Professors Beardsley and Wimsatt, and telling us that poems *never* mean what they were intended to mean. Perhaps that is forgiveable romantic exaggeration, but it might be as well not to feel too sure. In any case we ought, I think, to take it as evidence that *sometimes* poems do not mean what they were intended to mean. Again, when a poet changes expressions in a poem during revision, is that not sometimes[1] because he considers that the words he is rejecting do not express as well as the new words, what he meant? A mere change would not by itself be evidence; but the setting of the words in the poem *might* be the only additional factor requiring consideration, to make it clear that the old words did not express what the poet meant. On the other hand, other evidence *might* be required, and might actually be *forthcoming*, e.g. the poet might himself tell us that the old expressions did not convey what he had meant, and he might even tell us *how* they failed to do so.

Thus both of the assertions of Professors Beardsley and Wimsatt seem to me to be wrong. There could be evidence, both internal and external, as to the meaning that the poet intended a poem to have, even where that meaning would differ from the meaning of the poem as it stands. On the other hand, there seems to be definite point in what they say with regard to internal evidence. If it is clear 'from within the four corners of the poem itself' (to adapt an expression from English legal interpretation to new purposes), that some of the words in the poem do not convey the poet's meaning, then at all events the poem as a whole has at least revealed the poet's meaning. Might there not therefore be colour for saying that the poem as a whole, as it stands, *does* convey the poet's meaning? And would it not be an easy step from that to saying that the poem as a whole has the meaning that the poet intended it to have? There is some plausibility in this. All the

---

[1] I say 'sometimes', because there are certainly also cases where the poet has new ideas during revision, so that although the old expressions were good enough for the old wine they are not good enough for the new.

same, the last step, at least, would be a dangerous one. And I believe the second step would also be objectionable. The indication as to what the poet really intended the poem to mean might be a mere hint here and there, and in that case it would surely be a mistake to say that the poem *as a whole* conveyed the meaning the poet intended it to convey, when the greater part of it did not?

Let us leave this point now, and go on to another point about the assertions of Professors Beardsley and Wimsatt. There was an important difference between assertions (1) and (2). The first poured ridicule on the claim that the author's aim *can be detected* internally in the work even when it is not realized. The second expressed the larger opinion that there *can be no evidence that* the author had conceived something which he did not execute. Now Shelley's statement seems to me, as I have said, strong evidence in favour of the view that authors have at least sometimes intended their works to mean something different from what they do in fact mean: but it is no evidence that *what* the authors intended their works to mean *can be detected* either by internal or by external evidence. Shelley might well have admitted that 'the original conceptions' of the poet could not be detected by readers of his poem, and might even have agreed that the poet himself could not say in what way the poem as it stands differs from his 'original conception'. Possibly, then, Professors Beardsley and Wimsatt could have enlisted Shelley's support for their first point, even though he was a powerful adversary of their second point. But Shelley's statement as it stands does not give their first point any support either. He says nothing about a poet's subsequent knowledge of his 'original conceptions'. In any case, though, surely a poet might sometimes be able to recapture his 'original conceptions', and to describe them to some extent, even though he had failed to express them in the poem which he actually wrote? Alternatively, even if a poet could never do *this*, surely, before writing his poem, he might have acquiesced in the reduction of his intentions to something which he could easily *describe*, yet failed to *express* in the poem?

My own view, then, is that there could be both internal and external evidence of the meaning which the poet intended a poem to have, even where that meaning differed from the meaning of the poem as it stands. This is also *part* of an answer to the original question: 'Is the meaning of a poem the meaning the poet intended it to have?' If I am right, we should at least answer to this: 'Not always.'

That by no means exhausts the matter, though. We must go on to ask whether the meaning of a poem is *ever* the meaning the poet intended it to have. Mr. T. S. Eliot, in an article in *The Partisan Review* (November-December 1942), writes (on p. 457): 'There may be much more in a poem than the author was aware of.' It is important to notice that Mr. Eliot does not say that there *must* be much more in a poem than the author was aware of, or even that there *is always* much more in a poem than the author is aware of, but only that there *may* be much more in a poem than the author is aware of. He leaves open the possibility that in *some* poems there is neither more nor less than the author was aware of. This is perhaps the point at which to say a brief word as to the relation between 'being aware of' a meaning, and 'intending' a meaning. In the most common sense of the terms 'intention' and 'intended', the sense in which it would be reasonable to take the term 'intended' in the question we are considering, a meaning in a poem being written could not be 'intended' without the poet 'being aware of' it. So that when Mr. Eliot says that there may be much more in a poem than the author was aware of, we must take it that he is at least saying that there may be much more in a poem than the author intended. That statement we may, I think, accept. It seems very unlikely that in the case of every poem that has ever been written, the poet has always intended everything that the poem means, especially if we take the 'meaning' of the poem in a full sense, such as that described by Professor I. A. Richards in his book *Practical Criticism*, i.e. as including intellectual, emotive, tonal and intentional elements. It seems very unlikely that every poet in writing every poem has been in full conscious control of all these.[1] Even in the case of *good* poems it seems that poets are at

---

[1] And even if we take the term 'meaning' more narrowly, the same is true. Even in the narrowest construction of the term 'meaning', as *bare sense*, it is surely unlikely that every poet in writing every poem has realized the full sense of the words he is writing. And we are certainly at liberty to construe 'meaning' more widely than that.

least sometimes, as Socrates found them to be, 'like prophets and oracular persons, who say many fine things without knowing what it is that they are saying'. There may be much more in a poem, then, than the author intended.

But *must* there be more in a poem than the author intended? To answer in the affirmative would be to enunciate a necessary proposition, which ought immediately to be suspect. What is there to exclude the *possibility* that, substantially at least, there may be in some poems neither more nor less than the author intended? It is difficult, even in comparatively simple cases, to tell for certain whether this is so: but a probable estimate would seem often possible.

So far then, it seems that a poem may mean something different from what the poet intended it to mean, may mean less than the poet intended it to mean, may mean more than he intended it to mean; may perhaps sometimes mean substantially what he intended.

But if this is so, it would certainly seem that the poet's intention cannot be used as a *universal* criterion of the meaning of a poem, and can hardly even always be used as a *leading* criterion in the search for the meaning even if that intention can easily be discovered, which may often not be the case. On the other hand, the probable intention of the poet does at least sometimes afford a criterion by which to judge whether a certain meaning which is attributed to a poem is probably correct or not. The situation is therefore confusing. Is part of the confusion due to the fact that the use of the term 'intention' or 'intended', in the question under consideration, lets in such awkward cases as those envisaged by Shelley? Very possibly. While admitting, then, that in such cases the meaning of a poem is not the meaning the poet intended it to have, let us try to clear up the rest of the situation by asking a slightly different question, namely: 'Is the meaning of a poem what the poet *meant* by it?' Some people would say: 'Yes, certainly, otherwise it would not be the poet's poem.' Professor G. E. Moore expressed such a view to me about two years ago when I was discussing this very point with him. He said that he did not see how a poem could be called the poem of the poet who wrote it, unless it meant what the poet meant by it. (I should not like to misrepresent that fine philosopher's views about anything, and I cannot help thinking that he must have had *good* poems in mind: for it seems to me that a *bad* poem could only too easily mean something different from what the poet meant by it.) In the opposite camp to that of those who would say that the meaning of a poem *is* what the poet meant by it, we might expect to find those who would say that the meaning of a poem is *never* what the poet meant by it; but I think the population of such a camp would be rather sparse. On the other hand, there would, I believe, be plenty of people who would maintain that, although the meaning of a poem may often be what the poet meant by it, that would be a pure contingency; on the ground that the meaning of the poem itself is neither more nor less than the meaning it has for an intelligent and sensitive reader or for intelligent and sensitive readers, who understand the language in which it is written. In this camp, as can be seen, there would be included both people who consider that a poem has *one* meaning, and people who consider that it has *many* meanings, the meanings, namely, that it would have for all the intelligent and sensitive readers who come to read it. There is, in my opinion, a crippling objection to this view, namely, that even intelligent and sensitive readers are liable to make mistakes. Yet another camp would be represented by the late John Dewey, who, in his book *Art as Experience*, writes as follows: 'It is absurd to ask what an artist "really" meant by his product; he himself would find different meanings in it at different days and hours and in different stages of his own development. If he could articulate, he would say "I meant just *that*, and *that* means whatever you or anyone can honestly, that is in virtue of your own vital experience, get out of it".'[1] This position of Dewey's is a somewhat curious one. Substantially, he seems to be mediating between the two opposing camps by saying that the meanings of the work *are* what the artist meant by it: while, on the other hand, there are many meanings, and what these meanings are is determined by what he calls 'whatever anyone can honestly, that is, in virtue of that person's vital experience, get out of it'. Dewey, it will be noticed,

[1] John Dewey, *Art as Experience*, New York, 1934, pp. 108-9.

alleges that the artist 'would say' all those things. Now that is an empirical proposition which I, for one, believe to be untrue. Those things are indeed what Dewey would have *liked* the artist to say: but it is more than doubtful whether artists are all and always so liberal. Still, we must not undervalue Dewey's point. Even if artists *would not* always say those things, perhaps those are the things they *ought* to say. Yet, facing this suggestion, we can legitimately ask: 'Why should they? Why *should* a poet say: "I meant by my poem everything anyone can honestly, that is in virtue of that person's vital experience, get out of it"?' At least in one important sense it would seem fantastic to suggest, for instance, that Shakespeare *meant* by his plays just everything which that vital Professor, George Wilson Knight, to take one person only, may 'honestly' get out of them at any time. It might not be wholly unreasonable, though this also would take some swallowing, to say that Shakespeare's *plays* 'meant' all these things; but it appears to me ridiculous to suppose that *Shakespeare himself* 'meant' all these things by them. A better attitude on that point would seem to me to be expressed by Mr. Eliot's remark that there may be much more in a poem than the author was aware of. Even if Shakespeare himself might be forced, were he alive, to confess that he *ought* to have meant all these things by his plays, there seems no good reason why, were he alive, he *ought* to *confess*, that he *did* mean them. Dewey's position, then, seems to me to be untenable, but it is, nevertheless, an instructive one to consider. Dewey is trying to satisfy two apparently conflicting urges which many of us who consider these matters cannot help feeling. We do not want to have to say, when we think of or come across a satisfying interpretation of a good poem, that it does not matter at all whether this is what the poet *meant* by the poem. On the other hand, we do not wish to say that what the poem means to different people, however sensitive and intelligent, is always precisely the same. Dewey tries to satisfy both these urges by saying that the poem means many different things, and that the poet meant by his poem all of them. Now I feel certain that many people, like me, will not be satisfied by his attempt. Many of us do not want to have to say that a poet means utterly disparate, even contrary or contradictory things, by his poem, according as readers, even sensitive and intelligent[1] readers, may interpret his poem in disparate, contrary or even contradictory ways.

We should be willing to admit that a poem may really mean disparate things to different intelligent and sensitive readers: that a poem may sometimes even mean *contrary* or even *contradictory* things to different intelligent and sensitive readers, but it does not follow from such propositions, that the poet *meant* all these disparate, contrary or contradictory things by his poem. The puzzle is, which are we going to call '*the* meaning' of the poem, *in an unqualified way*, what it means to the readers, or what the poet meant by it? The prize term '*the* meaning' seems to float between the two parties, like a balloon floating above two parties of children, each of which wishes to reach and appropriate it. Some people faced with our present puzzle about the meaning of a poem, might feel like applying a needle-point to the balloon, and denying that there is such a thing as '*the* meaning' of a poem at all. Yet this would not be satisfying either, for it would make nonsense of all those occasions on which readers ask each other such questions as: 'What do *you* think this poem means?' or 'What do *you* take the meaning of this poem to be?' and so on. It might be claimed that all such questions are pseudo-questions: but that would take a great deal of showing, and they would in any case be very queer pseudo-questions, for they time and again receive answers which entirely satisfy the questioners. Again, there are other contexts in which we constantly speak of 'the meaning' of a poem. You may remember, for instance, that in the early part of this lecture I frequently spoke of 'the meaning' of a poem, and distinguished it from such things as 'what the poet intended his poem to mean', as if I knew what 'the meaning' of a poem was. To speak of 'the meaning' of a poem, in this unperturbed way, is, I would claim, a legitimate thing for us to do on many occasions. We many of us know what 'the meaning' of a poem is, in the sort of way in which St. Augustine said he knew what time was, in the passage in the *Confessions*,[2] often quoted by Wittgenstein in his

[1] 'Honesty' is clearly not enough; but there is no time to take Dewey up on that point
[2] Augustine, *Confessions*, XI, 14.

AA

lectures:[1] What is time? If you don't ask me, I know: but if you ask me, I don't know.' We are many of us familiar *enough* with what we would call 'the meaning' of a poem, but it is hard indeed to give an analysis of that concept. Not so hard, however, to see the shortcomings of certain analyses or parts of analyses which may be proposed. For instance, from what we know of 'the meaning' of a poem it seems to me that we could not be satisfied with an analysis so strictly tied to the poet as one which might be suggested by Moore's remark: or with one so freely accommodating to the reactions of readers as the analysis proposed by Dewey. In this respect, at least, the meaning of a *poem* is not unlike the meaning of a *word*. A word uttered by someone on some occasion may not mean what the speaker meant by it; and it may not mean what it means for many intelligent and sensitive hearers who know the language:[2] though each of these possibilities is perhaps *in general* less likely in the case of a word than in the case of a sentence, and less likely in the case of a sentence than in the case of a poem.

Although there are many further difficulties that could be considered, let me make a rough constructive suggestion, which may help towards a satisfactory analysis: Perhaps the meaning of a poem is a class of similar experiences, one or other of which those words in that order and arranged in that form, *ought* to evoke in a reader familiar with the language (or languages) in which the poem is written.[3]

Some such account would seem to accord with our practice of asking such questions as 'What is the full meaning of this poem?' On this account the question would be tantamount to asking: 'What set of experiences ought the poem to evoke in a reader?' It would also satisfy the desire to restrict that welter of allowable meanings which Dewey would permit. It would further fulfil the wish to distinguish between what the poet intended to mean or actually did mean by his poem, and what his poem in fact means. The account certainly seems to have these advantages: but accounts of this sort are only too liable to be wrong.

Before concluding I wish to do two things: (1) to distinguish this rough suggestion of mine from a suggestion made by Professor I. A. Richards in his epoch-making book *Principles of Literary Criticism*, first published in 1924; (2) to make one or two comments on the form of my suggestion, and, in particular, to consider briefly (very briefly, I fear) what factors would decide what experiences the words of a poem *ought to evoke*.

First, then, as to the distinction between the present suggestion and that of Professor I. A. Richards. In *Principles of Literary Criticism*[1] Richards writes that 'the only workable way of defining a poem' is as 'a class of experiences which do not differ in any character more than a certain amount, varying for each character, from a standard experience', adding that we might take as this standard experience 'the relevant experience of the poet when contemplating the completed composition.' Now the idea of a class of experiences seems to me very important in this connection, and I have gratefully borrowed the idea from Richards, but I cannot agree with the use he has made of it here, and, as I hope will be clear, I have, in my suggestion, made a very different use of it. There is indeed much to be said about Richards's interesting definition, but at present I only want to draw attention to two points on which my suggestion differs from it. First, Richards is offering a suggestion for the definition of *a poem*, not of *the meaning of a poem*. This is not a trivial point. I believe that the Riccardian suggestion leads into difficulties. We want to speak of being able to *read* poems, and *write* poems, and we cannot very well say

[1] At pp. 226-9.

that we read experiences or even (except in an elliptical way) that we *write* experiences. When we read a poem we read *words*, and when we write a poem we write *words*. We also want to be able to speak of the words *of* a poem, and we cannot very well speak of the words *of* a class of experiences. And there are other such difficulties. To define a *poem* as a class of experiences is to fail to conform to common usage, and there seems here no sufficient justification for that failure to conform. It would seem better to think of a poem as a set of symbols (generally, and certainly for our purpose, *words*) functioning within a language system. Yet some philosophers and aestheticians certainly seem to feel driven to think of *poems* as *experiences*. This may perhaps be due to some phobia that otherwise they would have to consider them as marks on paper, or mere sounds in the air. John Dewey in *Art as Experience* seems to exhibit this phobia. Another acute writer who seems to have suffered from it was A. C. Bradley. Bradley writes:[1] 'Poetry being poems, we are to think of a poem as it actually exists; and, without aiming here at accuracy, we may say that an actual poem is a succession of experiences — sounds, images, thoughts, emotions — through which we pass when we read as poetically as we can'. What Bradley has done here is simply invent or take over an artificial sense of the word 'poem', to connote a succession of experiences. This must be what he has done, if we are to interpret his remark charitably: since otherwise what he would be saying would be nonsense. This can easily be seen. For I take it that what we read 'as poetically as we can', is a *poem*. And, if so, he would be saying that 'an actual poem is a succession of experiences through which we pass when we read a succession of experiences through which we pass when we read a succession of experiences through which we pass when we read . . .' and so on, *ad infinitum*, which would seem to be absurd. But there is no need to be caught in the dichotomy that a poem is *either* marks on paper (or sounds in the air) *or* experiences. There is a third alternative, namely, that a poem is *words*, symbols functioning within a language system. The poem can, and does indeed, in my view, con-

[1] In the Inaugural Lecture called 'Poetry for Poetry's Sake', delivered by him at Oxford on his assumption of the Chair of Poetry (publ. 1901), reprinted in his *Oxford Lectures on Poetry*, 1909 (1923 edition, at p. 4).

sist of *words*. The *meaning* of the poem, on the other hand, may well be *experiences*, and, indeed, that is my suggestion.

I now want to pass to my second point of dissent from Richards's suggestion. I cannot agree that the standard experience should be taken to be the relevant experience of the poet when contemplating the completed composition. That cannot be right, I think. The poet may sometimes never contemplate the completed composition: he might even die before he could do so. If the poem were a long one he might never think over the whole thing again. There are many possible forms of this objection. Another objection was seen by Richards himself, who added in a footnote that the poet might be dissatisfied without reason. But there are other difficulties, too. Even the *relevant* experience of the poet when contemplating the completed composition, may fail in adequacy to the full meanings of the words of the poem. The contemplating poet may be no more infallible as a judge of the meaning of his creation than the creating poet was.

This is a convenient point at which to pass to my concluding remarks:

If we take seriously the suggestion I have made that perhaps the meaning of a poem is a class of similar experiences[1] which those words in that order and in that form *ought* to evoke in a reader familiar with the language in which the poem is written, we must obviously consider the question as to what factors would decide what experiences the words of a poem *ought* to evoke. One factor, I suggest, is the meanings of the words in that order in the language system which prevailed *at the time when they were written*. If the words or the order would have been novel at that time, evidence such as other writings of the poet, or even statements of intention, may be relevant: and these may also be relevant in cases of ambiguity. There may be other sorts of evidence relevant in such cases, e.g. known influences, evidence of literary imitation and allusion. Even in these cases of novelty and ambiguity, though, there may be limits to the pains we ought to take to ascertain *what the poet meant* by his poem, as a means of finding out what the poem *means*. Sometimes, where a poet attaches a novel

[1] 'Similar', not, by the way, to any standard experience, but to one another.

sense to a word, or intends the word to have a special novel effect, this may not come out in the poem as it stands, and we certainly sometimes say that if the poet intended the word to bear that sense or to have that effect, he should have made it clearer, for it does not bear that sense or have that effect in the poem as it stands. The words of the poem do not mean what he meant by them. And it seems to me often legitimate that we should say such things. In such cases the only experiences which the poem ought to evoke in us are not the same as those the poet intended his readers to have. Again, sometimes we say that we are not sure what certain words of a poem mean, that their meaning is obscure, whereas at other times we say quite confidently that the meaning of the words is clear enough, though we are certain that they do not mean what the poet meant by them. In the latter case we definitely think that this is a defect in the poem. In the former case (the case of obscurity) we sometimes regard it as a defect, but not always; and whether we regard it as a defect or not, we sometimes look further, and try to find out what the words *do* mean, and this we may succeed in doing, either by making use of internal evidence or even by making use of external evidence. On the other hand, sometimes we refuse to make use of external evidence: we say that the meaning of a poem cannot be given to it by the external evidence; that that would be *importing* a meaning into the poem which it has not got in its own right. We seem, therefore, in some cases more inclined, and in some cases less inclined, to regard the meaning of a poem as being something other than the meaning which the words would naturally have borne or would naturally bear, in the language system in which the poem was written. We seem in some cases more inclined, and in some cases less inclined, to attach importance in determining what is the meaning of a poem, to what the poet meant by it. I suggest that there is no universal rule that we ought to attach the same importance in all cases to what the poet meant by his poem, in determining the meaning of the poem: but that the degree of importance we should attach to it in any particular case is a matter for *aesthetic decision*. The *meaning* of a poem, then, like its value, is something which we shall only arrive at if we make a right aesthetic decision. The meaning of the poem, moreover, will correspond to that right decision, in making which we have given their due weight (whether by careful consideration or by some more or less automatic process) to the different factors involved, in determining that class of experiences one or other of which the words of the poem, in that order, and in that form, *ought to evoke* in a reader familiar with the language (or languages) in which the poem is written.

(II) THE RELATIONS BETWEEN EVALUATIONS, REASONS AND DESCRIPTIONS IN AESTHETICS

Suppose someone were asked why he thought Jane Austen's *Emma* a good novel, and replied (whether justifiably or not is not in question) that it was a good novel for many reasons, and, in particular, because it showed a deep knowledge of human nature, and because its moral judgments were always well-grounded, and because it showed a subtle sense of the finer points of day-to-day living, and because the language was always alive and clear, and often striking, and the whole work was strewn with touches of shrewd humour. And, to prevent any misunderstanding, let us take all the reasons given for the overall value-judgment as themselves value-judgments. With regard to such a case an interesting question is whether the relations between the reasons and the overall value-judgment (meaning value-*proposition*, not the psychological act of judgment), are *logical*. A closely allied but different question, carefully to be distinguished from our first question, is whether the relation between the *consideration* that the novel had these various good qualities, and the overall evaluation that *Emma* is a good novel, would be *merely causal*. Now the *consideration* referred to would often also be called a '*reason*' for the final judgment; and so our two questions could both be called questions as to the relations between reasons and aesthetic value-judgments (value-propositions or evaluations, as the case may be). These two questions, then, are the first questions I wish to consider in this lecture.

Let us look into the first question.

One way of cutting near to the root of the matter is perhaps to ask: Could there be a novel which showed a deep knowledge of human nature, gave well-grounded moral judgments, showed a subtle sense of the finer points of day-to-day living, and was written in language always alive and clear, and often striking, and was strewn with touches of shrewd humour, and yet was not a good novel?

I am afraid we should have to admit that there *could* be such a novel. However much all the good qualities mentioned might be taken to weigh, there might still be some radical defect, say, for instance, a strong tendency to needless digression, or a hopeless weakness of plot construction, which even in a novel with all those good qualities, would nevertheless spell ruin to overall value.

Jane Austen's *Emma*, however, is itself deficient in neither of these two respects. It is admirably economical, and the plot, on a careful reading, gives almost as much cause for wonder as the insight into human nature. This suggests the possibility that if we went on long enough with our list of good qualities we might eventually bar out any chance of some sneaking defect putting paid to our overall value-judgment. *If* such a list were possible, moreover, it would seem as if the relation between the complete list and the overall value-judgment would quite certainly be a logical one: for any novel with the good qualities $q^1_g\, q^2_g\, q^3_g \cdots q^n_g$, would *necessarily* be a good novel.

Is it possible to compile such a list of good qualities? I myself cannot *see* that it would be impossible: but I am not proposing to attempt the feat of compiling one in this lecture. Indeed, though I cannot *see* that it would be impossible to compile such a list, I believe it might be difficult to do so. One reason for thinking this seems to me to be as follows: Suppose we compiled a list of good qualities which seemed satisfactory, and then some great moral or aesthetic teacher were to arise in course of time, and either suggest some important criterion of value, which seemed to outweigh in importance all that we had previously considered, or show that the criteria we had employed were, in any case, of small importance, then our list might no longer appear satisfactory to us. A

Tolstoy, for instance, might persuade us that we had overvalued the qualities which had made us think the work of Shakespeare great: another St. Thomas Aquinas might see something which made all his writings seem useless, and, by telling us so, might bring us to believe that we ourselves had shallowly overrated them. The ways of evolution are so incalculable that we cannot rule out such possibilities. On the other hand, as far as our question goes, the existence or non-existence of some further awkward criterion, the consideration of which might upset the connexion between our list of good qualities and the overall value-judgment, would not affect the point that the relation between the reasons and whatever overall value-judgment were then valid, would still be logical. The 'reasons' would in that case militate against the new judgment, just as they had supported the old one.

But ignoring the difficulties of compiling such a list, and assuming for a moment that such a list is possible, let us consider its logical status. The complete list would be a statement of a *sufficient condition* of any novel's being good. On the other hand, it would not be a statement of any *necessary* condition of a novel's being good. A novel might not have any of the good qualities listed, and might still be a good novel. Moreover, the list would only be a statement of *a* sufficient condition of any novel's being good. There might well be another list or other lists of good qualities which would also be the statement or statements of *a sufficient condition* of any novel's being good. *This* list of good qualities, however, would be the statement of *a sufficient condition* of any novel's being good, and so, as I have said, the relation between the proposition that any particular novel had all the qualities contained in this list, and the overall value-judgment that the novel was a good one, would be a *logical* relation.

Let us now assume, though, that it would not be possible to compile a list of good qualities such that any novel which possessed them all would *necessarily* be good. It might still be possible to compile a list of good qualities such that any novel which possessed them would *almost certainly* be good, or at least would *probably* be good. Unfortunately, the same difficulty arises here as with the other list already discussed, namely that it would always be *possible* that some criterion might come to light which would make it clear that a work with the good qualities listed would not even be probably good. Consider the case of Tolstoy and Shakespeare. Tolstoy promulgated criteria of value, such as contribution to the love of God or the love of one's fellow men,[1] according to which (among other more usual criteria[2]) the work of Shakespeare seemed to him inferior. Now Tolstoy was a very great man, and these criteria have a certain impressiveness. The reconsideration of Shakespeare's work in the light of them may even lessen its value in the eyes of some of us. On the other hand, there is little doubt that except with fanatics such reconsideration will not prevent people from thinking Shakespeare's works *good*. Even in Soviet Russia, where one could expect Tolstoy's anti-aristocratic strictures against Shakespeare, based on the second of the above criteria, to have had some powerful and lasting effect, the reputation of Shakespeare is as high as ever. This may indeed be partly due to critical opinion there not having agreed whole-heartedly with Tolstoy as to the tendencies of Shakespeare's work; but it is hard to believe that it is not also partly due to the value attached even in Russia to other literary criteria, though it may also be partly due to disagreement with the judgments Tolstoy based on some of *those*. This sort of case suggests that it might be feasible to make a list of good qualities of a novel or other literary work, such that, although it would still be *possible* that the consideration of other criteria would reverse the judgment that the novel was good, such a *possibility* would itself be *highly improbable*. In the case of Shakespeare's work, for instance, we might say that though indeed at some future time some criteria of value might be applied which would reveal that Shakespeare's work was, after all, not good, yet it is very improbable that any such criteria will be applied. Moreover, if that were so, then the relation between the proposition that the literary work in question had the good qualities in the list, and the overall judgment that the novel was a good one, would still be one of probability. To me at least it would seem

---

[1] See Tolstoy, 'What is Art?' (*Works*, tr. Maude, Oxford, 1929, Vol. XVIII, pp. 241-2).

[2] E.g. Sincerity, naturalness of situation, appropriateness of speech to character, sense of proportion. See Tolstoy's essay, 'Shakespeare and the Drama' (*Works*, tr. Maude,. Oxford, 1929, Vol. XXI, especially pp. 363-4).

that such a list of good qualities could be compiled. It might, indeed, not be much longer in the case of a novel, for instance, than the list of good qualities mentioned in connection with *Emma* at the start of this lecture. Now, suppose we had such a list, would the relation between the proposition that a novel had all the qualities in the list, and the overall value-judgment (value-proposition) that the novel was good, be a *logical* relation? The answer seems to me clearly to be that, if we call probability a logical relation, then the relation between those propositions is a logical relation. The answer, therefore, depends ultimately on whether probability is a logical relation. This is, as you know, a highly controversial issue, on which great brain-power has been exerted.[1] It would be presumptuous even to start to attack that difficult problem in this lecture. I shall only say that I personally feel attracted, as far as this case goes, by Keynes's view that probability *is* a logical relation. That being so, I feel inclined to the view that the relation between the proposition that a novel has all the qualities in the supposed list, and the overall value-judgment (value-proposition) that the novel is good, is a logical relation.

Let us now turn to the second question, namely, whether the relation between the *consideration* that a novel had all the good qualities in a list of either of the two main types considered, and the overall value-judgment (act of evaluation), would be a *logical* relation or a *merely causal* relation. The answer to this question seems to me to be that we should not be stretching usage at all to say that the relation would be at least partly a logical relation, and not a merely causal relation. Let us look into the matter. Certainly, if a person A on some occasion considers the fact that a certain novel has the *bare* qualities[2] $q^1 q^2 q^3 \ldots q^n$, that consideration may or may not *cause* him to hold that the novel is a good one. If he

[1] For exposition of the view that probability is a logical relation see J. M. Keynes, *A Treatise on Probability*, Macmillan, 1921; H. Jeffreys, *Theory of Probability*, Oxford, 1939; C. D. Broad in *Mind*, 1918, 1920, and in *Proceedings of the Aristotelian Society*, Vol. 28 (1927-28). For opposing views see R. von Mises, *Probability, Statistics and Truth*, London, 1939; K. R. Popper, *Logik der Forschung*, Vienna, 1935; Hans Reichenbach, *Logical Foundations of Probability*, Berkeley, 1949; R. A. Fisher, *Statistical Methods for Research Workers*, Edinburgh, 1923.

[2] By 'bare qualities' I mean qualities considered without any value-charge which may be attached to them, e.g. *complexity*, which may or may not be valued by some critic or some culture.

himself *thinks* that $q^1 q^2 q^3 \ldots q^n$ *are* good qualities, i.e. are $q^1_g q^2_g q^3_g \ldots q^n_g$, the consideration that the novel has those qualities could hardly cause him to think that the novel is a bad one. On the other hand, if he himself *thinks* that $q^1 q^2 q^3 \ldots q^n$ are bad qualities, i.e. are $q^1_b q^2_b q^3_b \ldots q^n_b$, then the consideration that the novel has those qualities might well *cause* him to hold that the novel is a bad one. It might be suggested, then, that whether a person will be caused to think the novel good or bad, will depend on whether the person concerned *thinks* the qualities are good or bad. Thus the consideration that the novel has the bare qualities $q^1 q^2 q^3 \ldots q^n$ will have a *mere causal relation* to a judgment that the novel is good, if by 'mere causal relation' we mean (and this seems the most important sense) a relation such that there would be no contradiction involved if the consideration that the novel had the qualities $q^1 q^2 q^3 \ldots q^n$ caused the judgment that the novel was a bad one. This argument, in my opinion, may be perfectly sound, but is quite irrelevant to our question. For the relation we are considering in our second question is *not* the relation between the consideration that a novel has the *bare* qualities $q^1 q^2 q^3 \ldots q^n$ and the overall judgment that the novel is good: but the relation between the consideration that the novel has the *good* qualities $q^1_g q^2_g q^3_g \ldots q^n_g$ and the overall judgment that the novel is good. Now a contradiction would certainly be involved if A should assert: 'the fact that the novel has the good qualities $q^1_g q^2{}_g q^3_g \ldots q^n_g$ makes it probable that it is a bad novel' or if he should assert: 'the fact that the novel has the good qualities $q^1_g q^2_g q^3_g \ldots q^n_g$ goes no way towards making it probable that it is a good novel' or if he should assert: 'the fact that the novel has the good qualities $q^1_g q^2_g q^3_g \ldots q^n_g$ goes no way towards making it true that the novel is a good one'. And the type of case we are discussing is of this sort, and not one involving bare qualities. The supposed critic mentioned at the beginning of this lecture clearly considered that the qualities of *Emma* which he enumerated were *good* qualities, and if he had said that the fact that *Emma* had these qualities made it a bad novel; or (by themselves) made it probable that *Emma* was a bad novel; or went no way towards making it probable that it was a good novel: that would have involved a contradiction. The relation between the consideration that a novel has qualities deemed by the critic to be good, and his judgment that the novel is good, cannot therefore be a mere causal relation, in the sense indicated earlier in this paragraph.

I hope I have now shown that the relation between the consideration that a novel has certain good qualities and the subsequent value-judgment that the novel is good, is not a merely causal one.

Thus in the sort of case (the case about *Emma*) mentioned at the beginning of this lecture, the relation between the 'reasons' or 'reason' for the value-judgment that the novel is good, and the value-judgment itself, is at least partly logical, whether the 'reasons' be taken to be (a) the *facts* that *Emma* has this good quality, that good quality and the other good quality, in which case the relation is *wholly* logical, or the 'reason' be taken to be (b) the *consideration* by a critic that *Emma* has this good quality, that good quality and the other good quality, in which case the relation is *partly* logical.

Both our questions have been concerned, as you know, with good qualities attributed to a work, or at least with qualities clearly *taken* to be good by the critic concerned. It will readily have occurred to you that analogous questions could be raised with regard to *bare* qualities, that is, qualities considered without any value-charge which may be attached to them. These questions might be expressed (restricting them somewhat so as to make them more pointed) as follows: (1) Is the relation between the fact that a novel has a certain bare quality, and the value-proposition that the novel has at least one good quality, a logical relation? and (2) Is the relation between the *consideration* that a novel has a certain bare quality, and the *act of evaluation* that the novel has at least one good quality, a merely causal relation?

I wish to spend most of the remainder of my lecture discussing the first of these two questions, to follow this with a brief passage on the second question, and finally to say something about the relation between our two *sets* of questions.

Let us consider question (1), then, and for the sake of clarity let us at first focus attention on one of the bare qualities forming the descriptive (as opposed to evaluatory) element of one of the good qualities attributed to *Emma* by the supposed critic at the start of my lecture. We may ask the following question: Is the relation between the fact that a novel shows a deep knowledge of human nature, and the fact that it has at least one good quality, a logical relation? The term 'deep knowledge', in this question, is to be taken *purely descriptively* (at least with respect to a novel), abstracting completely the evaluatory element or value-charge present in the phrase on so many occasions when it is used in criticism. It is to be taken, that is, as meaning, *roughly*, correct plumbing of human motive, accurate description of less obvious human reactions, correct prediction of basic human behaviour, a full and precise sense of human feeling. (I do not wish to insist on the detail of this particular analysis.) Now to this question taken in this sense I am inclined to think we ought to reply in the negative. As it happens, the best judges consider that a deep knowledge of human nature is a point in favour of a novel: but they might equally well have found deep knowledge of human nature, where shown in any novel, an *execrable* quality. Admittedly the best judges may often have *reasons* for the view they *do* hold on this point; and the relation between these *reasons* and their judgment that a deep knowledge of human nature *is* a good point in a novel, would be a logical relation, or at least not a merely causal one: but however long the chain of reasons might be, I for one find it hard to believe that there will not come a point at which a brute preference is reached. (Indeed I do not think that the chain of reasons likely to be adduced in the present case is a long one at all.) Now if in fact there always *does* come a point at which a brute preference is reached, then between the fact that the novel has a certain bare quality, and the fact that it has at least one good quality, there is at a certain point a logical gap, the only bridge over which is the brute preference itself. I said a moment ago that 'I for one find it hard to believe' that there will not come a point in the chain of reasons for the positive evaluation of a quality, at which a brute preference is reached. Now it might well appear that such a difficulty of belief is not definite enough evidence for strict philosophical thinking. It might be suggested that if it could be shown that there *must* come a point in the chain of reasons, at which a brute preference is reached, then that would be more satisfying. *Can* it be shown? It seems clear that it could only be shown by deduction from some proposition or propositions admitted to be true. Now a proposition which clearly presents itself as a candidate for the premiss of such a deduction is the general proposition that no value-judgment follows logically from a purely descriptive proposition. Is this proposition true? That is a crucial point.

It might be said against the view that this proposition is true, that when we make aesthetic value-judgments we often give as reasons propositions which are purely descriptive. For instance, we often give as a reason for saying that a portrait is good, that it is 'like' the person of whom it purports to be a portrait. (For the purposes of our argument let us take the slippery word 'like' to mean in this context 'bearing a strong physical resemblance to'.) With regard to this sort of case I want to raise the following problem, namely, whether *any* value-judgment really *follows* from the reason given; and, in particular, whether it *follows* that the portrait has at least one good point. In favour of the view that this *does* follow, it might be urged that a portrait *is* something which should be like the person it purports to be a portrait of; that part at least of the meaning of the term 'portrait' is: 'picture that should be like the person whom it purports to represent'. If that is so, the argument would continue, then, to say that a certain portrait is like the person whom it purports to represent, is to say something from which it follows that the portrait has at least one good point, since to say that a certain portrait is like the person whom it purports to represent is to say that a certain picture which *should be like* the person it purports to represent, *is* like that person; and if it *is* what it should be, that is obviously a point in favour of it. Thus, it might be concluded, this one value-judgment, slight though it may be, *follows* from a purely descriptive statement. This argument seems to me formally sound; so that much if not everything seems to hinge on whether a portrait *is* something which *should be* like the person whose portrait it purports to be: or, to put the point in linguistic terminology (without suggesting any exact equivalence), much if not everything seems to hinge on whether part at least of the *meaning* of the term 'portrait' is: 'picture that should be like the person whom it purports to represent'.

This is rather a hard question. Suppose that up till now portraits had in fact been like the persons they purported to represent, but that a new technique of what its exponents called 'portrait-painting' were evolved, such that a 'portrait' of this new type was a representation of a person, but was not required to be like that person physically. (I can remember that when I was an undergraduate here there was a woman student at Newnham College who used to draw pictures of the 'souls' of her male acquaintances, to whom the pictures were quite clearly not required to bear any physical resemblance.) Should we call such a picture a 'portrait'? There would probably be some people who would say: 'That picture is not a "portrait" ' or 'That picture does not deserve to be called a "portrait".' On the other hand, we could expect some others to rejoin: 'Why not? It is a "portrait" all right: you are just narrow-minded.'

What is the situation here? It seems to me to be as follows: The first party is regarding it as an essential criterion of a portrait that it *should be* like (i.e. that it *ought to be* like) the person of whom it purports to be a portrait: or (in linguistic terms) the first party would hold that the term 'portrait' cannot be correctly used to refer to a picture unless that picture ought to be like the person of whom it purports to be a portrait. The second party, on the other hand, does not regard it as an essential criterion of a portrait that it ought to be like the person of whom it purports to be a portrait: or (in linguistic terms) the second party would hold that the term 'portrait' *can* be correctly used to refer to a picture even if it is not true that that picture ought to be like the person of whom it purports to be a portrait. The second party *might* perhaps add that it would be quite enough for the picture to be required to be in some way a representation of that person (e.g. a highly distorted projection, or one of the Newnham student's 'soul'-pictures) without it needing to be required to resemble that person physically.

The situation we have been considering has actually arisen in connection with some ultra-modern pictures which certain people would call 'portraits', while other people would deny them that title, even though some of the latter class of people might admire them as works of art, all the same.

Now which of our two parties would be right? This again is a hard question. It might seem that we could only answer it, if at all, by reference to the correct idea of a portrait: or (in linguistic terms) by reference to the meaning of the word 'portrait' as it is correctly used in the English language. Now what is the correct idea of a portrait: or (in linguistic terms) what is the meaning of the word 'portrait' as it is correctly used in the English language? The true answer seems to me to be that we do not know exactly. We do know a fair amount about these matters: for instance, we know that a portrait is a picture and not a sort of cricket-bat, and (in linguistic terms) we know that it *is* part of the meaning of the term 'portrait' (in at least one of its most important uses) that it is a picture. On the other hand, there are points on which we are in the dark, and one such point is as to whether to be a portrait at all a picture must be *required to be like* (*not* must *be like*, of course) the person of whom it is a picture: and we are in the dark as to whether (in linguistic terms) it is at least part of the meaning of the word 'portrait' as correctly used in the English language, that it is a picture which ought to be like the person whose portrait it purports to be. We are in the dark on these points, I suggest: but that is not, I believe, because there is some true answer; but because our ideas and correct usage are on these points *indeterminate*. If this is so, then, of our two parties, the first was wrong in holding that it is definitely an essential criterion of a portrait that it ought to be like the person whose portrait it purports to be: while the second was wrong in holding that the term 'portrait' can correctly (i.e. according to established usage) be used to refer to a picture even if it is not true that that picture ought to be like the person of whom it purports to be a portrait. Whether it will *become* correct usage is a question. The issue is being fought out: and while it is being fought out, we can only say that it is *better* to extend the use of the term to cover such cases, or that it is *better not* to extend the use of the term to cover such cases, not that it is *correct* to do so, or *correct* not to do so. It might be *better*, for instance, in view of the practical effects, e.g. the encouragement or discouragement of a looser or freer style of painting. A new style 'portrait' by any other name might still be as good a work of art: but if it was not called a 'portrait' there might not be as many commissions for its painter. Another way in which it might be better to extend or not to extend the use of the term 'portrait' to cover the new cases, would be that it would emphasize the likenesses or differences between these new portraits and the 'respectable' old ones. If it were more important to emphasize the likenesses, that would be a point in favour of extending the use. If, on the other hand, it were more important to emphasize the differences, that would be a point in favour of *not* extending the use.

If I am right in my analysis of this matter so far, it is uncertain whether it should be part of the meaning of the term 'portrait' that it ought to be like the person whose portrait it purports to be. That issue is not yet fought out. Now, if that is so, it is also uncertain whether to say that a certain portrait is like the person whom it purports to represent is to say something from which it *follows* that the portrait has at least one good point. It might be instructive here to compare this case of the portrait with the case of sugar. It is certainly part of the meaning of the term 'sugar' that it *ought to be* sweet. There the doubtful matter is not whether it is part of the meaning of the term 'sugar' that it *ought to be* sweet, but whether it is part of the meaning of the term 'sugar' that it *is* sweet.[1] (That is quite a different point, however, and we need not go into it.) We should certainly not call anything 'sugar' if it ought not to be sweet. That is a point in our language that has been decided: whereas in the case of the portrait, whether we should call a picture a 'portrait' if that picture has no need to be like the person it purports to represent, has *not* been decided. But there is a further, and I think, deeper point. When it is decided, if ever it is decided, *either* that the term 'portrait' *cannot* be correctly used to refer to a picture unless that picture ought to be like the person it purports to represent, *or* that the term *can* be correctly used to refer to a picture even if it is not true that that picture

---

[1] It is interesting to find that in the American dictionary of Funk and Wagnall the primary sense of 'sweet' is given as 'Agreeable to the sense of taste; having a flavor like that of sugar . . . .'

ought to be like the person whom it purports to represent, then the meaning of the term 'portrait' in the English language will be different from what it is now, and, putting the point in non-linguistic terms, the concept of a portrait will be different from what it is now. For now the usage of the term 'portrait' is vague, and the concept of a portrait is radically indeterminate: whereas then the usage of the term 'portrait', and the concept of a portrait, will be in this respect fixed and definite. From this it follows that nothing decided by that change would provide an answer to the questions we have asked: for the questions we have asked concern the situation as it is now. And in the situation as it is now, there are two views on this point as to the meaning of the term 'portrait', and those two views correspond to the tendencies in people to emphasize the likeness or the difference between the old 'respectable' portraits and the new type of pictures. These new pictures, of course, are just as like or unlike the old ones as they are, and nothing we can say about them can make them more or less like the old ones than they in fact are. *In this respect* (and I should wish these words to bear considerable emphasis) it is a matter of indifference whether we *call* the new type of picture a 'portrait' or not. But it is not at all a matter of indifference with respect to the answer to our original question, namely, whether it *follows* from the fact that a portrait is like the person whom it purports to represent, that the portrait has at least one good point. For, as we saw, the answer to that question hinged on whether or not a portrait *is* a picture which ought to be like the person whose portrait it purports to be, or, to put the point in linguistic terminology, whether part, at least, of the *meaning* of the term 'portrait' is: 'picture that should be like the person whom it purports to represent'. The original question was about *portraits*, that is, about those things referred to by the term 'portrait' as it is at present used in English: and, as I have said, in my view it is quite uncertain whether only a picture that *ought to be like* the person whom it purports to represent can be a portrait. And that being so, it seems to me quite uncertain whether it *follows* from the fact that a portrait is like the person whom it purports to represent, that the portrait has at least one good point. It seems to me, therefore, quite uncertain whether any value-judgment *follows* from the supposedly purely descriptive proposition that the portrait is like the person whom it purports to represent.

But suppose it had turned out in this case that portraits *are* in fact pictures that *ought to be like* the persons whom they purport to represent, or, in linguistic terms, that part at least of the meaning of the term 'portrait' is: 'picture that ought to be like the person whom it purports to represent', then would it really *be* a purely descriptive proposition (i.e. a proposition making no value assertion), that a certain portrait was like the person it purported to represent? Let us consider the sentence:

'The portrait P is like A whom it purports to represent'.

Now *ex hypothesi* part of the meaning of this sentence is:

The picture P which ought to be like A *is* like A.

And this is a value proposition. Thus what may have seemed to be a purely descriptive proposition would, if the very condition required for the argument had been fulfilled (i.e. if part of the meaning of the term 'portrait' had been 'picture that ought to be like the person it purports to represent'), have in fact been merely a value proposition in disguise.

The case of the portrait, then, fails on two grounds to provide an instance where a value proposition follows from a purely descriptive proposition.

Yet this seemed a plausible case in favour of the view that value propositions sometimes follow from purely descriptive propositions. Can some more plausible cases be suggested, and, if so, will they turn out on analysis not really to be instances of value-judgments *following* from *purely descriptive* propositions? Finally, if we are unable to find any cases which stand up to analysis, and feel therefore led, as we might be, to maintain that perhaps no value-judgment ever follows from a purely descriptive proposition, we shall then naturally be called upon, I think, to try to describe as precisely as possible the relationship between value-judgments and the apparently purely descriptive propositions which are often quite rightly given as reasons for them.

One thing that is certain is that if we are eventually led to the conclusion that no value-judgment ever follows from a purely descriptive proposition, then we shall have to admit that the relation between the *consideration* that a work of art has a certain bare quality, and the judgment that the work has at least one good quality, may well be merely causal.

I shall end by trying very briefly to fulfil my promise to say something about the connexion between the two sets of questions which have formed the subject of this lecture. The situation seems to me to be this: When we make aesthetic value-judgments, we sometimes support them by other value-judgments. In that case, it seems to me, the relation between the supporting value-judgments and the main value-judgment is, where the support is valid, a logical relation, sometimes one of probability, sometimes perhaps one of necessity. Moreover, the relation between the consideration that the work has the qualities which we attribute to it in the supporting value-judgments, and our overall evaluation, is more than merely causal, in that it would involve us in contradiction to assert that positive value elements failed to contribute to overall value.

On the other hand, sometimes we give in support of our aesthetic value-judgments what may seem to be purely descriptive propositions. The existence of such cases might suggest that value-judgments sometimes *follow* from purely descriptive propositions. In one plausible case, however, which I investigated in some detail, it did not appear that we could definitely say that *any* value-judgment *followed* from the supposedly purely descriptive proposition, if it was indeed a purely descriptive proposition. On the other hand, examination of the case showed that if we could have said that the value-judgment *followed* from the proposition in question, then that proposition would not have been a purely descriptive proposition, but a value-judgment in disguise.[1]

Once we are within the magic circle of value-judgments, then, logical relations seem to hold between some value-judgments and

[1] Dr. Ernst Topitsch, Lecturer in the Philosophical Institute at Vienna University, one of the Course Members, has pointed out to me the close relation between these and other points made in this lecture, and certain positions maintained by Henri Poincaré in his paper 'La Science et la Morale' in *Dernières Pensées*.

other value-judgments which seem to support them: but the questions remain as to whether we can be compelled to enter that magic circle of value-judgments by the logical force of purely descriptive propositions sometimes offered as reasons for value-judgments, and, if not, what the precise relation is between these purely descriptive propositions and both the overall value-judgments they are used to support, and the lesser value-judgments which these logically include. And corresponding questions concern the relations between 'considerations' and 'evaluations'. Anything like an adequate attempt to answer these questions, however, would require at least another lecture: and I shall therefore now leave them with you in the hope that what I have said here may have both sharpened the questions and at least cleared the ground for satisfactory answers.

H. BONDI

Some Philosophical Problems in Cosmology

HERMANN BONDI, M.A. (Cantab.), F.R.S.: born in Vienna, November 1st, 1919; educated in Austria and at Trinity College, Cambridge; Fellow of Trinity College, 1943-51; Professor of Mathematics at King's College, London, since 1954; Research Associate, Cornell University, 1953-54; Fellow of Royal Astronomical Society since 1946 and Secretary since 1956; married 1947, C. M. Stockwell, a graduate in Mathematics of Newnham College, Cambridge, with whom he has collaborated in research and publication.

Chief publications: 'Review of Cosmology', *Mon. Not. R. Astr. Soc.*, 1948. 'On the Interpretation of the Hertzsprung-Russell Diagram', *Mon. Not. R. Astr. Soc.*, 1950. 'Modern Theories of Cosmology', *The Advancement of Science*, 1954. 'Relativity and Indeterminacy', *Nature*, 1952. 'Gravitational Waves', *Endeavour*, 1961, 'Why Scientists Talk', *Advancement of Science*, 1962. Together with other papers in collaboration with Mrs. C. M. Bondi, T. Gold and F. Hoyle.

H. BONDI

SOME PHILOSOPHICAL PROBLEMS
IN COSMOLOGY

(1) I shall try to present to you some of the philosophical problems the physicist meets when he wishes to discuss the properties of the universe as a whole. The first problem concerns the definition of the term 'universe'. Several different answers to this question have been given and are current amongst physicists. These differing definitions may well account for some of the differences amongst present-day theories of cosmology. This problem of definition will be discussed later.

(2) There is an interesting difference between cosmology and the rest of physics. In physics we are primarily interested in *laws* describing common features of a variety of phenomena.

As an example consider the law of free fall on the surface of the Earth. This can be regarded as an abstraction from a large number of experiments in which it is found that every object moves with the same constant downward acceleration. A distinction is drawn between, on the one hand, the 'accidental' feature of the velocity and direction of projection, which is largely under our control and distinguishes the trajectories of different projectiles from each other, and on the other hand the 'general' feature of the unique constant downward acceleration common to all projectiles. The law of gravitation is solely concerned with this general feature. Similarly, on the larger scale of the solar system, the law of gravitation describes the features common to the orbits of all planets and satellites, while the question of the 'accidental' circumstances of projection is left to the far more difficult and obscure subject of the origin of the solar system.

In cosmology a unique object is studied (the universe) and

accordingly this process of abstraction becomes inappropriate. Any attempts to distinguish between 'general' and 'accidental' features of the unique universe is hence wholly arbitrary. The most complete 'explanation' that a theory of cosmology can give is therefore a description.

(3) There are two distinct ways of constructing a model of the universe:

(i) One can take the laws of physics as found locally and then try to apply them to the whole universe.

(ii) One can postulate (as a kind of working hypothesis) some general properties of the entire universe and then, by applying the known laws of physics as far as is possible, one can try to infer *local observable consequences* of the original postulates. The observational comparison that can now be made makes a disproof of the postulates possible and so gives them scientific status.

Method (i) is historically the oldest and is still possibly the most popular one. Newton used it to prove, by a typical cosmological argument, that matter must be more or less evenly distributed throughout the whole of space. For otherwise, (e.g. if there were no matter outside a finite region of the infinite space,) there would exist a centre of mass of all material, and by virtue of the law of gravitation, all the matter in the universe would tend to collapse towards this point. The absence of any observable motion of this kind was taken by Newton as a proof of an infinite and roughly uniform distribution of matter in the universe.

A difficulty arises in this approach to cosmology. A variation might be made in a locally established law of physics that would be *locally* unobservable and yet might be important on the very large scale, and there are clearly very many possible variations of this type. Consider for example the modification of the inverse square law of gravitational attraction that arises if a term of repulsion proportional to distance is added. If the coefficient of the new term is chosen so that the term is wholly negligible within the solar system then there could be no local disproof of the existence of this new term. Nevertheless on a sufficiently large scale, the new term could predominate since it increases with distance while the usual inverse square law term diminishes with distance. Such a term might therefore be of great cosmological importance, and yet would wholly escape local examination. In the second approach this difficulty is minimized. We merely ask what local laws are compatible with (rather than deducible from) a given postulated set of properties of the universe as a whole.

(4) Some of the philosophical points that arise can perhaps best be discussed by the illustrative use of a definite cosmological theory, and for this purpose the steady state theory of Bondi and Gold will be chosen.

If we can say anything about the Universe, then it can only be because what happens very far from us does have locally observable effects, i.e. it must not be nonsensical to talk of such effects.

Now, whatever we may assume about these influences, it is obvious that these effects cannot vary very rapidly, either in space or in time.

It follows that the whole body of knowledge we have was obtained from a very definite Universe. Now, if the Universe were (a) in a state of change in time, or (b) looked different from different places, or (c) both — then physics, investigated in different places, or at different times, might be very different from physics as it is known to us.

Any theory of cosmology contemplating a universe changing in space or in time or in both must therefore make definite assumptions about the effects of these changes on the laws of physics. Even the statement that there are no such effects is evidently an assumption, in fact a highly arbitrary assumption.

The only way to avoid the need to make any such assumption is to postulate that the large scale aspect of the universe is always the same irrespective of position and time. This postulate is called the perfect cosmological principle (P.C.P.). This postulate forms a good working hypothesis in that it enables us to construct a quite definite and unique model of the universe without the need to make any additional assumption. For if the universe looks the same from all places at all times then our physics is universally valid. This model can hence be worked out uniquely and its local aspects can be found. Comparison with observation becomes then possible and renders the P.C.P. liable to observational disproof.

This possibility of a clear-cut disproof establishes the scientific status of the P.C.P.

It turns out, in developing the consequences of the P.C.P.,that it is incompatible with the law of conservation of matter. What is required is a continual creation of matter at a rate which, though low by terrestrial standards, is of great cosmological importance. (The rate is approximately one hydrogen atom per litre volume every thousand million years.) There is therefore no practical possibility of a direct proof or disproof of this process of continual creation. The relation of this process to the classical law of conservation of matter can be considered as an interesting application of the simplicity postulate. There is direct experimental evidence that matter is conserved to a high degree of accuracy. In the context of terrestrial physics it is clear that the simplest theoretical formulation of this fact is the law of the absolute conservation of matter. The rate of creation (i.e. violation of this law) demanded by the P.C.P. is far lower than the accuracy of the experimental evidence in favour of the law. It is therefore argued that the greatest simplicity in relation to the entire range of physics including cosmology is achieved by adopting the more complicated law stating that there is a constant universal rate of continual creation but that apart from that matter is conserved. The complexity of this law is, it can be argued, more than counterbalanced by the gain in simplicity in cosmology.

The chief controversy in contemporary cosmology concerns this point, viz. whether to adopt the P.C.P. with its consequential modification of the law of conservation of matter or whether to stick firmly to the law of absolute conservation of matter, abandoning the idea of an unchanging universe. The most widely accepted theory of cosmology is of this latter type and is based on the general theory of relativity, which is believed to be the best formulation we have of the laws of conservation of matter and of gravitation. In this relativistic cosmology one works with perfectly definite laws of physics (the field equations of general relativity) which are assumed to be unchanging although the model of the universe so derived is necessarily a model varying in time. The decision between the steady state and relativistic model can be made purely observationally. Though present observations are still insufficient it seems likely that within ten to fifteen years the decision can be made.

Since the relativistic equations do not specify the model completely, further assumptions are required (at least until observation supplies more information than at present). These assumptions must be less restrictive than the P.C.P. The assumption usually made is the cosmological principle (C.P.) which states that at any given time the large scale aspect of the universe is the same from all points. In other words, just as in the P.C.P. spatial location is assumed to be irrelevant, but contrary to the P.C.P. location in time is taken to be of physical relevance. The status of the C.P. in relativistic cosmology is quite different from the status of the P.C.P. in the steady state theory. There the P.C.P. forms the basic assumption on which the entire theory is built, but in relativistic cosmology the C.P. is only the most plausible assumption concerning distant regions that can be made in accordance with the meagre observational data. An observational disproof of the C.P. would lead to mere minor modification of relativistic cosmology, but an observational disproof of the P.C.P. would completely destroy the steady state theory, since the P.C.P. is logically prior to the theory.

(7) The question of the direct verification of the C.P. and the P.C.P. raises philosophical questions closely connected with the problem of the definition of the universe that was mentioned earlier.

Consider first the status of the assertion that the surface of the Earth is more or less the same everywhere. A man belonging to the flat-earth school and therefore believing the earth to be infinite could correctly say that the assertion could never be established observationally. For however far observations might reach, changes beyond the reach of observation could still upset any conclusion of general homogeneity inferred from the observed region. On a finite Earth, however, observation can establish the degree of uniformity of the surface.

If the universe is finite, as some theories suggest, observation can discover the degree of homogeneity, but certain other complications arise. However, in addition to the possibility that the universe may be finite, there is another much subtler limitation of the range of observation that is of great importance.

It is observed (and it follows from both the C.P. and the P.C.P.) that the light of distant objects is shifted to the red, the extent of the red shift being roughly speaking proportional to the distance of the object. If the red shift is interpreted as due to a velocity of recession then the concept of the expanding universe results, together with the so-called velocity distance law.

It is a direct consequence of the laws of physics that if light is shifted to the red, it loses energy. Thus light received from distant objects has less energy and hence they look fainter than they would without the red shift. In addition to the inverse square law there is therefore another factor limiting the range of our instruments. Though this effect is negligible out to considerable distances it then becomes far more important than the inverse square law and leads to a far faster rate of diminution of observability with distance. The biggest existing telescopes are already appreciably affected by this. The 200 in. telescope sees far less than twice as far as the 100 in. telescope, and for telescopes say, three times as large a doubling of the aperture would only lead to an increase in range of a few per cent.

There is therefore a lack of coupling with the distant regions of the universe. Regions more than, say, 8000 million light years apart hardly interact. Their mutual observability is sharply reduced. The question is now whether this new type of barrier is to be regarded as the frontier of the universe. In particular the question is whether verification of the C.P. or P.C.P. within the region in which the red shift is less than some fixed value (say 90 per cent or 99 per cent) is to be regarded as establishing the C.P. (or P.C.P.). In the author's view such verification is sufficient, but in the view of some distinguished proponents of relativistic cosmology this is not so, and in their view any cosmological principle is incapable of direct observational verification. If the author's view is taken then there is already strong observational support for both C.P. and P.C.P.

It will be seen that the question at issue is precisely that of the definition of the universe. Broadly speaking there appear to me to be three possibilities.

(i) The totality of all objects to which physical theory can be applied, whether these objects are observable or not.

(ii) All objects that are observable now or at any time in the future.

(ii) All objects that are now observable.

On the basis of (iii) there is strong evidence that the universe is uniform and that at least the C.P. applies. On the basis of (ii) no evidence can be conclusive for all time but provisionally the existing evidence can be regarded as strong. On the basis of (i), however, the C.P. is either necessarily conjectural or merely a local statement of no particular interest for the universe as a whole. The question at issue here is philosophical, but the answer to it is of great physical interest.

POSTSCRIPT

THERE have been few developments in theoretical cosmology since 1956, but on the side of tests of the theories some matters of interest have happened. The first concerns the theory of the origin of the elements and is of exceptionally wide significance for many branches of science. It is also a model of how a theory such as the steady-state theory, however shaky, can yet be most fruitful, and is worth describing here.

It has been known for forty years that hydrogen, by far the simplest of all elements, is also the most common one in the universe, and that helium, the next simple, is the second most abundant, all others together accounting for barely 2 per cent of all matter. This has naturally led to the idea that somehow the other elements may have been built up from hydrogen, and perhaps helium, in nuclear reactions. Since the structure of the stars began to be understood due to Eddington's work, and particularly since the understanding of the nuclear reactions involved due to Bethe, it has been appreciated that the energy source for most stars is the conversion of hydrogen into helium, a nuclear reaction that proceeds at relatively low temperatures. However, during the entire development of nuclear physics until the midfifties it was argued on very strong grounds that the building up of more complicated elements required far higher temperatures than could reasonably be found in stars. In other words, when the nuclear physicists specified the conditions required for the synthesis of heavy elements, the astronomers could reply that they knew of no place in the present universe in which these conditions were realized. This appreciation of the situation gave an immense impetus to all theories of cosmology in which the past was very different and, in particular, much denser and hotter than the present, for the origin of the heavy elements could then be placed into the early phases of the history of such a universe. In a sense, the heavy elements could then be looked at as a fossil remaining from the youth of the universe. Though this thinking was already shaken by Hoyle's analysis of the production of very heavy elements in supernovæ, this process was unable to make heavy elements in the required quantities and therefore people continued to look back to the origin of the universe as a nuclear oven. This kind of thinking was clearly completely out of tune with the steady-state theory. If there were ever any places where heavy elements could be synthesized then, according to the steady-state theory, such places must exist now. Their absence would totally disprove the theory.

Spurred on by this, Hoyle, in collaboration with Fowler, E. M. Burbidge and G. R. Burbidge, Cameron, Salpeter and others began to rethink the problem of the origin of heavy elements. From the nuclear physics side the nature of the conditions of the origin was thought out afresh; from the astrophysical side the evolution of stars and, in particular, the conditions at their centres, were newly investigated. The end result of this work can only be described as a tremendous triumph, for not only was the existence of heavy elements accounted for in terms of known types of stars, but their distribution through space (through the explosion of such stars also known to occur) and their total quantity was predicted correctly. But far beyond this, the theory accounted with uncanny accuracy for the relative abundances not only of all the different chemical elements, but indeed of all the isotopes from which they are made.

The fascinating point in connection with the subject of this chapter is that a theory as uncertain as the steady-state theory should have inspired and directly caused one of the most important advances in physics during the last decade, an advance far more firmly grounded than the steady-state theory itself. This achievement will undoubtedly survive even if the steady-state theory should be disproved. On the other hand, by virtue of its very existence, this theory of the origin of heavy elements means that the steady-state theory has effectively passed a severe test.

The other matter of interest is that a very novel branch of astronomy, radio-astronomy, gives results that well may be of great cosmological interest. They may well be destructive of the steady-state theory, though the interpretation of the experiments is still open to a great deal of discussion. Many other tests are being discussed and actively attempted by astronomers. Here again the existence of rival theories of the structure of the universe has been a powerful stimulus to research and enterprise on the observational side.

(H. B. 1963)

INDEX

INDEX

ACCUSATIVES OF THINKING, 261
'Acts' of mind, 160ff, 261
Aesthetic evaluations, 375-90
Aesthetic interpretation, 361-75
Alexander, Samuel, 38, 128
Algebraical reasoning, W. E. Johnson on, 26
Analogical arguments, 31
Analysis, linguistic, 268ff
  paradox of, 318
  philosophical, 77, 119ff, 224ff, 236, 263
Antilogism, 22
Antinomies, 118ff
Aristotle, 104, 124, 129, 131, 239
Associationism, 99ff
Atomism, 91-101
Attitudes as a psychological concept, 107
Austin, J. L., 318
Ayer, A. J., 65, 87, 209, 287ff

BACON, FRANCIS, 17
Barfield, Owen, 295n
Barnes, F. W. H., 92n, 285
Beardsley, M. C., 362ff
Behaviourism, 106ff
  Analytic, 107-10
  Dispositional, 107
  Naive, 106
Berkeley, George, 25ff, 215, 229ff
Berlin, I., 230
Birkhoff, G., 327
Black, Max, 287n, 288
Boole, G., 18ff, 241, 327ff
Bosanquet, R. G., 347ff
Bradley, A. C., 372
Bradley, F. H., 35, 41, 156, 241
Braithwaite, R. B., 24, 33
Brentano, F., 241, 259
British Philosophy, characteristics of, 66ff, 77, 262
Broad, C. D., 72ff, 135, 361

CALCULUS AND LANGUAGE, 289
Cambridge philosophy, 13-61
Carnap, R., 137ff, 287
Carritt, E. F., 72
Carroll, Lewis (see also Dodgson), 21, 241
Categories and category mistakes, 104, 220
Causality, Aristotle's views on, 119
  W. E. Johnson's views on, 26ff
Causal properties, 26, 103
Causal theory of perception, 225ff
Collingwood, R. G., 293
Common Sense, 157ff
Common Sense ethical opinion, 88ff
Connotation and denotation, 246ff
Continuants, Psychical, 27
  W. E. Johnson on, 26
Cosmological principle, 395ff
Cosmology, philosophical problems of, 393

DECISIONS, AESTHETIC, 374
Demarcation of science, problems—of, 162ff
de Morgan, A., 18ff, 241
Denotation and Connotation, 246ff
Descartes, René, 101ff, 105ff, 216, 272ff
Descriptions, Russell's theory of, 58ff
Determinism-free will, 126
Dewey, John, 367ff
Discovery, philosophical, 128, 283ff
Dispositional properties, 26, 107ff
Dodgson, C. L. (see also Carroll, Lewis), 21
Dualism, 99-112

EINSTEIN, correspondence with Boon, 124-5
Eliot, T. S., 365

Ellis, L. C., 19
Emmet, Dorothy M., 290
Empson, William, 294ff
English Philosophy (*see* British Philosophy)
Ethical judgments, 65ff, 268ff
Ethology, 110
Existence, the concept of, 120
Existential statements, 278
Existentialism, 67

FACT *v.* INTERPRETATION, 115ff
Fisher, R. A., 279n
Free will-determinism, 126
Frege, 57, 241ff
Freud, Sigmund, 101
Fry, Roger, 362, 367

GALILEO, 103
'Given', nature of, 115ff
Gold, T., 395
'Good' as indefinable, 67ff
Grote, John, 14

HARE, R. M., 86
Hedonism, psychological and ethical, 47ff
Hegel, 43ff
Hobbes, Thomas, 107, 239, 241ff
Holftreter, J., 303ff
Hume, David, 85, 105, 135, 162, 215ff, 267, 273, 275, 287
Husserl, 163, 241ff, 254, 260

IDEOGRAPHIC LANGUAGE, 309ff
Induction, 30-3
Infinity, problems of, 118ff
Intellectualism, 99ff
Introspection, 108ff
Intuitionism in ethics, 68ff
   in the theory of perception, 223ff

JAMES, WILLIAM, 105, 110, 259
Jeffreys, Sir Harold, 135ff, 379n
Jevons, Stanley, 135, 241
Johnson, W. E., 13ff, 23-8
Joseph, H. W. B., 176
Just noticeable differences, 137

KANT, IMMANUEL, 83ff, 104, 124, 131, 135, 176ff, 197, 257
Karlgren, B., 316, 325n
Keynes, J. M., 13ff, 28-33, 135ff, 379
Keynes, J. N., 13ff, 21-2
Kneale, W., 137
Knowledge by acquaintance and knowledge by description, 59, 206ff

LADD-FRANKLIN, MRS., 22
Langer, Suzanne K., 297n
Language, Interpretation of, 267-78
   Metaphysical and Ideographic, 283-357
Law of great numbers, 140ff
Laws of Thought, 127
Leibnitz, 57
Linguistic analyses, 268ff, 283-357
Linguistic recommendations, 217
Lloyd, Morgan, C., 38
Locke, John, 104ff, 177, 215, 240
Logical constructions, 59
Logical empiricism, 283
Logical positivism, 284ff
'Looking', G. E. Moore on, 208ff

MACE, C. A., 40
Mansel, 28
Maurice, F. D., 14
McTaggart, J. E., 13ff, 42-5
Meaning, 239-64
   of a poem, 361ff
Meaningless expressions, 272ff
Meinong, A., 241ff, 260
Mencius, 350ff
Meriggi, H., 309
'Metaphysical directives', 123ff
Metaphysics, nature of, 283ff, 312ff
Meta-statements, 306ff
Method of ideal isolation, Moore's, 68
Mill's Four Experimental Methods, 25
Mill, J. S., 18, 135ff, 179, 188, 240ff, 267, 289ff

Mind, the concept of, 272ff
the philosophy of, 99-112
Mind, the journal, 40, 50
W. E. Johnson's articles in, 23
'Models', 105
Moral judgments (*see* Ethical judgments)
Moore, G. E., 13ff, 50-4, 65ff, 106, 156, 215, 241ff, 283ff, 361

NAMES AND WORDS, 242ff
Naturalism, Ward on, 37ff
Naturalistic definition of good, 75ff
Necessary connection, 135
Neyman, J., 149
Newton, Isaac, 17, 137, 394
Newtonian physics, 149

OBJECTIVITY OF ETHICAL JUDGMENTS, 65ff
'Occurrents', W. E. Johnson's views on, 26
Ogden, C. K., 361
Organic wholes, 74ff

PALGRAVE'S DICTIONARY OF POLITICAL ECONOMY, J. N. Keynes's contributions to, 22
Paradox, nature of, 295ff, 307ff
Parmenides, 158
Peano, 57
Perception, 110ff, 205-36
Direct, 210ff, 216-25
Indirect, 224-8
Phenomenalism, 106, 227ff
Phenomenological description, 108ff, 117ff
Philosophical thinking, 115-31
Pierce, C. S., 136, 144ff, 241
Plato, 128, 131, 239ff
Play, concept of, 333ff
Poetic creation, Shelley on, 362
Poincaré, 197
Popper, K. R., 137ff, 379
'Portrait', meaning of, 383ff
Price, H. H., 225, 294
Prichard, H. A., 51, 70ff

Primary and secondary qualities, 226
Principle of extensive abstraction, 56
of indifference, 29ff, 145
of limited independent variety, 31ff, 146
cosmological (C.P.), 397ff
perfect cosmological (P.C.P.), 395ff
'Pro-attitudes', 75ff
Probability, 29ff, 33ff, 135-51, frequency theory of, 143ff, limiting frequency interpretation of, 19, 29, 145
numerical *v.* comparative, 136ff
Problematic induction, 26, 135ff
Psychical Research, 49
Psycho-physical interaction, 38

RAMSEY, F. P., 14ff, 33-4, 289
Rashdall Hastings, 69
'Reasons' for aesthetic judgments, 275ff
Reductionism, 223
Reichenbach, Hans, 143, 379
Relativity, theory of, 56ff, 198ff
Richards, I. A., 295n, 361ff
Ross, Sir David, 72ff
Russell, Earl, 13ff, 57-61, 120, 206ff, 211, 215, 241, 284ff
Ryle, Gilbert, 50, 103, 150, 220ff, 273ff

SCEPTICISM REGARDING PHYSICAL OBJECTS, 223ff
Schröder, 21
'See', Moore on common usage of, 205ff
Sensationism, 99ff
Sense-data, 59, 205ff, 215ff
visual, 205-11, 215-36
Sidgwick, Henry, 13ff, 46-9, 67
Sorley, W. R., 13ff, 49-50
Spearman, Charles, 101ff
Spencer, Herbert, 37
Spinoza, Benedict, 308ff, 347ff
Statistics, general propositions, 139ff
Steady state theory, 395
Stebbing, L. S., 121

Stevenson, C. L., 87ff
Stout, G. F., 13ff, 39-42, 105
Strawson, P. F., 138, 147ff
Symbolic Logic, 18, 131, 241

TENNANT, F. R., 39
Theory of Types, 253
Thouless, R. H., 40
Titchener, E. B., 105
Tolstoy, Leo, 377ff
Toulmin, S. E., 92n

UNIFORMITY OF NATURE, 135
Universals, 251, 314
    and ideographs, 314ff
    of law and factual generalizations, 26
'Universe', physicists' definitions of, 393
Urban, W. M., 289ff
'Use', 254ff
Utilitarianism, 48, 67ff

VAGUENESS, 160
Venn, John, 13ff, 18-21, 241
Verification Principle, 162ff
Vienna Circle, 290
von Kries, 29
von Mises, 137, 139ff, 379n
von Wright, 14ff

WARD, JAMES, 13ff, 34-9, 100ff
Whewell, W., 14, 18
Wilkins, Bishop, 316
Wimsatt, N. K., 362ff
Wisdom, John, 14, 92n, 95n, 285, 293, 361
Wittgenstein, Ludwig, 13ff, 54-5, 155ff, 243, 254ff, 284ff, 361
Words and concepts, 267-79
Words and names, 242ff
Wrinch, D. M., 135

ZENO, HIS ARROW, 118ff

LECTURES ON PHILOSOPHY
G. E. MOORE
Edited by CASIMIR LEWY

G. E. Moore lectured at Cambridge every year from 1911 until his retirement in 1939. These lectures were often attended by philosophers from different parts of the world, and they were one of the chief means by which he extended his influence on the philosophical thought of his time. Dr Lewy has now edited a selection from some of these lectures. They discuss problems in epistemology, in philosophical logic and in the methodology of philosophy. They contain ideas which Moore did not publish elsewhere, and they should be of unusual interest to students of analytic philosophy.

Demy 8vo

30s. net

PHILOSOPHICAL ESSAYS
BERTRAND RUSSELL

This volume is essentially a reprint of a book, with the same title, published in 1910. But because two essays in that volume have since been reprinted in *Mysticism and Logic*, they have been replaced by an article on history and another on Poincare's 'Science and Hypothesis'. Otherwise the essays stand exactly as originally published and the author has made no attempt to modify them to accord with changes in his opinions which have developed in the interval. The collection includes 'The Elements of Ethics', 'Pragmatism', 'The Monistic Theory of Truth', 'James' Conception of Truth' and 'On the Nature of Truth and Falsehood'.

Demy 8vo

30s. net

GEORGE ALLEN & UNWIN LTD

GEORGE ALLEN AND UNWIN LTD

London: 40 Museum Street, W.C.1

Auckland: P.O. Box 36013, Northcote Central, Auckland N.4
Bombay: 15 Graham Road, Ballard Estate, Bombay 1
Barbados: P.O. Box 222, Bridgetown
Buenos Aires: Escritorio 454–459, Florida 165
Calcutta: 17 Chittaranjan Avenue, Calcutta 13
Cape Town: 68 Shortmarket Street
Hong Kong: 44 Mody Road, Kowloon
Ibadan: P.O. Box 62
Karachi: Karachi Chambers, McLeod Road
Madras: Mohan Mansions, 38c Mount Road, Madras 6
Mexico: Villalongin 32–10, Piso, Mexico 5, D.F.
Nairobi: P.O. Box 4536
New Dehli: 13–14 Asaf Ali Road, New Delhi 1
Ontario: 81 Curlew Drive, Don Mills
São Paulo: Caixa Postal 8675
Singapore: 36c Prinsep Street, Singapore 7
Sydney, N.S.W.: Bradbury House, 55 York Street
Tokyo: 10 Kanda-Ogawamachi, 3-Chome, Chiyoda-Ku

British Philosophy in Mid Century